Empowerment Evaluation

Second Edition

Empowerment Evaluation

Knowledge and Tools for Self-Assessment, Evaluation Capacity Building, and Accountability

Second Edition

David M. Fetterman
Fetterman & Associates and Stanford University

Shakeh J. Kaftarian
Kaftarian & Associates

Abraham Wandersman
University of South Carolina

Editors

Los Angeles | London | New Delhi
Singapore | Washington DC

Los Angeles | London | New Delhi
Singapore | Washington DC

FOR INFORMATION:

SAGE Publications, Inc.
2455 Teller Road
Thousand Oaks, California 91320
E-mail: order@sagepub.com

SAGE Publications Ltd.
1 Oliver's Yard
55 City Road
London EC1Y 1SP
United Kingdom

SAGE Publications India Pvt. Ltd.
B 1/I 1 Mohan Cooperative Industrial Area
Mathura Road, New Delhi 110 044
India

SAGE Publications Asia-Pacific Pte. Ltd.
3 Church Street
#10-04 Samsung Hub
Singapore 049483

Printed in the United States of America

Cataloging-in-publication data is available for this title from the Library of Congress.

ISBN 978-1-4522-9953-2

This book is printed on acid-free paper.

Acquisitions Editor: Helen Salmon
Production Editor: Amy Schroller
Editorial Assistant: Anna Villarruel
Copy Editor: Colleen Brennan
Typesetter: C&M Digitals (P) Ltd.
Proofreader: Theresa Kay
Indexer: Jean Casalegno
Cover Designer: SAGE India (Design)
Marketing Manager: Nicole Elliott

SFI Certified Sourcing
www.sfiprogram.org
SFI-00453

SFI label applies to text stock

14 15 16 17 18 10 9 8 7 6 5 4 3 2 1

Table of Contents

Foreword

The field of evaluation has grown by leaps and bounds over the past two decades. For example, recent estimates suggest more than 34,000 professionals are now participating in evaluation societies and more than 80 universities provide evaluation degree and certificate programs worldwide (Donaldson, 2014). The quest for credible and actionable evidence to improve decision making, foster improvement, enhance self-determination, and promote social betterment is now a global phenomenon.

Without a doubt, this positive social epidemic spreading across the globe is largely due to the discovery and development of innovative evaluation approaches that better meet stakeholder, organization, community, and societal needs. In these past two decades, evaluation theorists and practitioners alike have responded to and overcome the challenges that limited the effectiveness and usefulness of traditional evaluation approaches primarily focused on seeking rigorous scientific knowledge about social programs and policies. No modern evaluation approach has received a more robust welcome from stakeholders across the globe than empowerment evaluation.

This book marks the 21st anniversary of empowerment evaluation, an approach that has literally altered the landscape of evaluation. David M. Fetterman introduced the approach as part of his presidential address to the American Evaluation Association in 1993. Since that time, it has gone viral and is practiced vigorously throughout the United States and in more than 16 countries.

Empowerment evaluation has been a leader in the development of stakeholder involvement approaches to evaluation, setting a high bar for quality and rigor. In addition, empowerment evaluation's respect for community knowledge and commitment to the people's right to build their own evaluation capacity has influenced the evaluation mainstream, particularly concerning evaluation capacity building. One of empowerment evaluation's most significant contributions to the field has been to improving evaluation use and knowledge utilization.

This book represents the culmination of decades of dialogue. This collection of scholars and practitioners, led by David M. Fetterman, Abraham Wandersman, and Shakeh J. Kaftarian, have engaged in an honest and sincere dialogue with their colleagues, seeking critical feedback at every juncture. In addition to exchanges in the *American Journal of Evaluation* with numerous colleagues, I organized and moderated a pivotal debate about the value of empowerment evaluation between David M. Fetterman, Michael Quinn Patton, and Michael Scriven at the Claremont Colleges in August 2009. While the exchanges were invigorating and overflowing with evaluation wisdom, the most remarkable memory was how David modeled empowerment evaluation's characteristic orientation to openly and honestly engage in self-reflection and critique throughout the debate (see Donaldson, Patton, Fetterman, & Scriven, 2010). David and his colleagues have used this critical feedback to refine and improve their conceptual clarity and methodological specificity. This book, building on these exchanges, represents the cutting edge of insight and understanding into empowerment evaluation.

This collection presents the history of empowerment evaluation, from its turbulent first steps to its well-established and institutionalized stages, including the establishment of a special division within the professional association. It includes theory, principles, concepts, and steps of empowerment evaluation. The book highlights the breadth and depth of the approach, including the views of authors from foundations, as well as international case examples. The authors provide domestic examples ranging from corporate philanthropy to government-sponsored engagements.

True to the title of the book, this volume is not at a loss when it comes to tools. The authors provide clear case examples and instruments ready to be adapted and applied to a variety of settings. Finally, as a measure of the maturity of the approach, it includes research on its practice.

I have had the great pleasure of traveling down evaluation byways with David over the past decade. It is amazing to observe David facilitating empowerment principles in practice. I can attest this man practices what he preaches and serves as a wonderful spokesperson and role model for the evaluation profession. David and his colleagues have created a brilliant evaluation path that provides discipline to one of the most pervasive forms of evaluation going on today throughout governments, universities, for profit and not-for-profit organizations, and communities across the globe—that is, self-evaluation.

David has convinced me and others that, contrary to popular belief, self-evaluation is without a doubt the most common form of evaluation being practiced throughout the world today. However, most of this pervasive self-evaluation work is rather superficial, practiced by amateurs without professional evaluation training, and is not informed by professional evaluation standards, principles, and ethics. One of the greatest evaluation innovations of the past two decades has been the development of a professional and systematic approach to self-evaluation called empowerment evaluation. This book offers you the latest cutting-edge understanding of this powerful innovation and evaluation approach. May you be inspired and empowered as you adventure through the chapters in this outstanding volume!

Stewart I. Donaldson

President-Elect, American Evaluation Association

Dean & Professor, School of Social Science, Policy & Evaluation

Dean & Professor, School of Community & Global Health

Director, Claremont Evaluation Center

Claremont Graduate University

Claremont, CA

References

Donaldson, S. I. (2014). Examining the backbone of contemporary evaluation practice. In S. I. Donaldson, C. A. Christie, & M. M. Mark (Eds.), *Credible and actionable evidence: The foundation of rigorous and influential evaluations.* Newbury Park: Sage.

Donaldson, S. I., Patton, M. Q., Fetterman, D., & Scriven, M. (2010). The 2009 Claremont Debate: The promise of utilization-focused and empowerment evaluation. *Journal of MultiDisciplinary Evaluation, 6*(13), 15–57.

Preface

"**E**mpowerment evaluation served as the theme of the 1993 American Evaluation Association annual meeting as well as the basis for Fetterman's presidential address. The topic stimulated conversations and arguments that spilled out into the hallways during the conference." This is how the preface began in our first empowerment evaluation book 21 years ago. The liveliness of the conversations has not subsided. They simply became more refined and precise. Empowerment evaluation continues to grow in scope and depth. It has also served to expand the roles of evaluators and practitioners in evaluation.

What many people may not remember is that one of the plenary speakers at the 1993 conference was Kenneth Arrow, a Nobel Laureate from Stanford University. He spoke eloquently about the increasing importance of evaluation in society and the significance of this new approach, about to be introduced to the field.

One of the colleagues who came up to the podium to thank and agree with David M. Fetterman about the tenets of empowerment evaluation was Shakeh Kaftarian. At the time, she was the deputy director of the Office of Scientific Analysis at the Center for Substance Abuse Prevention (CSAP). Shakeh, along with many of her colleagues, observed the need for development, evaluation, and accountability in communities with major service needs. During this time, the federal government and the private sector were launching hundreds of community-based services programs and requiring their grantees to show that they were making the promised changes in their communities. These requirements by funding organizations were not aligned with clear, affordable, and practical models for program development, self-evaluation, and accountability. It was also clear to the social scientists working for the federal government and in academia that local communities didn't know how to select or develop interventions that fit their problems, evaluate their programs, and work with their "expert" program developers and evaluators—even if they had access to such "experts."

Empowerment evaluation tools and techniques were conceived during this time to deal with a void that didn't have many practical solutions. Empowerment evaluation–based practical models were quickly developed and tested in a few real-life settings and rolled out to national and international communities. Shakeh was instrumental in helping to deploy empowerment evaluations in the substance abuse community throughout the United States.

Shakeh and Abe (Abraham Wandersman) had met when she was a CSAP project officer, and Abe was an academician serving on the advisory board for one of CSAP's evaluation studies. Abe had already developed the widely disseminated program evaluation manual called *Prevention Plus III*, which was a capacity building tool and was being used by many CSAP grantees during the early 1990s. Shakeh invited Abe to participate in a panel at the 1992 American Evaluation Association (AEA) annual meeting in Seattle, to address the critical issue of how local communities who had received community service grants from CSAP could become "empowered" to better develop and evaluate their local grants. This meeting was well attended, although sometimes contentious in mood. The concept of "empowerment" was a new and sensitive approach to doing "business"—by the feds, grantees, and evaluation experts. Attendees from scientific and practice communities were not sure about the impact of "empowerment" on their respective work at the community and national levels.

Shakeh was also instrumental in connecting David and Abe by inviting Abe to participate in a panel at the 1992 AEA conference. At the conference, Abe ran into Len Bickman (a SAGE evaluation series editor). Len was speaking to a very energetic guy and invited Abe to join him for a walk to get some Seattle coffee with "that guy." Abe did, and the rest is part of empowerment evaluation history. The energetic guy was David M. Fetterman. They started talking and a few hours later realized how many common interests they shared. Abe shared his work with coalitions with David. David shared his work with public school systems in the United States and townships in South Africa. A bond was created.

David invited Abe to participate in an AEA presidential plenary panel in 1993 in Dallas. They brainstormed about building on David's presidential address, Abe's work on local capacity building, and Shakeh's work on the national evaluation of a large grant program. David, Shakeh, and Abe joined forces for the development of a book on the topic of empowerment evaluation. This three-way connection planted the seeds for the first empowerment evaluation book—*Empowerment Evaluation: Knowledge and Tools for Self-Assessment and Accountability*. This is the book we are revisiting after 21 years.

We reflect on and are thankful for the series of circumstances, and a healthy dose of serendipity, that brought us together. We held positions in academia and government, with an overlapping commitment to community settings. Over the years, we have tried to bring our scientific knowledge to bear on practice with an openness we each felt toward pressing, real-life issues in communities. Clearly each of us felt and heard his or her thoughts expressed by the other two, and found that partnering together was an organic process, which flowed naturally. Individually and collectively, we saw the practical utility of an iterative approach to evaluation that was mindful of both the scientific process and practical problem solving. This book, we think, continues to broaden and deepen empowerment evaluation. Each author in this book has a journey that motivates him or her to work with individuals, organizations, and communities in a collaborative and empowering way to use the knowledge and tools of evaluation. We hope the efforts of our colleagues and ourselves over the past couple of decades contribute to your own journey to help people help themselves.

David M. Fetterman

Shakeh J. Kaftarian

Abraham Wandersman

Acknowledgments

We conducted focus groups of evaluators to help guide us as we developed this collection. One of the frequent recommendations is that we consolidate what has been written over the past 21 years, minimizing the need for the reader to find relevant passages in our various publications. We have done our best to honor that request. As such, we would like to thank the following sources for permission to reprint passages in part or whole:

Fetterman, D. M. (2005). A window into the heart and soul of empowerment evaluation: Looking through the lens of empowerment evaluation principles. In D. M. Fetterman & A. Wandersman (Eds.), *Empowerment evaluation principles in practice*. New York: Guilford Press.

Fetterman, D. M. (2013). The drivers: The three Digital Villages. In D. M. Fetterman, *Empowerment evaluation in the Digital Villages: Hewlett-Packard's $15 million race toward social justice*. Stanford, CA: Stanford University Press.

Fetterman, D. M. (2013). Empowerment evaluation: Learning to think like an evaluator. In M. Alkin (Ed.), *Evaluation roots: A wider perspective of theorists' views and influences* (2nd ed.). Thousand Oaks, CA: Sage.

Fetterman, D. M. (2013). The engine: Empowerment evaluation. In D. M. Fetterman, *Empowerment evaluation in the Digital Villages: Hewlett-Packard's $15 million race toward social justice*. Stanford, CA: Stanford University Press.

In addition, concerning Chapter 8, we add the following disclaimer: *Support for this work was provided by and administered through the Center for Substance Abuse Prevention, Contract Number #HHSS277200800004C, Reference number 277–08–0218. The content of this publication does not necessarily reflect the views or policies of the Department of Health and Human Services, and the views expressed in this paper are those of the authors.*

We are grateful for the valuable feedback from the following reviewers: Robert Shumer, University of Minnesota and Gary J. Skolits, University of Tennessee.

PART I
INTRODUCTION

CHAPTER 1
Introduction

History and Overview

David M. Fetterman

Fetterman & Associates and Stanford University

Empowerment evaluation is the use of evaluation concepts, techniques, and findings to foster improvement and self-determination. (Fetterman, 1994)

[Empowerment evaluation is] an evaluation approach that aims to increase the likelihood that programs will achieve results by increasing the capacity of program stakeholders to plan, implement, and evaluate their own programs. (Wandersman et al., 2005, p. 28)

Empowerment evaluation is a global phenomenon. It has been used in over 16 countries and in places ranging from the corporate offices of Hewlett-Packard to squatter settlements and townships in South Africa to create sustainable community health initiatives. Empowerment evaluation has been applied by the U.S. Department of Education's Office of Special Education and Rehabilitation Services to foster self-determination, as well as by Native Americans in reservations stretching from Michigan to San Diego. Empowerment evaluation has also been used in higher education in accreditation self-studies at Stanford University and the California Institute of Integral Studies.

Youth are conducting their own empowerment evaluations. It can be found operating in child abuse prevention programs, as well as after school program collaborations. Empowerment evaluation has even dared to reach for the stars by contributing to the NASA/Jet Propulsion Laboratory's efforts to educate youth about the prototype Mars rover (Fetterman & Bowman, 2002). (A sample of the breadth and scope of empowerment evaluation is captured in Table 1.1.)

Table 1.1 A Sample of the International Scope of Empowerment Evaluation in Practice

Countries	Foundations	Government	Higher Education	Native American Reservations	Community-Based Social Programs
Australia Brazil* Canada Ethiopia Finland† Israel Japan Korea Nepal Mexico New Zealand South Africa Spain Thailand United Kingdom United States	Health Foundation of Central Massachusetts John S. and James L. Knight Foundation Marin Community Foundation Mary Black Foundation W. K. Kellogg Foundation	NASA/Jet Propulsion Laboratory Schools • Academic distress (Fetterman, 2005a, pp. 107–120) • High performing • Gifted and talented U.S. Department of Education U.S. DOE's Office of Special Education and Rehabilitation Services U.S. Substance Abuse and Mental Health Services Administration	California Institute of Integral Studies (Fetterman, 2001, 2012) Hebrew Union College (Rhea Hirsch School of Education) Stanford University's School of Medicine (Fetterman, 2009; Fetterman, Deitz, & Gesundheit, 2010)	National Indian Child Welfare Association, Michigan Native Aspirations, Washington Tribal Digital Village, San Diego, CA	Alcohol, Tobacco, and other Drug Prevention Programs (CBOs) Family Support Services (Keener, Snell-Johns, Livet, & Wandersman, 2005) Squatter Settlement Assistance (South Africa) The Night Ministry‡ Tobacco Prevention (Fetterman & Wandersman, 2007)

CBOs, Community-based organizations; DOE, Department of Education.

* Dr. Thereza Penna Firme (2003) at the Federal University of Rio de Janeiro and the Cesgranrio Foundation in Brazil is applying empowerment evaluation to the Educational Program in Amazonian Brazil.

† Riitta Haverinen from Stakes National Research and Development Centre for Welfare and Health; Liisa Horelli, Research Fellow at the University of Helsinki; Juha Siitonen (Siitonen & Robinson, 1998) from the University of Oulu; and Heljä Antola Robinson from Bradley University are applying empowerment evaluation.

‡ The Night Ministry is a nondenominational church–based organized that reaches out to Chicago's nighttime street communities through a street and health outreach program (see Wandersman et al., 2004).

HISTORY

The history of empowerment evaluation has been one of evolving conceptual clarity and methodological specificity. Empowerment evaluation was introduced in a presidential address at the American Evaluation Association (AEA; Fetterman, 1994). The empowerment evaluation approach was painted with broad strokes focusing on the definition, conceptual roots, and developmental facets or stages, including training, facilitation, advocacy, illumination, and liberation. In addition, caveats and concerns were raised. The new approach created a tremendous amount of intellectual and emotional excitement, commentary, and debate. It was an idea "whose time had come." The approach spread like wildfire and was embraced by evaluators from around the world. The depth and breadth of adoption was so rapid it was called a movement (Scriven, 1997; Sechrest, 1997). It challenged the status quo and thus touched a nerve among many traditional evaluators, resulting in highly charged exchanges in the journal *Evaluation Practice* (Fetterman, 1994, 1995; Stufflebeam, 1994). Nevertheless, while making it clear that "empowerment evaluation is not a panacea," empowerment evaluators seized the moment and applied the approach to a wide variety of programs and diverse populations. Empowerment evaluation spoke to issues at the very heart of evaluation. What is the purpose of evaluation? Who is in control? Who am I (as an evaluator)?

The introduction of empowerment evaluation to the AEA and the resulting dialogues led to the first collection of works concerning this approach. It was titled *Empowerment Evaluation: Knowledge and Tools for Self-Assessment and Accountability* (Fetterman, Kaftarian, & Wandersman, 1996). The collection provided an introduction to the theory and practice of this approach. It also highlighted the scope of empowerment evaluation, ranging from its use in a national educational reform movement to its endorsement by the former W. K. Kellogg Foundation's director of evaluation. The book also presented examples of empowerment evaluation in various contexts, including federal, state, and local government; HIV prevention and related health initiatives; African American communities; and battered women's shelters. This first volume also provided various theoretical and philosophical frameworks as well as workshop and technical assistance tools. The first book helped to launch a new approach to evaluation, setting the stage for future developments. It also sparked additional debate and discussion with some of the most prominent leaders in the field of evaluation (Fetterman, 1997a, 1997b; Patton, 1997; Scriven, 1997). Wild's review of the book captured the spirit of the times: "Fetterman et al. have nailed their theses to the door of the cathedral. Now the question is, How tolerant is the establishment of dissent?" (Wild, 1996, p. 172).

Foundations of Empowerment Evaluation (Fetterman, 2001), the second empowerment evaluation book, raised the bar in empowerment evaluation, building on the previous collection of knowledge and shared experience. The approach was less controversial at the time. The book was pragmatic, providing clear steps and examples of empowerment evaluation work, including a high-stakes higher education accreditation self-study. The book also applied the standards to empowerment evaluation, including utility, feasibility, propriety, and accuracy standards (see Joint Committee on Standards for Educational Evaluation, 1994; Yarbrough, Shulha, Hopson, & Caruthers, 2011). *Foundations of Empowerment Evaluation* made several additional contributions, including the following:

1. Explaining the role of process use (as people conduct their own evaluations, they enhance their ownership of the evaluation)

2. Comparing collaborative, participatory, and empowerment evaluation

3. Discussing similarities with utilization-focused evaluation

4. Discussing the multiple purposes of evaluation, including program development, accountability, and knowledge

The collection was followed by a number of articles and contributions to encyclopedias and leading texts in the field (e.g., Fetterman 2004a, 2004b; Wandersman et al., 2004). Empowerment evaluation, at that stage of development, had become a part of the intellectual landscape of evaluation.

Empowerment Evaluation Principles in Practice (Fetterman & Wandersman, 2005) represented a milestone in the development of empowerment evaluation. In pursuit of additional conceptual clarity, it elaborated on the existing definition of empowerment evaluation, emphasizing capacity building, outcomes, and institutionalization. In addition, although empowerment evaluation had been guided by principles since its inception, many of them were implicit rather than explicit. This led to some inconsistency in empowerment evaluation practice. This motivated a cadre of empowerment evaluator leaders and practitioners (contributors to the collection) to make these principles explicit. The 10 principles are as follows:

1. Improvement

2. Community ownership

3. Inclusion

4. Democratic participation

5. Social justice

6. Community knowledge

7. Evidence-based strategies

8. Capacity building

9. Organizational learning

10. Accountability

These principles should guide empowerment evaluation from conceptualization to implementation. The principles of empowerment evaluation serve as a lens to focus an evaluation. (They are discussed in detail in Chapter 2 and in Fetterman & Wandersman, 2005.) Case examples from educational reform, youth development programs, and child abuse prevention programs were used to highlight the use of these guiding principles. This book, like past collections, generated a lively debate among many of the same leaders in the field (Fetterman, 2005b; Patton, 2005; Scriven, 2005; Wandersman & Snell-Johns, 2005).

A 2005 AEA conference panel session titled "Empowerment Evaluation and Traditional Evaluation: 10 Years Later" provided another opportunity to engage in this ongoing dialogue in the field and reflect on the development and evolution of empowerment evaluation. Speakers included Drs. Robin Miller, Christina Christie, Nick Smith, Michael Scriven, Abraham Wandersman, and David Fetterman. Based on the 2005 panel at AEA, a substantial and systematic review[1] of empowerment evaluation was published (Miller & Campbell, 2006). They highlighted types or modes of empowerment evaluation, settings, reasons for selecting the approach, who selects the approach, and degree of involvement of participants. The relationship between the type of empowerment evaluation mode and related variables was useful. They provided many insights, including the continuum of flexibility to structure and standardization in empowerment evaluation wording, based on the size of the project. Miller and Campbell (2006) also noted that the reasons for selecting empowerment evaluation were generally appropriate, including capacity building, self-determination, accountability, making evaluation a part of the organizational

---

1. See also Christie (2003) for an insightful comparison of empowerment evaluation with deliberative democratic evaluation (House & Howe, 2000), highlighting theoretical similarities and differences in practice. The focus was on degree of stakeholder involvement. See also Fetterman (2003). Sheldon (2014) also presents survey results of empowerment evaluators.

routine, and cultivating staff buy-in. Nick Smith complemented their work with his application of an ideological lens to the analysis of empowerment evaluation (Smith, 2007).

This same 2005 AEA session was responsible for a series of additional empowerment evaluation related publications. One of the publications was titled "Empowerment Evaluation: Yesterday, Today, and Tomorrow" (Fetterman & Wandersman, 2007). It consolidated over a decade of critiques and responses concerning empowerment evaluation. It helped to further clarify the purpose and objectives of empowerment evaluations and discussed misperceptions and misunderstandings. The article addressed issues of people empowering themselves, advocacy, role of consumers, complementarity of internal and external evaluation, as well as traditional and empowerment evaluation, practical and transformative empowerment evaluation, bias, ideology, and social agenda. It was one of the *American Journal of Evaluation*'s most downloaded articles, which speaks to the relevance[2] of empowerment evaluation in the field at the time.

This book marks the 21st anniversary of the approach. *Empowerment Evaluation: Knowledge and Tools for Self-Assessment, Evaluation Capacity Building, and Accountability* builds on a wealth of empowerment evaluation discussions, presentations, publications, and practice. This collection takes one more step toward enhancing conceptual clarity and methodological specificity.

First, this collection (building on the last one) highlights the role of the empowerment evaluation principles in practice. Selected principles are discussed throughout the collection. The chapters demonstrate how the principles serve as a guiding force in each of the empowerment evaluations.

Second, this book brings to the surface a central theme in empowerment evaluation: evaluation capacity building. "Evaluation capacity building (ECB) is an intentional process to increase individual motivation, knowledge, and skills, and to enhance a group or organization's ability to conduct or use evaluation" (Labin, Duffy, Meyers, Wandersman, & Lesesne, 2012, p. 308). This concept was a driving force in our first empowerment evaluation book (Fetterman, Kaftarian, & Wandersman, 1996) and a light motif or refrain in our second book (Fetterman, 2001). It is listed as one of the 10 principles in our third book (Fetterman & Wandersman, 2005). After 21 years of empowerment

---

2. Empowerment evaluation continued to play a central role in the field as evidenced by an internationally broadcast debate between Fetterman, Scriven, and Patton at Claremont Graduate University in 2009. It is in the university's virtual library at http://ccdl.libraries.claremont.edu/cdm/singleitem/collection/lap/id/69. See Donaldson, Patton, Fetterman, and Scriven (2010).

evaluation practice, evaluation capacity building has emerged as an overriding focal point and is discussed explicitly in many of the chapters of this book.

Third, this latest edition helps to document the empowerment evaluation continuum (Fetterman, 2001, p. 114; Fetterman, 2005, pp. 42–72; see also Cousins, 2005, p. 188). The first book emphasized themes of transformative empowerment evaluation, explaining how "the investigation of worth or merit and plans for program improvement were typically viewed as the means by which self-determination is fostered, illumination generated, and liberation actualized" (Fetterman, 1996, p. 381). Examples of illumination and liberation were presented, based on work in a township in South Africa, as well as in the Oakland public school system in California. The transformative tone of empowerment evaluation was captured by one empowerment evaluator who exclaimed in the middle of their presentation: "I get it: It is not formative, it is transformative" (Fetterman, 2001, p. 38). In contrast, the *Foundations of Empowerment Evaluation* book acknowledged the value of classifying some efforts as the application of empowerment evaluation concepts and techniques (as compared with a more comprehensive empowerment evaluation). This book complements (but does not replace) the earlier volumes, emphasizing the practical empowerment evaluation end of the spectrum. This stream focuses on utilization and specifically program decision making and problem solving to increase the probability of achieving outcomes.

OVERVIEW OF THE BOOK

This book contains a wealth of wisdom, in terms of both theory and practice. This introductory chapter, containing a brief history of the approach, is followed by a chapter about the theory, principles, concepts, and steps of empowerment evaluation. It should be used as a lens with which to read the remaining chapters.

Part II of the book highlights the scope and breadth of the approach. It presents the views of authors from a community health foundation and a national foundation. It is followed by two international case examples, including one in Peru and the Visible Learning program operating in 10 countries, including Australia, Canada, Denmark, Holland, New Zealand, Norway, Sweden, United Kingdom, and the United States. Part II also includes chapters on empowerment evaluations in the United States. Corporate philanthropy and government-sponsored examples also help document the range of empowerment evaluation settings.

Tools are needed to translate theory into practice. In Part III, five tools are highlighted within the context of concrete case examples; they are Getting To Outcomes®, Caseload Evaluation Tracking System, Evaluation Capacity Assessment Instrument, Quality Implementation Tool, and Empowerment Evaluation Dashboard. In addition, the use of conventional tools such as focus groups, concept mapping, and questionnaires are discussed.

It is consistent with the spirit of empowerment evaluation to continually reflect on practice. The collection concludes with a chapter about some of the research that has been conducted concerning the approach and a discussion about emergent themes and next steps.

Highlights

Theory, Principles, Concepts, and Steps

David M. Fetterman summarizes empowerment evaluation theories, principles, concepts, and steps in Chapter 2. Theories guide behavior, providing an overall road map or conceptual map of the terrain. Instrumental empowerment evaluation theories shaping practice include empowerment, self-determination, and process use, as well as theories of use and action. Principles represent the next logical level to inform practice. The 10 empowerment evaluation principles help ensure empowerment evaluations remain focused and authentic.

Empowerment evaluation concepts provide additional conceptual clarity. They are intellectual landmarks on the landscape. Key concepts include critical friends, culture of evidence, cycles of reflection and action, communities of learners, and reflective practitioners. There are many ways to conduct an empowerment evaluation. The two most common approaches—the 3-step and 10-step models—are discussed to help inform practice. Both are designed to build capacity and enhance the probability of program success. Chapter 2 also briefly discusses the role of the empowerment evaluator, as a collaborator, facilitator, and critical friend.

Scope and Breadth

One test of an approach is its adoption and use. The entire book speaks to the breadth and scope of empowerment evaluation, from domestic to international contexts and from government to corporate philanthropic settings. Foundations play a particularly unique role in society. They are powerful catalysts for change. Empowerment evaluation is philosophically and strategically in alignment with many foundations. Foundations' choices have both symbolic and substantive impacts in the field. Therefore, their views and use of empowerment evaluation are important to discuss.

Foundations

Two authors from two foundations highlight their views as they apply and reflect on the power of empowerment evaluation. Jan B. Yost, author of Chapter 3, is the president of the Health Foundation of Central Massachusetts, a regional community health foundation. She describes the evolving philanthropic landscape from disinterested benevolence to an interest in accountability. Empowerment evaluation is viewed as a conduit for achieving results. Jan explains how funders can operationalize empowerment evaluation using her foundation as an example, focusing on the partnership between grantee, funder, and evaluator.

Laura C. Leviton is the senior advisor for the Robert Wood Johnson Foundation, one of the largest foundations devoted to health in the United States. Laura describes how the foundation is driven by its philanthropic strategy for social change, including its choice of evaluation approaches. In Chapter 4, she describes the potential role of empowerment evaluation in achieving such a strategy. Laura focuses on several empowerment evaluation principles, including capacity building, inclusion, and community knowledge.

International

Empowerment evaluation is international in scope, operating in more than 16 countries. Two international examples are presented in this section of the collection. In Chapter 5, Susana Sastre-Merino, Pablo Vidueira, José María Díaz-Puente, and María José Fernández-Moral, members of the Planning and Management of Sustainable Rural Development Research Group at the Universidad Politécnica de Madrid, describe a Peruvian empowerment evaluation. They explain how rural Aymara women used empowerment evaluation to transform their craft activities into a successful and sustainable business. They highlight the utility of the following empowerment evaluation principles in guiding their work: improvement, inclusion, democratic participation, capacity building, community knowledge, community ownership, and accountability.

Janet Clinton and John Hattie, from the University of Melbourne, provide an international example, in Chapter 6, of an empowerment evaluation in action, that is, building capacity in an educational setting. Their Visible Learning approach has operated in 10 countries. It is based on more than 800 meta-evaluations about what impacts student learning. They highlight the importance of teachers "knowing their impact" and being interpreters of evidence, above and beyond being data collectors. They demonstrate how empowerment evaluation principles have been incorporated into the Visible Learning model of schooling, helping to maximize student learning and achievement. Principles driving their efforts include improvement, culture of evidence, community ownership, capacity building, social justice, and accountability.

United States

Corporate Philanthropy. Shifting gears to domestic programs and initiatives, in Chapter 7, David M. Fetterman provides an insight into Hewlett-Packard's Digital Village initiative. It was a $15 million effort to bridge the digital divide in communities of color. Empowerment evaluation was used to drive community efforts to create economic sustainability, provide educational opportunity, and preserve cultural heritage. This initiative is an example of corporate philanthropy. Principles of improvement, respect for local knowledge, and organizational learning helped shape the empowerment evaluation. However, the focus of the discussion is on evaluation capacity building and outcomes.

Government. In Chapter 8, Pam Imm, Matthew Biewener, and Kim Dash, from the Education Development Center, and Dawn Oparah, from Amadi Leadership Associates, describe a U.S. Substance Abuse and Mental Health Services Administration (SAMHSA) initiative. The logic behind the initiative was to help communities conduct more rigorous evaluations of "practitioner-initiated" programs and in turn implement more effective substance abuse prevention programs. They applied empowerment evaluation principles, such as improvement, inclusion, democratic participation, capacity building, respect for community knowledge, evidence-based strategies, social justice, organizational learning, and accountability. They describe how the principles were operationalized and applied to cultivate local ownership of evaluation practices and enhance program sustainability. The authors also discuss the role of the critical friend in helping to facilitate the evaluation.

Tools

Empowerment evaluation is about use. Tools are continually being introduced, applied, tested, and refined. They help practitioners operationalize and transform empowerment evaluation principles into practice. The six chapters in Part III describe how empowerment evaluation principles guided these practitioners' efforts. However, they also highlight tools that can be adapted for wider use; these tools include the Getting To Outcomes® model; Caseload Evaluation Tracking System; focus groups, concept mapping, and questionnaires; the Evaluation Capacity Assessment Instrument; the Quality Implementation Tool, and the Empowerment Evaluation Dashboard. These tools are provided in each of the chapters.

Getting To Outcomes® (CDC-Funded Teenage Pregnancy Prevention Program)

Getting To Outcomes® (GTO®) is one of the most popular tools used to conduct an empowerment evaluation. It involves asking and answering 10 accountability questions, which are (1) What are the underlying needs and conditions to address? (2) What are the goals, priority populations, and objectives? (3) Which science (evidence-based) methods and best practices can be useful in reaching the goals? (4) What actions need to be taken so the selected program fits the community context? (5) What organizational capacities are needed to implement the program? (6) What is the plan for this program? (7) How will the quality of program and/or initiative implementation be assessed? (8) How well did the program work? (9) How will continuous quality improvement strategies be incorporated? (10) If the program is successful, how will it be sustained?[3]

GTO, described in Chapter 9, explicitly provides stakeholders with tools for assessing the planning, implementation, and self-evaluation of their programs. GTO manuals or how-to workbooks have been developed for substance abuse prevention, positive youth development, underage drinking prevention, and teenage pregnancy prevention. An initiative on teenage pregnancy prevention, funded by the Centers for Disease Control and Prevention (CDC), is used to highlight GTO features.

Caseload Evaluation Tracking System (Charter School Social Workers)

Described in Chapter 10, the Mastery Charter Schools is an example of a school turnaround success story. President Obama recognized the charter school for its "no excuses" approach and its high-stakes, performance-based culture. Ivan Haskell, director of Social and Psychological Services at the Mastery

---

3. Adapted from Chinman, Imm, and Wandersman (2004).

Charter Schools, and Aidyn L. Iachini, from the University of South Carolina, describe an empowerment evaluation of the Mastery Charter school social work program. Their work focused on (1) helping social workers develop and take ownership of a new evaluation tracking system; (2) understanding the impact of their services on youth; and (3) improving social work practitioners' evaluation capacity in order to improve the effectiveness of their work with individual students. Their caseload evaluation tracking system spreadsheet is a useful tool that can be adapted for many other purposes. Capacity building, community ownership, and continuous improvement were hallmarks of their efforts.

Focus Groups, Concept Mapping, and Questionnaires (Elementary School Youth)

Empowerment evaluations are also conducted by youth. In Chapter 11, Regina Day Langhout and Jesica Siham Fernández describe an empowerment evaluation conducted by fourth and fifth graders in California. It was part of an ongoing collaborative community-based research project. Youth identified a problem in their schools, set goals, and developed a strategy to achieve their goals. However, the real story is how they evaluated their initiative and, based on their findings, reshaped their ongoing initiative. Their tools included focus groups, concept mapping, and questionnaires. Guiding empowerment evaluation principles in the initiative included social justice, inclusion, improvement, evidence-based strategies, capacity building, and community ownership.

Evaluation Capacity Assessment Instrument (University-Community Based Organization Partnership)

Yolanda Suarez-Balcazar, Tina Taylor-Ritzler, and Gloria Morales-Curtin (a member of the community-based organization), in Chapter 12, highlight the empowerment evaluation efforts of a 7-year university-community–based organization partnership. They describe their work in terms of the developmental stages of empowerment evaluation, including training, facilitation, advocacy, illumination, and liberation (Fetterman, 1996). In essence, they describe a process of organizational transformation. As the transformation unfolded, the evaluators' role changed from facilitators and coaches to critical friends. Evaluation capacity building was a fundamental component of this effort. The Evaluation Capacity Assessment Instrument proved to be a useful evaluation needs assessment tool in the process. Organizational learning, improvement, inclusion, social justice, and accountability were also guiding empowerment evaluation principles in this initiative.

Quality Implementation Tool
(School District Mobile Computing Initiative)

Andrea E. Lamont, Annie Wright, Abraham Wandersman, and Debra Hamm conducted an empowerment evaluation, described in Chapter 13, of a technology integration initiative in a school district in South Carolina. The initiative provided students in Grades 3 through 12 with their own mobile computing devices (e.g., iPads and Chromebooks). The focus of the initiative was on building capacity to ensure the program was implemented with quality. Implementing with quality is considered a key to success and sustainability in the implementation science literature. These authors describe the use of the Quality Implementation Tool to build capacity and facilitate quality implementation. One of the coauthors, Debbie Hamm, was the school superintendent in charge of the initiative.

Evaluation Dashboard (State of
Arkansas Tobacco Prevention Program)

David M. Fetterman, Linda Delaney, and Beverly Triana-Tremain conducted a decade-long empowerment evaluation of a statewide tobacco prevention initiative in Arkansas, which they discuss in Chapter 14. Marian Evans-Lee, the program coordinator, is a coauthor. The initiative was funded by the Tobacco Master Settlement Agreement and administered by the University of Arkansas at Pine Bluff, under the auspices of the Minority Initiative Sub-Recipient Research Grant Office (MISRGO). The tobacco prevention initiative was guided by the Centers for Disease Control and Prevention guidelines. There were 20 grantees across the state conducting tobacco prevention and cessation programs. An evaluation dashboard was developed to help grantees monitor their own performance. It consists of goals, benchmarks or milestones, baselines, and actual performance. Grantees used it to determine if they were making progress toward stated annual goals. It allowed them to make mid-course corrections as needed. The dashboards also enabled the sponsor (Arkansas Health Department), grant administrators (MISRGO), and evaluators to monitor grantee progress as a group throughout the state. The same dashboard findings were reported to the legislature to respond to accountability concerns and future fund allocations.

Research and Reflections

One of the milestones of an approach as it matures is critique and exchange. Empowerment evaluation has been engaged (and, at times, embroiled) in critique, exchange, discourse, and review for two decades (Alkin & Christie, 2004; Altman, 1997; Brown, 1997; Cousins, 2005, 2013; Fetterman, 1994, 1995, 1997a, 1997b, 2005b; Fetterman & Wandersman, 2007; Patton, 1997, 2005; Scriven, 1997, 2005; Sechrest, 1997; Smith, 2007; Stufflebeam, 1994; Wandersman & Snell-Johns, 2005; Wild, 1996). Empowerment evaluation has benefited greatly from this phase of its development, helping to enhance conceptual clarity and methodological specificity.

A second milestone in the evolution of an approach is when research is conducted about it. Research about empowerment evaluation has been growing for over a decade. For example, Christie (2003) conducted a comparison between empowerment evaluation and deliberative democratic evaluation (House & Howe, 2000). She highlighted theoretical similarities and differences in practice, focusing on the degree of stakeholder involvement (see also Fetterman, 2003). Miller and Campbell (2006) conducted a systematic review of empowerment evaluation, as discussed earlier. They found that the reasons for selecting the approach were appropriate. Jeffrey Sheldon (2014) conducted a survey of empowerment evaluators. The findings provided insight into empowerment evaluation theories and mechanisms, as well as the conditions associated with realizing empowerment and self-determination.

In Chapter 15, Matthew Chinman, Joie Acosta, Sarah B. Hunter, and Patricia Ebener summarize 11 years of research on empowerment evaluation. They discuss six studies focused on Getting To Outcomes®, a 10-step result-based approach to accountability that is an operationalization of empowerment evaluation. It is designed to increase the capacity of community-based practitioners to plan, implement, and evaluate quality programs and produce desired outcomes. These authors document how empowerment evaluation improves capacity and performance of key programming activities. They also demonstrate how their measures of capacity predict measures of performance.

David M. Fetterman, Abraham Wandersman, and Shakeh J. Kaftarian bring this volume to a conclusion in Chapter 16. They provide their reflections on emergent themes and next steps, just as they concluded the first volume 21 years ago. However, this time the collection reflects the international scope of the approach. It is a measure of the global acceptance and use of empowerment evaluation. In addition, the tenure of the approach has allowed for colleagues to conduct, study, and learn from long-term (10-year) empowerment evaluations. The aim is to improve practice. The adaptability of empowerment evaluation is also acknowledged, as it operates in a wide variety of settings, including government, corporate, nonprofit, and foundation-funded environments.

However, on reflection, the most significant observation about empowerment evaluation over the past two decades is its growth, in terms of its conceptual clarity and methodological specificity. This includes guiding principles and specific steps and tools.

Fetterman, Wandersman, and Kaftarian venture to consider next steps for empowerment evaluation in the conclusion, recognizing their ideas are based on past practice and experience. As McLuhan phrased it, "We look at the present through a rear-view mirror. We march backwards into the future" (McLuhan & Fiore, 1967, pp. 74–75).

Although no one can predict the future, calculated guesses, probable scenarios, and thoughtful speculations are presented about the future of empowerment evaluation.

CONCLUSION

This book is a paradox much like Plutarch's ship of Theseus. Plutarch raised the question of whether a ship, once restored by replacing every piece, is still the same ship. This collection began as a "simple" revision of the book that helped launch the empowerment evaluation approach—*Empowerment Evaluation: Knowledge and Tools for Self-Assessment and Accountability*. However, in the process of creating a "simple" revision and update, we have replaced every single chapter. In addition, we have added principles and tools that did not exist when the approach was first launched. The revision is so radical that even the title of the book has been changed to explicitly include the term *evaluation capacity building*. Part of the paradox is that many of the principles were implicit. Capacity building was always a fundamental part of the approach. Nevertheless, we believe this collection represents a transformation, literally decades beyond our first voyage. Ultimately, we leave it to the reader to determine if this is the same ship with new sails or an entirely new vessel as they chart their own journey across this book's ocean of discourse, insight, and experience.

REFERENCES

Alkin, M., & Christie, C. (2004). An evaluation theory tree. In M. Alkin (Ed.), *Evaluation roots: Tracing theorists' views and influences* (pp. 381–392). Thousand Oaks, CA: Sage.

Altman, D. (1997). [Review of the book *Empowerment evaluation: Knowledge and tools for self-assessment and accountability*, by Fetterman, Kaftarian, and Wandersman]. *Community Psychologist, 30*(4), 16–17.

Brown, J. (1997). [Review of the book *Empowerment evaluation: Knowledge and tools for self-assessment and accountability,* by Fetterman, Kaftarian, and Wandersman]. *Health Education & Behavior, 24*(3), 388–391.

Chinman, M., Imm, P., and Wandersman, A. (2004). *Getting To Outcomes: Promoting accountability through methods and tools for planning, implementation, and evaluation.* Santa Monica: RAND Corporation. Retrieved from http://www.rand.org/pubs/technical_reports/TR101/

Christie, C. (2003, Spring). What guides evaluation? A study of how evaluation maps on to evaluation theory. *New Directions for Evaluation, 97,* 7–36.

Cousins, B. (2005). Will the real empowerment evaluation please stand up? A critical friend perspective. In D. M. Fetterman & A. Wandersman Eds., *Empowerment evaluation principles in practice.* New York: Guilford Press.

Cousins, B. (2013). Arguments for a common set of principles for collaborative inquiry in evaluation. *American Journal of Evaluation, 34*(1), 7–22.

Donaldson, S. I., Patton, M. Q., Fetterman, D. M., & Scriven, M. (2010, February). The 2009 Claremont debates: The promise and pitfalls of utilization-focused and empowerment evaluation. *Journal of MultiDisciplinary Evaluation, 6*(13).

Fetterman, D. M. (1994). Empowerment evaluation. 1993 Presidential address. *Evaluation Practice, 15*(1), 1–15.

Fetterman, D. M. (1995). [Response to Dr. Daniel Stufflebeam's Empowerment evaluation, objectivist evaluation, and evaluation standards: Where the future of evaluation should not go, where it needs to go, October 1994, 321–338]. *American Journal of Evaluation, 16,* 179–199.

Fetterman, D. M. (1996). Conclusion: Reflection on emergent themes and next steps. In D. M. Fetterman, S. Kaftarian, & A. Wandersman (Eds.), *Empowerment evaluation: Knowledge and tools for self-assessment and accountability.* Thousand Oaks, CA: Sage.

Fetterman, D. M. (1997a). Empowerment evaluation: A response to Patton and Scriven. *Evaluation Practice, 18*(3), 255–260.

Fetterman, D. M. (1997b). [Response to Lee Sechrest's book review of *Empowerment evaluation: knowledge and tools for self-assessment and accountability,* by Fetterman, Kaftarian, and Wandersman]. *Environment and Behavior, 29*(3), 427–436.

Fetterman, D. M. (2001). *Foundations of empowerment evaluation.* Thousand Oaks, CA: Sage.

Fetterman, D. M. (2003). Fetterman-House: A process use distinction and a theory. *New Directions for Evaluation, 97,* 47–52.

Fetterman, D. M. (2004a). Empowerment evaluation. In S. Mathison (Ed.), *Encyclopedia of evaluation.* Thousand Oaks, CA: Sage.

Fetterman, D. M. (2004b). Empowerment evaluation. In A. R. Roberts & K. R. Yeager (Eds.), *Evidence-based practice manual: Research outcome measures in health and human services.* Oxford, UK: Oxford University Press.

Fetterman, D. M. (2005a). Empowerment evaluation: From the digital divide to academic distress. In D. M. Fetterman & A. Wandersman (Eds.), *Empowerment evaluation principles in practice.* New York: Guilford Press.

Fetterman, D. M. (2005b). In response to Drs. Patton and Scriven. *American Journal of Evaluation, 26,* 418–420.

Fetterman, D. M. (2009). Empowerment evaluation at the Stanford University School of Medicine: Using a critical friend to improve the clerkship experience. *Ensaio, 17*(63), 197–204.

Fetterman, D. M. (2012). Empowerment evaluation and accreditation case examples: California Institute of Integral Studies and Stanford University. In C. Secolsky & D. B. Denison (Eds.), *Handbook on measurement, assessment, and evaluation in higher education.* New York: Routledge.

Fetterman, D. M., & Bowman, C. (2002). Experiential education and empowerment evaluation: Mars rover educational program case example. *Journal of Experiential Education, 25*(2), 286–295.

Fetterman, D. M., Deitz, J., & Gesundheit, N. (2010). Empowerment evaluation: A collaborative approach to evaluating and transforming a medical school curriculum. *Academic Medicine: Journal of the Association of American Medical Colleges, 85*(5), 813–820.

Fetterman, D. M., Kaftarian, S., & Wandersman, A. (Eds.). (1996). *Empowerment evaluation: Knowledge and tools for self-assessment and accountability.* Thousand Oaks, CA: Sage.

Fetterman, D. M., & Wandersman, A. (2005). *Empowerment evaluation principles in practice.* New York: Guilford Press.

Fetterman, D. M., & Wandersman, A. (2007). Empowerment evaluation: Yesterday, today, and tomorrow. *American Journal of Evaluation, 28*(2), 179–198.

Firme, T. (2003, November). *Designing evaluation in international contexts: Lessons from the external evaluation of the educational program in Amazonian Brazil.* Paper presented at the annual meeting of the American Evaluation Association, Reno, NV.

House, E., & Howe, W. R. (2000, Spring). Deliberative democratic evaluation. *New Directions for Evaluation, 85,* 3–12.

Joint Committee on Standards for Educational Evaluation. (1994). *The program evaluation standards.* Thousand Oaks, CA: Sage.

Keener, D.C., Snell-Johns, J., Livet, M., & Wandersman, A. (2005). Lessons that influenced the current conceptualization of empowerment evaluation: Reflections from two evaluation projects. In D. M. Fetterman & A. Wandersman (Eds.), *Empowerment evaluation principles in practice.* New York: Guilford Press.

Labin, S. L., Duffy, J. L., Meyers, D. C, Wandersman, A., & Lesesne, C. A. (2012). A research synthesis of the evaluation capacity building literature. *American Journal of Evaluation, 33,* 307–338.

McLuhan, M., & Fiore, Q. (with Agel, J.). (1967). *The medium is the massage: An inventory of effects.* New York: Random House.

Miller, R. L., & Campbell, R. (2006). Taking stock of empowerment evaluation: An empirical review. *American Journal of Evaluation, 27*(9), 296–319.

Patton, M. Q. (1997). Toward distinguishing empowerment evaluation and placing it in a larger context. *Evaluation Practice, 18*(2), 147–163.

Patton, M. Q. (2005). Toward distinguishing empowerment evaluation and placing it in a larger context: Take two. *American Journal of Evaluation, 26,* 408–414.

Plutarch (75 A.C.E.). *Theseus* (J. Dryden, Trans.). Retrieved from http://classics.mit.edu/Plutarch/theseus.html

Scriven, M. (1997). Empowerment evaluation examined. *Evaluation Practice, 18*(2), 165–175.

Scriven, M. (2005). [Review of the book *Empowerment evaluation principles in practice*]. *American Journal of Evaluation, 26*(3), 415–417.

Sechrest, L. (1997). [Review of the book *Empowerment evaluation: Knowledge and tools for self-assessment and accountability*, by Fetterman, Kaftarian, and Wandersman]. *Environment and Behavior, 29*(3), 422–426.

Sheldon, J. A. (2014). *Evaluation as social intervention and the predictability of psychological well-being outcomes from the practice and principles of empowerment evaluation.* Unpublished doctoral dissertation, Claremont Graduate University, Claremont, CA.

Siitonen, J., & Robinson, H. A. (1998). Empowerment: Links to teachers' professional growth. In R. Erkkila, A. Willman, & L. Syrjala (Eds.), *Promoting teachers' personal and professional growth* (pp. 165–191). Oulu, Finland: University of Oulu, Department of Teacher Education.

Smith, N. (2007). Empowerment evaluation as evaluation ideology. *American Journal of Evaluation, 28*(2), 169–178.

Stufflebeam, D. (1994). Empowerment evaluation, objectivist evaluation, and evaluation standards: Where the future of evaluation should not go, where it needs to go. *Evaluation Practice, 15*(3), 321–338.

Wandersman, A., Keener, D.C., Snell-Johns, J., et al. (2004). Empowerment evaluation: Principles in action. In L. A. Jason, C. B. Keys, Y. Suarez-Balcazar, et al. (Eds.), *Participatory community research: Theories and methods in action.* Washington, DC: American Psychological Association.

Wandersman, A., & Snell-Johns, J. (2005). Empowerment evaluation: Clarity, dialogue, and growth. *American Journal of Evaluation, 26*(3), 421–428.

Wandersman, A., Snell-Johns, J., Lentz, B., et al. (2005). The principles of empowerment evaluation. In D. M. Fetterman & A. Wandersman (Eds.), *Empowerment evaluation principles in practice.* New York: Guilford Press.

Wild, T. (1996). [Review of the book *Empowerment evaluation: Knowledge and tools for self-assessment and accountability*]. *Canadian Journal of Program Evaluation, 11*(2), 170–172.

Yarbrough, D. B., Shulha, L. M., Hopson, R. K., & Caruthers, F. A. (2011). *The program evaluation standards: A guide for evaluators and evaluation users* (3rd ed.). Thousand Oaks, CA: Sage.

CHAPTER 2

Empowerment Evaluation

Theories, Principles, Concepts, and Steps

David M. Fetterman

Fetterman & Associates and Stanford University

This discussion highlights the theories, principles, concepts, and steps of empowerment evaluation. They represent the conceptual building blocks of the approach. Together, they link theory to practice. The sequence, from the abstract to specific concrete steps, is designed to help practitioners understand and implement empowerment evaluation practice.

OVERVIEW

Empowerment evaluation is guided by empowerment, self-determination, and evaluation capacity building theories. It is also informed by specific evaluation theories, including process use and theories of use and action. In turn, these theories help define 10 overarching principles that provide empowerment evaluation with an explicit direction and purpose, beginning with improvement and continuing to accountability. Key concepts that help define empowerment evaluation include critical friends, cultures of evidence, cycles of reflection and action, communities of learners, and reflective practitioners (Fetterman, 2009, 2012; Fetterman, Deitz, & Gesundheit, 2010; Fetterman & Wandersman, 2005, 2007).

There are many ways to implement an empowerment evaluation. However, two of the most popular approaches are the 3-step and 10-step models.[1] These steps help to further

_____

1. There is also an equally popular 10-step approach referred to as Getting to Outcomes, developed by Chinman, Imm, and Wandersman (2004).

explicate the nature of empowerment evaluation in practice. The theories, principles, concepts, and steps are interrelated and reinforcing. The theories provide a birds-eye view of the approach, while the steps provide turn-by-turn insights. Together they provide a rich and layered map of the dynamic terrain of empowerment evaluation.

THEORIES

An exploration into the theories guiding empowerment evaluation practice will help to illuminate the integral relationship between method and use in empowerment evaluation. The pertinent theories guiding empowerment evaluation are empowerment theory, self-determination theory, evaluation capacity building, process use, and theories of use and action. *Empowerment theory* is divided into processes and outcomes. This theory has implications for the role of the empowerment evaluator or facilitator, which can differ from that of a traditional evaluator. *Self-determination* is one of the foundational concepts underlying empowerment theory, and it helps to detail specific mechanisms or behaviors that enable the actualization of empowerment. *Process use* represents much of the rationale or logic underlying empowerment evaluation in practice, because it cultivates ownership by placing the approach in community and staff members' hands. Finally, the alignment of *theories of use and action* explains how empowerment evaluation helps people produce desired results.

Empowerment Theory

Writings in community psychology have developed an area called empowerment theory. Empowerment theory is about gaining control, obtaining resources, and understanding one's social environment. It is also about problem solving, leadership, and decision making. It operates on many levels, and distinguishing between empowering processes and outcomes is critical. According to Zimmerman (2000):

> Empowerment processes are ones in which attempts to gain control, obtain needed resources, and critically understand one's social environment are fundamental. The process is empowering if it helps people develop skills so they can become independent problem solvers and decision makers. Empowering processes will vary across levels of analysis. For example, empowering processes for individuals might include organizational or community involvement,

empowering processes at the organizational level might include shared leadership and decision making, and empowering processes at the community level might include accessible government, media, and other community resources. (pp. 44–45)

Similar to the distinctions of process and outcome in evaluation, empowerment theory processes contribute to specific outcomes. Linking the processes to outcomes helps draw meta-level causal relationships or at least a chain of reasoning. When specified outcomes are achieved, it is possible to retrace steps to determine which processes were most effective. Similarly, when specific processes are implemented poorly, it is easy to see the causal relationship or at least the contributing factors associated with a failure to achieve specified outcomes. Zimmerman (2000) provides additional insight into the outcome level of analysis to further explicate empowerment theory:

> Empowerment outcomes refer to operationalization of empowerment so we can study the consequences of citizen attempts to gain greater control in their community or the effects of interventions designed to empower participants. Empowered outcomes also differ across levels of analysis. When we are concerned with individuals, outcomes might include situation-specific perceived control, skills, and proactive behaviors. When we are studying organizations, outcomes might include organizational networks, effective resource acquisition, and policy leverage. When we are concerned with community level empowerment, outcomes might include evidence of pluralism, the existence of organizational coalitions, and accessible community resources. (pp. 44–45)

Self-Determination Theory[2]

The theoretical level of empowerment processes and outcomes requires mechanisms to link it to action. Mithaug's (1991, 1993, 1996) extensive work with individuals with disabilities to explore the concept of self-determination provided theoretical inspiration and guidance. The concept of self-determination details specific mechanisms that help program staff members and participants implement

---

2. Mithaug's work in this area is typically referred to as self-regulation theory, with self-determination as a guiding concept in his work. For the purposes of clarity and as it relates to instructing empowerment evaluation, self-determination is being used as the umbrella term in this discussion.

an empowerment evaluation. Self-determination was one of the foundational concepts in the study that informs empowerment evaluation today.

Self-determination is defined as the ability to chart one's own course in life. It consists of numerous interconnected capabilities, such as the ability to identify and express needs; establish goals or expectations and a plan of action to achieve them; identify resources; make rational choices from various alternative courses of action; take appropriate steps to pursue objectives; evaluate short- and long-term results, including reassessing plans and expectations and taking necessary detours; and persist in the pursuit of those goals. A breakdown at any juncture of this network of capabilities—as well as various environmental factors—can reduce a person's likelihood of being self-determined.[3]

Mithaug and Fetterman, as part of an American Institutes for Research team, completed a 2-year grant funded by the U.S. Department of Education on self-determination and individuals with disabilities. They conducted research designed to help both providers for students with disabilities and the students themselves become more empowered. They learned about self-determined behavior and attitudes and environmentally related features of self-determination by listening to self-determined children with disabilities and their providers.

Evaluation Capacity Building Theory

Capacity building has been a driving force in empowerment evaluation since its inception (Fetterman, 1994; Fetterman, Kaftarian, & Wandersman, 1996; Fetterman & Wandersman, 2007). The evaluation capacity literature has coincided and intersected with the empowerment evaluation literature. (For more information about evaluation capacity building, see Boyle, 1999; Duffy & Wandersman, 2007; Gibbs et al., 2002; Kotter, 1996; Milstein & Cotton, 2000; Owen, 2003; Preskill & Boyle, 2008; Sanders, 2003; Stockdill et al., 2002; Suarez-Balcazar et al., 2010; Taylor-Ritzler et al., 2010.)

Labin, Duffy, Meyers, Wandersman, and Lesesne (2012) conducted a research synthesis on the topic and define evaluation capacity building (ECB) as "an intentional process to increase individual motivation, knowledge, and skills, and to enhance a group or organization's ability to conduct or use

---

3. See also Bandura (1982) for more detail on issues related to self-efficacy and self-determination.

evaluation" (p. 2). The assumption is that ECB strategies will improve individual attitudes, knowledge, and skills as evidenced by behavioral changes. In addition, ECB strategies will facilitate sustainable organizational learning. Strategies include formal and informal training, face-to-face communications, and remote meetings. In empowerment evaluation, training is typically by doing or conducting the evaluation (with the assistance of an empowerment evaluator). In addition, ECB cultivates a sense of ownership that increases the probability that the individual and/or group will use the findings and recommendations. This, in turn, helps produce desired outcomes.

Organizational contexts, such as adequate resources and supportive leadership, represent critical ECB factors encouraging individual learning and behavior, as well as organizational growth. Empowerment evaluation has adopted ECB as one of its guiding principles, and ECB is a central tenet of the approach (Fetterman & Wandersman, 2005).

Process Use Theory

One of the most significant problems facing the field of evaluation is inadequate knowledge utilization. Evaluation reports often sit and gather dust. Decisions are made without the benefit of being informed by evaluation findings. Empowerment evaluation is designed to be used by people. It places evaluation in the hands of community and staff members. The more that people are engaged in conducting their own evaluations, the more likely they are to believe in them, because the evaluation findings are theirs. In addition, a byproduct of this experience is that they learn to think evaluatively. This makes them more likely to make decisions and take actions based on their evaluation data. This way of thinking is at the heart of process use.[4]

According to Patton (2002), "Helping people learn to think evaluatively by participating in real evaluation exercises is what I've come to call 'process use' (Patton 1997, 1998). I have defined process use as relating to and being indicated by individual changes in thinking and behaving that occur among those involved in evaluation as a result of the learning that occurs *during the evaluation process*" (p. 189). In an empowerment evaluation, thinking evaluatively is a product of guided immersion. This occurs when people conduct their own evaluation as guided by an empowerment evaluator. Teaching

---

4. There is a substantial literature concerning the use of evaluation. However, most of it is devoted to lessons learned after the evaluation. The discussion of process use in this context focuses on use during an evaluation.

people to think evaluatively is like teaching them to fish. It can last a lifetime and is what evaluative sustainability is all about—internalizing evaluation (individually and institutionally).

Empowerment evaluation requires participation. Participation or immersion is a form of experiential education. This guided immersion helps people to see the world through an evaluative lens. Participation also creates an authentic, credible, and almost palpable sense of ownership. It is this combination of evaluative thought and ownership, through immersion, that makes empowerment evaluation work, improving knowledge utilization in the process.

Theories of Action and Use

Once the groundwork is laid with empowerment, self-determination, and ECB theory, as well as process use theories, conceptual mechanisms become more meaningful. Theories that enable comparisons between use and action are essential. The approach works when the pieces are in place. When things go wrong, which is normal in life, it is possible to compare and identify the areas needing attention.

Empowerment evaluation relies on the reciprocal relationship between theories of action and use at every step in the process. A *theory of action* is usually the espoused operating theory about how a program or organization works. It is a useful tool, generally based on program personnel views. The theory of action is often compared with the theory of use. Theory of use is the actual program reality, the observable behavior of stakeholders (see Argyris & Schon, 1978; Patton, 1997). People engaged in empowerment evaluations create a theory of action at one stage and test it against the existing theory of use during a later stage. Similarly, they create a new theory of action as they plan for the future. Because empowerment evaluation is an ongoing and iterative process, stakeholders test their theories of action against theories in use during various microcycles to determine whether their strategies are being implemented as recommended or designed. The theories go hand in hand in empowerment evaluation.

Theories of action and use are used to identify significant differences between the ideal and the real. For example, communities of empowerment evaluation practice compare their theory of action with their theory of use to determine whether they are even pointing in the same direction. Three common patterns that emerge from this comparison are *in alignment, out of alignment,* and *alignment in conflict* (Figure 2.1). In alignment is when the two theories are parallel or pointed in the same direction. They may be distant or close levels of alignment, but they are on the same general track. Out of alignment occurs when actual practice is divergent from the espoused theory of how things are supposed to work. The theory of use is not simply distant or closely aligned, but actually off target or at least pointed in another direction. Alignment in conflict occurs when the theory of action and use are pointed in diametrically opposite directions. This signals a group or organization in serious trouble or self-denial.

After making the first-level comparison, a gross indicator, to determine whether the theories of action and use are even remotely related to each other, communities of empowerment evaluation practice compare their theory of action with their theory of use in an effort to reduce the gap between them. This assumes they are at least pointed in the same direction. The ideal progression is from distant alignment to close alignment between the two theories. This is the conceptual space where most communities of empowerment evaluation practice strive to accomplish their goals as they close the gap between the theories (Figure 2.2).

The process of empowerment embraces the tension between the two types of theories and offers a means for reconciling gaps. This dialectic, in which theories of action and use are routinely juxtaposed in daily practice, creates a culture of learning and evaluation.

Figure 2.1   Contrasting patterns of alignment

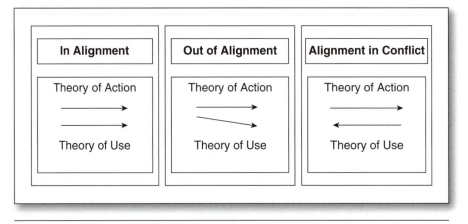

SOURCE: © 2001 by Fetterman and Eiler. Reprinted from *Empowerment Evaluation and Organizational Learning: A Path Toward Mainstreaming Evaluation.* American Evaluation Association, St. Louis, MO.

Figure 2.2 Aligning theories of action and use to reduce the gap

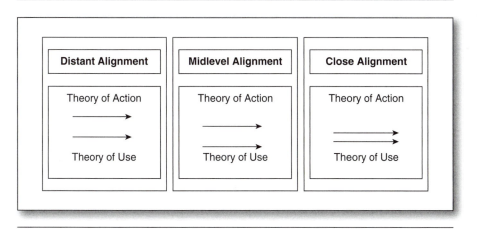

SOURCE: © 2001 by Fetterman and Eiler. Reprinted from *Empowerment Evaluation and Organizational Learning: A Path Toward Mainstreaming Evaluation.* American Evaluation Association, St. Louis, MO.

PRINCIPLES

The theoretical foundations of empowerment evaluation lead to specific principles required to inform quality practice. Empowerment evaluation principles provide a sense of direction and purposefulness throughout an evaluation. Empowerment evaluation is guided by 10 specific principles (Fetterman & Wandersman, 2005, pp. 1–2, 27–72). These principles are as follows:

1. Improvement: Empowerment evaluation is designed to help people improve program performance; it is designed to help people build on their successes and reevaluate areas meriting attention.

2. Community ownership: Empowerment evaluation values and facilitates community control; use and sustainability are dependent on a sense of ownership.

3. Inclusion: Empowerment evaluation invites involvement, participation, and diversity; contributions come from all levels and walks of life.

4. Democratic participation: Participation and decision making should be open and fair.

5. Social justice: Evaluation can and should be used to address social inequities in society.

6. Community knowledge: Empowerment evaluation respects and values community knowledge.

7. Evidence-based strategies: Empowerment evaluation respects and uses the knowledge base of scholars (in conjunction with community knowledge).

8. Capacity building: Empowerment evaluation is designed to enhance stakeholders' ability to conduct evaluation and to improve program planning and implementation.

9. Organizational learning: Data should be used to evaluate new practices, inform decision making, and implement program practices; empowerment evaluation is used to help organizations learn from their experience (building on successes, learning from mistakes, and making mid-course corrections).

10. Accountability: Empowerment evaluation is focused on outcomes and accountability; empowerment evaluation functions within the context of existing policies, standards, and measures of accountability; did the program or initiative accomplish its objectives?

Empowerment evaluation principles help evaluators and community members make decisions that are in alignment with the larger purpose or goals associated with capacity building and self-determination. The principle of inclusion, for example, reminds evaluators and community leaders to include rather than exclude members of the community, even though fiscal, logistic, and personality factors might suggest otherwise. The capacity building principle reminds the evaluator to provide community members with the opportunity to collect their own data, even though it might initially be faster and easier for the evaluator to collect the same information. The accountability principle guides community members to hold one another accountable. It also situates the evaluation with the context of external requirements and credible results or outcomes (see Fetterman & Wandersman, 2005, p. 2).

CONCEPTS

Empowerment evaluation concepts provide a more instrumental view of how to implement the approach. Key concepts include critical friends, cultures of evidence, cycles of reflection and action, communities of learners, and reflective practitioners (see Fetterman, Deitz, & Gesundheit, 2010).[5] A critical friend is an evaluator who facilitates the process and steps of empowerment evaluation. This evaluator believes in the purpose of the program but provides constructive feedback designed to promote improvement. A critical friend helps to raise many of the difficult questions and, as appropriate, tells the hard truths in a diplomatic fashion. In addition, this person helps to ensure the evaluation remains organized, rigorous, and honest (Fetterman, 2009, 2012; Fetterman, Deitz, & Gesundheit, 2010).

Empowerment evaluators help cultivate a culture of evidence by asking people why they believe what they believe. They are asked for evidence or documentation at every stage, so that it becomes normal and expected to have data to support one's opinions and views. Cycles of reflection and action involve ongoing phases of analysis, decision making, and implementation (based on evaluation findings). It is a cyclical process. Programs are dynamic, not static, and require continual feedback as they change and evolve. Empowerment evaluation is successful when it is institutionalized and becomes a normal part of the planning and management of the program.

Empowerment evaluation is driven by a group process. It is a community of learners. Group members learn from each other, serving as their own peer review group, critical friend, resource, and norming mechanism. Individual members of the group hold each other accountable concerning progress toward stated goals. Finally, empowerment evaluations help create reflective practitioners. Reflective practitioners use data to inform their decisions and actions concerning their own daily activities. This produces a self-aware and self-actualized individual who has the capacity to apply this worldview to all aspects of their life. As individuals develop and enhance their own capacity, they improve the quality of the group's exchange, deliberation, and action plans (see Lentz, Imm, Yost, et al., 2005).

STEPS

There are many ways in which to implement an empowerment evaluation. In fact, empowerment evaluation has accumulated a warehouse of useful tools. The 3-step (Fetterman, 2001) and 10-step Getting To Outcomes (Chinman, Imm, & Wandersman, 2004) approaches to empowerment evaluation are the most popular tools in the collection.

---

5. These concepts are influenced by traditional organizational development and transformation theorists, including Argyris and Schon (1978) and Senge (1994), as well as evaluators associated with organizational learning (e.g., Preskill).

Three-Step Approach

The three-step approach includes helping a group (1) establish their mission, (2) take stock of their current status, and (3) plan for the future. The popularity of this particular approach is in part a result of its simplicity, effectiveness, and transparency.

Mission. The group comes to a consensus concerning their mission or values. This gives them a shared vision of what's important to them and where they want to go. The empowerment evaluator facilitates this process by asking participants to generate statements that reflect their mission. These phrases are recorded on a poster sheet of paper (Figure 2.3) and may be projected using an LCD projector depending on the technology available. These phrases are used to draft a mission statement (crafted by a member of the group and the empowerment evaluator). The draft is circulated among the group. They are asked to "approve" it and/or suggest specific changes in wording as needed. A consensus about the mission statement helps the group think clearly about their self-assessment and plans for the future. It anchors the group in common values.

Figure 2.3 Mission

Mission

1. Democratic
2. Transparent
3. Group values
4. Honor existing mission but go where the energy is in the room
5. Giving voice and making meaning

Taking Stock. After coming to a consensus about the mission, the group evaluates their efforts (within the context of a set of shared values). First, the empowerment evaluator helps members of the group generate a list of the most important activities required to accomplish organizational or programmatic goals. The empowerment evaluator gives each participant five dot stickers and asks the participants to place them by the activities they think are the most important for accomplishing programmatic and organizational goals (and thus the most important to evaluate as a group from that point on). Their use of the dots can range from putting one sticker on five different activities to putting all five on one activity if they are concerned that activity will not get enough votes (Figure 2.4). The top 10 items with the most dots represent the results of the prioritization part of taking stock. The 10 activities represent the heart of part two of taking stock: rating.

Figure 2.4 Taking stock, part I

Taking Stock

Part I

- List activities
- Prioritize (dots)

Activities	Prioritization with Dots
Communication	○ ○ ○ ○
Product Development	○ ○ ○ ○ ○ ○ ○
Fundraising	○ ○ ○

The empowerment evaluator asks participants in the group to rate how well they are doing concerning each of the activities selected, using a 1 (low) to 10 (high) scale (Figure 2.5). The columns are averaged horizontally and vertically. Vertically, the group can see who is typically optimistic and/or pessimistic. This helps the group calibrate or evaluate the ratings and opinions of each individual member. It helps the group establish norms. Horizontally, the averages provide the group with a consolidated view of how well (or poorly) things are going. The empowerment evaluator facilitates a discussion and dialogue about the ratings, asking participants why they gave a certain activity a 3 or a 7, for example.

The dialogue about the ratings is one of the most important parts of the process. In addition to clarifying issues, evidence is used to support viewpoints and "sacred cows" are surfaced and examined during dialogue. Moreover, the process of specifying the reason or evidence for a rating provides the group with a more efficient and focused manner of identifying what needs to be done next, during the planning for the future step of the process. Instead of generating an unwieldy list of strategies and solutions that may or may not be relevant to the issues at hand, the group can focus its energies on the specific concerns and reasons for a low rating that were raised in the dialogue or exchange.

Figure 2.5 Taking stock, part II

Taking Stock

Part II

- Rating 1 (low) – 10 (high)
- Dialogue

Activities	DF	DE	SEC	Average
Communication	3	6	3	4
Teaching	4	5	9	6
Funding	5	2	1	2.67
Prod. Develop	1	8	4	4.33
Average	3.25	5.25	4.25	4.25

Planning for the Future. Many evaluations conclude at the taking stock phase. However, taking stock is a baseline and a launching-off point for the rest of the evaluation. After rating and discussing programmatic activities, it is important to do something about the findings. It is time to plan for the future (Figure 2.6). This step involves generating goals, strategies, and credible evidence (to determine if the strategies are being implemented and if they are effective). The goals are directly related to the activities selected in the taking stock step. For example, if communication was selected, rated, and discussed, then communication (or improving communication) should be one of the goals. The strategies emerge from the taking stock discussion, as well, as noted earlier. For example, if communication received a low rating and one of the reasons was because the group never had agendas for their meetings, then preparing agendas might become a recommended strategy in the planning for the future exercise.

Figure 2.6 Planning for the future

Planning for the Future

- Goals
- Strategies
- Evidence

Monitoring the Strategies. Many programs, projects, and evaluations fail at this stage for lack of individual and group accountability. Individuals who spoke eloquently and/or emotionally about a certain topic should be asked to volunteer to lead specific task forces to respond to identified problems or concerns. They do not have to complete the task. However, they are responsible for taking the lead in a circumscribed area (a specific goal) and reporting the status of the effort periodically at ongoing management meetings. Similarly, the group should make a commitment to reviewing the status of these new strategies as a group (and be willing to make mid-course corrections if they are not working). Conventional and innovative evaluation tools are used to monitor the strategies, including online surveys, focus groups, interviews, as well as the use of a quasi-experimental design (where appropriate). In addition, program-specific metrics are developed, using baselines, benchmarks or milestones, and goals (as deemed useful and appropriate). For example, a minority tobacco prevention program empowerment evaluation in Arkansas has established (Figure 2.7):

1. Baselines (the number of people using tobacco in their community)

2. Goals (the number of people they plan to help stop using tobacco by the end of the year)

3. Benchmarks or Milestones (the number of people they expect to help stop using tobacco each month)

4. Actual Performance (the actual number of people they help to stop smoke at each interval throughout the year)

These four metrics are used to help a community monitor program implementation efforts and enable program staff and community members to make mid-course corrections and substitute ineffective strategies with potentially more effective ones as needed. These data are also invaluable when the group conducts a second taking stock exercise (3 to 6 months later) to determine if they are making progress toward their desired goals and objectives. Additional metrics enable community members to compare, for example, their baseline assessments with their benchmarks/milestones or expected points of progress, as well as their goals (see Chapter 14 for an example of this metric or Empowerment Evaluation Dashboard).

Figure 2.7 Baseline

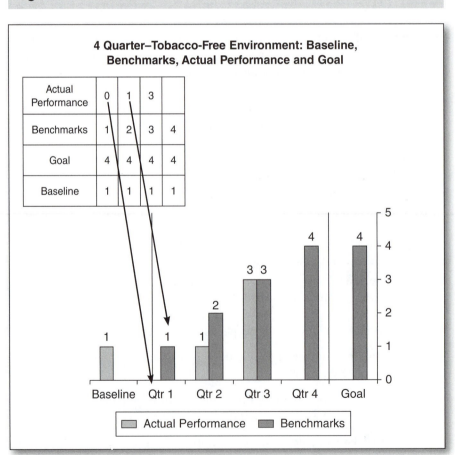

Ten-Step Getting To Outcomes® Approach

The 10-step approach is called Getting To Outcomes® (GTO®; Chinman et al., 2004). GTO is a method for planning, implementing, and evaluating programs in order to achieve success. GTO provides a framework of 10 accountability questions. When answered with quality, they provide a pathway to help programs achieve results and demonstrate accountability (see Table 2.1).

The first step is to conduct a needs and resource assessment to determine what the important issues are in the community, school, or agency. This involves collecting both qualitative and quantitative data about the problem, for example, using community forums, interviews, surveys, and archival documentation. The orienting question is: What are the needs and resources in your organization/community/state?

The second step is to identify the goals, target population, and desired outcomes. Set up short- and long-term (realistic) objectives to help assess progress toward desired objectives. An orienting question is: What are the goals, target population, and desired outcomes (objectives) for your organization/community/state?

The third task is to review the literature and similar programs to find best practices. It is not necessary to reinvent the wheel. Programs should be selected with an established evidence base. An orienting question is: How does the intervention incorporate knowledge or science and best practices in this area?

The fourth step is to determine how well the program or initiative (selected in step 3) fits the needs of the target population and community. This is an important stage in which to consult with community leaders about the value of the proposed program. An orienting question is: How does the intervention fit with other programs already being offered?

Fifth, determine if your organization has the capacity to implement the selected program with quality. This includes funding, staffing, expertise, and community contacts. This will help to prevent program failure. One of the orienting questions is: What capacities do you need to put this intervention into place with quality?

Sixth, make a plan to implement your program. This includes determining (1) who will implement the program; (2) what needs to be done; (3) when, where, how, and why the tasks will be completed; and (4) what and how much will happen as a result of community participation in the program. An orientation question is: How will this intervention be carried out?

Seventh, ask if the program is being implemented faithfully and with quality (at least in spirit). Describe what was done, how program activities were executed, who was served, and what detours were required along the way. An orientation question is: How will the quality of implementation be assessed?

Eighth, think about how you will measure if the program met its goals and produced desired outcomes. This involves selecting or designing an appropriate evaluation design, data collection tools, and data analysis plans. An orienting question is: How well did the intervention work?

Ninth, plan for continuous quality improvement. Use existing evaluation findings to inform ongoing decision making about program operations. Develop a culture of organizational learning. An orienting question is: How will continuous quality improvement strategies be incorporated?

Table 2.1 GTO Accountability Questions

1. Needs Assessment	• What are the needs and resources in your organization/school/community/state?
2. Goal Setting	• What are the goals, target population, and desired outcomes (objectives) for your school/community/state?
3. Science and Best Practices	• How does the intervention incorporate knowledge or science and best practices in this area?
4. Collaboration; Cultural Competence	• How does the intervention fit with other programs already being offered?
5. Capacity Building	• What capacities do you need to put this intervention into place with quality?
6. Planning	• How will this intervention be carried out?
7. Implementation/Process Evaluation	• How will the quality of implementation be assessed?
8. Outcome and Impact Evaluation	• How well did the intervention work?
9. Total Quality Management; Continuous Quality Improvement	• How will continuous quality improvement strategies be incorporated?
10. Sustainability and Institutionalization	• If the intervention is (or components are) successful, how will the intervention be sustained?

SOURCE: Adapted from Chinman, Imm, and Wandersman (2004).

Finally, tenth, review sustainability considerations. Does the problem continue to exist? Do the data merit future funding? If so, identify program advocates and search for continued funding streams. An orienting question is: If the intervention is (or components are) successful, how will the intervention be sustained?

These steps and guiding questions are designed to build evaluation capacity and improve the probability of program success and sustainability. There are many GTO manuals with worksheets designed to address how to answer each of the 10 questions (e.g., Chinman et al., 2004). GTO has been used in multiple domains, including substance abuse prevention, underage drinking (Imm, Chinman, Wandersman, Rosenbloom, Guckenburg, & Leis, 2006), promoting positive youth development (Fisher, Imm, Chinman, & Wandersman, 2006), and home visiting programs (Mattox, Hunter, Kilburn, & Wiseman, 2013). (See Chapter 9, this volume, for a discussion about GTO and evaluation capacity building and Chapter 15 concerning research on GTO.)

In addition, empowerment evaluations are using many other tools, including photo journaling, online surveys, virtual conferencing formats, blogs, shared Web documents and sites, infographics and data visualization (Fetterman, 2013), ethnography (Fetterman, 2010) and creative youth self-assessments (Sabo, 2001).

ROLE

While steps are useful and necessary, relationships play a pivotal role in the process of conducting an empowerment evaluation. The role of the critical friend merits attention because it is like a fulcrum in terms of fundamental relationships. Applied improperly, it can be like a wedge inhibiting movement and change; applied correctly, this role can be used to leverage and maximize the potential of a group. The empowerment evaluator can differ from many traditional evaluators. Instead of being the "expert" and completely independent, separate, and detached from the people he or she works with, so as not to get "contaminated" or "biased," the empowerment evaluator works closely with and alongside program staff members and participants. Empowerment evaluators are not in charge. The people they work with are in charge of the direction and execution of the evaluation. Empowerment evaluators are critical friends or coaches. They believe in the merits of a particular type of program, but they pose the difficult questions (in a diplomatic fashion). Some people ask, How can empowerment evaluators be objective and critical if they are friends and in favor of a particular type of program? The answer is simple:

Empowerment evaluators are critical and objective because they want the program to work (or work better).

Zimmerman's (2000) characterization of the community psychologist's role in empowerment activities is easily adapted to the empowerment evaluator. It also demonstrates the impact of theory on practice, shaping the approach, including the evaluator's role.

> An empowerment approach to intervention design, implementation, and evaluation redefines the professional's role relationship with the target population. The professional's role becomes one of collaborator and facilitator rather than expert and counselor. As collaborators, professionals learn about the participants through their cultures, their worldviews, and their life struggles. The professional works *with* participants instead of advocating *for* them. The professional's skills, interest, or plans are not imposed on the community; rather, professionals become a resource for a community. This role relationship suggests that what professionals do will depend on the particular place and people with whom they are working, rather than on the technologies that are predetermined to be applied in all situations. (pp. 44–45)

Empowerment evaluators are trained evaluators with considerable expertise. They provide it as needed to keep the evaluation systematic, rigorous, and on track. They are able to function in this capacity by advising, rather than directing or controlling an evaluation. They provide a structure or set of steps to conduct an evaluation. They recommend, rather than require, specific activities and tools. They listen and rely on the group's knowledge and understanding of their local situation. The critical friend is much like a financial advisor or personal health trainer. Instead of judging and making pronouncements about successes or failure, compliance or noncompliance, the empowerment evaluator serves the group or community in an attempt to help them maximize their potential and unleash their creative and productive energy for a common good. Important attributes of a critical friend include creating an environment conductive to dialogue and discussion; providing or requesting data to inform decision making; facilitating rather than leading; and being open to ideas, inclusive, and willing to learn.

An eloquent literature on empowerment theory by Zimmerman (2000); Zimmerman, Israel, Schulz, and Checkoway (1992); Zimmerman and Rappaport (1988); and Dunst, Trivette, and LaPointe (1992) also informs empowerment evaluation.

CONCLUSION

This chapter summarizes the theories, principles, concepts, and primary steps of empowerment evaluation, all of which provide additional conceptual and methodological rigor to the field and guidance for practitioners in the field. Theory is often derided in the field, cited as being out of touch or at best irrelevant. A humorist captured this view of ivory tower theory:

> A young student ran madly into the classroom proclaiming the value of his program: "Professor, it worked. My program worked in practice." In response the professor asked, "Wonderful, but does it work in theory?"

Lamentably, this is not a completely apocryphal story. Too often, the scholarly focus on theory has been to the exclusion of valuing practice. Lewin helped to reclaim the role of theory in practice. He wrote, "There is nothing more practical than a good theory" (1952, p. 169). Theory can provide a social road map where there is none to be seen by the naked eye. It helps guide practice. Theory can help communities chart their course across a vast ocean of uncertainty and despair.

However, theory not grounded in reality is of dubious value. Bledow, Frese, Anderson, Erez, and Farr (2009) countered the conventional wisdom when they argued there is "nothing as theoretical as a good practice."[6] This complementary and dialectic perspective is a useful reminder that theory can be built from the ground up, for example, grounded theory (Glaser & Strauss, 1999). It is built on people's daily practice and thus produces a strong foundation to build understanding.

This chapter highlights the role of theory to guide empowerment evaluation. However, theory, concepts, principles, and practice are mutually reinforcing and feed into each other. Together they are tools forged in the real world and designed to help people help themselves as each chapter demonstrates throughout this collection.

REFERENCES

Argyris, C., & Schon, D. A. (1978). *Organizational learning: A theory of action perspective.* Reading, MA: Addison-Wesley.

Bandura, A. (1982). Self-efficacy mechanism in human agency. *American Psychologist, 37,* 122–147.

---

6. See Friedman and Rogers (2009) as applied to action research.

Bledow, R., Frese, M., Anderson, N., Erez, M., & Farr, J. (2009). Extending and refining the dialectic perspective on innovation: There is nothing as practical as a good theory; nothing as theoretical as a good practice. *Industrial and Organizational Psychology, 2*(3), 363–373.

Boyle, R. (1999). Professionalizing the evaluation function: Human resource development and the building of evaluation capacity. In R. Boyle & D. Lemaire (Eds.), *Building effective evaluation capacity* (pp. 135–151). New Brunswick, NJ: Transaction.

Chinman, M., Imm, P., & Wandersman, A. (2004). *Getting To Outcomes: Promoting accountability through methods and tools for planning, implementation, and evaluation.* Santa Monica, CA: RAND Corporation. Retrieved from http://www.rand.org/pubs/technical_reports/TR101/

Duffy, J. L., & Wandersman, A. (2007, November). *A review of research on evaluation capacity-building strategies.* Paper presented at the annual conference of the American Evaluation Association, Baltimore, MD.

Dunst, C. J., Trivette, C. M., & LaPointe, N. (1992). Toward clarification of the meaning and key elements of empowerment. *Family Science Review, 5,* 111–130.

Fetterman, D. M. (1994). Empowerment evaluation. *Evaluation Practice, 15*(1), 1–15.

Fetterman, D. M. (2009). Empowerment evaluation at the Stanford University School of Medicine: Using a critical friend to improve the clerkship experience. *Ensaio, 17*(63), 197–204.

Fetterman, D. M. (2010). *Ethnography: Step by step* (3rd ed.). Thousand Oaks, CA: Sage.

Fetterman, D. M. (2012). Empowerment evaluation and accreditation case examples: California Institute of Integral Studies and Stanford University. In C. Secolsky (Ed.), *Measurement and evaluation in higher education.* London: Routledge.

Fetterman, D. M., Deitz, J., & Gesundheit, N. (2010). Empowerment evaluation: A collaborative approach to evaluating and transforming a medical school curriculum. *Academic Medicine, 85*(5), 813–820.

Fetterman, D. M., Kaftarian, S., & Wandersman, A. (1996). *Empowerment evaluation: Knowledge and tools for self-assessment and accountability.* Thousand Oaks, CA: Sage.

Fetterman, D. M., & Wandersman, A. (2005). *Empowerment evaluation principles in practice.* New York: Guilford Press.

Fetterman, D. M., & Wandersman, A. (2007). Empowerment evaluation: yesterday, today, and tomorrow. *American Journal of Evaluation, 28*(2), 179–198.

Fischer, D., Imm, P., Chinman, M., & Wandersman, A. (2006). *Getting To Outcomes with developmental assets: Ten steps to measuring success in youth programs and communities.* Minneapolis, MN: Search.

Friedman, V., & Rogers, T. (2009). There is nothing so theoretical as good action research. *Action Research, 171*(1), 31–47.

Gibbs, D., Napp, D., Jolly, D., Westover, B., & Uhl, G. (2002). Increasing evaluation capacity within community-based HIV prevention programs. *Evaluation and Program Planning, 25,* 261–269.

Glaser, B., & Strauss, A. (1999). *The discovery of grounded theory: Strategies for qualitative research.* New Brunswick, NJ: Aldine Transition.

Imm, P., Chinman, M., Wandersman, A., Rosenbloom, D., Guckenburg, S., & Leis, R. (2006). *Preventing underage drinking: Using Getting To Outcomes with the SAMHSA strategic prevention framework to achieve results.* Santa Monica, CA: RAND Corporation.

Kotter, J. (1996). *Leading change.* Cambridge, MA: Harvard Business School Press.

Labin, S., Duffy, J. L., Meyers, D. C., Wandersman, A., & Lesesne, C. A. (2013). A research synthesis of the evaluation capacity building literature. *American Journal of Evaluation, 33*(3), 307–338.

Lentz, B. E., Imm, P. S., Yost, J. B., Johnson, N. P., Barron, C., Lindberg, M. S., et al. (2005). Empowerment evaluation and organizational learning: A case study of a community coalition designed to prevent child abuse and neglect. In D. M. Fetterman & A. Wandersman (Eds.), *Empowerment evaluation principles in practice* (pp. 155–183). Thousand Oaks, CA: Sage.

Mattox, T., Hunter, S. B., Kilburn, M. R., & Wiseman, S. H. (2013). *Getting To Outcomes® for home visiting: How to plan, implement, and evaluate a program in your community to support parents and their young children.* Santa Monica, CA: RAND Corporation. Retrieved from http://www.rand.org/pubs/tools/TL114.html

Milstein, B., & Cotton, D. (2000). *Defining concepts for the presidential strand on building evaluation capacity.* Working paper circulated in advance of the November 2000 meeting of the American Evaluation Association.

Mithaug, D. E. (1991). *Self-determined kids: Raising satisfied and successful children.* New York: Macmillan.

Mithaug, D. E. (1993). *Self-regulation theory: How optimal adjustment maximizes gain.* New York: Praeger.

Mithaug, D. E. (1996). Fairness, liberty, and empowerment evaluation. In D. M. Fetterman, S. Kaftarian, & A. Wandersman (Eds.), *Empowerment evaluation: Knowledge and tools for self-assessment and accountability* (pp. 234–258).Thousand Oaks, CA: Sage.

Owen, J. M. (2003). Evaluation culture: A definition and analysis of its development within organizations. *Evaluation Journal of Australasia, 3,* 43–47.

Patton, M. Q. (1997). *Utilization-focused evaluation: The new century text* (3rd ed.). Thousand Oaks, CA: Sage.

Patton, M. Q. (2002). *Qualitative research and evaluation methods.* Thousand Oaks, CA: Sage.

Preskill, H., & Boyle, S. (2008). A multidisciplinary model of evaluation capacity building. *American Journal of Evaluation, 29,* 443–459.

Preskill, H., & Torres, R. T. (1999). *Evaluative inquiry for learning in organizations.* Thousand Oaks, CA: Sage.

Sabo, K. (2003, August). Youth participatory evaluation: A field in the making. *New Directions in Evaluation, 98.*

Sanders, J. R. (2003). Mainstreaming evaluation. *New Directions for Evaluation, 99,* 3–6.

Scriven, M. (1997). Empowerment evaluation examined. *Evaluation Practice, 18*(2), 165–175. Available online at http://www.davidfetterman.com/scrivenbkreview1997.pdf

Senge, P. (1994). *The fifth discipline: The art and practice of the learning organization.* New York: Doubleday.

Stockdill, S. H., Baizerman, M., & Compton, D. W. (2002). Toward a definition of the ECB process: A conversation with the ECB literature. *New Directions for Evaluation, 93,* 7–25.

Suarez-Balcazar, Y., Taylor-Ritzler, T., Garcia-Iriarte, E., Keys, C., Kinney, L., & Rush-Ross, H., et al. (2010). Evaluation capacity building: A cultural and contextual framework. In F. Balcazar, Y. Suarez-Balcazar, T. Taylor-Ritzler, & C. B. Keys (Eds.), *Race, culture and disability: Rehabilitation science and practice* (pp. 307–324). Sudbury, MA: Jones & Bartlett.

Taylor-Ritzler, T., Suarez-Balcazar, Y., & Garcia-Iriarte, E. (2010). *Results and implications of a mixed-methods ECB model validation study.* Paper presented at the American Evaluation Association annual meeting, San Antonio, TX.

Zimmerman, M. A. (2000). Empowerment theory: Psychological, organizational, and community levels of analysis. In J. Rappaport & E. Seldman (Eds.), *Handbook of community psychology* (pp. 2–45). New York: Kluwer Academic/Plenum.

Zimmerman, M. A., Israel, B. A., Schulz, A., & Checkoway, B. (1992). Further explorations in empowerment theory: An empirical analysis of psychological empowerment. *American Journal of Community Psychology, 20*(6), 707–727.

Zimmerman, M. A., & Rappaport, J. (1988). Citizen participation, perceived control, and psychological empowerment. *American Journal of Community Psychology, 16*(5), 725–750.

PART II
SCOPE AND BREADTH

CHAPTER 3
Mission Fulfillment

How Empowerment Evaluation Enables Funders to Achieve Results

Janice B. Yost

The Health Foundation of Central Massachusetts, Inc.

EVOLVING PHILANTHROPIC LANDSCAPE

The founding of America through the development of the colonies and democracy was accompanied by the Puritans' call for Christian charity to share the surplus in brotherly affection with those who had less. A practice of benevolence began and has continued for centuries in the United States as a humanitarian act of simply sharing wealth. Philanthropists' generosity was typified by their disinterested nature. In recent decades, however, a growing donor and funder interest in the effective use of charitable contributions and grants has given rise to a culture of accountability in giving. This shift began with foundations seeking to make strategic grants and with donors designating their gifts for specific purposes. Newly described as investors and stakeholders, philanthropists began demonstrating self-interest in their giving. This philanthropic quest for cost beneficial interventions and a return on investment has recently extended to taxpayers and state and federal governments seeking both social and financial returns on their allocations and social impact bonds. The philanthropic evolution now demands a responsive recipient, essentially the nonprofit sector, that is fully capable of designing sophisticated research models and documenting the results of an investment.

EMPOWERMENT EVALUATION AS A CONDUIT FOR ACHIEVING RESULTS

As the nonprofit sector responds to funders in this new era of accountability, it faces the challenge with limited resources and experience, especially in evaluation. Addressing solutions to substantive social issues often requires a collaborative approach that applies a set of integrated, multifaceted, evidence-based interventions for a significant duration in order to effect change. One key to achieving outcomes from an initiative is the intentional use of evaluation throughout the process. Yet few nonprofit organizations who step forward to lead collaborative efforts or develop comprehensive interventions have the internal capacity to provide the initiative with professional evaluation assistance. In addition, applicants and funders rarely negotiate for funding to include a robust evaluation component.

A proactive alternative is for funders to provide grantees with support for an evaluation component that will help to shape their work and enhance the likelihood of achieving outcomes. Thus, funders should prioritize evaluation as a significant grantmaking function. Grants should include sufficient resources to support a substantive evaluation component, and funders should commit significant internal staffing to support and participate in the evaluation process.

Empowerment Evaluation

Definition

Empowerment evaluation has demonstrated its efficacy in facilitating grantee results and funder impact. Empowerment evaluation is an evaluation approach that aims to increase the probability of achieving program success by (a) providing program stakeholders with tools for assessing the planning, implementation, and self-evaluation of their program, and (b) mainstreaming evaluation as part of the planning and management of the program/organization (Wandersman et al., 2005, p. 28). Because nonprofits typically lack the capacity to systematically plan for, monitor, and capture results in their programming, the empowerment evaluation framework offers funders an alternate approach that embraces a philosophy of partnership between the funder, the applicant/ grantee, and the evaluator, promoting the mutual goal of achieving successful results. This interactive partnering approach is distinctly different from the traditional model of grantmaking in which evaluation may occur only after the grant has concluded but is typically unable to ascertain if the programming per se produced any outcomes.

The traditional grant evaluation model depicted in Figure 3.1 shows two disconnected stages. In stage 1, the grantee has little, if any, involvement with the funder or an evaluator. After the project has concluded, an evaluator may be hired by the funder to assess the project. This traditional model assumes the grantee has selected interventions that are best practices or evidence based and that the grantee has identified measurable objectives and valid measurement tools at the outset. The model also assumes that data are gathered methodically throughout the duration of the project, including the initial benchmarks. Further, the use of comparison or control groups is rare. Thus, the traditional evaluation model frequently concludes that the project's outcomes cannot necessarily be attributed to the project's interventions. Such conclusions often leave the grantee frustrated with the practice of evaluation and unable to gain support for sustaining the project. Moreover, the grantee, and the nonprofit sector in general, may become disillusioned with the value of pursuing new strategies and interventions in the future.

The empowerment evaluation partnership model depicted in Figure 3.2 reflects an interactive and collaborative partnership throughout the project. The partnership model intends to integrate evaluation as a process within the project, acting as a normal part of planning and management, rather than as a separate function often occurring outside the project, as is the case with the traditional evaluation model. Thus, the partnership model ensures the assumptions made in the traditional evaluation model are realized. The partners are connected and are able to share their perspectives and skills, adding value throughout the duration of the project and thereby increasing the likelihood of achieving outcomes that can be attributed to the project's interventions.

Guiding Theories and Principles

The empowerment evaluation approach is guided by the "theory of process use," meaning that if project staff are involved in conducting the

Figure 3.1 Traditional grant evaluation model

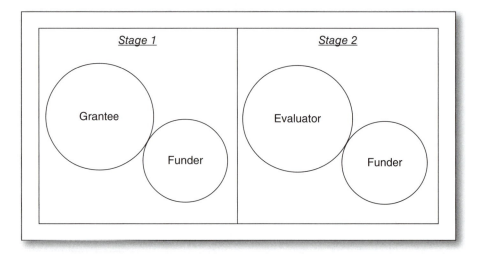

Stage 1	Stage 2
Grantee Funder	Evaluator Funder

Figure 3.2 Empowerment evaluation partnership model

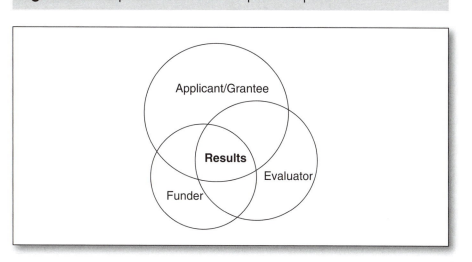

evaluation, the results are credible and more likely to be acted on. In addition, the empowerment evaluation approach facilitates the alignment of the "theory of action," or the espoused rationale for the project, with the "theory of use," or what the project actually does (Wandersman et al., 2005, 30–38). The empowerment evaluation partnership model helps to provide a process for those designing and implementing a project with clarity of purpose and action.

These theories work in conjunction with 10 specific principles of empowerment evaluation (Fetterman & Wandersman, 2005). These principles, described in Table 3.1, provide the lens through which to focus the evaluation.

Role of the Grantee, Funder, and Evaluator as Partners

The empowerment evaluation partnership model brings together unique assets represented by the partners' differing experiences and expertise as well as other resources, such as the funder's capacity to convene others to support or participate in the project. With each partner sharing in the responsibility to foster a successful project, the interaction of their varied skills and resources compounds the value of their unique contributions. The partners' interactive process, from planning the project through monitoring its implementation and capturing the outcomes, yields results beyond those typically emanating from a traditional evaluation model.

Table 3.1 Empowerment Evaluation Principles

Improvement	Empowerment evaluation is designed to help people improve program performance; it is designed to help people build on their successes and re-evaluate areas meriting attention.
Community Ownership	Empowerment evaluation values and facilitates community control; use and sustainability are dependent on a sense of ownership.
Inclusion	Empowerment evaluation invites involvement, participation, and diversity; contributions come from all levels and walks of life.
Democratic Participation	Participation and decision making should be open and fair.
Social Justice	Evaluation can and should be used to address social inequities in society.
Community Knowledge	Empowerment evaluation respects and values community knowledge.
Evidence-based Strategies	Empowerment evaluation respects and uses the knowledge base of scholars (in conjunction with community knowledge).
Capacity Building	Empowerment evaluation is designed to enhance stakeholders' ability to conduct evaluation and to improve program planning and implementation.
Organizational Learning	Data should be used to evaluate new practices, inform decision making, and implement program practices; empowerment evaluation is used to help organizations learn from their experience (building on successes, learning from mistakes, and making mid-course corrections).
Accountability	Empowerment evaluation is focused on outcomes and accountability; empowerment evaluation functions within the context of existing policies, standards, and measures of accountability; did the program or initiative accomplish its objectives?

SOURCE: Adapted from Fetterman and Wandersman (2005).

The partnership process generates a culture of evidence-based decision making and demystifies the evaluation function. Moreover, it builds the capacity for effective programming within nonprofit organizations by transferring the skills learned through this process to the administration of other programming.

Role of the Grantee

The grantee's role often includes taking the lead in designing and implementing the project; seeking advice from the evaluator on best practices or evidence-based strategies; choosing measurements and methods of data collection; participating in cycles of reflection and action to continuously improve the project by reviewing data, and when appropriate, proposing and implementing programmatic revisions to overcome barriers to implementation. In addition, the grantee's role includes seeking assistance from the funder, when appropriate, to broaden or strengthen program or funder partnerships; facilitating advocacy activities to build public awareness of a societal issue and support its alleviation using the project's interventions; and developing credible progress and outcome evaluation reports with assistance from the evaluator to augment advocacy efforts, including lobbying for changes in public policy.

Role of the Evaluator

The evaluator's role often includes informing the planning process by assessing the selection of evidence-based strategies or best practices; adapting those selected strategies to the community and implementing the strategies with fidelity; identifying valid measurement tools and assisting in the development of data gathering practices; fostering the monitoring of data collection to assist the process of continuous quality improvement or cycles of reflection and action; and coaching the grantee on preparing credible progress and summary reports that can assist in securing future funding and institutionalizing the project.

Role of the Funder

The funder's role often includes assisting in inviting key community leaders and representatives from other organizations to support the grant project; participating in cycles of reflection and action, and authorizing real-time decisions regarding programmatic or budget changes; assisting in seeking other funders for the project; and assisting in advocating for changes in public policy to remove barriers to the resolution of societal issues targeted by the project and/or to institutionalize the project's interventions.

Ten Accountability Questions

With the partnership model in place, an empowerment evaluation problem-solving framework—as fully described by Chinman, Imm, and Wandersman (2004) in *Getting To Outcomes 2004: Promoting Accountability Through Methods and Tools for Planning, Implementation, and Evaluation*—uses the 10 accountability questions presented in Table 3.2. These questions provide

Table 3.2   Ten Accountability Questions

Accountability Questions	Relevant Literature
1. What are the underlying needs and conditions in the community? (NEEDS/RESOURCES)	Needs/resources assessment
2. What are the goals, target populations, and objectives (i.e., desired outcomes)? (GOALS)	Goal setting
3. Which evidence-based models and best practice programs can be useful in reaching the goals? (BEST PRACTICE)	Consult literature on science-based and best practice programs
4. What actions need to be taken so the selected program "fits" the community context? (FIT)	Feedback on comprehensiveness and fit of program, including cultural competence
5. What organizational capacities are needed to implement the program? (CAPACITIES)	Assessment of organizational capacities
6. What is the plan for this program? (PLAN)	Planning
7. How will the quality of program and/or initiative implementation be assessed? (PROCESS)	Process evaluation
8. How well did the program work? (OUTCOMES)	Outcome and impact evaluation
9. How will continuous quality improvement strategies be incorporated? (CQI)	Total quality management; continuous quality improvement
10. If the program is successful, how will it be sustained? (SUSTAIN)	Sustainability and institutionalization

the structure for an effective problem-solving process and underpin the facilitation of project planning and monitoring, the documentation of outcomes, and the sustainability of interventions by the partners. Each question must be satisfied in varying degrees of specificity as the project proceeds. For example, answers should be fully vetted during the planning stage of a project to questions 1 through 6 (What are the underlying needs and conditions in the community? What are the goals, target populations, and objectives [i.e., desired outcomes]? Which evidence-based models and best practice programs can be useful in reaching the goals? What actions need to be taken so the selected program "fits" the community context? What organizational capacities are needed to implement the program? What is the plan for this program?). Once the piloting of the project is under way, questions 7 through 9 become the foci (How will the quality of program and/or initiative implementation be assessed? How well did the program work? How will continuous quality improvement strategies be incorporated?). Answers to these questions inform change in the project's design and operation as full implementation gets under way. During full implementation, the answers to questions 7 and 9 remain critical functions (How will the quality of program and/or initiative implementation be assessed? How will continuous quality improvement strategies be incorporated?), while questions 8 and 10 rise in priority (How well did the program work? If the program is successful, how will it be sustained?).

HOW FUNDERS CAN OPERATIONALIZE EMPOWERMENT EVALUATION

Funders have a fundamental responsibility to help grantees satisfy the philanthropic quest for results. First, funders should demonstrate recognition that generating outcomes is not a short-term proposition; indeed, funders should adopt a long-term view by budgeting multiyear support of up to 5 years when requesting proposals. Funders should also initiate the use of the empowerment evaluation partnership model and, depending on the sophistication of the research design, should expect to provide an additional 10% to 15% of the programmatic budget to enable the participation of evaluators throughout the duration of the project.

In addition, funders should commit to active participation in the partnership and, at a minimum, should establish and maintain the 10 accountability questions as the structure for the partnership's focus and interaction throughout the project. This can be achieved by embedding the 10 accountability questions in the announcement of a funding cycle, when calling for proposals or letters of intent, as well as in the grant application form, process evaluation form, and grant summary reporting form.

If the grantmaking portfolio includes smaller grants of a 1-year duration, funders may also consider embedding the accountability questions in that avenue's application form, process evaluation form, and grant summary report to shape the grantee's problem-solving approach. With these smaller grants, the funder may also interact to a lesser degree with the grantee, and an evaluator would typically not be a partner in the process.

Case Study: The Health Foundation of Central Massachusetts' Experience Using the Empowerment Evaluation Partnership Model

The Health Foundation of Central Massachusetts, Inc. was created in 1999 from the sale of Central Massachusetts Health Care (CMHC), a nonprofit HMO initiated in the 1970s by physicians, with the mission of using its resources to improve the health of those who live or work in the Central Massachusetts region, with particular emphasis on vulnerable populations and unmet needs. Nearly all health care conversion foundations across the country were created as private foundations from the sale of nonprofit health plans or hospitals to for-profit entities. The Health Foundation of Central Massachusetts, Inc., however, sought and gained approval from the Massachusetts attorney general and probate court to retain the CMHC's 501(c)(4) tax status with the agreement to limit its lobbying activities to that allowed by the Internal Revenue Service for publicly supported charities and to target an annual payout of 5% of its assets. The allowance of some flexibility in the annual payout, and more important, the capacity to lobby for public policy changes in order to institutionalize effective grant strategies, have been recognized as significant to the foundation's ability to make an impact. Specifically, as the foundation's grant projects have addressed accountability question 10 (If the program is successful, how will it be sustained?), the capacity for the nonprofit grantee to be joined by foundation staff in lobbying has led to sustained funding streams from the state and federal governments.

Operationalization of the Empowerment Evaluation Partnership Model

Despite a modest asset base of $65 million and the extreme volatility of the investment market during the foundation's 13-year history, the foundation has made grants totaling $26 million. To make an impact with a modest grant investment in the range of $2 million per year, the foundation made two critical decisions. The first was to adopt the empowerment evaluation partnership model. The approach was operationalized through the co-development with Dr. Abraham Wandersman of a planning, implementation, and evaluation system called Results-Oriented Grantmaking and Grant-Implementation (ROGG), specifically tailored to the foundation's funding avenues. The 10 accountability questions formed the basis for ROGG, and the questions are embedded in the foundation's applications, process evaluation, and summary report forms.

The second fundamental decision, to focus the foundation's grantmaking on impact, resulted in the creation of the Health Care and Health Promotion Synergy Initiative as the primary funding avenue for grants. Approximately 75% of the foundation's annual grantmaking is channeled to support 3- to 5-year projects through its Health Care and Health Promotion Synergy Initiative funding avenue. Typically operating on a 5-year cycle, this initiative solicits proposals that target significant health issues in Central Massachusetts with collaborative, comprehensive prevention and treatment strategies. Projects are expected to progress from planning, to piloting, to full implementation, with the ultimate goal of documenting evidence-based practices and securing public policy to create systems change, thus continuing those evidence-based practices after the foundation's funding concludes. Each funding cycle typically supports four projects for 5 years, with total funding for each project in the $2 million range.

The foundation does not identify specific health issues as its funding priorities, but instead relies on community leaders stepping forward to identify a substantive health issue and demonstrate that a coalition of organizations is in place to address the issue. This approach recognizes a key ingredient of a successful project: community leadership and commitment. Foundation staff work with prospective applicants to ascertain that the intended project fits with the foundation's guidelines. Once the project has been funded, staff function as the funder partner in the empowerment evaluation partnership model throughout the duration of the project.

Prospective grantees to the Health Care and Health Promotion Synergy Initiative are first asked to submit a letter of intent to apply. When the foundation selects those who are invited to submit an application, applicants are provided with a guidebook explaining ROGG and the empowerment evaluation partnership model.

Selecting Empowerment Evaluation Partners

With each cycle calling for applications to the Health Care and Health Promotion Synergy Initiative, the foundation identifies a pool of professional evaluators familiar with the empowerment evaluation approach from which invited applicants may select an evaluation partner. The pool often includes evaluators who have prior experience with the health issues to be addressed by the applicants. As the invited applicants begin preparing an application for a planning grant, the foundation hosts a "speed dating" event designed to introduce the potential evaluators and applicants. Before the event, the evaluators are asked to read the applicants' letters of intent and the applicants are given the opportunity to review the evaluators' resumes. After meeting, both parties complete a form that is submitted to the foundation indicating their respective interest in potential partnerships. Foundation staff then match an applicant with an evaluator and provide a modest consulting fee to the evaluator to work with the applicant in preparing the planning grant application. This practice gives the partners a trial experience to assess their working relationship.

Evaluators are able to bring expertise to the initial phase of developing the proposed project, providing valuable assistance to the applicant in focusing the proposed project, especially with regard to accountability question 1 (What are the underlying needs and conditions in the community?) and question 2 (What are the goals, target populations, and objectives?). Evaluators are incentivized to help the applicant produce a clear and focused proposed project with the anticipation that they will be hired by the grantee as the planning grant empowerment evaluation partner. Foundation staff also act as the funder partner during the preparation of the application, typically meeting with, and responding to questions from, both the evaluator and applicant.

To support the empowerment evaluation partnership model during the planning, pilot, and implementation grant phases of the project, the foundation targets 10% to 15% of Health Care and Health Promotion Synergy Initiative project budgets for the evaluation component. Applications for each phase of a 5-year project include a specific evaluation component and are typically submitted on an annual basis. This range in allocation for the evaluator partner's participation has been designed to accommodate varying levels of sophistication in the research design. A useful resource to both the funder and the grantee, *Evaluation for Improvement: A Seven-Step Empowerment Evaluation Approach for Violence Prevention Organizations* (Cox, Keener, Woodard, & Wandersman, 2009) offers detailed advice on hiring evaluators. When the planning grant and subsequent pilot and implementation grants are awarded, the grantee and the evaluator enter into a memorandum of agreement, or subcontract, for the specific evaluation activities included in the application.

Empowerment Evaluation
Partnership and ROGG Orientation

After planning grants are awarded, the foundation hosts a ROGG orientation workshop involving the four Health Care and Health Promotion Synergy Initiative project grantees, including the project director, project coordinator, key collaborating organizational representatives, and the evaluator. The main purpose of the workshop is to explain more fully the empowerment evaluation partnership model and the 10 accountability questions. A professional evaluator knowledgeable about empowerment evaluation is hired by the foundation to facilitate the session. A partnership approach between the evaluator, funder, and grantee throughout the project is a relatively new experience for most grantees, and this orientation helps to clarify relationships and begin to build camaraderie among the partners.

As part of the grant contract, the foundation also requires that the grantee and evaluator participate with the funder in quarterly grant management team meetings. The grantee is responsible for convening the meetings and preparing the agenda with input from the other partners, as well as preparing the minutes or summary notes highlighting action items agreed on during the meeting. Grant management team meetings serve a fundamental function in operationalizing ROGG. These meetings allow the partners to bring their perspectives and expertise to the discussion in monitoring data, assessing progress, and addressing concerns or barriers, which often results in real-time adjustments to the project. Substantive changes are subsequently formalized by amending the grant contract.

In addition, the grantee drafts the process evaluation and grant summary reports in consultation with the evaluator and funder partners before submitting the reports. The preparation of applications for continued funding typically follows a similar process and includes a meeting of the three partners to fully vet the proposal before it is submitted. Evaluators are asked to prepare process- and outcome-related reports in a formal format, which includes an executive summary that can also be used for advocacy and lobbying purposes. The evaluator takes the lead in drafting these reports, and feedback is solicited from the grantee and funder. This sharing of input from the partners ensures accuracy and readability of the reports while enhancing the partners' engagement in the project.

In a further effort to provide shared learning sessions across the projects, the foundation also hires a professional evaluator with empowerment evaluation experience to facilitate periodic telephone conference calls involving the four project evaluators and foundation staff. This provides an opportunity for the evaluators to learn from each other as the projects progress through the planning, pilot, and implementation phases, while also informing each other's projects. In addition, these conference calls provide an avenue for presenting new learning opportunities identified by the evaluators and supported by the foundation (e.g., a webinar on economic evaluation) that can enhance the evaluators' contributions to their respective projects.

Impact

The foundation has been recognized for its effective use of evaluation in several reports that assess foundation grantmaking and through presentations at American Evaluation Association, Grantmakers for Effective Organizations, Grantmakers In Health, and the Independent Sector conferences. Released by FSG Social Impact Advisors, *From Insight to Action: New Directions in Foundation Evaluation* (Kramer, Graves, Hirschhorn, & Fiske, 2007) highlighted the foundation's use of empowerment evaluation as one of eight case studies of performance-centered evaluation approaches. The foundation was also featured in *Evaluation in Philanthropy: Perspectives From the Field,* a report co-released by Grantmakers for Effective Organizations and the Council on Foundations (2009), as one of 19 foundations from across the country that uses evaluation to drive learning and improvement and capture results.

Prodding philanthropy's attention to impact investing, Kania and Kramer (2011) introduced the concept of collective impact and described its usefulness:

> Large-scale social change requires broad cross-sector coordination, yet the social sector remains focused on the isolated intervention of individual organizations. . . . Collective Impact Initiatives are long-term commitments by a group of important actors from different sectors to a common agenda for solving a specific social problem. Their actions are supported by a shared measurement system, mutually reinforcing activities and continuous communication, and are staffed by an independent backbone support organization. (pp. 36, 39)

The Independent Sector's 2011 annual conference showcased Kania and Kramer's new thinking with a session titled "Working Collectively for Greater Impact," which included a presentation connecting the empowerment evaluation partnership model and the 10 accountability questions framework as responsible for the impact made by the foundation's grantmaking.

The foundation is in the midst of the third funding cycle of its Health Care and Health Promotion Synergy Initiative, having successfully completed two five-year cycles. Lentz, Imm, and Yost, et al. (2005) used the foundation's round one grant project titled Child Abuse Prevention and Protection Collaborative as a case study to describe the implementation of empowerment evaluation's principles and practices. Since that time, the foundation's grantees have achieved outcomes with varying levels of impact. Indeed, four projects (described in the next few paragraphs) have created a sea change in how certain health issues are addressed and have received ongoing governmental support to sustain effective interventions.

Oral Health Improvement

In its first funding cycle, the foundation focused nearly $6 million to introduce and expand dental services for vulnerable populations in the Worcester area and North Central Massachusetts via two grant projects, the Central Mass Oral Health Initiative (CMOHI) and the Oral Health Initiative of North Central Mass (OHINCM). OHINCM helped to introduce a dental clinic at a community health center offering Medicaid and free dental services in that area for the first time. That dental clinic was then able to expand preventive dental services to 43 schools throughout the area. CMOHI helped double dental services provided by two other community health centers, who have sustained that enhanced capacity, in part due to the development by CMOHI of a graduate dental residency program at those centers. The two projects joined forces in advocating for a series of changes in public policy to remove barriers that prevented dentists in private practice from accepting Medicaid. At the outset of the projects, fewer than 10 dentists in Central Massachusetts were accepting Medicaid; by its conclusion, nearly 200 dentists accepted Medicaid, boosting participation rates to 50%.

Children's Mental Health Improvement

The foundation's first funding cycle also provided $1.8 million for the Together For Kids project, which developed and documented the efficacy of a mental health consultation model to aid the social-emotional development of preschoolers in child care settings who presented with challenging behaviors. Following advocacy and lobbying efforts, the state began funding these services statewide in 2010 and has continued the services, providing more than $8 million to date.

Ending Adult Chronic Homelessness

During the second funding cycle, the foundation provided $2.2 million for the Home Again project to end adult chronic homelessness in Worcester. The project first documented the efficacy of using a "housing first" approach and was instrumental in persuading the state to transition its funding from sheltering to a housing first approach. In January 2011, the U.S. Interagency Council on Homelessness recognized Worcester as the first community of its size in the country to essentially end adult chronic homelessness. Other advocacy efforts resulted in changing public policy to gain state (i.e., Medicaid) and federal government (i.e., Medicare) funding for the provision of case management services to this population statewide to ensure they remain housed.

Cautionary Acknowledgments in Using the Empowerment Evaluation Partnership Model

While the foundation's experience with the empowerment evaluation partnership model and the 10 accountability questions has created impact and justifies its continuation, there are cautionary acknowledgments that accompany its endorsement. Perhaps the most obvious objection some funders may have is that funding a robust evaluation component throughout a multiyear project requires resources that could otherwise go to support additional grants. If funders with this objection are comfortable with the outcomes and impact of their grantmaking, then adopting the empowerment evaluation partnership model may not be advised.

For those funders considering adoption of the empowerment evaluation partnership model and 10 accountability questions, it is important to understand that a partnership process requires additional resources to support staffing at the foundation level, as well as within the grant budget. As with the development of any relationship, the empowerment evaluation partnership will require some extra attention to interpersonal communication and chemistry. Grantees may initially be hesitant to lead and somewhat intimidated by having the funder and the evaluator as partners in the process of planning and implementing the project. The funder may be perceived as too dominant in the partnership. Similarly, the evaluator may take a rather academic approach that may result in the evaluation essentially overwhelming the project, especially with regard to the project staff's time and effort in data collection. Evaluators are advised to present a practical approach that can be translated to service in the field, while maintaining scientific standards.

To be effective partners with the grantee, funders and evaluators must quickly become well informed on the issue being addressed by the project, including its root cause and efficacious solution. In addition, given the occasional turnover of key players among the partnership during a multiyear project, the partnership will experience some interruption and attention must be given to orienting new players and rebuilding relationships.

EMPOWERMENT EVALUATION'S ADDED VALUE

The empowerment evaluation partnership offers a model for collaborative learning and problem solving. With the evaluator's involvement, the 10 accountability questions provide an effective framework for designing comprehensive programming to systematically plan for, monitor, and document results.

In addition, the interactive empowerment evaluation partnership process builds the capacity of nonprofits to generalize the experience to other aspects of their work. Funders benefit by having a clear understanding and rationale for making continuation grants to support the project. Most important, results are well documented and often lead to changes in how society best serves its most vulnerable. The call for accountability is answered.

Evidence of outcomes and impact should be the driving force in determining the use of philanthropic and governmental investment in programming to serve vulnerable populations and alleviate societal issues and concerns. All talent should be brought together to focus on that goal. Funders and nonprofits have long been engaged in this endeavor, and elevating their efforts to a higher level of effectiveness should remain an ongoing consideration. Evaluators bring a skill set to those efforts that can add value well beyond the cost of their involvement. Using science to address societal issues and then translating that science into practice is a worthy purpose indeed.

REFERENCES

Chinman, M., Imm, P., & Wandersman, A. (2004). *Getting To Outcomes 2004: Promoting accountability through methods and tools for planning, implementation, and evaluation.* Santa Monica, CA: RAND Corporation. Retrieved from http://www.rand.org/publications/TR/TR101

Cox, P. J., Keener, D., Woodard, T. L., & Wandersman, A. H. (2009). *Evaluation for improvement: A seven-step empowerment evaluation approach for violence prevention organizations.* Atlanta, GA: Centers for Disease Control and Prevention.

Fetterman, D., & Wandersman, A. (2005). *Empowerment evaluation principles in practice.* New York: Guilford Press.

Grantmakers for Effective Organizations & Council on Foundations. (2009). *Evaluation in philanthropy: Perspectives from the field.* Washington, DC: Authors. Retrieved from http://www .geofunders.org/geo-publications/569-evaluation

Kania, J., & Kramer, M. (2011, Winter). Collective impact. *Stanford Social Innovation Review,* 36–41.

Kramer, M., Graves, R., Hirschhorn, J., & Fiske, L. (2007). *From insight to action: New directions in foundation evaluation.* FSG Social Impact Advisors. Retrieved from http://www.fsg.org/ tabid/191/ArticleId/177/Default.aspx

Lentz, B. E., Imm, P. S., Yost, J. B., Johnson, N. P., Barron, C., Lindberg, M. S., et al. (2005). Empowerment evaluation and organizational learning: A case study of a community coalition designed to prevent child abuse and neglect. In D. M. Fetterman & A. Wandersman (Eds.), *Empowerment evaluation principles in practice* (pp. 155–182). New York: Guilford Press.

Wandersman, A., Snell-Johns, J., Lentz, B. E., Fetterman, D. M., Keener, D. C., Livet, M., et al. (2005). The principles of empowerment evaluation. In D. M. Fetterman & A. Wandersman (Eds.), *Empowerment evaluation principles in practice* (pp. 27–41). New York: Guilford Press.

CHAPTER 4

Foundation Strategy Drives the Choice of Empowerment Evaluation Principles

Laura C. Leviton

T he Robert Wood Johnson Foundation (RWJF) is the fourth largest private foundation in the United States and the largest devoted to health (Lavizzo-Mourey, 2010). Since 1972, its mission has been to improve health and health care for all Americans. It recently announced a new strategic direction:

> We, as a nation, will strive together to create a culture of health enabling all in our diverse society to lead healthy lives, now and for generations to come. . . . It is a nation in which everyone has the information and the means to make choices that promote healthy lifestyles and behaviors. In a flourishing culture of health, private and public leaders will keep the health of the entire population foremost in their minds when making decisions. And business, government, schools, individuals, and organizations will work together to build and bridge good health care with communities that promote healthy lifestyles. (Lavizzo-Mourey, 2013)

RWJF's strategic planning process, still under way as of this writing, will have many implications for how it conducts evaluation, and in particular, for the use of selected empowerment evaluation principles. The foundation is aiming for greater transparency and inclusiveness in decision making. "Work together to build and bridge good health care with communities that promote healthy lifestyles" implies joint problem solving and improvement strategies, principles that we believe are necessary to achieve improved health and health care. Empowerment evaluation is consistent with these aspirations.

RWJF's choice of evaluation approaches and methods is driven by RWJF's philanthropic strategy. With 20 to 40 evaluations in the field at any given time, the foundation has never endorsed the exclusive use of any single approach to evaluation. As RWJF has learned about philanthropic strategy, it has also learned about evaluation to improve that strategy. It is in the area of strategy improvement that RWJF has most consistently employed principles associated with empowerment evaluation. Given the new focus on a culture of health, however, RWJF may employ these principles more broadly in future.

Fetterman (1996) notes that empowerment evaluation can address societal change as well as program improvement. This chapter begins with a description of what constitutes a philanthropic strategy for social change and the potential role of empowerment evaluation in achieving such a strategy. It is followed by an outline of how RWJF generally conducts evaluations and why the evaluations include selected (not all) empowerment evaluation principles. The history of RWJF evaluation and its organizational learning for improving strategy are presented next. The chapter concludes with a statement about the future of RWJF and where the potential may be for using empowerment evaluation going forward.

PHILANTHROPIC STRATEGY

Not a Piggy Bank

Philanthropic strategy is defined as grantmaking informed by clear goals for social change, as contrasted with responsive charitable support for a scatter-shot though worthy set of projects (Leviton & Bass, 2004). Strategy takes the foundation mission statement and makes it operational through a theory of change, both predetermined and emergent based on experience (Patton & Patrizi, 2010). Thus, strategy considers an entire group of grants aimed at a goal or strategic objective, not individual grant or program success and failure. RWJF's work was always based, to some degree, on strategy. However, strategic philanthropy came into more common parlance in the late 1990s as private fortunes swelled and a variety of entrepreneurs started their own foundations.

These entrepreneurs were used to achieving specific aims and wanted to apply that same approach to philanthropy. An influential *Harvard Business Review* article crystallized the challenge:

> If foundations serve only as passive middlemen, as mere conduits for giving, then they fall far short of their potential and of society's high expectations. Foundations can and should lead social progress. They have the potential to make more effective use of scarce resources than either individual donors or the government. Free from political pressures, foundations can explore new solutions to social problems with an independence that government can never have. And compared with individual donors, foundations have the scale, the time horizon, and the professional management to create benefits for society more effectively. (Porter & Kramer, 1999, pp. 121–122)

To be strategic, foundations need to focus their grants on a smaller set of aims and make fewer, bigger grants to achieve those aims. To address a social problem, such as preventing childhood obesity or improving human rights, strategic philanthropy uses several tactics in combination, such as building a needed field of research or practice (Hirschhorn & Gilmore; 2004); supporting community organizers, coalitions, or media efforts to advocate for policy changes (Coffman, 2009); or empirically demonstrating the effectiveness of model social policy and programs (Knickman & Hunt, 2007; RWJF, 2010). (For an illustration of how the Heinz Endowment applied evaluation to strategy on improving education, see Leviton & Bickel, 2004.)

Foundation strategy is usually emergent, not fixed, requiring reexamination and often, a change in underlying assumptions about what will produce the desired changes (Patrizi, 2010). From this perspective, principles of empowerment evaluation can be of assistance to the foundation staff, advisers, and grantees that want to produce a social change (Fetterman, 1996, 2013). The evaluations of individual programs and funding initiatives contribute to the tactics. By examining how and why programs succeed or fail, foundations can refine both their tactics and strategy.

RWJF evaluation for strategy focuses most often on national initiatives such as a fellowship program or a campaign to cover the uninsured. Empowerment evaluations can be done at this level, and they have been used to address state and national social issues (Fetterman, 2005, 2010, 2013; Fetterman & Wandersman, 2007). However, the most common use of empowerment evaluation principles is for improvement of individual, local program sites. Some

RWJF grantees utilize foundation funds to address local improvement. This may be strategic for the individual grant, but only rarely for a cross-site, national program.

An example illustrates how RWJF develops strategy based on experience. In the 1990s and 2000s, a major goal was improving medical care at the end of life: better management of pain, abiding by the wishes of the patient and family, and the promotion of advance directives—the "living wills" that directed medical staff to terminate life support if a person had no chance for recovery. RWJF and the Open Society Institute were the only major funders to advance these aims. RWJF programs reflected several tactics: a large-scale demonstration and evaluation, various fellowships, quality improvement and research programs, and various advocacy efforts. Patrizi, Thompson, and Spector (2011) documented how the successes and failures of these programs sharpened the emergent strategy and helped to revise tactics. Along with the advocates and champions of these changes, RWJF learned that the usual methods of diffusing innovations in medicine (education, training, exhortation) were not sufficient to change end-of-life care. Not every physician or nurse needed or wanted this information—it was much more important for oncologists and cardiologists, for example, than for primary care doctors. Experience taught us that hospitals manage end-of-life care better when (1) medical and nursing licensure tests demand content knowledge, and (2) the hospital has a specialist on pain management to guide and support the staff. These were not just static "lessons learned." Having identified these leverage points for change, RWJF pushed on them and pushed hard. RWJF can be credited with contribution, not attribution, but most large U.S. hospitals now have appropriate pain management and honor patients' advance directives.

Although RWJF did not use empowerment evaluation in this example, it does illustrate how empowerment evaluation can inform foundation program development, tactics, and overall strategy. Evaluation of strategy focuses on a portfolio of grants and whether they are effective to address social change. The primary evaluation users are the foundation officers responsible for achieving progress toward a social aim, who are holding themselves accountable to the foundation board of trustees.

Not a Democracy

Private foundations, unlike community foundations or public charities, take no public funding and are accountable only to their board of trustees and to the Internal Revenue Service. In the past, this led many foundations to work in a highly elitist fashion, unresponsive to voters and lacking diversity at both the staff and board levels (Leviton & Bass, 2004). Yet, as Porter and Kramer (1999) note, private foundations get major tax advantages in comparison with other organizations, so they need to demonstrate value. For many large foundations, this has taken the form of evaluating outcomes, whether commissioned independently or by supporting program capacity. And although some foundations espouse support for empowerment evaluations and others are highly responsive to community constituencies, both the process and the results are highly variable.

RWJF is generally the primary client on behalf of "building a field," not the programs themselves and not program participants or recipients (although three interesting exceptions appear later). Also, the evaluations are mostly funded and conducted independent of the programs. Independent evaluation is believed to offer greater credibility, although that does not have to be the case (Fetterman, 1996; Fetterman & Wandersman, 2005, 2007). It is RWJF's experience that direct oversight of these visible, high-stakes evaluations offers a higher quality evaluation product, given the low evaluation capacity issues so prevalent among nonprofit organizations. RWJF evaluations are usually collaborative with programs and usually aim to assist self-reflection, both by RWJF staff and grantees. However, the line is drawn quite differently about whose questions take priority. With very few exceptions, independent evaluations try to maximize information for RWJF, grantees, and (often) external stakeholders about a way forward for an overall strategy of social change.[1]

RWJF evaluations aim at social justice in the broadest sense of addressing issues such as access to health care, coverage of the uninsured, and disparities in health. Some evaluations are inclusive of key stakeholders, particularly when a strategic aim requires the buy-in of outside stakeholders. Community knowledge is sought when it is deemed appropriate, for example, in RWJF's work on changing community policies and environmental factors to prevent childhood obesity by promoting a healthier diet and physical activity (Brennan et al., 2012). Capacity building, organizational learning, and other principles also are employed as the program, tactics, or overall strategy appears to require them.

Three examples illustrate the selective use of these principles for foundation strategy. First, RWJF regularly conducts training sessions with certain individual grantee organizations on evaluation, followed by access to 6 months of technical assistance on grantee-driven evaluations in progress. The grantees,

---

1. Although Fetterman notes that outsiders can do empowerment evaluation by serving as a coach and facilitating improvement by program insiders, this is only rarely an exclusive goal for RWJF.

however, often have evaluations pending that were viewed as strategic for field building—or they were located in New Jersey, where RWJF operates more like a community foundation. Second, RWJF recently commissioned evaluability assessments to identify promising programs for intimate partner violence prevention in immigrant and refugee communities, then worked with these programs, along the lines of empowerment evaluation, to build evaluation capacity to test their models (RWJF, 2011; Uehling et al., 2011). In this case, the strategy dictated that ethnic communities were more likely to accept and utilize the findings if they emerged from community organizations that shared their cultural expectations and shared sense-making.

A third example, and one that does illustrate a democratic approach, was the evaluation of Allies Against Asthma, an approach to improving asthma care through community coalitions (Clark et al., 2006). Over 5 years, the seven coalitions made a total of 89 changes to policy and systems, improving the ability of families, schools, and health care providers to care for children's asthma. Children experienced significantly fewer symptoms than the comparison children, and parents felt less helpless, frightened, and angry. Importantly, greater changes were seen in community coalitions reporting the most highly engaged partners (Clark et al., 2010). In this case, the democratic approach to evaluation was strategic because no one organization in a community had resources or power to address the wide variety of policy and systems changes that were needed, and their buy-in was imperative. At the same time, the evaluation team was composed of arguably some of the foremost practitioners of community-based participatory research in the country—making it more likely that an efficient, effective evaluation process could be achieved.

Accountability for the Evidence, or Accountability for Compliance?

At RWJF, both evaluation and programs aim either to use evidence-based strategies in some way, or they try to produce the evidence for the strategies. In empowerment evaluation terms, the latter represents the principle of accountability, in that it assists organizations and programs to hold themselves accountable for results. This is a worthy aim, one that RWJF has endorsed since 1972. However, it is not how most people think of the term *accountability*. It is important to distinguish empowerment evaluation's accountability from accountability as compliance with grantee assurances about the use of the funder's money. Grantee organizations commonly view evaluation as addressing compliance accountability—yet nothing could be further from the truth at RWJF. As Chelimsky (1997) pointed out, evaluations for compliance accountability are generally incompatible with improvement and learning. Wandersman (Chapter 9, this book) believes that Getting To Outcomes could in fact achieve both accountability and learning. However, we find that grantee concerns about compliance accountability regularly distort both collaboration and the uses of evaluation. The power imbalance in such evaluations imposed by the funder often impairs the ability to learn together. Compliance accountability is just not necessary for evaluation at RWJF. A foundation is not like government: It is not accountable to the public for the way it spends the money, so it does not need to do compliance accountability evaluations. Also, there are many other systems in place to ensure compliance with what the grantee proposed to do.[2] Consequently, RWJF seldom uses evaluation for compliance accountability, a strategic decision because of the desire for learning and improvement.

RWJF'S ROAD FORWARD IN USING THE EMPOWERMENT EVALUATION PRINCIPLES

History

Cases like Allies Against Asthma are the exception that proves the rule. In general, RWJF's evaluation practice has evolved in ways that mirror the national experience. From 1972 onward, an important assumption was that research and evaluation evidence would inform high-level decisions and guide improvements in health care policy and practice. For example, access to medical care was a central focus in RWJF's first decade, work that continues to this day in RWJF's efforts to cover the uninsured (Rosenblatt, 2006). Through research and evaluation, access to care came to be understood as a theoretical construct, reflecting barriers and facilitators of health care utilization such as ability to pay, trust in providers, and availability of care (Aday, Fleming, & Andersen, 1984). RWJF viewed better measurement and tracking of access as essential tools to improve policy and change systems—consistent with empowerment evaluation principles, but even more consistent with advocating for needed changes in federal health policy. Evaluation's own Howard Freeman was an important contributor to this research and an advisor to RWJF until his untimely death (Freeman et al., 1987).

---

2. There are many other kinds of accountability for RWJF grants and contracts, such as financial accountability, monitoring by program officers, and oversight of deliverables.

In the mid-1980s and well into the 1990s, RWJF funded a wide variety of innovations under the assumption that government would adopt them and they would therefore be sustained over time. Colby and Isaacs (2011) have documented how RWJF-funded innovations contributed to shaping the McKinney-Vento Act to provide health care for homeless individuals and to the federal Ryan White Comprehensive AIDS Resources Emergency Act to provide community services to people living with HIV/AIDS (Colby & Isaacs, 2011). The end-of-life care initiatives also fit this category. And finally, a recent RWJF-funded randomized experiment persuaded Medicaid to waive regulation and permit people with disabilities to select their own personal care attendants rather than receiving this service from a stranger through a social service agency. The experiment concluded that costs did not rise and people reported better quality of life when they received counseling on how to choose and pay for personal care attendants (Mathematica Policy Research, 2013). All 50 states now permit this practice (RWJF, 2012). This study was the culmination of years of discussion and testing of various systems to improve independent choices on behalf of people with disabilities. That development process resonates with empowerment evaluation. However, the culminating study had quite a different purpose: demonstrating cost-effectiveness to Medicaid and state medical assistance programs.

Another central assumption in this era, and well into the 2000s, was that the grantees were more than capable of implementing their ideas well—implementation was the test of a concept, not the test of whether the concept could spread. Calls for proposals deliberately selected the most highly capable organizations to participate in demonstration programs. In a pool of 200 grant applicants, for example, it should come as no surprise if the top 10 proposals come from organizations that could implement almost any idea pretty well. One is permitted, however, to speculate about the generalizability of any results if implemented by lower capacity organizations and practitioners. Moreover, within that top-10 list, implementation and outcomes were still uneven. Would empowerment evaluation approaches have assisted the grantees to improve their efforts?

A third assumption was that, to persuade government to adopt innovations, credibility required independent third-party evaluation to avoid the appearance of a conflict of interest. Yet independence sometimes came at the cost of evaluations that were less useful to assist practitioners and managers. Initially, there was a strict separation of program and evaluation, such that evaluation teams did not always have access to the thought process and evaluation questions that program staff would want to pose. Later, the process became more collaborative, but the focus on evaluation to inform foundation strategy and tactics has sometimes come at the cost of useful information for program staff. Would empowerment evaluation have ensured that both strategic and programmatic questions could be asked?

Increasing Use of Capacity Building, Inclusion, and Community Knowledge

When government policy devolved to the states in the late 1990s, foundation staff needed to reconsider RWJF's strategy. In such areas as covering the uninsured and in tobacco control, the focus shifted to state and local, as well as federal, policy (Center for Public Program Evaluation, 2011). This strategy required cooperation between program and evaluation, although independent evaluation was still the priority. RWJF gained more awareness, and provided more support, for evaluation to improve programs. For example, the Scholars in Health Policy Research program recruits mainstream economists, political scientists, and sociologists into the study of health policy. Evaluation established that the fellowship salary was not competitive for recruiting top-flight economists (Palmer, 2000). The program director and three universities housing the fellowships used the information to better attract economists. Evaluative feedback has also worked to improve other research programs, such as Active Living Research (to promote children's physical activity) and Healthy Eating Research (to promote children's healthy diet) (Emont & Emont, 2009; Ottoson et al., 2008).

Another example of evaluation that informed program improvement comes from the Active for Life program, which implemented two evidence-based interventions to encourage physical activity in older people in real-world settings ranging from health plans to faith-based organizations. The evaluation focused, in part, on establishing whether a 12-week version of one intervention would operate as well as the evidence-based 20-week version: 12 weeks achieved the same effect size, attracted more of the working population, and was more sustainable in community organizations (Lattimore, 2010; Wilcox, 2008). This example is notable because the test of the shorter program came at the request of the organizations implementing the program. This substudy was consistent with empowerment evaluation principles, in that it focused on a potential program improvement that would make spread and sustainability more likely.

By the 1990s, government was less likely to fund new programs. Would private insurers, nonprofit and voluntary organizations, or other funders pick up the innovations? If so, a revised focus on spread and scale was needed. Technical assistance became a more important focus in RWJF national program initiatives, and RWJF realized that good implementation was essential to achieve real spread and scale. It became clear over time that organizational capacity was not always what it should be and, in selected areas, evaluation should focus on assisting practitioners and managers with implementation and program improvements.

A notable shift to technical assistance and capacity building was seen in RWJF's work on quality improvement in medicine. Under a grant from RWJF, the RAND Corporation documented that the health care system was only providing the right care 50% of the time (McGlynn et al., 2003). During this period, RWJF championed the work of the Institute for Healthcare Improvement, which applied industry's rapid cycle improvement approach to quality improvement in medicine (Berwick & Davidoff, 2004; Kohn, Corrigan, & Donaldson, 2000; Perla, Provost, & Parry, 2013). Several RWJF initiatives focused on technology transfer and technical assistance. For example, Improving Chronic Illness Care (Pearson et al., 2005) employed technical assistance and coaching to implement Edward Wagner's Chronic Care Model in physician offices, and Prescription for Health (Cohen et al., 2008) sought ways to incorporate lifestyle counseling into primary care practices. The focus on technical assistance and timely feedback in these initiatives look like empowerment evaluation. Indeed, Wandersman and his colleagues later adopted the rapid cycle improvement strategy as part of their Getting To Outcomes framework (Chinman et al., 2008), and Wandersman's interactive systems framework for dissemination and implementation aims to support implementation with quality (Wandersman, Chien, & Katz, 2012). However, RWJF and its partners did not recognize such technical assistance as a form of evaluation. Instead, technical assistance in evaluation crept in the back door— for example, the evaluators of Prescription for Health found themselves offering a certain amount of technical assistance to grantees in the natural course of their interactions around evaluation.

A New Focus on Spread and Scale

The foundation reevaluated its approaches to technical assistance. With more experience, it became clear that certain approaches were simply not suited to the capacity of the implementing organizations. In other cases, technical assistance was labor intensive and might not be worth the cost. For spread and scaling of good models, the question has become this: What kind of technical assistance is appropriate under what conditions, for which kinds of organizations, to achieve program improvement? This also resonates with empowerment evaluation.

A case in point is the Healthy Schools Program of the Alliance for a Healthier Generation, created by the William J. Clinton Foundation and the American Heart Association to prevent childhood obesity. A grant from RWJF permitted the Healthy Schools Program to offer coaching and technical assistance to schools on policy and environmental changes that can help students maintain a healthy weight. Predominantly low-income schools are recruited by relationship managers and coached in-person to achieve changes. Other schools enroll and participate online, using a wealth of resources and technical assistance. As of this writing, approximately 18,000 schools participate nationwide. RWJF evaluated low-income schools' progress from 2006 to 2011 (Beam et al., 2012a, 2012b). Over 80% of the low-income schools that were approached enrolled; of those, 79% completed data collection; and of those, 79% made at least one improvement. Effect sizes were moderate to large.

At the same time, the onsite coaching was labor intensive, and the large majority of schools participated online, giving the program greater reach. The JPB Foundation funds onsite coaching, while RWJF now funds the online model primarily. The two foundations are now collaborating on a randomized experiment to compare the effects of the onsite versus online models, specifically for low-income schools. In addition, we will be testing a priori hypotheses about the characteristics of schools that benefit more from one model or the other. It may well be that onsite technical assistance produces bigger effect sizes for many improvements, but online help can reach more schools and may be more cost-effective. Either way, the results will be extremely helpful to the program for its strategy and execution and as a guide to the two foundations on future investments and a focus on program improvement and foundation strategy.

Empowerment Evaluation Principles in the Future

Evaluation's purposes and practices are being reexamined as part of RWJF's strategic planning process, and the repertoire is likely to include more of the principles associated with empowerment evaluation. RWJF may invest more in capacity building, for example, especially when engaging with a nonprofit organization to strengthen and test the organization's good ideas. Inclusiveness and community wisdom will receive more emphasis as the foundation engages a diverse society in the problem solving necessary to reduce health disparities and foster demand for policies and environments conducive to health. Also, translating research into practice is likely to be emphasized even more in the future, for example, to assist public health departments with quality improvement and to offer evidence-based solutions to public health problems.

Why consider empowerment evaluation as opposed to related strategies and cognate concepts for these efforts? There are three reasons to do so. First, RWJF's experience with its "exceptional" evaluations, such as Allies Against Asthma or Active for Life, illustrate the advantages of working more closely with program developers and managers to bring the best out of implementation. As long as the strategy is emergent, the programs themselves are unlikely to be fully developed and, under those conditions, it only makes sense to collaborate more fully and systematically with those implementing the programs. The second reason is grantee buy-in. I was able to witness firsthand how empowerment evaluation can engage, even enthrall, a receptive audience of intelligent non-profit organizational leaders. They immediately understood the concepts behind Getting To Outcomes and were highly enthusiastic about the approach. The third reason is that, with spin-off products such as Getting To Outcomes and the interactive systems framework for dissemination and implementation, it is my belief that the relevant issues and experiences of empowerment evaluation have been processed and formalized in ways that can help RWJF grantees to improve health and health care for Americans. The models and processes are consistent with how program managers do their business and how good ideas get implemented well in health and social programs. These features are consistent with RWJF's continuing focus on evaluation for quality improvement and accountability to the field, not the funder, for showing results.

REFERENCES

Aday, L. A., Fleming, G. V., & Andersen, R. (1984). *Access to medical care in the U.S.: Who has it, who doesn't*. Chicago: University of Chicago, Center for Health Administration Studies.

Beam, M., Ehrlich, G., Donze Black, J., Block, A., & Leviton, L. C. (2012a). Evaluation of the Healthy Schools Program: I. Interim progress. *Preventing Chronic Disease, 9*, 110106. doi:http://dx.doi.org/10.5888/pcd9.110106

Beam, M., Ehrlich, G., Donze Black, J., Block, A., & Leviton, L. C. (2012b). Evaluation of the Healthy Schools Program: II. The role of technical assistance. *Preventing Chronic Disease, 9*, 110105. doi:http://dx.doi.org/10.5888/pcd9.110105

Berwick, D. M., & Davidoff, F. (2004). *Escape fire: Designs for the future of health care*. San Francisco: Jossey-Bass.

Brennan, L. K., Brownson, R. C., Leviton, L. C., Strunk, S. L., Schmid, T. L., & Cohen, D. A. (Eds.). (2012). Evaluation of active living by design. *American Journal of Preventive Medicine, 43*(5 Suppl 4).

Center for Public Program Evaluation. (2011). *The tobacco campaigns of the Robert Wood Johnson Foundation and collaborators, 1991–2010.* Princeton, NJ: Robert Wood Johnson Foundation. Retrieved from http://www.rwjf.org/content/dam/farm/reports/evaluations/2011/rwjf70005

Chelimsky, E. (1997). The coming transformations in evaluation. In E. Chelimsky & W. R. Shadish (Eds.), *Evaluation for the 21st century: A handbook.* Thousand Oaks, CA: Sage.

Chinman, M., Hunter, S. B., Ebener, P. A., Paddock, S. M., Stillman, L., Imm, P., et al. (2008). The Getting to Outcomes demonstration and evaluation: An illustration of the prevention support system. *American Journal of Community Psychology, 41*(3–4), 206–224.

Clark, N. M., Doctor, L. J., Friedman, A. R., Lachance, L. L., Houle, C. R., Geng, X., et al. (2006). Community coalitions to control chronic disease: Allies Against Asthma as a model and case study. *Health Promotion Practice, 7*(2 Suppl), 14S–22S.

Clark, N. M., Lachance, L. L., Doctor, L. J., Gilmore, L., Kelly, C., Krieger, J., et al. (2010). Policy and system change and community coalitions: Outcomes from Allies Against Asthma. *American Journal of Public Health, 100*(5), 904–912.

Coffman, J. (2009). *A user's guide to advocacy evaluation planning.* Cambridge, MA: Harvard Family Research Project. Retrieved from http://www.hfrp.org/evaluation/publications-resources/a-user-s-guide-to-advocacy-evaluation-planning

Cohen, D., Crabtree, B. F., Etz, R. S., et al. (2008). Fidelity versus flexibility: Translating evidence-based research into practice. *American Journal of Preventive Medicine, 35,* S381–S389.

Colby, D. C., & Isaacs, S. L. (2011). From idea to mainstream: The Robert Wood Johnson Foundation experience. In S. L. Isaacs & D. C. Colby (Eds.), *To improve health and health care* (Vol. 14). San Francisco: Jossey-Bass.

Emont, S., & Emont, N. (2009). *Healthy Eating Research program tracking indicators.* Danbury, NH: White Mountain Research Associates.

Fetterman, D. M. (1996). Empowerment evaluation: An introduction to theory and practice. In D. M. Fetterman, S. J. Kaftarian, & A. Wandersman (Eds.), *Empowerment evaluation: Knowledge and tools for self-assessment and accountability* (pp. 3–48). Thousand Oaks, CA: Sage.

Fetterman, D. M. (2005). Empowerment evaluation: From the digital divide to academic distress. In D. M. Fetterman & A. Wandersman (Eds.), *Empowerment evaluation principles in practice* (pp. 92–122). New York: Guilford Press.

Fetterman, D. M. (2010). *Ethnography: Step by step.* Thousand Oaks, CA: Sage.

Fetterman, D. M. (2013). *Empowerment evaluation in the digital villages: Hewlett-Packard's $15 million race toward social justice.* Stanford, CA: Stanford University Press.

Fetterman, D. M., & Wandersman, A. (2005). *Empowerment evaluation principles in practice.* New York: Guilford Press.

Fetterman, D. M., & Wandersman, A. (2007). Empowerment evaluation: Yesterday, today, and tomorrow. *American Journal of Evaluation, 28*(2), 179–198.

Freeman, H. E., Blendon, R. J., Aiken, L. H., Sudman, S., Mullinix, C. F., & Corey, C. R. (1987). Americans report on their access to health care. *Health Affairs, 6*(1), 6–18.

Hirschhorn, L., & Gilmore, T. N. (2004). *Ideas in philanthropic field building: Where they come from and how they are translated into action.* New York, NY: Foundation Center. Retrieved from http://foundationcenter.org/gainknowledge/research/pdf/practicematters_06_paper.pdf

Knickman, J. R., & Hunt, K. A. (2007). The Robert Wood Johnson Foundation's approach to evaluation. In S. L. Isaacs & J. R. Knickman (Eds.), *To improve health and health care* (Vol. 11). San Francisco: Jossey-Bass.

Kohn, L. T., Corrigan J. M., & Donaldson, M. S. (Eds.). (2000). *To err is human: Building a safer health system.* Washington, DC: National Academies Press.

Lattimore, D., Griffin, S. F., Wilcox, S., Rheaume, C., Dowdy, D., Leviton, L. C., et al. (2010). Understanding the challenges and adaptations made by community organizations for translation of evidence-based behavior change physical activity interventions: A qualitative study. *American Journal of Health Promotion, 24*(6), 427–434.

Lavizzo-Mourey, R. (2009). *Health care's all-American journey.* Princeton, NJ: Robert Wood Johnson Foundation. Retrieved from http://www.rwjf.org/en/research-publications/find-rwjf-research/2010/04/health-care-s-all-american-journey.html

Lavizzo-Mourey, R. (2013). *Envisioning a healthy America.* Princeton, NJ: Robert Wood Johnson Foundation. Retrieved from http://www.rwjf.org/en/about-rwjf/annual-reports/president-s-message-20131.html

Leviton, L. C., & Bass, M. (2004). Using evaluation to advance a foundation's mission. In M. Braverman, N. Constantine, & J. K. Slater (Eds.), *Foundations and evaluation: Contexts and practices for effective philanthropy* (pp. 3–26). San Francisco: Jossey-Bass.

Leviton, L. C., & Bickel, W. E. (2004). Integrating evaluation into foundation activity cycles. In M. Braverman, N. Constantine, & J. K. Slater (Eds.), *Foundations and evaluation: Contexts and practices for effective philanthropy* (pp. 119–144). San Francisco: Jossey-Bass.

Mathematica Policy Research. (2013). *Cash and counseling evaluation changes policymakers' approach to consumer-directed care.* Princeton, NJ: Author. Retrieved from http://www.mathematica-mpr.com/health/cashcounseling1.asp

McGlynn, E. L., Asch, S. M., Adams, J., Keesey, J., Hicks, J., DeCristofaro, A., et al. (2003). The quality of health care delivered to adults in the United States. *New England Journal of Medicine, 348,* 2635–2645.

Ottoson, J., Green, L. W., Beery, W. L., Senter, S. K., Cahill, C. L., Greenwald, H. P., et al. (2008). Policy contribution assessment and field-building analysis of the Robert Wood Johnson Foundation's Active Living Research Program. *American Journal of Preventive Medicine, 36*(2 Suppl), S34–S43.

Palmer, J. (2000). *Evaluation report to the Robert Wood Johnson Foundation on the Scholars in Health Policy Research Program.* Syracuse, NY: Syracuse University, Maxwell School of Citizenship and Public Affairs.

Patrizi, P. A. (2010). Death is certain, strategy isn't: Assessing the Robert Wood Johnson Foundation's end-of-life grant making. *New Directions for Evaluation, 128,* 47–68.

Patrizi, P., Thompson, L., & Spector, A. (2011). *Improving care at the end of life: How the Robert Wood Johnson Foundation and its grantees built the field.* Princeton, NJ: Robert Wood Johnson Foundation. Retrieved from http://www.rwjf.org/content/dam/farm/reports/reports/2011/rwjf69582

Patton, M. Q., & Patrizi, P. A. (2010). Strategy as the focus for evaluation. *New Directions for Evaluation, 128,* 5–28.

Pearson, M. L., Wu, S. Y., Schaefer, J., Bonomi, A. E., Shortell, S. M., Mendel, P. J., et al. (2005). Assessing the implementation of the chronic care model in quality improvement collaboratives. *Health Services Research, 40*(4), 978–996.

Perla, R. J., Provost, L. P., & Parry, G. J. (2013). The seven propositions of the science of improvement. *Quality Management in Health Care, 22*(3), 170–186.

Porter, M. E., & Kramer, M. R. (1999, November/December). Philanthropy's new agenda: Creating value. *Harvard Business Review,* 121–130.

Rosenblatt, R. (2006). The Robert Wood Johnson Foundation's efforts to cover the uninsured. In S. L. Isaacs & J. R. Knickman (Eds.), *To improve health and health care* (Vol. 9, Chap. 3). San Francisco: Jossey-Bass.

RWJF (Robert Wood Johnson Foundation). (2010). *Research and evaluation*. Retrieved from www .rwjf.org/content/dam/files/rwjf-web-files/Framing-Strategy/RE%20Framing%20Doc%20 061110.pdf

RWJF (Robert Wood Johnson Foundation). (2011). *Evaluating models for prevention of intimate partner violence in immigrant and refugee communities*. Retrieved from http://www.rwjf.org/ en/about-rwjf/newsroom/newsroom-content/2011/07/evaluating-models-for-prevention-of-intimate-partner-violence-in.html

RWJF (Robert Wood Johnson Foundation). (2012). *Cash & counseling: Empowering choice, improving health*. Retrieved from www.rwjf.org/en/about-rwjf/newsroom/newsroom-content/ 2012/05/cash-and-counseling-empowering-choice-improving-health1.html

Uehling, G., Bouroncle, A., Roeber, C., Tashima, N., & Crain, C. (2011). Preventing partner violence in refugee and immigrant communities. *Forced Migration Review, 50*–51. Retrieved from http:// www.fmreview.org/technology/uehling-et-al.html#sthash.3V4rbMIG.dpuf

Wandersman, A., Chien, V. H., & Katz, J. (2012). Toward an evidence-based system for innovation support for implementing innovations with quality: Tools, training, technical assistance, and quality assurance/quality improvement. *American Journal of Community Psychology, 50*(3–4), 445–459.

Wilcox, S., Dowda, M., Leviton, L. C., Bartlett-Prescott, J., Bazzarre, T., Campbell-Voytal, K., et al. (2008). The Active for Life initiative: Final results of translating two evidence-based physical activity programs into practice. *American Journal of Preventive Medicine, 35*(4), 340–351.

CHAPTER 5

Capacity Building Through Empowerment Evaluation

An Aymara Women Artisans Organization in Puno, Peru

Susana Sastre-Merino
Universidad Politécnica de Madrid

Pablo Vidueira
Universidad Politécnica de Madrid

José María Díaz-Puente
Universidad Politécnica de Madrid

María José Fernández-Moral
Universidad Politécnica de Madrid

INTRODUCTION

Empowerment evaluation was applied to a rural development project to promote leadership among rural women artisans in Puno (Peru). They are developing their skills to become the leaders of their own project and transform their craft activities into a successful and sustainable business. This case study demonstrates how empowerment evaluation is a useful tool to promote capacity building in rural areas and to help programs achieve their goals. The rural project and its evaluation were guided by the empowerment evaluation principles of improvement, inclusion, democratic participation, and capacity building, as well as a respect for community knowledge, community ownership, and accountability.

AYMARA COMMUNITIES

This project is being developed in several Aymara communities located in the Andean region of Puno (Peru) around Titicaca Lake. The local communities are among the poorest in the country, with a poverty rate between 51% and 70% (INEI, 2009). This is due to a variety of factors, including high altitudes and extreme temperatures (SENAMHI, 2009); poor communication and transport infrastructure; low technological level of agricultural production activities; land fragmentation; and a lack of irrigation systems (Arias & Polar, 1991).

The economy of the region is based on sheep and alpaca wool production, as well as cattle and the cultivation of potatoes, quinoa, and barley (Cazorla, De los Ríos, Hernández, & Yagüe, 2010). Non-agricultural activities have proliferated as a means of diversifying the economy, combined with the temporary migration of male household members (Forstner, 2012).

At the household level, the husband's salary is the main source of income for Aymaran families. The majority of women lack access to educational opportunities and economic resources. In addition, there is little income associated with agriculture and farming because they are almost exclusively devoted to subsistence. In this context, craft production and the hand knitting of textiles, dominated by women, has been a significant strategy for diversifying the communities' rural livelihood (Forstner, 2012). Efforts to capitalize on textile production–related opportunities, however, have been thwarted by intermediaries profiting from their low product pricing (Forstner, 2012). Aymaran women have made efforts to seek international markets in order to sell their products at a higher price than in local markets or to intermediaries. Several institutions—such as nongovernmental organizations (NGOs), religious organizations, and state development agencies—support these groups (Forstner, 2012). The aim of support is often to strengthen the women's economic role or to increase their political participation (Forstner, 2012). Empowerment evaluation has been instrumental in making this a reality.

THE PROJECT BACKGROUND: INTEGRATING THE PRODUCTIVE FUNCTION INTO THE SOCIAL ORGANIZATION

This case study focuses on one organization: Coordinadora de Mujeres Aymaras. It is a women's organization in the Puno region that is comprised of 400 women organized in 22 groups that are distributed among 6 districts: Huancané, Moho, Vilquechico (northern area), Platería, Chucuito (central area), and Juli (southern area). This organization was set up in 1982 by the Maryknoll Society as Coordinación Pastoral de Mujeres de la Prelatura de Juli (CPM) and included several women's support groups that were related to the Catholic Church. In its origins, the association's objectives included evangelization, defending women's rights, and combating domestic violence. Over time, other objectives were added, such as the pursuit of personal, group, and community development; institutional strengthening; and the improvement of health and training. During the 1990s, they worked with external institutions such as Caritas, Instituto de Educación Rural de Juli (IER), and Prelature of Juli and Vicaría Solidaridad, among others. They provided training in agricultural activities, crafts, and human rights. In the late 1990s, some members of the association started to train other members and neighboring communities in hand knitting, natural medicine, and leadership.

Over two decades the women of the organization had developed a strong social capital. However, the religious order that supported them left the area. They had been exporting some crafts with this organization, but as a side activity. Their role was only as artisans, and they were not involved in the marketing or in developing the capacity to operate a business. Nevertheless, they developed an incipient interest in enhancing the productive part of the organization. However, they no longer received support from any organization to sell their crafts.

THE DEVELOPMENT PROJECT AND ITS EVALUATION

The purpose of this project was to help these women market their products. In 2006, the organization, through the Bishop of Juli, contacted researchers of the Research Group on Planning and Management of Rural Development (GESPLAN) of the Technical University of Madrid (UPM) and requested assistance.

In 2007, four workshops were carried out based on the empowerment evaluation methodology developed by Fetterman (2001). One was conducted with the executive committee and the others were held in each of the three geographic areas of the organization.

The aims of the project were established during the initial empowerment evaluation workshops. These aims were to increase the personal and leadership skills of the artisan women involved in this project; to enhance the organizational capacity of the project for better access to markets; and to develop a sustainable business model for their communities. The framework for skills development was based on a scheme, which was proposed by the International Project Management Association (IPMA, 2006). This was important, given the context of rural projects where local people can become leaders of projects and need to manage these projects in a sustainable manner. People involved in this project needed technical skills and the ability to develop and manage relationships and the business aspect of the project.

A strengths, weaknesses, opportunities, and threats analysis was carried out by GESPLAN. The project was presented to the Council of Madrid (Spain) and was later approved for funding and implementation for a period of 2 years. Other institutions provided funding, and the project continued through 2012. Although other ideas were explored, textile crafts turned out to be the most successful line of economic development (Cazorla et al., 2010).

From 2008 to 2012, the project applied empowerment evaluation principles and practices. A local manager from GESPLAN acted as a facilitator (Díaz-Puente, Gallego, Vidueira, & Fernández-Moral, 2013) of the process, focusing on a critical friend role (Fetterman, 2009; Fetterman, Deitz, & Gesundheit, 2010; Fetterman & Wandersman, 2005) to help in the systematization and monitoring of the strategy as defined by Fetterman et al. (2010). The executive committee held regular meetings. They invited the local managers from each of the regions to help them monitor the development of the project, set priorities, and develop action plans (encouraging a cycle of reflection and action).

In November 2012, a new set of training sessions were carried out, following the same empowerment evaluation principles but focusing more heavily on improvement, inclusion, democratic participation, and capacity building. This time the aim was to help prepare the women of all regions to lead their own training sessions.

IMPROVEMENT

Regarding the productive process, new materials, working tools, and designs were incorporated. In addition, a local quality control committee was created to establish and implement international quality standards (Negrillo, Yagüe, Hernández, & Sagua, 2011). This enhanced the marketability of their products. Previously they could sell their crafts only to intermediaries or in local markets.

Figure 5.1   Participants in one of the 2012 empowerment evaluation workshops

Courtesy of Susana Sastre

Now they had stable clients in Spain, Australia, and Norway and were receiving an average of three times the previous price for their work. Most important, these artisan women continued to use traditional materials such as alpaca fiber in creating products that incorporated some new elements in their traditional designs. This demonstrates how it is possible to promote community-based knowledge and skills as well as local culture and traditions in generating marketable products.

After each production period, the whole process was evaluated within the principles of empowerment evaluation, using information gathered from the leaders and clients of each of the three areas. Meetings in which these evaluations were carried out allowed participants to enhance their decision-making processes, identify elements that were important in product quality, and understand how access to better markets can lead to more profitable business.

These sessions also improved labor division, transparency, and equity between areas. Participants moved from specialized local designs and products to a system where women from all three areas learned to knit all the designs. This was accomplished through an internal training program with the goal of responding to large and varied orders in a timely manner.

In addition, the group requested and received training to improve their business skills and production capacities in the garment industry. According to their 2011 survey, 94% of these women reported they had increased their technical abilities.

One of the most significant accomplishments in this regard is that they are now reaching a global market. They have opened a local store and an online shop, and are selling their crafts through several national and international outlets. Sales have increased steadily from $7,734 in 2009 to $8,659 in 2010 and finally to $11,263 in 2011. Additionally, they are working with tourism operators to establish the store as a stopover for tours.

INCLUSION

Following the first empowerment evaluation workshop, other women in these communities who were interested in participating in the project were quickly welcomed and included in the training. Broader participation was promoted and guided on the basis of the empowerment evaluation principle of inclusion. By including the voices of all stakeholders through an open assembly system, these women were able to solve many of the problems they faced and generate

Figure 5.2   2012 CMA artisan products catalog

Courtesy of Asociacion Diseno para el Desarrollo

new ideas. It should be reported that membership in this empowerment evaluation project increased considerably, from 320 women in 2010 (Negrillo, Yagüe, García, & Montes, 2010) to 408 women in 2012 (Sastre-Merino, Negrillo, & Hernández-Castellano, 2013).

Initial evaluation of this project carried out in 2010 showed that because of the distance from the central office, the northern region was not participating well enough in planned activities (Sastre-Merino & De los Ríos, 2012). Through improved communication and more frequent visits by the executive board, this area became more involved in activities and became a more integral part of the group.

In addition, the women agreed to alternate the position of president among themselves to promote meaningful participation and inclusion. Furthermore, the establishment of a new repository for raw materials to complement the existing one facilitated equal and easy access to raw materials, thus reducing travel time for women who lived in more distant regions. This in turn increased production and made production more timely in all three regions.

Training for new designs further promoted a sense of inclusion and access to knowledge transfer. Two women from each group attended and assisted with these training sessions and workshops, and were made responsible for training their groups when they returned to their communities.

DEMOCRATIC PARTICIPATION

The project is based on the model of planning as social learning (Cazorla, De los Ríos, & Salvo, 2007; Friedman, 1991). This model proposes the involvement of people in all stages of the project in a continuous learning process. This learning process is bidirectional, as both the facilitators and the local people share their expert knowledge and experience. Furthermore, the role that the facilitators adopted (i.e., as resource mobilizers and catalysts of both public and private interests) helped the women find innovative solutions in their territories.

All of the major decisions made by the executive committee were made in consensus with the groups. This committee, supported by the facilitators, has led a process of continuous monitoring, to reorient work strategies and enhance many aspects related to both the organization's structure and the productive process. They defined the rhythm of the project, which produced a sense of ownership. This is not common in the area, where other NGOs apply a top-down approach and women do not take part in the decision-making process. According to a survey conducted in 2011 by GESPLAN (Sastre-Merino, 2014),

55.7% of the women thought their participation in decision making had increased as a result of their participation in this enterprise.

CAPACITY BUILDING

Strong local leadership and continuous evaluation of the project have proven to be important capacity building elements in this endeavor. For example, a woman who served on the executive committee emerged as a leader who made training accessible for all women, even those who were not part of the project. This kind of leadership is invaluable in building broad-based capacity at the community level. Empowerment evaluation also emphasized the importance of continuous self-evaluation and improvement. When women asked for help in 2007, they thought they just needed support in accessing international markets. However, by using the empowerment evaluation principle of critical self-reflection (Fetterman et al., 2010), they were able to refine their thinking and quickly realized that they were not ready to meet international market dictates. They also realized that before worrying about access to markets, they should first improve their quality standards, organizational structure, and business skills. Through self-evaluation, they were able to reorient themselves and the project, as well as become better prepared to face marketing challenges. It was only then that they were able to move toward a more profitable and sustainable business model. It should also be mentioned that although this continuous and rigorous self-assessment process was important, it did not always provide positive and encouraging outcomes. Nevertheless, it was certainly invaluable in gradually resolving problems and building local capacity for success.

ADDITIONAL EMPOWERMENT EVALUATION PRINCIPLES

This group was guided by additional empowerment evaluation principles, including respect for community-based knowledge, community ownership, and accountability. For example, since knitting is at the heart of Aymara women's culture, and their knitting patterns symbolize much of their worldview (Nostas & Sanabria, 2009), integrating these cultural patterns into their designs and products represented a profound respect for community knowledge.

Community ownership was another guiding principle for both the business and evaluation aspects of the project. Although it took 8 months to select an assistant in the technical office and 4 months to renew the executive committee positions, these women did not rush to judgment. They wanted to make sure they had the right people in the right positions. The process of deliberating over each candidate, and assessing the merits of each one for the organization, created a sense of ownership (for both the evaluative process and the business).

The empowerment evaluation principle of accountability was also manifested throughout the endeavor. It ranged from establishing internal quality controls to making a profit. Workshops for ensuring everyone's alignment with the project mission, monitoring product quality (i.e., women agreeing to write their names on their products to accept both credit and responsibility), and adhering to timelines were meaningful practices that brought about internal accountability.

It should be added that although the previously mentioned empowerment evaluation principles have been discussed separately, they often overlapped and had synergistic value in practice settings.

CONCLUSION

This case study highlighted the utility of empowerment evaluation principles and processes in guiding the development, evaluation, and implementation of a local business model. It demonstrated how the empowerment evaluation process was instrumental in helping a rural group of women take an idea and transform it into a successful, competitive, and profitable business. It showed how empowerment evaluation principles and process can help define and set realistic goals and objectives and how they can help build the necessary capacity for achieving those goals and objectives.

This example also demonstrated how empowerment evaluation principles and process can be instrumental in significant social change and how following them can assist in establishing and institutionalizing shared values and common vision over geographically disparate areas. Most important, women involved in this empowerment evaluation project reported feelings of belonging, collaboration, and self-worth. These once economically disenfranchised women are now significant contributors to the financial well-being of their families and communities and can be used as beacons of hope for other disenfranchised groups of women across the world.

REFERENCES

Arias, A., & Polar, O. (1991). *Pueblo aymara: realidad vigente* [The Aymara people: Current reality]. Cusco: Instituto de Pastoral Andina.

Cazorla, A., De los Ríos, I., Hernández, D., & Yagüe, J. L. (2010). *Working with people: Rural development with Aymara communities of Peru.* Paper presented at the International Conference on Agricultural Engineering, Clermont-Ferrand, France.

Cazorla, A., De los Ríos, I., & Salvo, M. (2007). *Desarrollo rural: modelos de planificación* [Rural development: Planning models]. Madrid: Ediciones Mundiprensa.

Díaz-Puente, J. M., Gallego, F. J., Vidueira, P., & Fernández, M. J. (2013). Facilitation in community development. Twenty-five years of experience in rural territories in Cuenca, Spain. *European Planning Studies.* doi:10.1080/09654313.2013.830695

Fetterman, D. M. (2001). *Foundations of empowerment evaluation.* Thousand Oaks, CA: Sage.

Fetterman, D. M. (2009). Empowerment evaluation at the Stanford University School of Medicine: Using a critical friend to improve the clerkship experience. *Ensaio: Avaliação e Políticas Públicas em Educação, 17*(63), 197–204.

Fetterman, D. M., Deitz, J., & Gesundheit, N. (2010). Empowerment evaluation: A collaborative approach to evaluating and transforming a medical school curriculum. *Academic Medicine, 85*(5), 813–820.

Fetterman, D. M., & Wandersman, A. (2005). *Empowerment evaluation principles in practice.* New York: Guilford Press.

Forstner, K. (2012). Women's group-based work and rural gender relations in the southern Peruvian Andes. *Bulletin of Latin American Research, 31*(1), 46–60.

Friedman, J. (1991). *La planificación en el ámbito público* [Planning in the public domain]. Madrid: Instituto Nacional de Administración Pública.

Instituto Nacional de Estadística e Informática (INEI). (2009). *Informe técnico: evolución de la pobreza al 2009* [Technical report: The evolution of poverty, 2009]. Lima: Author.

International Project Management Association (IPMA). (2006). *ICB-IPMA competence baseline,* version 3.0. Nijkerk, Netherlands: Author.

Negrillo, X., Yagüe, J. L., García, A., & Montes, A. (2010). Aprendizaje social en los proyectos de desarrollo rural: el caso de la Coordinadora de Mujeres Aymaras en Juli (Puno, Perú) [Social learning in rural development projects: The case of Coordinadora de Mujeres Aymaras de Juli (Puno, Peru)]. In *Selected Proceedings from the 14th International Congress on Project Engineering,* Madrid, Spain.

Negrillo, X., Yagüe, J. L., Hernández, D., & Sagua, N. (2011). *El Aprendizaje social como modelo de planificación y gestión de proyectos de desarrollo: la Coordinadora de Mujeres Aymaras* [Social learning as a planning and management model of development projects: The Coordinadora de Mujeres Aymaras]. Paper presented at the 15th International Congress on Project Engineering, Huesca, Spain.

Nostas, M., & Sanabria, C. E. (2009). *Detrás del cristal con que se mira: órdenes normativos e interlegalidad mujeres quechuas, aymaras, sirionó, trinitarias, chimane, chiquitanas, y ayoreas.* La Paz, Peru: Coordinadora de la Mujer.

Sastre-Merino, S. (2014). *Desarrollo de capacidades para el liderazgo en proyectos de desarrollo rural. Aplicación a comunidades aymaras.* Unpublished doctoral thesis, Universidad Politécnica de Madrid, Spain.

Sastre-Merino, S., & De los Ríos, I. (2012). *Project management competence analysis in rural communities through territorial representation: Application to Aymara women communities in Puno (Peru).* Paper presented at the 2nd International Conference on Applied Social Science, February 1–2, 2012, Kuala Lumpur, Malaysia.

Sastre-Merino, S., Negrillo, X., & Hernández-Castellano, D. (2013). Sustainability of rural development projects within the working with people model: Application to Aymara women communities in the Puno Region, Peru. *Cuadernos de Desarrollo Rural, 10* (70), 219–244.

SENAMHI. (2009). *Reporte anual del clima por regiones* [Annual report of weather by region]. Lima, Perú: Edición regional del Servicio Nacional de Meteorología e Hidrografía.

CHAPTER 6

Teachers as Evaluators

An Empowerment Evaluation Approach

Janet Clinton and John Hattie[1]

University of Melbourne

Empowerment evaluation is concerned with fostering improvement, evaluating impact, and developing the capacity to monitor and evaluate one's own performance. Specifically, Fetterman (1994) defined empowerment evaluation as "the use of evaluation concepts, techniques, and findings to foster improvement and self-determination" (p. 1). The definition later was expanded to provide users with additional guidance and insight into the approach: "Empowerment evaluation is an evaluation approach that aims to increase the likelihood that programs will achieve results by increasing the capacity of program stakeholders to plan, implement, and evaluate their own programs" (Fetterman, 2005, p. 11). This involves mainstreaming evaluation as part of program/organization planning and management (cf. Wandersman et al., 2005).

EVALUATORS OF IMPACT: A CULTURE OF EVIDENCE

Empowerment evaluation in action in the school sector provides the basis for this chapter. It demonstrates how educators can profitably adopt an empowerment evaluation approach, build evaluation capacity, and see themselves primarily as "evaluators of their impact." The educator's role is portrayed not merely as collecting data, creating reports, and filling in surveys, but as being excellent interpreters of evidence. Empowerment

---

1. We thank Abraham Wandersman, David Fetterman, Amy Gullickson, and Debra Masters for their improvements to this chapter.

86

evaluation assists in the cultivation of a continuous culture of evidence by asking educators for evidence to support their views and interpretations and to engage in continual phases of analysis, decision making, and implementation. Such evaluation requires making judgments about their impact, their leadership with others to engage in this evaluation of impact, and their practice. The chapter further illustrates how the nine principles of empowerment evaluation can be incorporated into a visible learning model of schooling. The fundamental assumption of the visible learning model is that when educators focus on defining, evaluating, and understanding their impact, this leads to maximizing student learning and achievement.

Know Thy Impact

The visible learning message can be summed up by the phrase "Know thy impact." A synthesis of more than 1,000 meta-analyses of various influences on student achievement (Hattie, 2009, 2012; Hattie & Anderman, 2013; Hattie & Yates, 2014) provides the basis for the visible learning model for schooling. Educators who see their fundamental role as evaluators of the impact of their work are more likely to have a sustained impact. This notion of "know thy impact" goes to the heart of the empowerment evaluation approach. This approach raises critical issues about the nature of the impact, the magnitude of the impact, the extensiveness of who is impacted, and the teacher's discovery about his or her effectiveness in having a real and measureable impact concerning student knowledge and understanding. This means that educators must have a deep understanding of evaluation methods, think as evaluators, and make evaluation the core of their professional responsibilities.

Visible Learning Premises

The major premises of visible learning include teachers believing their major role is to evaluate their impact, working together to know and evaluate their impact, clearly knowing students' prior learning, being explicit to students about what success looks like near the start of a series of lessons, implementing programs that have the optimal proportion of emphasis on surface and deep learning, and setting appropriate levels of challenge for students instead of merely telling them, "Do your best." This means that teachers need to take an empowerment evaluation stance: fostering improvement, evaluating impact, and making evaluation or response to interventions their major mind-set. This involves being clear about their notions of success, the appropriate balance of surface versus deep knowing as part of this notion of success, understanding where students are relative to these notions of success, and ensuring that the success criteria are sufficiently challenging for all students. A key question is how to build the capacity of teachers and school administrators, in order to collectively build and evaluate successful teaching programs and learning experiences.

The Current Scene in Education

The professionalism of teaching often is enshrined in the autonomy of teachers to choose best how to teach. This has led to a proliferation of teaching methods and major debates about optimal teaching methods (as if there ever could be but one). Often teachers are implored to use method X or method Y (e.g., reciprocal teaching or direct instruction) *because* successful teachers have used these methods. This confuses the correlates of effectiveness with the causes. Scriven (1971, 1975, 2005a) has long written about mistaking correlates of learning with causes. His claim is that various correlates of school outcomes—for example, the use of advance organizers, the maintenance of eye contact, or increased time on task—should not be confused with good teaching. Although these may indeed be correlates of learning, it is still the case that good teaching may include none of these attributes. It may be that increasing these behaviors in some teachers also leads to a decline in other attributes (e.g., caring and respect for students). Correlates, therefore, are not to be confused with causes.

A systematic observation of classroom practice over the past 150 years, however, shows that there is one dominant "method" of teaching that is evident in most Western classrooms. This method, dubbed by Tyack and Cuban (1995) the "grammar of schooling," sums up how many schools and classrooms function: concentrating the work of a teacher in one grade, splintering knowledge into subjects, a uniform curriculum, similar assessed outcomes, self-contained classrooms, bells and periods, batch processing through years, compulsory attendance, teachers monitoring and controlling students, assigning and ensuring students accomplish tasks and do their homework, and teachers dominating the classroom with their talk. In this grammar of schooling, the teachers' role is to choose engaging resources; use textbooks or worksheets; have the students sit in rows or groups to work individually; ask questions and elicit responses, usually one at a time; and talk, talk, and talk. The efficiency of the teacher talking and the belief that this is an optimal method for imparting instruction are such that, even when class sizes are reduced, teacher talking increases (Hattie, 2006)!

This is not to imply that this grammar has not been effective. The grammar is clearly claimed by many teachers to be an optimal and efficient model when there are 25 to 35 students in a class: It highlights the skills of management and discipline to focus all students on similar tasks, and it allows the bulk of the class to advance in step while allowing for the bright and struggling students to do more or less, respectively. It has stood the test of time as the dominant model of teaching. The evaluation skills under this model relate more to monitoring whether students are on task, ensuring all students complete (to whatever level) their assignments on time, choosing differentiated activities for students of varying abilities, optimizing student turn-taking via questioning, and setting tasks for students so they know what success looks like.

EFFECT SIZES AND THE VISIBLE LEARNING PERSPECTIVE

The synthesis of the many meta-analyses—based on more than 55,000 studies or about a quarter billion students (Hattie, 2009, 2012)—showed an average effect size of teachers of about .20 to .30, and an average across all interventions of .40.[2] Figure 6.1 presents the distribution of effect sizes from the 1,000 meta-analyses (based on approximately 250 million students). The key question in visible learning relates to ascertaining the underlying story to explain the differences between those influences above and below the average of .40.

The most notable feature of this distribution of effects is that almost everything has a positive impact on student learning (i.e., $d > .0$). Hence, asking in schools "What works?" is close to a meaningless question since almost everything does. This helps explain why teachers always can find evidence to support whatever teaching program they implement, why academics always find support for their pet innovation, and why politicians and evaluators can find success stories for their policies. The more important question is "What works

---

2. Effect sizes are standardized measures of the magnitude of influences—in this case, influences on student achievement. Cohen (1988) argued that an effect size of $d = 1.0$ should be regarded as a large, blatantly obvious, and grossly perceptible difference. The results in visible learning determined that an effect size greater than .60 in influences on achievement can be considered large. This is similar to the difference between the average IQ of PhD graduates and high school students, or to the naked eye the difference between a person who is 5'3" (160 cm) and a person who is 6'0" (183 cm). Effect sizes greater than .40 are above average, and effect sizes below .20 are small.

Figure 6.1 The frequency of effect sizes from 1,000+ meta-analyses

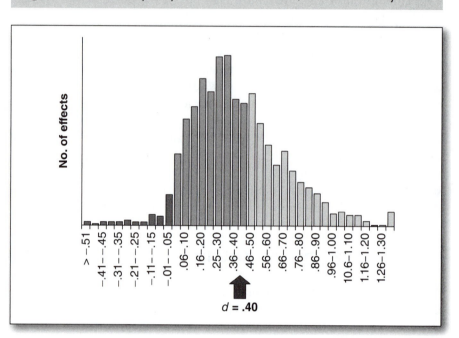

best?" where *best* is defined as at least greater than the typical effect from all possible interventions ($d > .40$).

Among the most common claims is that changing the structures of schooling can lead to improvements. Certainly, the funders (politicians, parents, voters) can physically see many of these effects. Such structural changes include new forms of schools (e.g., charter schools), changes in classroom structure (e.g., smaller class sizes, different classroom architecture such as open classrooms), grouping of the students (e.g., tracking), and more money. In nearly every case, the structural reforms of schooling are below average in their effects (Table 6.1 shows the rank of various structural influences out of 200 comparisons and their average effect sizes). This is not to say structural changes are unimportant, but it does say that major attention to these matters will make little difference to student outcomes.

Similarly, there are long debates about the optimal method of teaching in schools—as if one method would suffice for all students. There are many programs that fail to gain above the average hinge-point of .40 (left side of Table 6.2) and there are programs with high probabilities of success (right side of Table 6.2). The programs on the left-hand side of Table 6.2 tend to favor deep over surface learning, whereas the programs on the right-hand side tend to

Table 6.1   Ranking (out of 200) and Effect Sizes for Various Structural Influences on Student Achievement

Rank	Influence	Effect Size (d)
140	Summer school	0.23
141	Finances	0.23
142	Religious schools	0.23
147	Class size	0.21
159	Within class grouping	0.18
171	Ability grouping	0.12
177	Distance education	0.11
179	Changing school calendars/timetables	0.09
180	Detracking	0.09
183	Charter schools	0.07
185	Diversity of students	0.05
187	Multi-grade/age classes	0.04
192	Open vs. traditional	0.01
194	Welfare policies	−0.12
195	Retention (holding back a year)	−0.13

favor both deep and surface thinking. A focus on "deep learning" without attention to the domains of knowing what the thinking is built on tends not to be very successful. Determining the right mix of surface and deep learning requires a deep knowledge by the teacher as to when to focus on surface and when to move from the surface to the deeper tasks and thinking.

Teacher Expertise

The greatest effects relate to teacher expertise in the evaluation of his or her impact (Table 6.3). The first major dimension of effective teaching is the

Table 6.2   The Ranking (out of 200) and Effect Sizes for Various Teaching Programs

Rank	Influence	d	Rank	Influence	d
91	Inquiry-based methods	0.31	5	Conceptual change programs	1.16
136	Values/morals education programs	0.24	18	Meta-cognitive strategies	0.69
139	Programmed instruction	0.23	19	Acceleration	0.68
143	Individualized instruction	0.22	21	Vocabulary programs	0.67
144	Visual/audiovisual methods	0.22	22	Repeated reading programs	0.67
164	Matching styles of learning	0.17	23	Creativity programs	0.65
168	Problem-based learning	0.15	28	Problem-solving teaching	0.61
169	Sentence-combining programs	0.15	30	Comprehension programs	0.60
182	Perceptual-motor programs	0.08	31	Concept mapping	0.60
184	Whole language	0.06	35	Mastery learning	0.58
188	Homework in elementary classes	0.05	60	Second/third chance programs	0.50

evaluative skill to know when to make the move from surface to deep. The second and most powerful dimension is when teachers and school leaders believe their major role in classrooms is to know their impact. The premise "Know thy impact" can be operative within the current grammar of schooling, and indeed this emphasis does not dictate any methods, any program of work, or any format for the class. Instead, it highlights the capacity of educators to design effective programs, implement them with quality, and critically determine the magnitude of the impact of their educational programs on student

Table 6.3 The Effect Sizes of the Greatest Teaching Effects

	d
Teachers believing their major role is to evaluate their impact	.91
Teachers working together to know and evaluate their impact	.91
Teachers clearly knowing students' prior learning	.85
Teachers being explicit to students about what success looks like near the start of a series of lessons	.77
Teachers implementing programs that have the optimal proportions of surface and deep learning	.71
Teachers setting appropriate levels of challenge instead of merely telling students, "Do your best"	.57

learning. This emphasis on magnitude of change is paramount, especially given that 95%+ of methods employed to enhance learning lead to a positive impact on learning (Hattie, 2009). Merely enhancing learning is not enough—for maximum student outcomes, the teacher needs to know the magnitude of his or her impact and then evaluate whether this impact is sufficient.

The key to success is not only the *evaluative stance* of educators but also (given the emphasis on "know thy impact") a focus on educators determining the nature of "impact." Such impact is unlikely to be merely results on test scores, but it also includes students' attitudes, dispositions, and preparedness to reinvest in learning; tolerance for dealing with mistakes; collaboration; and keenness to be successful. When teachers communicate and students understand what the concept of desired impact or success is from any series of lessons, then there is greater probability that learning will be enhanced. Further, discussion about the sufficiency of this notion of success/impact goes to the heart of one of the definitions of evaluation—the evaluation of the merit, worth, and significance of impact (Scriven, 1991).

Working Collaboratively to Evaluate Impact on Learning

The impact on students is enhanced when teachers, school leaders, and students work collaboratively to evaluate their impact on learning—by working together to agree on the nature of success before beginning a series of lessons, by agreeing on multiple interventions such that when one does not have impact they are adept at changing the intervention, and by assisting each other to understand the specific impact of the teaching on each of the students. The latter can be accomplished, for example, not by observing the teachers in the act of teaching but by observing the impact of the teachers on the actions and understandings of the students.

VISIBLE LEARNING APPROACH: A MODEL OF EMPOWERMENT EVALUATION

The visible learning approach to teaching bridges the divide between education, evaluation, and teaching. It starts with a needs assessment of the degree to which a school can be deemed a visible learning school. The needs assessment not only indicates what a successful school looks like, but it also asks educators to evaluate the quality of the evidence they can provide relating to four major themes: (1) strategic planning and self-review that incorporates feedback about interventions and teaching impact; (2) the presence of deliberate strategies for raising teaching impact, monitoring the evaluative mind frames of teachers; (3) the use of student voice as part of the responses to interventions; and (4) the gathering and analyses of data about impact. The acronym teachers use is to DIE for; that is, they participate in *Diagnosing* the status of students as they begin lessons, they have multiple *Interventions* that they can apply if their current intervention is not having the desired impact, and they *Evaluate* the students' responses to their interventions.

The visible learning model starts with a day-long exposure to the research base. The 150 to 200 meta-analyses are introduced with an emphasis on the story—knowing thy impact. Overviews of two critical bonding notions—self-regulation and feedback—are provided with the message that it is about how we think about our work and it is receiving feedback about the impact of this work. Finally, the nine mind frames of teachers and school leaders, which will become the focus of the subsequent sessions, are introduced: (1) I am an evaluator of my impact; (2) I am a change agent; (3) I explicitly inform students what successful impact looks like from the outset; (4) I see assessment as providing feedback about my impact; (5) I work with other teachers to develop common conceptions of progress; (6) I engage in dialogue, not monologue; (7) I strive for challenge and not just "doing your best"; (8) I use the language of learning; and (9) I see errors as opportunities for learning.

In the first "evidence into action" session, the participants are introduced to the concepts and processes for collecting evidence against the visible learning matrix. This matrix is fundamentally a needs analysis, and the emphasis is on the nature and quality of evidence that is convincing not only to the school but also to others (peers, parents, system). The day involves planning how to collect the evidence. This matrix includes six major dimensions:

1. Teacher appraisal and impact (e.g., We seek and respond to student feedback as part of the appraisal process. Our appraisal system includes teachers setting goals and targets based on student achievement data and student feedback.)

2. Trust and welcome errors (e.g., Teachers feel it is okay to take risks, to say "I don't know" or "I need help." Our school culture encourages students to actively seek feedback from their teacher and peers.)

3. Teacher collaboration (e.g., The timetable allows for opportunities for teachers to meet to plan and moderate assessments. Teachers collaboratively plan series of lessons with learning intentions and success criteria.)

4. Visible learners (e.g., Our staff and team meetings focus on how to develop the characteristics of assessment—capable, visible learners. Lesson plans show deliberate efforts to develop assessment—capable, visible learners.)

5. Impact coaching (e.g., The person or team responsible for monitoring progress does so throughout the year and over time and makes this information available to teachers. There is a person or team in our school who has explicit responsibility for ensuring student success.)

6. Teacher observations and impact (e.g., Senior staff carry out regular walkthroughs and observations.)

On the second day (2 months or so later), they meet to evaluate the evidence with colleagues. This evidence is shared and critiqued, and implementation plans are devised to make enhancements that lead to positive impacts on student learning. Specific planning of both the implementation of these enhancements and the pre- and post-evaluation of the impact of implementations is devised. Other educators in the session collaborate in interrogating each other's evidence, deciding on evidence-based interventions, and improving the evaluation plan relating to both the fidelity of implementation and the nature of evidence to evaluate the implementation.

In the Visible Learning into Action for Teachers program, teachers focus on effective classroom practice. Teachers consider the visible learning research evidence to learn what practices have the highest probability for successful student learning and achievement. They then plan an impact cycle to focus on making changes to their teaching and learning. They collect the evidence with regard to current practice, complete their own learning, and then make changes. The impact of these changes is tracked, and they consider the success of the impact cycle and plan for the next cycle.

The Visible Learning Inside series provides more specificity about the research on high probability interventions. These include feedback that makes learning visible, using data to evaluate your impact, creating effective teacher-made tests, and developing assessment-capable learners. If requested, a specific set of sessions are provided that delve deeper into the meta-analysis method, specific meta-analyses, and ways to use effect sizes in the classroom and school context.

Finally, support for education systems (e.g., districts, state authorities) is also supported through the Visible Learning Collective Impact Program. The components of this program are similar to those listed previously but are aimed to support change at scale and build capacity for system-wide impact. These supports include the establishment of a guiding coalition, a school baseline capability analysis (using the individual's school matrix, described earlier, as the basis for this), and the training of impact coaches who support the collection of evidence as well as the planning and implementation of the visible learning program, school visits, and online support. The program has been designed to maximize the visible learning approach with intensive support for schools while building the capability and sustainability for the education system.

At its core, empowerment evaluation has various principles, and there is much synergy between visible learning's practical approach to schooling and empowerment evaluation. The following section illustrates how major principles of empowerment evaluation (Wandersman et al., 2005) relate to the visible learning approach.

1. **Guided Immersion and Ownership (Empowerment evaluation values and facilitates *community ownership* and control; use and sustainability are dependent on a sense of ownership.)**

The focus of visible learning is on teachers and school leaders becoming evaluators of their impact within the classroom and school; in doing so, they thus take ownership of the process. These educators need to adopt the visible learning mind frame (see Hattie, 2012), which involves a structured process leading to determining success and improvement options, agreeing on measurement of their impact that is shared by and with all, and working together to understand and enhance progression in learning. Visible learning is neither a program nor a scripted text; rather, it is an empowerment approach within classes, schools, and systems. It works by showing participants how to think in terms of evaluating their impact.

Fetterman (2013) argued that in an empowerment evaluation, thinking evaluatively is a product of guided immersion. "This occurs when people conduct their own evaluation as guided by empowerment evaluators. Teaching people to think evaluatively is like teaching them to fish. It can last a lifetime and is what evaluative sustainability is all about—internalizing evaluation (individually and institutionally)" (p. 308). This demands participation and immersion to see their impact through an evaluative lens, leading to a sense of ownership, and "it is this combination of evaluation thought and ownership, through immersion, that makes empowerment evaluation work, improving knowledge utilization in the process" (p. 308). This is one of the key mind frames of the visible learning model.

It is critical to note that the evaluation involves the impact of the interventions on learning. Too often, teachers evaluate the impact of the resources they use, and administer many tests to inform students about their progress—but it is critical that teachers see the impact of resources and student assessments as feedback about their impact. Similarly, some teachers see students as bright or struggling, as hard workers or disengaged, as motivated or not, as committed to classroom norms or disobedient—and indeed students can be all of these. However, this viewpoint places too much responsibility for learning on the student alone. Instead, the locus of responsibility in visible learning is with teachers—in their critical acumen to understand their impact, about what, and with whom. They need to see their teaching as based on diagnoses, multiple interventions, and evaluation of their impact—if students do not learn, then teachers need to change their practice.

2. **Collective Impact (Empowerment evaluation emphasizes collaboration with program stakeholders as communities of learners as guided by principles of inclusion and democratic participation.)**

The collective impact part of the visible learning model is attuned to moving all parts of the education community (from head office to classrooms) to ensure everything is aligned for maximum impact. It is about the collective from all pulling together in the same direction. This is similar to the notion of collective impact as described by Kania and Kramer (2011), who see collective impact initiatives as a process that involves "a centralized infrastructure, a dedicated staff, and a structured process that leads to a common agenda, shared measurement, continuous communication, and mutually reinforcing activities among all participants" (p. 38). When applied to the school setting, collective impact means school and system leaders developing a common agenda (maximizing their impact on learning), common progress measures (of progress and achievement), mutually reinforcing activities (each person's expertise is leverage as part of the overall impact), a culture of collaboration and communication, and a strong backbone organization (from systems throughout) to manage the collaboration and understanding of impact (Figure 6.2). Collective impact requires the development of evaluation methods among all in the school to best understand the impact. While the focus is the evaluation skills of the teachers, it assists in a major way to also teach the students these evaluation methods so they become evaluation-capable to optimize their investment in their own learning.

Collaboration and engagement are fundamental to school communities. The visible learning framework requires the adults in a school to work together, as this is a significant precursor of learning and helps make explicit the notions of what success for all in the school should be aiming for. Providing visibility, knowledge, and the means to track progress (and understanding specifically what is required to achieve progress) is empowering for the adults and for the

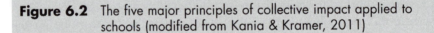

Figure 6.2 The five major principles of collective impact applied to schools (modified from Kania & Kramer, 2011)

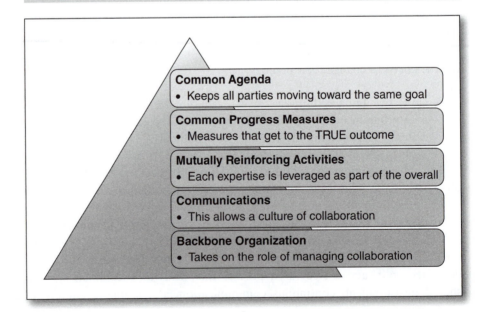

students. These all relate to key concepts of empowerment evaluation such as the presence of critical friends, cultures of evidence, impact cycles, and communities of learners—provided the focus is on understanding and maximizing the impact of the adults on the learning of the students.

3. **Impact Leader (Empowerment evaluation aims to influence and improve the quality of programs.)**

An emphasis on the collective means that school and system leaders need to be instructional leaders, and this demands far more than the more common transformational leaders. Most school leaders (Marks, 2013, estimates 90% of all principals) adopt a transformation form of leadership. This involves setting the vision, school goals, and expectations; providing instructional support; buffering staff from external demands and maximizing their class time; ensuring that staffing is fair and equitable; and securing a high degree of autonomy for school staff. In contrast, the instructional or high-impact leader thinks evaluatively and ensures that there are several formal classroom observations per year, interprets test scores from multiple sources with teachers, insists teachers collaborate in devising and evaluating the teaching program across grades, insists teachers have high expectations for all students, and ensures that class climate is conducive to learning for all students. The effects of the high-impact leader are two to three times greater than those of the transformational leader (Robinson, Lloyd, & Rowe, 2008). The focus of the high-impact leader is on the quality of the teachers delivering the programs to make a worthwhile difference to each student. It may be that instructional leaderships is built on transformational notions, but the key difference is the focus on the impact on the students, building a team devoted to this focus, and ensuring it is shared, delivered, and esteemed. It is via such leadership that the quality of programs can be evaluated in a collaborative, systematic, and improvement focused manner.

4. **Culture of Evidence and Capacity Building (Empowerment evaluation is based on evidence-based strategies: It respects and uses both community and scholarly knowledge.)**

Evidence is among the most contested notions in education. Biesta (2007) argued that what counts as "effective" crucially depends on judgments about what is educationally desirable—and certainly there are many outcomes of schooling beyond achievement. Social, moral, physical, and affective outcomes are important, as is learning the love of learning, the willingness and skills to reinvest in further learning, and respect for self and others. Evidence-based methods appear to offer a *neutral* framework that can be applied across areas (such as education or medicine) and central to the method is the idea of effective intervention. Evidence, like education, is never neutral,[3] as their fundamental purpose is intervention or behavior change.

This non-neutrality is what makes teaching a moral profession, with fundamental issues such as "Why teach this rather than that?" "How does one teach in defensible and ethical ways?" Snook (2003) has argued that teaching involves close personal relationships: between teachers and students, between one student and another, and between one teacher and another. Teaching involves a mission to change people in certain ways, and it often occurs in schools where there are hierarchies of control and rules to be obeyed. The "power" in these interactions and contests is very real. Hence, Snook claims, teaching involves ethics in its aims, its methods, and its relationships. He argues that the role of the teacher involves a respect for autonomy and a respect for reason. He cautions that "when we hear too much of the technicist teacher, the competent teacher, the skilled teacher, we should remind ourselves that education is essentially a moral enterprise and in that enterprise the ethical teacher has a central role to play" (p. 8). As Dewey (1938) noted, evidence does not provide us with rules for action but only with hypotheses for intelligence problem solving, and for making inquiry about our ends of education.

It is a critical part of visible learning that teachers and school leaders work together to decide on the nature of evidence, to seek disconfirmation as well as confirmation evidence about their impact, and to ensure that the impact is maximized on all students. The visible learning evidence shows that professional development starts with discussions and evidence about the impact of the educators in a school and then asks: What knowledge and skills do we as educators need? How can we deepen our professional knowledge and refine our skills to achieve this greater impact? How would we then know of the impact of our changed actions? To achieve this in school settings, capacity for evaluation needs to be built so that all can evaluate their impact. In empowerment evaluation, the process of evaluation is an integral part of teaching and learning that then includes organizational learning. This may require professional development in evaluation capacity building, typically with the assistance of a critical friend or empowerment evaluator. The professional development programs in the school need to be based on evaluation of impact in the school. This, of course, may mean bringing in outside expertise to assist

---

3. If it is not used to foster change, it is used to reinforce or reproduce the status quo.

in the evaluation or in the provision of enhanced processes (which also are subjected to evaluation of their impact).

5. **Improvement and Culture of Accountability (Empowerment evaluation stipulates that the power and responsibility for evaluation lies with the program stakeholders' ownership.)**

Evaluative thinking lies with the teachers and school leaders, hence creating a collective climate that is positive and forward-thinking. This may seem contrary to the usual claims about students taking responsibility for their own learning, but all learners need expertise to move beyond what they can do themselves. Often, students are not aware of the nature of success, and they need explicit instruction to move beyond what they know already. This is often termed the *zone of proximal development*, which refers to the distance between what a child can do on his or her own and what the child can complete with adult assistance. As Vygotsky (1978) claimed, "the zone of proximal development defines functions that have not matured yet, but are in a process of maturing, that will mature tomorrow, that are currently in an embryonic state; these functions could be called the buds of development, the flowers of development, rather than the fruits of development, that is, what is only just maturing" (pp. 86–87). This requires expertise—hence the importance of evaluating the impact of these experts on student learning.

In our work, we have discovered that a major problem in many education systems is that teachers and schools do not have a common conception of progress (Hattie, Brown, & Keegan, 2005). For example, within the New Zealand school system, schools were asked to provide evidence for accountability purposes of their "overall teacher judgments" rather than, as in the United States, to provide test scores. The basis of this request is that it is the teachers' interpretations of evidence of their impact that matters most. It is these interpretations that relate to the everyday decision making in classrooms, and they should be somewhat consistent across teachers and schools. These judgments are intended to be based on observing the process a student uses to complete a learning task; conversing with a student to find out what she knows, understands, and can do; and gathering results from formal assessments, including standardized tools. The claim is that when teachers do this moderation work together, with the explicit intent of supporting students' learning, pedagogical possibilities will accumulate in a manner that strengthens practice across the learning collective (Klenowski, Wyatt-Smith, & Gunn, 2010).

Ward and Thomas (2013) collected overall teacher judgments from a stratified sample of 96 New Zealand schools with Years 1 to 8 students, representative of the population of schools in terms of school type, school socioeconomic status, and geographic location. They concluded that teacher judgments "lack dependability, which is problematic as these judgements are the basis on which schools tailor teaching support with the ultimate aim of improving achievement" (p. 3). This indicates the critical importance of the educators working together to develop, within and across schools, common conceptions of progress. It should not be the case that a student's progress is determined by different judgments that teachers have about the standards expected of their students. Of course, the system needs to provide appropriate resources for moderating teacher judgments (and indeed this has been, until recently, a major deficiency of the New Zealand implementation of national standards).

Many systems also have inspection systems (e.g., Ofsted in the United Kingdom, Education Review Office in New Zealand) and they have a prime evaluation role. The visible learning argument is that there are two major evaluation questions that should dominate their work: "What is the evidence a school can provide to demonstrate that each student in the school is making at least a year's growth for a year's input?" and "What are the consequences for the school of this evaluation evidence?" Again, it is not a request for test scores but a request for evidence of evaluation capacity to understand impact and the consequential decisions based on this evidence. That is, what is their evidence of impact and what are they then doing in light of this evidence.

6. **Improvement and Culture of Evidence (Empowerment evaluation focuses on evidence, demystifies evaluation, and makes it additive and aimed at improvement instead of being punitive.)**

The use of evaluation methods in schools is optimized when a strengths-based approach is adopted, collectively building the capacity of all teachers (experienced and new) and developing a coalition of the successful teachers. The premise of developing an evaluation climate in the classroom and in the staff room is trust. Given that teachers have long considered their autonomy to teach as the essence of their professionalism, then it takes excellent leadership to replace "autonomy to teach" with "collaborative impact." (When there is convincing evidence of sustained high impact, then autonomy to choose how to teach can be granted.) Such trust needs to be high, as the most critical debates can be about what did not work, identifying those who did not make sufficient progress, and developing contingencies for the subgroups of students who did not have sufficient growth. A strengths-based approach can assist in ensuring that evaluation is additive and not punitive.

Many evaluation tools can be used to ascertain impact. These include starting with a systematic needs analysis to ascertain the success of the school to focus on visible learners, teachers, and schools; evaluating current levels of assessment-capable learners; using student voices and feedback; analyzing the data and evidence-based approaches driving practice in the school; identifying and determining priorities and targets; developing an action plan, including the monitoring of progress; evaluating the effectiveness of teacher-made assessments; using classroom observation to see the impact of teaching; and understanding the conceptions of progress used in the school. Program logic provides a valuable overview of plans for change and can be developed about how teachers collectively believe that impact can be enhanced, including a robust discussion on the nature of the outcomes from the program. Moderation and standard setting methods can also help demystify the appropriate magnitude of effects and the agreed-on conceptions of progress. For example, pre- and post student work on a series of lessons can be placed along a curriculum progression line to determine the degree of consensus as to the magnitude of impact and the understanding of levels of achievement. A matrix or crosswalk can be developed relating the key priorities to develop with various methods to collect evidence. Another tool is to use growth effect sizes (the change of pre- and post-test means divided by standard deviation; see Hattie, 2012, Appendix E) with the aim of understanding the size of effect, the comparison across different implementations/teachers, the growth of each student over time, and building evidence of sustained impact. Most critical to this approach is the development of effective leadership such that trust is high and the professional learning conversations in the school are focused on evaluating the program logic in light of the evidence of impact—the magnitude, the reach (i.e., how many students are positively impacted), and the efficiency. The quality of this evidence as to whether it is convincing enough to be used to determine progress is also a powerful discussion topic.

7. **Capacity Building and Organizational Learning (Empowerment evaluation builds stakeholders' capacity to conduct evaluation and to effectively use the results.)**

The key to enhancing educators' ability to evaluate and improve planning is to build their evaluation capacity. Evaluation capacity building is a process by which strategies are designed and implemented to assist individuals, groups, and organizations in the process of conducting effective, useful, and professional evaluation practice. Clinton (2013) has shown that the success of many interventions is not merely a function of the intervention activity alone. The capacity for the stakeholders (in schools, this includes system and school leaders, teacher, and parents) to enunciate the impact desired, the fidelity of the implementation, and the effects of the interventions of the implementers (e.g., teachers) are all key mediators to successful intervention. Process variables, such as organizational development and collaboration, are also critical contributors to the sustainability of a program (also see Labin et al., 2012). In this regard, Clinton argues that increasing the willingness and capacity of stakeholders to engage in evaluation is a worthwhile pursuit and one that should be at the forefront of any organization aiming at specific outcomes and sustainability. Often, this is related to building "assessment literacy." Unfortunately, this too often is exclusively about understanding the meaning of tests and test scores. Instead, what is needed is professional development to enhance evaluation skills, to work in a high trust collaborative environment, and to be focused on impact on learning. When educators work in professional learning communities, this can lead to clarifying exactly what students are to learn and then monitoring the educators' impact on each student's learning in a timely manner. The fundamental assumption is collaborative engagement; hence the importance of an instructional or impact leader, who is required to keep the community attentive to student learning.

Professional learning communities foster collaboration and continuous learning among educators for facilitating school improvement through cultural and organizational changes (DuFour & Fullan, 2013). Deliberative leadership is needed to ensure learning communities remain focused, for example, using multiple forms of evidence to demonstrate effectiveness, enhance the impact on all students, and move the focus from teaching to learning (by students and teachers, and what it is that is to be learned).

Harris and Jones (2010) also noted that collaborating is not enough: "If too loosely configured, it is easy for professional learning communities to pay attention to everything else except learning and teaching, and in so doing, to significantly reduce the potential impact of their work" (p. 172). Professional learning communities work only if they focus on improving learning outcomes. They can lead to closer observation of the impact of teaching on students, including students' impressions about their understanding of success and progress, and asking what is worth stopping and what is worth enhancing in light of the impact on learning. After reviewing the implementation of many professional learning communities, Harris and Jones concluded that the following are critical to their success: respect and trust among colleagues at the school and network level; possession of an appropriate cognitive and skill base that enables effective pedagogy and leads to effective learning; supportive leadership from those in key roles and shared leadership practices; the norms of continuous critical inquiry and continuous improvement; a widely shared vision or sense of purpose; a norm of involvement in decision making; collegial relationships among teachers; and a focus on impact and outcomes for learners.

8. **Continuous Quality Improvement (Empowerment evaluation uses evaluation results in the spirit of continuous quality improvement.)**

Continual growth and enhancement are fundamental to teaching and learning and although the spirit of continuous quality improvement is often seen through performance measurement systems, teachers' dialogue about continuous quality implementation and change provides evidence of evaluative thinking. The limited research about what teachers talk about in staff rooms shows a dominance of talking about students, curriculum, assessment, and work conditions. Deglau, Ward, O'Sullivan, and Bush (2006) listened to physical educator teachers' conversations and found that the conversations mainly related to assessment, liability issues, equipment needs within physical education programs, management strategies, classroom lessons when no gym is available, and strategies for dealing with difficult students. Ward et al. (2005) showed the predominant focus of teacher conversations was technical and situational, with teachers regularly describing, justifying, and critiquing their practice and work conditions. Too rarely is the dialogue about evaluating the impact of the educators on student learning. It is only via such a focus that there can be continuous quality improvement. Dialogue about impact needs to be part of a continuous quality cycle of improvement and also must relate to evaluating the fidelity of implementation of teaching program. Too often, great policies are thwarted by inadequate implementation. Barber (2008) developed an effective set of methods to accomplish successful implementation, based on four major steps; to these four steps, we add a fifth step.

First, develop a foundation for delivery that includes agreed-on criteria of success, such as ensuring all students gain at least $d > .40$ each year in this school on valued learning; a needs analysis reviewing the current state of delivery; and building the delivery unit. Second, agree on the delivery challenge based on evaluating past and present performance, understanding the drivers of performance and relevant systems activities. Third, plan for delivery, including specifying the reform strategy, setting targets and trajectories, and producing delivery plans. Fourth, drive the delivery via establishing routines to drive and monitor performance, solving problems early and rigorously, and sustaining and continually building momentum. Fifth, and critically, provide evidence of the quality of the measure of impact, celebrating success wherever it occurs.

This focus on continuous quality improvement, particularly when it leads to demonstrating there is sustained and systematic high impact on most students, can lead to reinforcing and valuing teacher success. Amabile and Kramer (2011) noted that "of all the things that can boost emotions, motivation, and perceptions during a workday, the single most important is making progress in meaningful work" (p. 22). Success at engendering high impact is meaningful work in classrooms, and thus evaluation evidence of high impact can be a major motivator for all, including the system leaders, school leaders, teachers, students, and parents. Thus, professional learning communities focused on high impact not only contribute to organizational success but also are motivated to further engage in worthwhile impact.

9. Social Justice (Empowerment evaluation embraces social justice, addressing social inequities in society.)

Schools are not just places where achievement is enhanced, where students are readied for employment and later life, but it is a worthwhile experience in itself. Further, students need to learn how to concentrate, engage in deliberate practice, develop resilience, and have respect for self and respect for others. Most critically, *all* students need to be impacted by schools. Thus, evaluation in schools needs to ask about the extent of the impact across all students, about whether schools are inviting places for all to learn, whether all students are being provided the tools of learning, and whether the appropriate range of outcomes is being enhanced for all students.

There are considerable inequities in outcomes from schooling. The Program for International Student Assessment (PISA) assesses students from more than 70 countries; results show that some countries have very wide dispersions of achievement. Shanghai (China) and Mexico are at the top and bottom of the PISA rankings, but both have very narrow spreads of scores in reading, numeracy, and scientific literacy. In reading, for example, the spread (standard deviation) of these two countries is about 250 to 260, whereas in other countries the spread is far greater, thus indicating major inequities (e.g., New Zealand is 347, Israel 374, and Singapore 329). In these high-spread countries, the data suggests major inequities in the progress made by students across the distribution. A common mistake is to believe that this spread is caused by more students in "the tail," near the bottom of the distribution, below average. Such claims have led to many mistaken policies to "close the gap" and reduce the tail, and these policies have had little impact because the problem is that there are students right across the distribution who are not making progress.

Another common policy in systems and schools is to set minimum standards (such as those designated in the No Child Left Behind Act) and then demand that all students exceed this minimum. This can detract from all students making sufficient progress and can mean that the top students are those who make little progress. For example, Ainley and Gebhardt (2013) showed that in Australia, the steady decline over the past 10 years is mostly related to the top 40% of students not making much, if any, progress. An alternative is for schools to combine the information and plot where the school, the classes, and the students fall on an "achievement by progress" chart (see Figure 6.3). Depending on where a school is placed, the consequential actions may be more obvious—moving from cruising to optimal may require different interventions than those used to move from a high progress zone to the optimal zone, or must change to the optimal zone.

CONCLUSION

Empowerment evaluation helps cultivate a continuous culture of evidence by asking educators for evidence to support their views and interpretations and to engage in continual phases of analysis, decision making, and implementation.

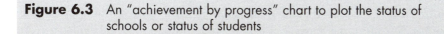

Figure 6.3 An "achievement by progress" chart to plot the status of schools or status of students

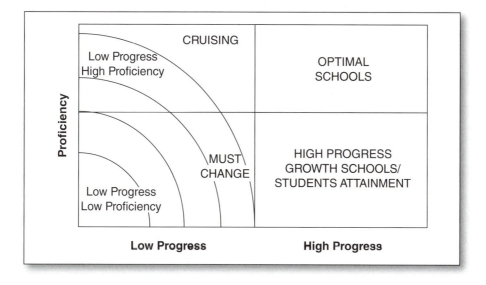

This chapter argues that school leaders need to be evaluators of the processes, programs, people, and products in their schools. Such evaluation requires determining and making judgments about the merit and worth of the effects of their leadership. This notion of educators as evaluators "implies deliberate change, directing of learning, and visibly making a difference to the experiences and outcomes for the students (and for the teachers)—and the key mechanism for this activation is via a mind frame that embraces the role of evaluation" (Hattie & Clinton, 2011, p. 99). Leaders are responsible for choosing the content of discussions in their school, and these discussions need to be about the nature of impact, the fidelity of implementation programs, and evaluations of the success or otherwise to attain this impact. Leaders do this by establishing goals and expectations, making decisions (most often between competing demands to resource strategically), evaluating teaching and the curriculum, promoting and participating in providing evaluative evidence relating to teacher learning and development, creating educationally powerful connections, ensuring that all in the school are engaged in constructive problem talk, and using evaluative evidence (e.g., from test scores, student work) as the underpinning of this talk.

A key notion is that the evidence for impact starts from within the school. The claim is that leaders are not expected to read the research literature and then ensure that top-rated implementations are in place in their school. Although it is the case that there are high and low probability interventions (see Hattie, 2009), the message is that it is the evaluation-based evidence from within the school based on the current practice that is the starting point for evidence and evaluation. As Senge (1990) noted, this notion requires school leaders who are sincerely interested in the world of practice, who are highly respectful of that world, and who are sincerely interested in using evaluative methods to make the school better for all.

> It is no longer sufficient to have one person learning for the organization, a Ford or a Sloan or a Watson. It's just not possible any longer to "figure it out" from the top, and have everyone else following the orders of the "grand strategist." The organizations that will truly excel in the future will be the organizations that will truly tap people's commitment and capacity to learn at all levels in an organization. (Senge, 1990, p. 4)

Moreover, Hattie and Clinton (2011) argued that there are many evaluation roles for school leaders: sense making, making priorities, ensuring equity, coaching, asking and framing questions, and evaluating their own impact on teachers and students. The leader's role also involves bringing expertise into evaluating the various interventions, developing partnerships, engaging communities, developing evaluation capacity, brokering knowledge into the school, promoting forward-thinking, and continuously attending to quality.

In a review of *Empowerment Evaluation Principles in Practice*, Scriven (2005b) argued that empowerment evaluation cannot be valid for formative evaluation unless "it is based on the most accurate evaluative conclusions that are feasible at midstream. Failure to achieve that standard means your client builds the improvements—for which formative evaluation is done—on sand, a pointless activity indeed" (p. 415). Because empowerment evaluation involves self-evaluation, so argued Scriven, it can be subject to positive bias, lacks an external evaluator, and can be too influenced by the relationship that is needed to enact empowerment evaluation. Scriven argued that empowerment evaluation "is simply amateur evaluation, with the only professional involved being self-excluded from exerting any control over the conclusions drawn" (p. 416). Thus, Scriven sees it as more akin to professional development or counseling. The claims based on visible learning, however, do have an external benchmark. From the multitude of meta-analyses, there is evidence for a benchmark that can be used for schools to evaluate their own impact, there are specific criteria for evaluating sufficient progression, there are many methods that the evaluator can bring into schools to expose programs and teachers lacking in sufficient impact; these methods can include an external evaluator to provide new directions, to reinforce success wherever it occurs, to help develop evaluation capacity, to assist in developing alternative methods to understand impact, and to meta-evaluate the schools' internal processes and findings. If there is an external agency (like an inspectorate), this group can evaluate the quality of in-school evaluations and how the information from these evaluations is being put to best use. In sum, visible learning and empowerment evaluation complement each other, with the external criteria of what is appropriate growth, the evidence base that provides high probability practices, and the focus on educators being evaluators of their own impact. The theme in this chapter is that educators could profitably adopt an empowerment evaluation approach, build evaluation skills, and see themselves mainly as evaluators of their impact: Know thy impact. Such a role is to not merely collect data, create reports, and fill in surveys, but to be excellent interpreters of evidence (Reeves, 2004). It is the *performance* of evaluation that makes the difference, and it is never ending but rewarding when there is sustained impact on all students.

REFERENCES

Ainley J., & Gebhardt, E. (2013). *Measure for measure: A review of outcomes of school education in Australia*. Camberwell, Australia: Australian Council for Educational Research. Retrieved from http://www.acer.edu.au/files/MeasureForMeasure—online.pdf

Amabile, T. M., & Kramer, S. J. (2011). *The progress principle: Using small wins to ignite joy, engagement, and creativity at work*. Cambridge, MA: Harvard Business Review Press.

Barber, M. (2008). *Instruction to deliver*. London: Methuen.

Biesta, G. (2007). Why "what works" won't work: Evidence-based practice and the democratic deficit in educational research. *Educational Theory, 57*(1), 1–22.

Clinton, J. M. (2013, October 29). The true impact of evaluation motivation for ECB. *American Journal of Evaluation*. doi:10.1177/1098214013499602. Retrieved from http://aje.sagepub.com/content/early/2013/10/24/1098214013499602

Cohen, J. (1988). *Statistical power analysis for the behavioral sciences* (2nd ed.). Hillsdale, NJ: Erlbaum.

Deglau, D., Ward, P., O'Sullivan, M., & Bush, K. (2006). Professional dialogue as professional development. *Journal of Teaching in Physical Education, 25*, 413–427.

Dewey, J. (1938). *Logic: The theory of inquiry*. New York: Holt, Rinehart & Winston.

DuFour, R., & Fullan, M. (2013). *Cultures built to last: Systemic PLCs*. Bloomington, IN: Solution Tree Press.

Fetterman, D. M. (1994). Empowerment evaluation. *Evaluation practice, 15*(1), 1–15.

Fetterman, D. M. (2005). A window into the heart and soul of evaluation. In D. M. Fetterman & A. Wandersman (Eds.), *Empowerment evaluation principles in practice* (pp. 1–26). New York: Guilford Press.

Fetterman, D. M. (2013). Learning to think like an evaluator. In M. Alkin (Ed.), *Evaluation roots: A wider perspective of theorists' views and influences* (2nd ed., pp. 304–322). Thousand Oaks, CA: Sage.

Harris, A., & Jones, J. (2010). Professional learning communities and system improvement. *Improving Schools, 13*(2), 172–181.

Hattie, J. A. C. (2006).The paradox of reducing class size and improved learning outcomes. *International Journal of Educational Research, 42*, 387–425.

Hattie, J. A. C. (2009). *Visible learning: A synthesis of 800+ meta-analyses on achievement*. Oxford, UK: Routledge.

Hattie, J. A. C. (2012). *Visible learning for teachers: Maximizing impact on achievement*. Oxford, UK: Routledge.

Hattie, J. A. C., & Anderman, E. (2013). *Handbook on student achievement*. New York: Routledge.

Hattie, J. A. C., Brown, G. T., & Keegan, P. (2005). A national teacher-managed, curriculum-based assessment system: Assessment Tools for Teaching & Learning (asTTle). *International Journal of Learning, 10*, 770–778.

Hattie, J. A. C., & Clinton, J. M. (2011). School leaders as evaluators. In *Activate: A leader's guide to people, practices and processes* (pp. 93–118). Englewood, CO: Leadership and Learning Center.

Hattie, J. A. C., & Yates, G. (2014). *Visible learning and the science of how we learn*. New York: Routledge.

Kania, J., & Kramer, M. (2011, Winter). Collective impact. *Stanford Social Innovation Review, 9*(1), 36–41.

Labin, S. N., Duffy, J. L., Meyers, D. C., Wandersman, A., & Lesesne, C. A. (2012). A research synthesis of the evaluation capacity building literature. *American Journal of Evaluation, 33*, 307–338.

Marks, W. (2013). *The late-career and transition to retirement phases for school leaders in the 21st century: The aspirations, expectations and reflections of late-career and recently-retired principals in New South Wales (2008–2012)*. Unpublished doctoral dissertation, University of Wollongong, NSW, Australia.

Reeves, D. B. (2004). *Accountability in action: A blueprint for learning organizations*. Englewood, CO: Advanced Learning Press.

Robinson, V. M. J., Lloyd, C., & Rowe, K. J. (2008). The impact of educational leadership on student outcomes: An analysis of the differential effects of leadership types. *Education Administration Quarterly, 41*, 635–674.

Scriven, M. (1971). The logic of cause. *Theory and Decision, 2*(1), 49–66.

Scriven, M. (1975). Causation as explanation. *Nous, 9*(1), 3–16.

Scriven, M. (1991). *Evaluation thesaurus*. Newbury Park, CA: Sage.

Scriven, M. (2005a). Causation. In S. Mathison (Ed.), *Encyclopedia of evaluation* (pp. 43–47). Thousand Oaks, CA: Sage.

Scriven, M. (2005b). [Review of the book *Empowerment evaluation principles in practice*]. *American Journal of Evaluation, 26*(2), 415–417.

Senge, P. (1990). *The fifth discipline: Mastering the five practices of the learning organization*. New York: Doubleday.

Snook, I. (2003). *The ethical teacher*. Palmerston North, New Zealand: Dunmore Press.

Tyack, D. B., & Cuban, L. (1995). *Tinkering toward utopia: A century of public school reform*. Cambridge, MA: Harvard University Press.

Vygotsky, L. S. (1978). *Mind in society: The development of higher psychological processes*. Cambridge, MA: Harvard University Press.

Wandersman, A., Snell-Johns, J., Lentz, B., Fetterman, D., Keener, D. C., Livet, M., et al. (2005). The principles of empowerment evaluation. In D. Fetterman & A. Wandersman (Eds.), *Empowerment evaluation principles in practice* (pp. 27–41). New York: Guilford Press.

Ward, J., & Thomas, G. (2013). *National standards: School sample monitoring and evaluation project, 2010–2012*. Wellington, New Zealand: Ministry of Education.

Ward, P., O'Sullivan, M., Deglau, D., Bush, K. A., & Segarra-Roman, Q. (2005). *Teacher dialogue as professional development*. Paper presented at the AAHPERD national convention and exposition, Chicago, IL.

Wyatt-Smith, C., Klenowski, V., & Gunn, S. (2010). The centrality of teachers' judgement practice in assessment: A study of standards in moderation. *Assessment in Education: Principles, Policy & Practice, 17*(1), 59–75.

CHAPTER 7

Hewlett-Packard's $15 Million Digital Village

A Place-Based Empowerment Evaluation Initiative

David M. Fetterman

Fetterman & Associates and Stanford University

People of color, rural communities, and individuals with lower incomes have less access to high-speed Internet. Smartphones have helped people bridge the digital divide (see Smith, 2011), but at this point in time, they are no substitute for high-speed bandwidth highways, required for job interviews, online courses, business meetings, and health care services. This digital problem is in many ways, and for many reasons, as pressing today as it was in 1995 when the U.S. Department of Commerce first identified the "digital divide" as a social justice issue—recognizing the racial, economic, and geographic gaps between the digital "haves" and "have nots." (*Social justice* is an important empowerment evaluation principle guiding practice.)

According to the Department of Commerce,

> 4 out of every 10 households with annual household incomes below $25,000 in 2010 reported having wired Internet access at home, compared with the vast majority—93 percent—of households with incomes exceeding $100,000. Only slightly more than half of all African-American and Hispanic households (55 percent and 57 percent, respectively) have wired Internet access at home, compared with 72 percent of whites. (Crawford, 2011)

Hewlett-Packard's bold $15 million corporate philanthropic endeavor was designed to address this issue, helping bridge the digital divide in communities of color (Bolt &

Crawford, 2000). The initiative was populated with success stories, ranging from building one of the largest wireless systems in the country to creating minority-owned small businesses (Fetterman, 2013a). Communities across the nation have built on many of these early tech successes over the decades, and the nation has made great strides bridging the digital divide. This chapter highlights how the empowerment evaluation principles[1] of *capacity building* and *accountability* were implemented in the context of Hewlett-Packard's Digital Village initiative.

DIGITAL VILLAGE INITIATIVE

Former HP chairman and chief executive officer Carly Fiorina, former U.S. president Bill Clinton,[2] and human rights activist Reverend Jesse L. Jackson, Sr., helped launch the HP Digital Village Initiative. It involved a partnership between Hewlett-Packard, Stanford University, and three ethnically diverse communities of color throughout the United States. It was a large-scale place- or community-based initiative. In place-based initiatives, citizens are engaged in a collaborative process to address issues in their own neighborhoods (Bellefontaine & Wisener, 2011). The initiative helped these communities build their own technologically oriented businesses, improve their education systems, and improve their economic health.

HEWLETT-PACKARD AND STANFORD UNIVERSITY

The Digital Village sponsor, Hewlett-Packard, invested their time and energy in the Digital Villages because they believed they could help communities accomplish their goals and objectives. Hewlett-Packard was confident about their

---

1. The 10 principles guiding empowerment evaluation are (1) improvement, (2) community ownership, (3) inclusion, (4) democratic participation, (5) social justice, (6) community knowledge, (7) evidence-based strategies, (8) capacity building, (9) organizational learning, and (10) accountability (see Fetterman & Wandersman, 2005).

2. This was an important opportunity for Clinton to announce a series of digital divide federal initiatives and help strengthen business collaboratives, such as HP's Digital Village. The original vision of the Initiative was to "create an informed, connected and empowered community by combining technology, brainpower, and collaborative energy." The inauguration ceremonies were held in East Palo Alto, one of the three Digital Village community sites in the United States.

ability to deliver the equipment and technical training. However, they were less confident about answering a few simple questions:

- How do you know if you have accomplished what you set out to do?
- How do you know if it made a difference?
- How do you do these things while keeping the program where it belongs—in the hands of the people living in their own communities?

Evaluation was the tool needed to address these critical questions, and Stanford had the requisite expertise. Stanford's empowerment evaluation team[3] agreed to conduct the evaluation and in the process provided faculty and students with real-world learning opportunities.

THE THREE DIGITAL VILLAGES

The overarching mission for the Digital Villages was simple: to leapfrog across the digital divide. The written mission was to:

> Provide people access to greater social and economic opportunity by closing the gap between technology-empowered and technology-excluded communities—focusing on sustainability for the communities and HP.

The Digital Villages ranged from urban to rural settings and could be found on both the east and west coasts. They included the Tribal Digital Village (San Diego area), Baltimore Digital Village (East Baltimore), and East Palo Alto Digital Village (northern California).

The Tribal Digital Village was comprised of 18 Native American tribes and reservations. The Baltimore Digital Village involved the Baltimore City Public School System and a collaboration of African American community–based organizations, including Blacks in Wax (an African American–featured wax museum). The East Palo Alto Digital Village consisted of programs ranging from Plugged In, a high-tech community resource center, to Opportunities Industrialization Center West, an employment training program. The residents were primarily African American, Latino, and Pacific Islander. HP provided each of the Digital Villages with $5 million in cash, equipment, and services over a 3-year period.

---

3. Fetterman was the director of Stanford's MA Policy Analysis and Evaluation Program in the School of Education at the time, with access to a vast array of faculty, students, and community members for this initiative.

These were communities left behind in the digital age, leaving them systematically disenfranchised from information and opportunities. HP's role was to provide each of the Digital Villages with the necessary funds, equipment, and consultants to pursue their strategies and accomplish their objectives.

EMPOWERMENT EVALUATION

Empowerment evaluation was selected to help plan, implement, assess, and improve their work. This approach differs from many other forms of strategic planning and evaluation because the groups or communities remain in control of the process. The definition of empowerment evaluation, as presented in previous chapters, provides a more concrete description of the approach.

> Empowerment evaluation is an evaluation approach that aims to increase the probability of achieving program success by (1) providing program stakeholders with tools for assessing the planning, implementation, and self-evaluation of their program, and (2) mainstreaming evaluation as part of the planning and management of the program/organization. (Wandersman et al., 2005, p. 28)

The theory behind empowerment evaluation is that the more that people participate in evaluating their own program, the more likely they are to buy into the findings and the recommendations—because they are their findings and recommendations. The approach cultivates pride and ownership. Empowerment evaluation helps people align what they say they are doing with what they are really doing, by providing them with a continuous feedback loop designed to refine and improve their practice. Empowerment evaluation is guided by many concepts, including (1) building a culture of evidence to make decisions; (2) using cycles of reflection—helping people think about their data, act on it, and then reflect on the impact of those decisions; (3) building a community of learners—where people learn from each other along the way; and (4) cultivating reflective practitioners—that is, people who think about how they can improve their performance on a daily basis. Empowerment evaluation is also guided by an evaluator, serving as a critical friend or coach, who values the effort but also asks the hard questions to keep things rigorous and on track (Fetterman, 2009; Fetterman, Deitz, & Gesundheit, 2010).

The Digital Villages used the three-step approach to empowerment evaluation; these steps are (1) mission, (2) taking stock, and (3) planning for the future (Fetterman, 2005). Once they agreed on their overall mission, they took some time to assess how well they were doing in relation to their goals. This honest critique set the stage for them to plan for the future and establish new goals to accomplish their objectives. The three-step cycle was simple, but the secret to its success is that there is no end to it. Once a Digital Village had implemented its plans for the future, it was immediately time to evaluate or assess its progress, make mid-course corrections, and implement a revised plan of action. It was a never-ending process, much like the continuous quality improvement approaches. (See Chapter 2 of this book and the empowerment evaluation webpage [www.davidfetterman.com] and blog [eevaluation.blogspot.com] for details and case examples.)

Empowerment evaluation is honest and rigorous. It is designed to help people accomplish their objectives. It is concerned more about contribution than attribution. It is almost impossible to attribute changes to specific treatments in large-scale, long-term initiatives, but it is possible to highlight the intervention's contributions (along with other interventions) to change in a community. Empowerment evaluation is not a short-term episodic observation and judgment; rather, it becomes internalized or institutionalized. Empowerment evaluation becomes a part of the fabric of an organization. It fosters life-long learning on both individual and organizational levels. Although there are no guarantees, empowerment evaluators improve the probabilities of success. Empowerment evaluation is designed to build capacity for the long haul, contributing to meaningful community sustainability.

EVALUATION CAPACITY BUILDING

Clearly, the selection of empowerment evaluation to guide this initiative was no random accident. Empowerment evaluation was selected because it was philosophically and practically in alignment with the Digital Village's commitment to capacity building and program improvement. *Capacity building* is one of the 10 principles guiding empowerment evaluation. It is such an important principle that if there is no capacity building present in a project or initiative, then it is not an empowerment evaluation.

There is no waiting period, delay, or probationary period in an empowerment evaluation. Empowerment evaluation begins with the community in control. Just as HP immediately handed over control to the Digital Village leadership, the Digital Village leadership handed over control to local community-based businesses and nonprofits, which were engaged in empowerment evaluation and capacity building.

The training ground in an empowerment evaluation is the evaluation. Instead of training to conduct an evaluation, Digital Village leadership, management, and community members simply conducted their own evaluation (with the assistance of a critical friend/evaluation coach). Conducting the evaluation was the training. They learned by doing (Dewey, 2009; Lewin, 1948). The immediacy of the experience propelled people into action. It also created a sense of owner-ship, which enhanced commitment and follow-through.

To help build evaluation capacity, the critical friend typically facilitated the initial or introductory exercises. In this case, the critical friend partnered with a member of the Digital Village or community member who had an interest in (and in one case some experience conducting) an evaluation. Quickly most responsibilities were transferred by the critical friend to the community "insider," leaving the critical friend as a support person as needed. For example, in the Tribal Digital Village, I facilitated the first exercise with Dr. Linda Locklear, one of the tribal members in the Digital Village. During the second exercise, I reversed the roles. Linda was in charge and I served as a support person. She was ready for it. Linda was used to crossing tribal lines. She was a boundary spanner (Daft, 1989). She was used to straddling the needs of social service agencies (and now the Digital Village) with the needs of individual tribes. She said, "They all know me. I have relatives in that tribe too [a tribe other than her own]. I am always knocking on doors to get things done."

I would still help her prepare for sessions and debrief her after them to learn from each experience. We maintained this partnership throughout the evalua-tion. However, she was the face of the evaluation for the Tribal Digital Village, not me. People learned to look to her instead of me during meetings and exer-cises. Most of the time this worked. Once in a while I was asked to step in or we brought in another tribal member because of some baggage or past experi-ence that got in the way. The same approach was applied to the other Digital Villages. This transition and substitution technique, "working myself out of a job," is an integral part of building capacity and institutionalizing evaluation. The same approach applied to using additional methods, including sorting data in spreadsheets, digital photography,[4] videoconferencing (Figure 7.1),[5] and online surveys.[6]

---

4. Digital photography was used extensively throughout the evaluation. The use of photogra-phy was guided by classics in the field of visual anthropology, including Collier and Collier (1986), Heider (2006), and Hockings (2003). See Rosenstein (2000) concerning the use of video for program evaluation. Digital photography also requires software to appropriately crop and to size pictures. Photoshop was used in this evaluation. See Sheppard (2011) and Carlson (2011) for instructions on the use of this software.

5. Videoconferencing was used throughout the evaluation, including connecting from my classroom in Wallenberg Hall at Stanford University and the Tribal Digital Village. See Fetterman (1996) for additional information about videoconferencing in educational settings.

6. Digital Village members used Zoomerang and SurveyMonkey throughout the evaluation to help determine if specific programs were viewed as working as designed both internally and by the larger community. See Ritter and Sue (2007) for examples and directions concern-ing the use of online surveys in evaluation.

Figure 7.1   Videoconferencing

Courtesy of David M. Fetterman

Members of the Digital Village added their collective thoughts to the formulation of a mission statement, used dots to set priorities for tasks, entered the taking stock ratings into an Excel spreadsheet, tabulated the results, and displayed the ratings by projecting the results on an LCD projector with the group. They also documented each activity with digital photography and used their pictures to tell their story. They observed critical activities, such as building a tower or computer skills training sessions, and documented them. They also conducted pre- and post-online surveys to assess community response to Digital Village interventions. They learned to think like evaluators by conducting the evaluation of their work by themselves (Fetterman, 2013b).

The skeptic might ask, How is this possible? People often ask the same question during my workshops.[7] They say, "evaluation is too complex to be handed off to amateurs." In response I ask one of them to take my camera and take a picture of me while I highlight an important point about people's native capacity to collect data and to evaluate in my presentation. The

---

7. Empowerment evaluation workshops are provided annually at the American Evaluation Association, in addition to organization-specific training workshops.

audience laughs as the participant snaps a photograph of me making such a serious point. I stop the demonstration and rhetorically ask, "What did I just do?"—aside from sharing a vain moment with them? My answer: "I just transferred a skill of evaluation, silently, transparently, and powerfully. That participant just helped us record part of the workshop—photographically." Of course, transferring evaluation skills involves hard work and takes time; however, this example highlights how simple and transparent the process can and should be.

The same simple and transparent empowerment evaluation approach used in communities was used to help HP leadership to evaluate the initiative, establishing baselines, goals, and benchmarks or milestones to evaluate their programs. Whether it is evaluation design, method, or management, people from all walks of life are capable of learning how to evaluate their own programs. There is no substitution for learning by doing in a psychologically "safe environment" guided by seasoned coaches, facilitators, and mentors.

Capacity building is about helping people learn new skills and competencies in order to more effectively manage their own affairs. Capacity building is a "hand up," not a "hand out," approach. The Digital Village provided community members with a nurturing and supportive training ground. They assumed new roles and exercised responsibilities in settings previously placed outside their reach. This opportunity allowed them to operate in what Vygotsky (1978) called the *proximal zone*. This is a place just beyond a person's reach and experience. It is somewhere between what a person can do on their own without help and what they can do with the assistance of a more experienced person. It placed them outside of their comfort zone. However, the proximal zone is a place conceptually where people learn to stretch themselves and reach another level of insight, understanding, and capacity. In this case, the Digital Village placed community members squarely in the proximal zone as planners, designers, managers, employers, employees, and *evaluators*. A few of the Digital Villages' most significant accomplishments, or outcomes, provide insight into the significance of evaluation capacity building—a hidden story behind many initiatives.

ACCOUNTABILITY AND OUTCOMES

Empowerment evaluation's 10th principle is *accountability*. It is focused on producing results or outcomes. The HP place-based initiative produced meaningful, real-world outcomes. Several examples are described next.

Tribal Digital Village

The most significant Tribal Digital Village accomplishment was the creation of one of "the largest unlicensed wireless systems in the United States," according to the former head of the U.S. Federal Communications Commission (FCC). The FCC continues to recognize the Tribal Digital Village's accomplishments, characterizing them as "one of the shining examples in wireless unregulated spectrums that's connected several tribes here" (U.S. Federal Communications Commission, 2009). It became the digital backbone of the tribes' communication system, connecting the 18 reservations, tribal offices, community centers, schools, and individual residences (Figure 7.2).

The HP initiative was designed to jump-start small entrepreneurial businesses in the community. The Tribal Print Source represented another Tribal Digital Village success story. It provided digital imaging and printing services. This generated a profitable alternative business to gaming and helped to support other programs on the reservations, focusing on improving health and education on the reservations and preserving the tribes' cultural heritage.

Figure 7.2   Tribal members constructing towers for increased bandwidth across the reservation and neighboring communities

Courtesy of Jack Ward

East Palo Alto Digital Village

One of the East Palo Alto Digital Village's notable achievements involved providing laptops to 400 students and their teachers in Grades 4 through 8 at Belle Haven School. The project transformed the learning environment for all those concerned, making the Internet a core resource for teaching and learning in the school. In addition, East Palo Alto Digital Village's Small Business Development Initiative contributed to the community's economic development by building the technological capacity of small businesses.

Baltimore Digital Village

The Baltimore Digital Village adopted five schools and integrated computer equipment and training into the Baltimore City Public School System's school curriculum. Over 185 teachers were provided with computers and technology training. According to Carmen V. Russo, former chief executive officer of the Baltimore City Public School System, "The technology and support that the Baltimore Digital Village has provided our teachers and students has proved invaluable in our efforts to develop an outstanding curriculum."

The Baltimore Digital Village's Small Business Development Initiative also provided 35 local business owners with technology packages, a 5-week skills training program, and business services consultations. The initiative fostered the development of 50 small businesses in the community. The Baltimore Digital Village also touched the lives of individual families, providing 300 families with their own computer equipment and computer skills training courses. These are solid outcomes with tremendous face validity, designed to generate sustainable economic and social development in the community long after this influx of seed money and support.

CONCLUSION

Digital Village learning was learning by doing. Digital Village members found this experiential approach to evaluation intellectually and emotionally exhilarating. They accomplished their goals. People began to see obstacles as opportunities. The Digital Village started as an effort to bridge the digital divide and evolved into a series of *learning organizations*[8] (another empowerment evaluation principle). The initiative flourished and continues to provide lessons learned to a diverse audience, through publications and invitations to radio programs throughout the United States (Figure 7.3).[9] The Digital Village provided an example of what's possible when a simple, transparent, and constructive approach to evaluation is applied to a large-scale community-based initiative.

The entire experience for Hewlett-Packard, Stanford, and three ethnically diverse communities became something much larger than a race to completion. The Digital Village became a race toward *social justice* (Fetterman, 2013a).

---

8. For additional examples of how to use evaluation to build organizational capacity, see Preskill and Russ Eft (2005) and Preskill and Torres (1999).

9. See http://www.davidfetterman.com/RadioInterviews.htm for a sample of radio interviews about a book about the initiative: Empowerment Evaluation in the Digital Villages: Hewlett-Packard's $15 Million Race Toward Social Justice.

Figure 7.3   Talk show radio host Vic McCarty (radio station1270 WMKT) interviewed Dr. Fetterman about his Digital Villages empowerment evaluation book.

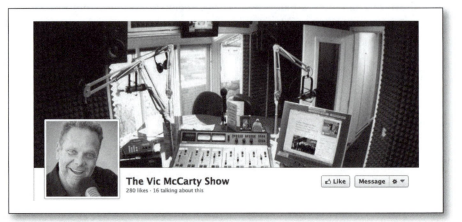

Courtesy of Vic McCarty

REFERENCES

Bellefontaine, T., & Wisener, R. (2011). *The evaluation of place-based approaches*. Ottawa, ON: Policy Horizons Canada.

Bolt, D., & Crawford, R. (2000). *Digital divide: Computers and our children's future*. New York: TV Books.

Carlson, J. (2011). *Photoshop elements 9 for Mac OS X: Visual QuickStart guide*. Berkeley, CA: Peachpit Press.

Collier, J., & Collier, M. (1986). *Visual anthropology*. Albuquerque: University of New Mexico Press.

Crawford, S. P. (2011, December 3). The new digital divide. *New York Times*. Retrieved from http://www.nytimes.com/2011/12/04/opinion/sunday/internet-access-and-the-new-divide.html?pagewanted=all&_r=0

Daft, R. L. (1989). *Organization theory and design* (3rd ed.). New York: West Publishing.

Dewey, J. (2009). *Democracy and education: An introduction to the philosophy of education*. New York: WLC Books. (Original work published 1916)

Fetterman, D. M. (1996). Videoconferencing on-line: Enhancing communication over the Internet. *Educational Researcher, 25*(4), 23–27.

Fetterman, D. M. (2005). Empowerment evaluation: From the digital divide to academic distress. In D. M. Fetterman & A. Wandersman (Eds.), *Empowerment evaluation principles in practice* (pp. 92–122). New York: Guilford Press.

Fetterman, D. M. (2009). Empowerment evaluation at the Stanford University School of Medicine: Using a critical friend to improve the clerkship experience. *Ensaio, 17*(63), 197–204.

Fetterman, D. M. (2013a). *Empowerment evaluation in the Digital Villages: Hewlett-Packard's $15 million race toward social justice.* Stanford: Stanford University Press.

Fetterman, D. M. (2013b). Empowerment evaluation: Learning to think like an evaluator. In M. Alkin (Ed.), *Evaluation roots: A wider perspective of theorists' views and influences* (2nd ed., pp. 304–322). Thousand Oaks, CA: Sage.

Fetterman, D. M., Deitz, J., & Gesundheit, N. (2010). Empowerment evaluation: A collaborative approach to evaluating and transforming a medical school curriculum. *Academic Medicine: Journal of the Association of American Medical Colleges, 85*(5), 813–820.

Fetterman, D. M., & Wandersman, A. (2005). *Empowerment evaluation principles in practice.* New York: Guilford Press.

Heider, K. G. (2006). *Ethnographic film.* Austin: University of Texas Press.

Hockings, P. (Ed.). (2003). *Principles of visual anthropology.* The Hague: Mouton de Gruyter.

Lewin, K. (1948). *Resolving social conflicts; selected papers on group dynamics* (G. W. Lewin, Ed.). New York: Harper & Row.

Preskill, H., & Russ-Eft, D. (2005). *Building evaluation capacity: 72 activities for teaching and training.* Thousand Oaks, CA: Sage.

Preskill, H., & Torres, R. (1999). *Building capacity for organizational learning through evaluation.* Thousand Oaks, CA: Sage.

Ritter, L., & Sue, V. (Eds.). (2007). *Using online surveys in evaluation.* San Francisco, CA: Jossey-Bass.

Rosenstein, B. (2000). Video use for program evaluation: A theoretical perspective. *Studies in Educational Evaluation, 26*(4), 373–394.

Sheppard, R. (2011). *Photoshop elements 9: Top 100 simplified tips and tricks.* New York: Wiley.

Smith, A. (2011). *Smartphone adoption and use.* Pew Research Internet Project. Retrieved from http://www.pewinternet.org/2011/07/11/smartphone-adoption-and-usage

U.S. Federal Communications Commission. (2009, December 3). [Meeting of the Advisory Committee on Diversity for Communications in the Digital Age]. Retrieved from http://transition.fcc.gov/DiversityFAC/120309/transcript-120309.doc

Vygotsky, L. S. (1978). *Mind and society: The development of higher psychological processes.* Cambridge, MA: Harvard University Press.

Wandersman, A., Snell-Johns, J., Lentz, B., Fetterman, D., Keener, D. C., Livet, M., et al. (2005). The principles of empowerment evaluation. In D. Fetterman & A. Wandersman (Eds.), *Empowerment evaluation principles in practice* (pp. 27–41). New York: Guilford Press.

CHAPTER 8

Empowerment Evaluation in Action in SAMHSA's Service to Science Initiative

Cultivating Ownership and Enhancing Sustainability

Pamela Imm

Education Development Center, Inc.

Matthew Biewener

Education Development Center, Inc.

Dawn Oparah

Amadi Leadership Associates, Inc.

AVPRIDE, Inc.

Kim Dash

Education Development Center, Inc.

Disclaimer: Support for this work was provided by and administered through the Center for Substance Abuse Prevention, Contract Number #HHSS277200800004C, Reference number 277–08–0218. The content of this publication does not necessarily reflect the views or policies of the Department of Health and Human Services, and the views expressed in this paper are those of the authors.

INTRODUCTION

This chapter highlights how the U.S. Substance Abuse and Mental Health Services Administration's (SAMHSA's) Service to Science (STS) initiative has applied empowerment evaluation principles—such as *capacity building*, *improvement*, and respect for *community knowledge*—to cultivate local ownership of evaluation practices and enhance program sustainability. STS operationalizes these principles to strengthen the ability of local organizations to conduct more appropriate, feasible, useful, and rigorous evaluation. Ultimately, the initiative helps communities develop and implement more effective substance abuse prevention programs. Although considerable literature has been published that describes the methods and principles of the empowerment evaluation approach as well as the theoretical and practical limitations of its tenets, few have described its expression on a national scale toward evaluation capacity building among substance abuse prevention programs. To that end, this chapter first describes how STS incorporates and applies empowerment evaluation methods and principles to build the evaluation capacity of local organizations and the prevention programs they implement, and then provides a case study of work conducted with a program in Fayette County, Georgia, to further illustrate empowerment evaluation in action.

THE IMPETUS FOR SAMHSA'S SERVICE TO SCIENCE INITIATIVE

Community-based organizations (CBOs) are under increasing pressure from federal, state, and local funders to implement substance abuse prevention programs with demonstrated evidence of effectiveness in producing changes in knowledge, attitudes, and behaviors among the populations they serve. Often, CBOs choose not to implement evidence-based interventions (EBIs) or model programs because they do not fit client or consumer needs, are incompatible with the organization's capacity to deliver them, or do not correspond to community values and frames (Everhart & Wandersman, 2000). Those organizations that do adopt model programs often struggle to implement them with fidelity (SAMHSA's Center for the Application of Prevention Technologies, 2003). Whether choosing to significantly adapt existing model programs or develop new approaches, CBOs often struggle to demonstrate program effectiveness because they lack the resources necessary for conducting well-designed evaluations with appropriate rigor (Connolly & York, 2002; Kegeles, Rebchook, & Tebbetts, 2005).

Recognizing gaps in local evaluation capacity, SAMHSA introduced the STS initiative to provide intensive technical assistance (TA) to community-based program developers, implementers, and evaluators on how to select and apply to their work appropriately rigorous evaluation methodologies. The STS initiative helps build the evaluation capacity of CBOs to demonstrate more credible evidence of their program's effectiveness, thereby increasing the number and array of locally developed evidence-based programs and practices from which states and communities can select to address substance abuse and other behavioral health problems. Thus, many programs participate in STS with the aim of achieving public recognition by meeting the criteria for evidence-based status applied by federal or other national registries. Among these is SAMHSA's National Registry of Evidence-Based Programs and Practices (NREPP)—a voluntary self-nominating system that employs independent content experts to assess programs and practices using transparent criteria related to the quality of a given program's evaluation research methods and readiness for dissemination (Brounstein, Gardner, & Backer, 2006).

EMPOWERMENT EVALUATION AND SAMHSA'S SERVICE TO SCIENCE INITIATIVE

SAMHSA's Center for the Application of Prevention Technologies (CAPT), a national substance abuse prevention training and TA system dedicated to strengthening prevention systems and the nation's behavioral health workforce, implements and monitors the STS initiative. As an evaluation capacity-building initiative, STS supports professional and organizational development by emphasizing "strategies to help individuals, groups, and organizations learn about what constitutes effective, useful, and professional evaluation practice" (Preskill & Boyle, 2008, p. 444). Professional development—designed to increase individuals' evaluation knowledge, attitudes, skills, and practices—includes a variety of strategies, such as structured guidance or training on evaluation methods as well as customized coaching and involvement in the evaluation process (Andrews, Motes, Floyd, Flerx, & Fede, 2006; Gibbs, Hawkins, Clinton-Sherrod, & Noonan, 2009; Preskill & Boyle, 2008). Organizational development—or systems change required to sustain appropriate evaluation practices—builds on professional development activities by including strategies such as preparing and making available evaluation materials, hiring expertise in evaluation, updating information management technology, making time for evaluation, and providing financial support and incentives (García-Iriarte, Suarez-Balcazar, Taylor-Ritzler, & Luna, 2011; Taylor-Powell & Boyd, 2008). Throughout the STS process, TA providers collaborate with program representatives to strengthen both professional and organizational evaluation capacity.

Since 2004, more than 500 programs have participated in STS, operating in diverse settings (e.g., CBOs, schools, health clinics), serving diverse populations (defined, for example, by race, ethnicity, gender, age, and sexual orientation), and addressing SAMHSA priorities related to substance abuse prevention and mental health promotion (SAMHSA, 2011). These programs are community-directed and practice-based, rather than research-directed and evidence-based—that is, they are developed with, or informed by, input from the target population and are rooted in the practical experience of working with that population in settings where the program is delivered. In addition to addressing substance abuse prevention, programs target disparities in access, quality, and outcomes among vulnerable populations that have been underserved or inappropriately served by the behavioral health system historically.

Operationalizing Empowerment Evaluation Methods in Service to Science Activities

Empowerment evaluation methods are well suited for an initiative like STS that focuses on building the evaluation capacity of innovative and practice-based programs. Empowerment evaluation is defined as an approach that "aims to increase the probability of achieving program success by (1) providing program stakeholders with tools for assessing the planning, implementation, and self-evaluation of their program, and (2) mainstreaming evaluation as part of the planning and management of the program/organization" (Wandersman et al., 2005, p. 28). The empowerment evaluation emphasis on evaluation ownership, detecting and documenting program outcomes, and helping programs to operate more effectively (Wandersman & Snell-Johns, 2005) is directly in keeping with the purposes of STS stated earlier. Moreover, and as is the case with empowerment evaluation, program staff participate directly in evaluation activities because they are well-versed in the unique needs of their clients and the organizational constraints and community factors that are likely to influence program development, implementation, and evaluation (e.g., Everhart & Wandersman, 2000).

STS consists of three main phases: program selection, intensive training and TA, and financial incentives (see Figure 8.1). After nomination and initial assessment, each program selected for participation is matched with an evaluation TA provider or coach [A] and takes part in a series of workshops on the fundamentals of evaluation capacity building [B]. Each program then meets with their assigned evaluation TA provider during an on-site consultation [C] to identify program and evaluation strengths and gaps as well as outline a series of proposed action steps to address those gaps and guide follow-up TA [D]. Approximately 10 months after selection for participation in the initiative, programs become eligible to submit proposals for subcontracts to further enhance evaluation capacity [E]. These phases incorporate several key empowerment evaluation methods, including determining program viability, fostering a "critical friend" relationship between the TA provider and program staff, and applying a three-step approach to evaluation planning; as well as other elements unique to STS and determined to be essential to evaluation capacity building, including providing customized evaluation TA and offering financial incentives for improvement. Each of these is explained in more detail in Figure 8.1.

Determining Viability When Selecting Programs for Participation in Service to Science

Building the capacity of the programs to improve their evaluation practices requires an existing level of individual and organizational capacity as well as motivation to move forward with this challenging task (Labin, Duffy, Meyers, Wandersman, & Lesesne, 2012). Therefore, programs are selected to participate based on their level of evaluation readiness (or *evaluability*) as well as their motivation to enhance their evaluation capacity. Single state agencies for substance abuse prevention and National Prevention Network representatives nominate substance abuse prevention programs that are innovative in design or focus, are responsive to local needs, fill gaps in the prevention evidence base, are informed by practical experience, focus on alleviating behavioral health disparities, and are committed to evaluation. Nominated programs then submit applications detailing how they meet these criteria, as well as plans for making use of STS TA. This systematized approach to assessing mission, assets, and evaluation gaps is essential to identifying those programs that are more viable and ready to participate (Leviton & Gutman, 2010; Leviton, Khan, Rog, Dawkins, & Cotton, 2010) and informs the operationalization of the empowerment evaluation principles through structured TA (Andrews et al., 2006; Schnoes, Murphy-Berman, & Chambers, 2000).

Fostering a "Critical Friend" Relationship

Following assessment and selection, program staff are assigned to work with an evaluation TA provider. These knowledgeable, capable, and respectful evaluation experts and prevention scientists serve as "critical friends" to their assigned programs. They work collaboratively with program stakeholders in-person and remotely to identify strengths and challenges in evaluation or

Figure 8.1 The Service to Science cycle

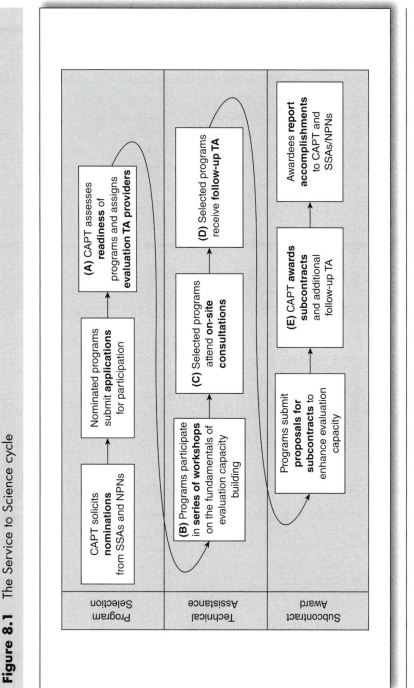

Program Selection

CAPT solicits **nominations** from SSAs and NPNs

Nominated programs submit **applications** for participation

(A) CAPT assesses **readiness** of programs and assigns **evaluation TA providers**

Technical Assistance

(B) Programs participate in **series of workshops** on the fundamentals of evaluation capacity building

(C) Selected programs attend **on-site consultations**

(D) Selected programs receive **follow-up TA**

Subcontract Award

Programs submit **proposals for subcontracts** to enhance evaluation capacity

(E) CAPT **awards subcontracts** and additional follow-up TA

Awardees **report accomplishments** to CAPT and SSAs/NPNs

CAPT, Center for the Application of Prevention Technologies; *NPN*, National Prevention Network; *SSA*, single-state agency; *TA*, technical assistance.

programming and, then, guide program staff through a series of steps to address such challenges (for more on the critical friend, see Fetterman, 2002, 2009; Fetterman, Deitz, & Gesundheit, 2010). The CAPT provides ongoing support and guidance to STS TA providers on assessing and diagnosing program evaluation needs, providing general foundational guidance on evaluation practices, preparing tailored action plans to guide evaluation TA, and using specific evaluation TA methods and tools. These methods, which are described in greater detail in the following paragraph, expand on the empowerment evaluation process described by Fetterman (1996, 1997, 2000) and include taking stock of the existing capacity, refining a clear purpose or mission, and planning for implementation with a focus on results and continued improvement.

Refining the Mission, Taking Stock, and Planning for the Future

The TA phase of STS begins with the three-step evaluation approach described in the empowerment evaluation literature (Fetterman, 1996, 2000; Fetterman & Wandersman, 2005). First, programs participate in a series of workshops on the fundamentals of evaluation capacity building that explore what it means to become an evidence-based program (SAMHSA, 2009), how to apply a five-step framework to guide evaluation planning (Centers for Disease Control and Prevention, 1999), and how to craft logic models to describe program and evaluation efforts. While becoming an evidence-based program may not be the mission of every program, these workshops encourage participants to take stock of their existing evaluation capacity, such as reviewing ways to design and deliver evaluations that are feasible, appropriate, and useful; considering evaluation issues or gaps worth addressing; and clarifying evaluation questions to guide work with the assigned TA provider. Initial guidance also includes the identification of how the various program stakeholders perceive the facilitating or hindering factors (e.g., financial resources, evaluation expertise) to implement an empowerment evaluation approach (Andrews et al., 2006; Schnoes et al., 2000). In earlier STS iterations, trained evaluators delivered this information in a face-to-face workshop format, but recent federal travel restrictions require distance-learning methods.

Providing Customized Technical Assistance That Meets Programs Where They Are

Following the webinar series, each program hosts an intensive on-site TA session during which program representatives and their assigned TA provider develop an initial action plan that outlines next steps for evaluation capacity building and follow-up TA. The on-site consultation also is an opportunity for TA providers and program representatives to build rapport, confidence, and trust in one another and in the ability of the program to achieve its evaluation goals. Evaluation TA providers deliver follow-up TA remotely, which is highly tailored and varied but often focuses on developing or refining a program logic model, implementing a more rigorous evaluation research design, implementing more rigorous data collection procedures, and developing and implementing valid or reliable instruments and measures of change (Harding et al., 2007). Because follow-up assistance is time-limited and capped at 30 hours, program representatives and the TA provider must prioritize the evaluation needs to ensure that the appropriate foundation is laid for subsequent evaluation efforts.

Offering Incentives for Improvement

Each year, approximately 10 months after their selection, participating organizations become eligible to compete for subcontracts to enhance further their evaluation capacity and demonstrate more credible evidence of their program's effectiveness. A committee of experts in prevention science and evaluation methodologies assesses the strength, clarity, and feasibility of each proposal, scoring programs according to their unique evaluation journey and the gaps identified through STS TA—not on the sophistication of the enhancements proposed. Funded organizations use subcontract funds primarily to strengthen evaluation research designs, develop and administer assessment tools that integrate reliable and valid measures of outcome and intervening variables, and run more complex analyses of collected evaluation data (Biewener, Viola, & Dash, 2012). During the 12-month funding cycle, programs submit midterm and final reports that document their progress in improving capacity to demonstrate more credible evidence of effectiveness.

Operationalizing Empowerment Evaluation Principles Through the Service to Science Directives

Empowerment evaluation is defined more by its principles than by its methods, as noted by Wandersman and Snell-Johns (2005). Although STS embodies methods similar to those described by others who implement empowerment evaluation approaches, the initiative's directives are derived from evaluation capacity-building models (Preskill & Boyle, 2008) and build on the empowerment evaluation principles of *inclusion, democratic participation, accountability, community ownership, improvement, capacity building, evidence-based strate-gies, social justice, community knowledge,* and *organizational learning* (Fetterman & Wandersman, 2007; Wandersman et al., 2005).

Democratic Participation and Inclusion (Service to Science Directive: Emphasize Collaboration With Local Programs and Organizations)

The STS approach to capacity building requires ongoing collaboration between TA providers and their assigned programs to shape the scope of work. Key participants and stakeholder groups possess critical knowledge and valuable insights that are included in the evaluation plan. Through *democratic participation* and true *inclusion*, the TA provider invites and works with all interested program staff to critically assess evaluation TA needs and capacities and develops a plan for refining evaluation efforts and identifying the assistance needed. All program staff are encouraged to participate fully in implementing the plan and work with the TA provider to clearly delineate their roles, responsibilities, and timelines as well as schedule opportunities for the TA provider and program staff to check in with each other periodically.

Internal Accountability and Community Ownership (Service to Science Directive: Acknowledge Program Decision Making and Ownership)

Participating programs are ultimately responsible for implementing their evaluation activities and are held accountable to their stakeholders. Thus, programs retain control of decision making and *ownership* over all evaluation capacity-building activities, such as identifying parts of the evaluation requiring assistance and determining how data results are reported and communicated. Similarly, they determine how to apply lessons learned and recommendations offered by their assigned TA provider. Additionally, *internal accountability* is built within the structure of the program and is fueled by internal pressures and institutionalized mechanisms developed by members of the group (Fetterman & Wandersman, 2005).

Capacity Building and Improvement (Service to Science Directive: Programs Will Be at Different Stages of Readiness)

STS takes a developmental approach to evaluation *capacity building* that is designed to move participants to higher levels of capacity. As a result, TA is tailored to meet programs where they are and to help set and meet realistic goals. TA providers help determine whether a program is in the early stages of evaluation planning or otherwise further along in terms of implementing evaluation activities. Frequently, this answer is dependent on the level of organizational support and its related culture in which the program exists. The supportive nature of an organizational culture is a critical factor in determining the degree to which the mainstreaming or routinization of the evaluation will be maintained (Labin et al., 2012). The assumption is that programs are more likely to achieve programmatic and methodological *improvements* if their staff/ organizations are sufficiently ready and motivated to engage in evaluation (Andrews et al., 2006; Schnoes et al., 2000; Wandersman, Chien, & Katz, 2012). In addition, ongoing resources to support the evaluation are necessary if the evaluation capacity building is going to be successful (Gibbs et al., 2009; Preskill & Boyle, 2008).

Evidence-Based Strategies (Service to Science Directive: Value Research Evidence From Multiple Social Science Disciplines)

STS draws on a cadre of scientific experts representing the fields of public health, public policy, sociology, psychology, economics, and education. This diversity allows for appropriate matching of content experts to the unique and innovative prevention approaches employed by participating programs. The experts work closely with programs to ensure that evaluation activities are informed by theories and methods that focus on the local or situational precursors to, and consequences of, substance abuse and mental health problems most pertinent to the populations served. STS is designed to help local organizations apply more rigorous evaluation methods in order to provide more credible *evidence* of their programs' effectiveness.

External Accountability and Social Justice (Service to Science Directive: Balance Program Needs With SAMHSA Priorities)

Although program staff play an important role in identifying their TA needs, evaluation TA providers take proactive steps to identify SAMHSA-identified priorities and assist organizations in meeting those priorities. Maintaining *external accountability* helps to ensure that programs meet the compliance requirements of the initiative's funder (Fetterman & Wandersman, 2005). Programs that apply for and participate in STS understand that they are doing so in order to focus on meeting specific substance abuse prevention outcomes and that these outcomes parallel substance abuse prevention priorities in their states. Moreover, STS explicitly addresses the empowerment evaluation principle of *social justice*, as it prioritizes recruiting programs that address disparities in prevention programming for historically underserved populations (SAMHSA, 2011). Conversely, TA providers relay to SAMHSA the challenges that participating programs face, such as the need to provide TA remotely or the balance of organizational resources for program development versus evaluation efforts. Thus, STS acknowledges that programs are accountable not only to SAMHSA and state nominating entities but also to their local constituents and stakeholders (thereby reinforcing *community ownership*).

Community Knowledge (Service to Science Directive: Respect Program Experiences, Practice, and Wisdom)

CBOs bring a wealth of practical experience in developing, implementing, and evaluating substance abuse prevention programming. Local program staff know what is required to deliver programming given local strengths and resource constraints and are most aware of those factors likely to influence the ability to undertake specific evaluation activities. Embracing the empowerment evaluation principle of *community knowledge*, STS encourages dialogue, illuminates strengths and accomplishments, and identifies gaps in capacity through on-site consultations as well as evaluation action planning and tailored follow-up TA. STS acknowledges that the ability to implement local solutions to prevent substance abuse resides with the programs themselves.

Improvement and Organizational Learning (Service to Science Directive: Focus on Improvements to Individual and Organizational Outcomes)

STS TA is designed to build capacities in evaluation knowledge, attitudes, and practices at the individual level, as well as to facilitate *organizational learning* and change. For this reason, the initiative includes a mix of educational activities focused on enhancing evaluation knowledge among program-level staff as well as more collaborative work designed to turn knowledge into action. TA providers recognize that program representatives who participate in educational and collaborative evaluation activities may become catalysts for change at the organizational level (García-Iriarte et al., 2011). Indeed, an earlier assessment of STS activities demonstrated some organizational learning as noted by self-reported *improvements* in developing or refining program logic models, implementing a more rigorous evaluation research design, implementing more rigorous data collection procedures, hiring or improving relationships with external evaluators, and developing and implementing more appropriate measures (Harding et al., 2007). More recent assessments have used performance indicators to determine organizational success in conducting activities and monitoring program progress along an evaluation capacity continuum. Conducted 15 months after programs are selected for participation, the impact assessment process is designed to indicate which enhancements programs have made to their evaluation efforts as a result of receiving evaluation TA (SAMHSA's Center for the Application of Prevention Technologies, 2013).

ASSOCIATION OF VILLAGE PRIDE, INC., CASE STUDY: SERVICE TO SCIENCE PARTICIPATION

To demonstrate empowerment evaluation in action, we provide an example of how STS methods and directives were applied to build the evaluation capacity of a single organization, the Association of Village Pride, Inc. (AVPRIDE) in Fayette County, Georgia. We begin with a description of the evaluation capacity-building trajectory of AVPRIDE through its participation in STS and conclude with a discussion of how the STS directives and empowerment evaluation principles were operationalized. The following AVPRIDE documents informed formulation of the case study: the STS application for the Leaders in Training (LIT) program, the TA action plan, the subcontract proposal, and subcontract midterm and final reports. In this section, we describe AVPRIDE's participation in STS, according to the initiative's three phases: program selection, TA delivery, and implementation of subcontract award.

Selection of AVPRIDE Into Service to Science

Nominated by the Georgia Department of Behavioral Health and Developmental Disabilities in 2010, AVPRIDE—an organization focusing on the development of youth leadership skills and related assets—submitted an application for its LIT program. AVPRIDE had been receiving prevention block grant funding from the state of Georgia for youth substance abuse prevention in Fayette County. Restrictions on those dollars, however, limited the organization's ability to evaluate the LIT program with appropriate rigor to demonstrate effectiveness. As initially conceived and at the time of selection, LIT consisted of a curriculum comprising didactic lessons, interactive activities, and service-learning opportunities for high school students in the county who were struggling academically, punished for disciplinary infractions, and more likely to drop out of school. Most students in the program were African American and Hispanic and more than one fifth were low income. Overrepresentation of ethnic and racial minority youth in these disciplinary practices (suspensions and expulsions) is especially troubling, as evidence suggests that such practices have negative long-term implications for youth (e.g., Fenning & Rose, 2007; Skiba, Michael, Nardo, & Peterson, 2002). Other AVPRIDE components included K–12 after-school programs, career exploration and mentoring, work-readiness skill development, and internship placement.

The essential elements of the program were designed to reduce risk factors for substance abuse and other behavioral health problems by enhancing protective factors associated with positive youth development (e.g., commitment to school, social connectedness, positive use of leisure time). The curriculum included a fragmented mix of lessons and activities that were not bound together by a clear theoretical framework; however, program staff expressed a desire to use the Developmental Assets® model developed by the Search Institute (Scales, Benson, Leffert, & Blyth, 2000; Scales & Leffert, 2004). Although AVPRIDE had collected and entered information on LIT program outputs (e.g., number of participants, number of events) into a state-mandated data management system, the organization had not conducted an outcome evaluation of LIT to determine whether or not program efforts were contributing to anticipated outcomes. The AVPRIDE interim executive director, who was also the LIT program developer, sought participation in STS because she knew that demonstrating program effectiveness using appropriately rigorous evaluation methods was important to key program stakeholders (namely, the AVPRIDE board of directors) and to organizational and LIT program sustainability.

The CAPT accepted the program for participation in STS, based on the organization's ability to demonstrate that LIT was an adaptation of an existing evidence-based program that included modifications to the original program's core elements and targeted a population different than the one with which the original intervention was tested. STS application reviewers (proficient in community-based evaluation) noted, however, that the program needed to better define its rationale for focusing on and tailoring the program to African American and Hispanic populations as well as provide a more comprehensive description of its core elements (e.g., amount of exposure, schedule of exposure) and links to the state's substance abuse prevention priorities. In addition to affecting risk factors for substance abuse behaviors, the program also was interested in documenting the extent to which youth participants showed improvements in protective factors, such as leadership, advocacy, and empathy for others. Comments and scores submitted by reviewers of the STS application suggested that the LIT program demonstrated "moderate" evaluation readiness. Although the program had previously gathered evaluation data to measure program outcomes tied to each age group and for each service component, it did not have a logic model that conveyed how program activities were expected to influence specific risk and protective factors and produce changes in substance abuse behaviors. Moreover, LIT did not have a process for measuring the quality of program implementation or program outcomes. The CAPT assigned a TA provider who had extensive experience working with CBOs to help program representatives identify and address evaluation gaps, according to the seven main directives of the STS approach (discussed in the previous section).

Service to Science Technical Assistance Provided to AVPRIDE

The LIT program developer invited her staff and the AVPRIDE board chairperson to participate in an initial on-site consultation with LIT's assigned TA provider so that they might understand the amount of effort required to conduct a more rigorous program evaluation. The AVPRIDE-STS team reviewed the program's evaluation TA needs, stakeholder priorities, and evaluation capacities to delineate and prioritize evaluation gaps. As a result of the on-site consultation, the AVPRIDE-STS team crafted an action plan for addressing those gaps, which included finalizing a program logic model that incorporated asset-building theory (Scales et al., 2000), conducting a literature review to substantiate links between youth leadership activities and strategies that promote developmental assets and other protective factors (Scales & Leffert, 2004; Scales et al., 2001), training new staff and board members on evaluation capacities, revising existing outcome data collection tools and measures, selecting and implementing an appropriately rigorous evaluation design, and developing a plan for analysis and reporting.

Reluctance

AVPRIDE expressed a strong desire to involve all LIT staff in the evaluation process. Still, the program developer and board chairperson indicated that program staff would require significant TA and guidance to develop a fundamental understanding of evaluation before making any decisions about the implementation of specific evaluation methods. Conversations with the board chairperson suggested that the board was reluctant to commit staff time to evaluation activities, even with guidance and coaching from the STS TA provider. To allay these concerns, the TA provider presented the chairperson with additional information on the STS initiative and its focus on working with local organizations to strengthen their evaluation capacity. She also detailed in writing the specific roles and responsibilities of all parties involved—noting that while AVPRIDE would be responsible for the work and have ownership of its products, the TA provider would provide ongoing support to the organization to help implement activities in which the staff had minimal expertise (e.g., survey development). With a greater understanding of the initiative and its expectations, and motivated especially by LIT's eligibility to compete for a $30,000 subcontract following its year of participation in the initiative, AVPRIDE's board decided to invest in the opportunity and commit staff resources toward the evaluation activities.

The AVPRIDE-STS team prioritized logic model development to articulate a clear rationale for the program and demonstrate to stakeholders how its activities were designed to achieve short- and long-term outcomes of interest, as well as how those outcomes would be measured. Staff agreed that with TA provider guidance they would investigate the Search Institute's Developmental Assets® model (one with which they were already familiar) more fully along with other youth development frameworks. This investigation would determine whether a theoretical framework existed that was consistent with LIT's overall goals and desired outcomes and that would facilitate subsequent identification of standard or reliable outcome measures for assessing those outcomes.

Developmental Assets

The Search Institute Developmental Assets® model organizes 40 youth assets that promote health and well-being into eight categories: support, empowerment, boundaries and expectations, and constructive use of time are considered "external assets"; commitment to learning, positive values, social competencies, and positive identity are considered "internal assets" (Search Institute, 2006). The TA provider encouraged LIT staff to crosswalk program activities with the model to ensure that the desired outcomes were consistent with the assets' definitions. A month later, the staff had identified the specific assets that they expected the program to address. Moreover, based on their research, LIT staff concluded that the program's long-standing curriculum needed to be rewritten to address all eight asset categories and that each component—didactic elements, activities, and community service—be matched with a measurable developmental asset. The final measurement tool included the Developmental Assets Profile[1] (Scales & Leffert,

---

1. AVPRIDE obtained permission to use this tool, now available at http://www.search-institute.org/survey-services/surveys/DAP.

2004) and items from the Georgia Student Health Survey[2] that assess substance abuse outcomes (e.g., 30-day use) and risk factors (e.g., perception of
risk or harm).

After 2 months of collaborative work following the on-site consultation, the
AVPRIDE-STS team finalized the LIT program's logic model and began prepa-
rations for pilot-testing the revised curriculum and corresponding measurement
tools. Due to resource limitations, the team decided to use a pretest-posttest
evaluation design without a comparison group. The TA provider collaborated
with the program developer to train staff on the purpose and methods of pretest-posttest administration. Specific challenges included the fact that the study
would need to be completed within 6 months (with only 4 months dedicated
to LIT implementation) and would require additional staff time to recruit participants and ensure high rates of participation and retention of youth. The
AVPRIDE-STS team consulted a representative of the Search Institute who
cautioned that students needed to be engaged in asset-building activities for at
least 6 months before meaningful changes could be observed using the
Developmental Assets Profile. Despite this caution, LIT staff moved forward
with the plan to implement and assess program outcomes after only 4 months
of implementation with support from the board, which was eager to see the
program's empirical results. LIT staff planned to closely observe and document
youth reactions to the newly revised curriculum as well as how programming
was implemented to determine whether modifications would be required in
subsequent LIT offerings.

Pretest and Posttest Results

LIT staff recruited 33 participants for the pilot's pretest, of which 13 completed posttests. Despite the fact that a number of participants did not provide
posttest information, subsequent analyses revealed that those participants who
completed their posttests demonstrated improvements, on average, in all eight
of the developmental assets categories—with significant improvement concerning "positive identity" and "empowerment." These categories were emphasized in the LIT programming and aligned with the objectives in the revised
curriculum. Thus, the pilot demonstrated that the data collection tools were
sensitive enough to register change in developmental assets targeted by the
revised curriculum. In addition, the STS work on logic model development
convinced AVPRIDE that the Developmental Assets® framework should guide

---

2. This survey is available at http://www.gadoe.org/Curriculum-Instruction-and-Assessment/
Curriculum-and-Instruction/GSHS-II.

all of its programming. However, as discussed with the TA provider during follow-up, LIT staff understood that in order to provide more credible evidence of program effectiveness, they needed to build on their pilot-test work: a larger sample size, a comparison group, and tracking fidelity of implementation. Additional financial support would be needed for these evaluation enhancements.

Service to Science Subcontract Awarded to AVPRIDE

In late 2011, AVPRIDE submitted a proposal for, and was awarded, a SAMHSA STS subcontract to further enhance evaluation capacity to demonstrate effectiveness of the LIT program. The TA provider did not assist AVPRIDE staff in preparing the proposal, as was stipulated in the request for proposals. With these funds, the organization hired an evaluator to help them to administer a larger-scale pretest-posttest, comparison group study to determine the effectiveness of its youth development training. In this design, students who participated in the LIT program (intervention condition) were compared with students who did not participate (comparison condition). Participants in both conditions completed assessments before and after the training using the tool developed during the STS TA phase.

The proposal detailed a series of evaluation activities that AVPRIDE and its board implemented in conjunction with their external evaluator. This included administering survey instruments, identifying students for and assigning them to the comparison group, identifying appropriate sites for survey administration, documenting the evaluation process for replication purposes, and developing a database to store contact and demographic information about respondents. The AVPRIDE board was responsible for a series of other activities that complemented and supported the AVPRIDE's overall evaluation efforts. They identified an evaluator (committed to stakeholder involvement approaches[3]) who not only led the LIT evaluation but also strengthened staff and board member evaluation capacities and worked to ensure that all AVPRIDE programs were evaluated (albeit, at different levels of rigor). Other priorities included continuing to embed program evaluation into program planning decisions and funding additional opportunities for staff to strengthen their evaluation capacity.

---

3. See Fetterman, Rodríguez-Campos, Wandersman, and O'Sullivan (2014) for additional discussion about stakeholder involvement approaches.

ASSOCIATION OF VILLAGE PRIDE, INC., CASE STUDY: OPERATIONALIZING EMPOWERMENT EVALUATION PRINCIPLES

In this section, we describe how empowerment evaluation principles guided the TA provided to AVPRIDE and helped the organization to realize its evaluation goals (organized by the seven STS directives).

Democratic Participation and Inclusion (Emphasized Collaboration With AVPRIDE and LIT Staff)

The STS action plan resulted from close collaboration between the TA provider and AVPRIDE staff and board chairperson during the initial on-site consultation. Because AVPRIDE was in the process of hiring a new executive director and additional LIT staff, the AVPRIDE-STS team determined that it would be important to involve the new director in the evaluation capacity-building activities. In keeping with empowerment evaluation principles of *inclusion* and *democratic participation*, the team agreed that any action plan should include all program representatives' input on the evaluation enhancements that would be feasible to implement. The TA provider prepared a draft action plan, which the LIT program developer shared with other key stakeholders for comment. The AVPRIDE-STS team remained in close contact throughout the TA phase that followed; program staff and AVPRIDE's executive director and board members provided ongoing input during each follow-up TA call, while the TA provider included program staff in all correspondence regarding the assistance and information that she provided.

Internal Accountability and Ownership (Acknowledged AVPRIDE Decision Making and Ownership)

AVPRIDE leadership recognized that by prioritizing inclusion and democratic participation, the evaluation capacity-building process would facilitate *community ownership* and shared commitment to the activities outlined in the STS evaluation action plan. Achieving true ownership and securing the requisite staff resources to implement the activities in the action plan, however, would constitute a paradigm shift for the board toward seeing evaluation through a capacity-building lens rather than one focused on external evaluation or evaluation by an outsider. LIT staff described the process of convincing the board and obtaining its buy-in as the jumping-off point from which they began to see themselves as catalysts for change; they recognized their *accountability*—to the board and to other stakeholders—for demonstrating program effectiveness by focusing its research design, collecting and analyzing data, making decisions based on those data, and using the information for continuous quality improvement.

Capacity Building and Improvement (Responded to AVPRIDE's Stage of Readiness for Evaluation)

By tailoring assistance to meet the specific evaluation gaps and capacity needs of LIT, the AVPRIDE-STS team established attainable evaluation goals and helped ensure that the LIT program would be likely to obtain its stated goals and objectives. Specifically, emphasis was placed on *improvement*—making sure the program rationale was sound and responsive to problems that LIT hoped to prevent and the youth assets they sought to strengthen. A focus on programming was considered an essential early step in evaluation planning (Centers for Disease Control and Prevention, 1999) as it helps organizations clarify what they are evaluating and channel limited resources and time into evaluation activities that produce results most meaningful to them. Similarly, once the logic model had been refined, the TA provider worked with AVPRIDE to distill evaluation action steps that the organization could implement with limited resources and that would provide them with essential information needed to *build their evaluation capacity* to implement more rigorous evaluation methods. These steps were critical for selecting outcome measures and developing and pilot-testing outcome data collection tools. Other structured guidance focused on how to be a better consumer of evaluation and what to look for when locating, hiring, and managing an evaluator.

Evidence-Based Strategies (Valued Research Methods and Evidence)

The first area of focus for STS TA was to refine the program's logic model to facilitate a recalibration of programming to increase the likelihood of positive results. For AVPRIDE, the logic modeling process prompted staff to better align the LIT program components with prior research on youth development and situate programming within a clear theoretical framework. Well-matched, both the TA provider and LIT program developer had previous experience applying the Developmental Assets® model to prevention programming (Fisher, Imm, Chinman, & Wandersman, 2006; Oparah, 2006). Together, they identified ways to revise the curriculum to be more in keeping with the eight developmental asset categories that LIT hoped to enhance through its curriculum and associated activities. For AVPRIDE, this process was arduous; however, it provided a framework not only for program revision and implementation but also for using established measures shown to register change associated with exposure to, or participation in, curricular activities (Scales & Leffert, 2004). Further, TA provider expertise in conducting program evaluation proved critical in helping LIT design and implement more rigorous and realistic evaluation methods. In addition to learning how to conduct evaluation activities, staff also experienced how difficult and time-consuming such activities could be—especially when implemented in addition to regular programmatic responsibilities.

External Accountability and Social Justice (Balanced AVPRIDE Needs With SAMHSA Priorities)

AVPRIDE maintained a focus on strengthening youths' developmental assets and promoting youth resilience—to address not only substance abuse but also the overrepresentation of African American and Hispanic youth in disciplinary actions (such as suspensions and expulsions) as well as other factors that place them at increased risk for poor economic and health outcomes (Chew, Osseck, Raygor, Eldridge-Houser, & Cox, 2010; Fenning & Rose, 2007; Skiba et al., 2002; Youngblade et al., 2007). Programmatic emphasis was not as much focused on risk abatement as on the cultivation and enhancement of existing strengths and assets—on what they had to offer themselves and others. For this *social justice* reason, AVPRIDE was most interested in measuring outcomes associated with those enhanced strengths or developmental assets rather than only risk behaviors. However, SAMHSA and other stakeholders were interested in outcomes associated with substance abuse. In this case, the TA provider and AVPRIDE staff worked together to reconcile these priorities and found a way to assess strengths-based outcomes and risk behaviors so that they would maintain both external *accountability* and community ownership.

Community Knowledge (Respected Program Experiences, Practice, and Wisdom)

The best illustration of STS TA respecting program experiences, practice, and wisdom in this case comes from the pilot test of the data collection instrument. The timing of the pilot test (May 1 through August 31) was not ideal; summer months presented unique challenges to participant retention and exposure to adequate program dosage. However, staff familiarity with their target population and the program greatly enhanced their capacity to reach out to and engage youth in evaluation activities, implement a revised program on short turnaround, monitor attendance, and collect surveys. The TA provider was required to trust that the program would be able to implement the pilot test despite the obstacles they faced. Indeed, compared to the TA provider, AVPRIDE had a more realistic understanding based on community knowledge concerning obstacles they were likely to encounter with regard to recruitment and retention and what might be required to overcome these obstacles. The results guided development and implementation of a larger-scale evaluation using SAMHSA STS subcontract funds. AVPRIDE also maintained control over specific aspects of the evaluation where they felt that their practical experience gave them an advantage (e.g., working with school system partners to identify an appropriate comparison group, recruiting and retaining youth participants, and implementing greater confidentiality and human protection mechanisms).

Improvement and Organizational Learning (Focused on Improvement to LIT and AVPRIDE Outcomes)

Individual-level gains in terms of specific evaluation knowledge, skills, and attitudes were not directly assessed. Instead, reviews of program documentation showed that, in keeping with the directives of the initiative, STS helped propel motivated individuals into roles of evaluation catalysts who would work to foster change at the organizational level (García-Iriarte et al., 2011). From assessment to subcontract implementation, AVPRIDE made major program- and organizational-level *improvements* in evaluation capacity, such as developing and refining their program logic model, revising the curriculum to ensure close alignment of goals and activities with asset-building strategies, developing and pilot-testing pre- and post-assessment surveys that included standard measures of youth development assets as well as substance abuse behaviors, hiring an evaluator committed to empowerment evaluation methods, increasing support and commitment of the board to secure additional funding for the LIT program and other activities, training staff on data collection and human protection protocols, and strengthening collaborative relationships with key youth service agencies and community partners.

In addition to these specific organizational improvements, STS TA fostered *organizational learning*. STS TA produced an overall transformation in how the LIT program was conceived, implemented, and evaluated. The results of the pilot test and the more rigorous evaluation effort conducted with subcontract funds encouraged the AVPRIDE board to incorporate evaluation activities into all of its programs and to invest in building and using data management systems to promote data-informed decision making. Participation in STS has resulted in numerous enhancements to evaluation capacities, which has helped AVPRIDE to grow from an annual budget of about $80,000 to over $500,000 in just 3 years. The LIT program developer indicated that staff and AVPRIDE board members attribute much of this success to the shift in the organization's culture and activities regarding evaluation of all programs—a shift that began with participation in the STS initiative.

CONCLUSION

Empowerment evaluation principles guided the STS TA provided to AVPRIDE staff. The process included a commitment to self-reflection and a focus on accountability that created a new lens through which the board could focus and view the organization's programs. The capacity-building approach facilitated the integration of evidence-based practice into the work, helped to maintain leadership for ongoing evaluation processes, and reinforced the understanding of the relationship between outcomes and continued funding. AVPRIDE staff and board leadership were essential catalysts in developing and sustaining a culture of accountability. This is consistent with a recent literature review conducted by Labin et al. (2012) showing that organizational resources (e.g., leadership) are critical to building organizational- and individual-level capacity outcomes.

In this example, individual capacity-building outcomes, as well as organizational outcomes for AVPRIDE, contributed to enhanced staff capacities and organizational success. At the individual level, staff improved their capacities in evaluation skills, including developing logic models, evaluation plans, and database systems for monitoring. At the organizational level, AVPRIDE improved their emphasis on the importance of ongoing evaluation and monitoring for all programs and became more competitive (and successful) at securing larger grant funds. This STS example offers a practical demonstration of how evaluation capacity-building models and empowerment evaluation processes and principles can be operationalized and applied in the translation of practice to science. Though STS targets substance abuse prevention outcomes specifically, the empowerment evaluation approach in this SAMHSA initiative can be applied more widely across many social and health service domains.

REFERENCES

Andrews, A. B., Motes, P. S., Floyd, A., Flerx, V. C., & Fede, A. L.-D. (2006). Building evaluation capacity in community-based organizations. *Journal of Community Practice, 13*(4), 85–104.

Biewener, M., Viola, R., & Dash, K. (2012). *Service to Science subcontracts to build evaluation capacity for evidence-based interventions: Cohort 6 (2010) subcontract aggregate report.* Newton, MA: Education Development Center.

Brounstein, P. J., Gardner, S. E., & Backer, T. (2006). Research to practice: Efforts to bring effective prevention to every community. *Journal of Primary Prevention, 27*(1), 91–109.

Centers for Disease Control and Prevention. (1999). Framework for program evaluation in public health. *Morbidity and Mortality Weekly Report, 48*(RR-11), 1–58.

Chew, W., Osseck, J., Raygor, D., Eldridge-Houser, J., & Cox, C. (2010). Developmental assets: Profile of youth in a juvenile justice facility. *Journal of School Health, 80*(2), 66–72.

Connolly, P., & York, P. (2002). Evaluating capacity-building efforts for nonprofit organizations. *OD Practitioner, 34*(4), 33–39.

Everhart, K., & Wandersman, A. (2000). Applying comprehensive quality programming and empowerment evaluation to reduce implementation barriers. *Journal of Educational and Psychological Consultation, 11*(2), 177–191.

Fenning, P., & Rose, J. (2007). Overrepresentation of African American students in exclusionary discipline: The role of school policy. *Urban Education, 42*(6), 536–559.

Fetterman, D. (1996). Empowerment evaluation: An introduction to theory and practice. In D. Fetterman, S. Kaftarian, & A. Wandersman (Eds.), *Empowerment evaluation: Knowledge and tools for self-assessment and accountability* (pp. 3–47). Thousand Oaks, CA: Sage.

Fetterman, D. (1997). Empowerment evaluation: A response to Patton and Scriven. *American Journal of Evaluation, 18*(3), 253–266.

Fetterman, D. (2000). *Foundations of empowerment evaluation.* Thousand Oaks, CA: Sage.

Fetterman, D. (2002). Empowerment evaluation: Building communities of practice and a culture of learning. *American Journal of Community Psychology, 30*(1), 89–102.

Fetterman, D. (2009). Empowerment evaluation at the Stanford University School of Medicine: Using a critical friend to improve clerkship experience. *Ensaio: Avaliação e Políticas Públicas em Educação, 17*(63), 197–204.

Fetterman, D., Deitz, J., & Gesundheit, N. (2010). Empowerment evaluation: A collaborative approach to evaluating and transforming a medical school curriculum. *Academic Medicine: Journal of the Association of American Medical Colleges, 85*(5), 813–820.

Fetterman, D., Rodríguez-Campos, L., Wandersman, A., & O'Sullivan, R. (2014). Collaborative, participatory, and empowerment evaluation: Building a strong conceptual foundation for stakeholder involvement approaches to evaluation. *American Journal of Evaluation, 35*(1), 144–148.

Fetterman, D., & Wandersman, A. (2005). *Empowerment evaluation principles in practice.* New York: Guilford Press.

Fetterman, D., & Wandersman, A. (2007). Empowerment evaluation yesterday, today, and tomorrow. *American Journal of Evaluation, 28*(2), 179–198.

Fisher, D., Imm, P., Chinman, M., & Wandersman, A. (2006). *Getting To Outcomes with developmental assets: Ten steps to measuring success in youth programs and communities.* Minneapolis, MN: Search Institute.

García-Iriarte, E., Suarez-Balcazar, Y., Taylor-Ritzler, T., & Luna, M. (2011). A catalyst-for-change approach to evaluation capacity building. *American Journal of Evaluation, 32*(2), 168–182.

Gibbs, D., Hawkins, S., Clinton-Sherrod, A. M., & Noonan, R. (2009). Empowering programs with evaluation technical assistance: Outcomes and lessons learned. *Health Promotion Practice, 10*(1 Suppl), 38S–44S.

Harding, W., Dash, K., Cummins, M., Sharma, A., Griffin, T., & Garrett, B., et al. (2007, November). *Testing a federal initiative designed to improve evaluation of innovative and emerging substance abuse prevention programs.* Paper presented at the American Public Health Association annual meeting, Washington, DC.

Kegeles, S., Rebchook, G., & Tebbetts, S. (2005). Challenges and facilitators to building program evaluation capacity among community–based organizations. *AIDS Education and Prevention*, *17*(4), 284–299.

Labin, S. N., Duffy, J. L., Meyers, D. C., Wandersman, A., & Lesesne, C. A. (2012). A research synthesis of the evaluation capacity building literature. *American Journal of Evaluation, 33*(3), 307–308.

Leviton, L., & Gutman, M. (2010). Overview and rationale for the systematic screening and assessment method. *New Directions for Evaluation, 125,* 7–31.

Leviton, L., Khan, L., Rog, D., Dawkins, N., & Cotton, D. (2010). Evaluability assessment to improve public health policies, programs, and practices. *Annual Review of Public Health, 31,* 213–233.

Oparah, D. C. (2006). *Make a world of difference: 50 Asset-building activities to help teens explore diversity.* Minneapolis, MN: Search Institute.

Preskill, H., & Boyle, S. (2008). A multidisciplinary model of evaluation capacity building. *American Journal of Evaluation, 29*(4), 443–459.

SAMHSA. (2009). *Identifying and selecting evidence-based interventions for substance abuse prevention: Revised guidance document for the Strategic Prevention Framework State Incentive Grant Program.* Rockville, MD: Author.

SAMHSA. (2011). *Leading change: A plan for SAMHSA's roles and actions 2011–2014.* Rockville, MD: Author.

SAMHSA's Center for the Application of Prevention Technologies. (2003). *Selecting the program that's right for you: A feasibility assessment tool.* Waltham, MA: Education Development Center.

SAMHSA's Center for the Application of Prevention Technologies. (2013). *Findings from the CAPT Service to Science 2011 Cohort Cumulative Service Assessment.* Waltham, MA: Education Development Center.

Scales, P. C., Benson, P. L., Leffert, N., & Blyth, D. A. (2000). Contribution of Developmental Assets to the prediction of thriving among adolescents. *Applied Developmental Science, 4*(1), 27–46.

Scales, P. C., Benson, P. L., Roehlkepartain, E. C., Hintz, N. R., Sullivan, T. K., & Mannes, M. (2001). The role of neighborhood and community in building developmental assets for children and youth: A national study of social norms among American adults. *Journal of Community Psychology, 29*(6), 703–727.

Scales, P. C., & Leffert, N. (2004). *Developmental Assets: A synthesis of the scientific research on adolescent development* (2nd ed.). Minneapolis, MN: Search Institute Press.

Schnoes, C., Murphy-Berman, V., & Chambers, J. (2000). Empowerment evaluation applied: Experiences, analysis, and recommendations from a case study. *American Journal of Evaluation, 21*(1), 53–64.

Search Institute. (2006). *40 Developmental assets for adolescents (ages 12–18).* Minneapolis, MN: Search Institute.

Skiba, R. J., Michael, R. S., Nardo, A. C., & Peterson, R. L. (2002). The color of discipline: Sources of racial and gender disproportionality in school punishment. *Urban Review, 34*(4), 317–342.

Taylor-Powell, E., & Boyd, H. (2008). Evaluation capacity building in complex organizations. *New Directions for Evaluation, 120,* 55–69.

Wandersman, A., Chien, V. H., & Katz, J. (2012). Toward an evidence-based system for innovation support for implementing innovations with quality: Tools, training, technical assistance, and quality assurance/quality improvement. *American Journal of Community Psychology, 50*(3/4), 445–459.

Wandersman, A., & Snell-Johns, J. (2005). Empowerment evaluation: Clarity, dialogue, and growth. *American Journal of Evaluation*, 26(3), 421–428.

Wandersman, A., Snell-Johns, J., Lentz, B., Fetterman, D., Keener, D., Livet, M., et al. (2005). The principles of empowerment evaluation. In D. Fetterman & A. Wandersman (Eds.), *Empowerment evaluation principles in practice* (pp. 27–41). New York: Guilford Press.

Youngblade, L. M., Theokas, C., Schulenberg, J., Curry, L., Huang, I.-C., & Novak, M. (2007). Risk and promotive factors in families, schools, and communities: A contextual model of positive youth development in adolescence. *Pediatrics*, *119*(Suppl 1), S47–S53.

PART III

TOOLS

CHAPTER 9

Getting to Outcomes®

An Empowerment Evaluation Approach for Capacity Building and Accountability

Abraham Wandersman

University of South Carolina

T he purpose of this chapter is to describe an empowerment evaluation approach called Getting To Outcomes® (GTO®),[1] which is designed to help individuals and organizations increase their capacity for implementing programs with quality, achieve desired outcomes, and become more accountable for their work. This chapter starts with a definition of empowerment evaluation and then describes GTO. It is followed by a brief overview of the rationale, components, scientific development, and practice of Getting To Outcomes (GTO). It also discusses some applications of "GTO thinking" to evaluation capacity building and accountability.

EMPOWERMENT EVALUATION

Empowerment evaluation is "an evaluation approach that aims to increase the probability of achieving program success by providing program stakeholders with tools for assessing the planning, implementation, and self-evaluation of their program, which mainstreams evaluation as part of the planning and management of the program/organization"

---

1. Getting To Outcomes and GTO are trademarks registered by the University of South Carolina and the RAND Corporation.

(Wandersman et al., 2005, p. 28). There are 10 principles guiding empowerment evaluation: *improvement, community ownership, inclusion, democratic participation, social justice, community knowledge, organizational learning, evidence-based strategies, capacity building,* and *accountability* (Wandersman et al., 2005).

The assumption behind empowerment evaluation is that if key stakeholders (including program staff members) had the capacity to use the necessary knowledge and tools for *planning* more systematically, *implementing* with quality, *self-evaluating*, and using the information for *continuous quality improvement (CQI)*, then they would be more likely to achieve their desired outcomes (Fetterman & Wandersman, 2005).

GTO AS AN EMPOWERMENT EVALUATION "HOW-TO" APPROACH

GTO is a 10-step, results-based approach to accountability. GTO and Fetterman's three-step approach are considered to be the most commonly applied empowerment evaluation models in the field. GTO is a results-based empowerment evaluation approach that provides detailed steps for capacity building and accountability. GTO involves asking and answering the following 10 accountability questions or "steps" at the beginning and throughout a program.

1. What are the needs and conditions to address? (NEEDS/RESOURCES)

2. What are the goals, priority populations, and objectives (desired outcomes)? (GOALS)

3. Which science (evidence-based) models and best practices can be useful in reaching the goals? (BEST PRACTICES)

4. What actions need to be taken so that the selected program fits with the community context? (FIT)

5. What organizational capacities are needed to implement the program? (CAPACITY)

6. What is the plan for the program? (PLAN)

7. How will the quality of the program and/or initiative be implemented? (IMPLEMENTATION/PROCESS EVALUATION)

8. How well did the program work? (OUTCOME EVALUATION)

9. How will continuous quality improvement strategies be incorporated? (CQI)

10. If the program is successful, how will it be sustained? (SUSTAIN)

See Table 9.1 for a more detailed description of the 10 steps and accountability questions.

Table 9.1   The Ten Accountability Steps in GTO Manuals (Guided by Key Questions)

1. What are the needs and resources to address? GTO step 1 provides information about conducting a community *needs* assessment to help inform program planning.
2. What are the goals and objectives? GTO step 2 has worksheets for creating measurable *goals & objectives* from the needs identified in step 1.
3. Which evidence-based programs can be useful in reaching the goals? GTO step 3 overviews *evidence-based programming* and how to select a program to address the goals outlined in step 2.
4. What actions need to be taken so the selected program fits the community context? GTO step 4 prompts readers to reduce duplication and facilitate collaboration with other programs.
5. What capacity is needed for the program? GTO step 5 prompts readers to ensure there is sufficient organizational *capacity* to conduct the selected program.
6. What is the plan for this program? GTO step 6 assists with *planning* the selected program.
7. How will implementation be assessed? GTO step 7 assists with conducting a program *process evaluation*.
8. How well did the program work? GTO step 8 assists with conducting a program *outcome evaluation*.
9. How will continuous quality improvement (CQI) strategies be incorporated? GTO step 9 prompts practitioners to reassess accountability steps 1–8 after completing the program to *improve* the program.
10. If the program is successful, how will it be sustained? GTO step 10 presents several ideas to consider when attempting to *sustain* an effective program.

SOURCE: Adapted from Chinman, Imm, and Wandersman (2004).

FAYETTEVILLE YOUTH NETWORK GTO EXAMPLE[2]

In this section, I present the Fayetteville Youth Network (FYN) example that is often used in trainings to illustrate what GTO looks like.

Fayetteville Youth Network (FYN) promotes positive youth development and provides substance abuse prevention services. Program staff noticed that a growing number of program participants were getting pregnant, and they were concerned about the effects of these early pregnancies. They decided to investigate this more closely and possibly add a teen pregnancy prevention component. A working group of staff members formed to take a look at the problem and plan a way to address it. They decided to use the GTO model to guide their efforts.

Step 1 (NEEDS AND RESOURCES). Program staff used existing databases as well as data they collected for their needs and resources assessment. First, state health department databases provided information on the number of pregnancies in each zip code within Fayetteville and the zip code where the majority of teen pregnancies were concentrated. Second, they collected information about the sexual behaviors of youth across the state from the Youth Risk Behavior Survey. Third, they surveyed high school students to assess different determinants of sexual behaviors (e.g., knowledge and attitudes about sexuality, sexually transmitted diseases [STDs], and contraception). Fourth, they conducted a focus group of school staff members to get perspectives on the risk factors facing youth in that school. These data helped staff identify high school–aged youth in zip code 12345 (pseudo zip code) as their priority target population. They decided to focus on reducing sexual activity and increasing correct and consistent condom use among sexually active youth.

Step 2 (GOALS). Having identified a target population, staff set the goal to reduce teen pregnancy in this school district by decreasing sexual activity and increasing the use of condoms and other forms of contraception. They identified determinants of teen sexual behavior and focused on increasing self-efficacy of teens using condoms and increasing teens' knowledge about HIV and other STDs. Next, staff developed a logic model based on the

---

2. FYN is a fictitious example developed by Jen Duffy (University of South Carolina) and enhanced by Gina Desiderio (Healthy Teen Network) for the Promoting Science-Based Approaches to Teen Pregnancy Prevention initiative funded by the Centers for Disease Control and Prevention.

health goal, behaviors, and determinants they wanted to change. They wrote the following outcome statement:

- By May 31, 2015, 75% of the students participating in Fayetteville High School's teen pregnancy prevention program will have increased knowledge about where to find condoms and contraception as recorded on surveys.

Step 3 (BEST PRACTICES). Once the group had identified their health goal and specific outcomes, they looked at lists of science-based programs to find some that might fit with what they wanted to do. They reviewed the Office of Adolescent Health website and easily identified a few programs that could meet their needs. The group especially liked two programs: *Becoming a Responsible Teen (BART)* and *Making Proud Choices*. Both programs had the same behavior outcomes among similar youth populations. They obtained copies of both programs for review and selection.

Step 4 (FIT). The group learned that both programs included eight sessions. After they reviewed both curricula, group members decided that *Making Proud Choices* fit best with the youth population and the values and mission of the organization. They decided to adapt some of the language used in the curriculum to incorporate terms that were commonly used in the school they planned to serve.

Step 5 (CAPACITY). After examining the curriculum, the group determined that FYN already had most of the capacities they needed to implement *Making Proud Choices* (e.g., appropriate personnel). Some capacities they needed to address included purchasing the curriculum and training staff members on how to use it.

Step 6 (PLAN). The group finalized their decision to use *Making Proud Choices*. They put together a detailed plan of how they would carry it out, which included purchasing the curriculum, getting training for the program facilitators, identifying strategies for recruiting youth to participate, deciding when and where the program would take place, and figuring out how to get the tools necessary to evaluate the program.

Step 7 (IMPLEMENTATION/PROCESS EVALUATION). As group members carried out the various parts of their plan, they referred back to the written copy of the plan to see if they were on track or if changes had to be made. They also kept track of the number of participants in the program, how often the participants attended, and how faithful the facilitators were to the *Making Proud Choices* curriculum.

STEP 8 (OUTCOME EVALUATION). Survey data were collected from program participants before and after the program, so that the group could track whether there were changes in the behaviors and determinants they intended to change (based on their goals and objectives in step 2).

Step 9 (CQI). The group then met to review and reflect on the previous eight steps they had already carried out. During this meeting, they talked about what aspects of the program had gone well and what areas could be improved.

Step 10 (SUSTAIN). Their successful experience with implementing *Making Proud Choices* led the group to decide to continue implementing the program as long as it fit with the needs of teens in their community. They explored funding sources to support the program. They looked for ways they could collaborate with other community organizations to increase the availability of science-based teen pregnancy prevention programs across the community.

Research and Development of GTO

Since 1999, we have been developing and implementing strategies and tools to enhance all 10 steps of GTO, with special attention to its capacity building component and with the overarching goal of producing desired outcomes (Wandersman, Chinman, Imm, & Kaftarian, 2000). Toward that end, we developed GTO manuals—"how-to" workbooks. They provide practitioners with the knowledge and tools used to perform each of the steps. GTO manuals have been developed in several content areas, including substance abuse prevention (Chinman, Imm, & Wandersman, 2004; Chinman et al., 2001; Wandersman, Imm, Chinman, & Kaftarian, 1999, 2000); positive youth development (Fisher, Imm, Chinman, & Wandersman, 2006); preventing underage drinking (Imm et al., 2006); teen pregnancy prevention (Lesesne et al., 2012); homeless veteran programs (Hannah, McCarthy, & Chinman, 2011), and home visiting programs (Mattox, Hunter, Kilburn, & Wiseman, 2013). We found, however, that providing manuals was necessary but not sufficient. To fully utilize GTO manuals, we have had to include key support components of training and technical assistance (e.g., Chinman et al., 2008; Lesesne et al., 2012).

Over the years, we realized that to achieve the full impact of the GTO model in building high-capacity programs, a more comprehensive approach was needed. Therefore, we included an evidence-based approach to supporting innovations (programs, policies, and practices that are new to an organization). The evidence-based system for innovation support (EBSIS) model uses a GTO frame to promote and categorize an accountability approach to four key support components: tools, training, technical assistance, and quality assurance/ quality improvement (Wandersman, Chien, & Katz, 2012).

EMPIRICAL RESULTS

Several studies have empirically studied the effects of using GTO (see Chinman, Acosta, Hunter, & Ebener, Chapter 15, this volume). For example, in a 2-year longitudinal trial funded by the Centers for Disease Control and Prevention (CDC), Chinman et al. (2008) tested the effectiveness of using GTO to improve prevention capacity and prevention programming of community coalitions. Results indicated significant improvements in staff capacity and program performance among programs that use GTO versus comparison programs. A dose-response relationship trend between GTO and improved capacity to engage in prevention activities was observed. In other words, greater exposure to GTO was associated with greater gains in prevention capacity, at the individual and program levels. In addition, programs that used GTO documented greater outcomes.

In a formative evaluation project, Chinman, Tremain, Imm, and Wandersman (2009) found that programs using iGTO (a web-based application of GTO) demonstrated an increase in the quality of performance of key prevention practices over non-iGTO programs. Chinman et al. (2013) presented interim findings from a randomized test of GTO called Assets-Getting To Outcomes (AGTO). This was a 2-year intervention to build prevention practitioners' capacity to implement positive youth development–oriented prevention practices in 12 prevention coalitions in Maine. The results show that opportunity to learn AGTO was not enough; that is, just being in the GTO intervention group was not sufficient. Those in the intervention group who used GTO improved their prevention capacity and the program quality (there was a dose-response relationship). (A more detailed description of these and other research projects on GTO is described in Chinman et al., Chapter 15, this volume.)

GTO IN PRACTICE

GTO is being used to help community-based organizations plan, implement, evaluate, use CQI, and sustain evidence-based programs. An example of the use of GTO is in a CDC-funded 2010–2015 initiative on teen pregnancy prevention called *Integrating Services, Programs, and Strategies Through Communitywide Initiatives: The President's Teen Pregnancy Prevention Initiative.* "The purpose of this program is to demonstrate the effectiveness of innovative, multicomponent, communitywide initiatives in reducing rates of teen pregnancy and births in communities with the highest rates, with a focus on reaching African American and Latino/Hispanic youth aged 15–19 years" (http://www.cdc.gov/ TeenPregnancy/PreventTeenPreg.htm). One of the five key components of this initiative (budgeted at over $50 million) is to implement evidence-based programs using the GTO process.

Several of the manuals (Chinman et al., 2004; Imm et al., 2007; Mattox et al., 2013) are available for free downloading from the RAND website http://www.rand.org/health/projects/getting-to-outcomes.html, and there have been over 100,000 downloads of the manuals. In the next section, the connections between GTO, evaluation capacity building, and accountability are discussed.

GTO AND EVALUATION CAPACITY BUILDING

Capacity building is one of the most important principles guiding empowerment evaluation practice. In their synthesis of the ECB literature, Labin, Duffy, Meyers, Wandersman, and Lesesne (2012) define evaluation capacity building (ECB) as "an intentional process to increase individual motivation, knowledge, and skills and to enhance a group or organization's ability to conduct or use evaluation" (p. 307). The assumption underlying ECB is that evaluation can lead to program improvement and greater outcomes (Clinton, 2014; Labin et al., 2012). Labin and colleagues (2012) presented an ECB logic model to guide their research synthesis (Figure 9.1). The logic model includes the need for ECB (including motivation and goals), the what and how of ECB (e.g., strategies, implementation, and evaluation of ECB), and the outcomes of ECB (individual, organizational, and program outcomes). Wandersman (2014) suggested that Labin et al.'s logic model can be reorganized into a "hands-on" practical approach to building ECB using the 10 GTO steps to plan, implement, evaluate, continuously quality improve, and sustain an ECB initiative (Figure 9.2). By following the 10 steps of GTO (similar to following GTO in the manuals), there is a pathway for planning, implementing, evaluating, improving, and sustaining ECB.

For example, if we are looking to build evaluation capacity in a specific community based organization, what are the needs for evaluation capacity and what are the resources? Given the needs and resources for evaluation capacity, what are the goals, desired outcomes, and target groups for evaluation capacity building? What best practices can be used to build ECB, and how do they fit with the current capacities and values of the target groups? What capacities are needed to do the ECB practices? What is the plan for providing ECB activities? How will implementation of the plan be monitored? What are the outcomes of the ECB efforts, how can continuous quality improvement of ECB occur, and how can ECB gains be sustained? One of the benefits of using GTO is as an accountability diagnostic. Figure 9.2 suggests that the ECB logic model doesn't clearly address step 3 (best practices—there is little evidence for ECB best practice strategies, and activities in step 6 are likely to be used), step 5 (the capacities involved to deliver ECB practices), or step 10 (sustaining ECB gains). GTO can provide valuable guidance for building accountable ECB approaches.

Figure 9.1   Integrative evaluation capacity building model*

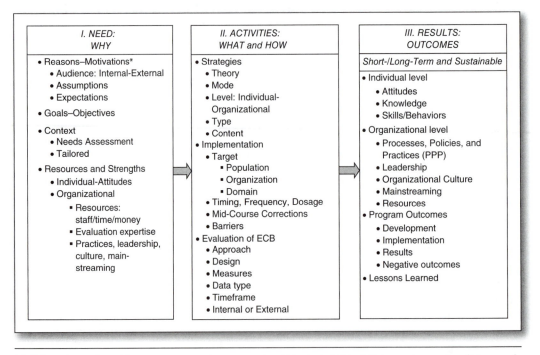

*Collaborative and participatory aspects and processes should be included in defining and operationalizing nearly all elements of the model.

Figure 9.2 GTO and the ECB Logic Model: Planning, Implementing, Evaluating, Improving and Sustaining ECB

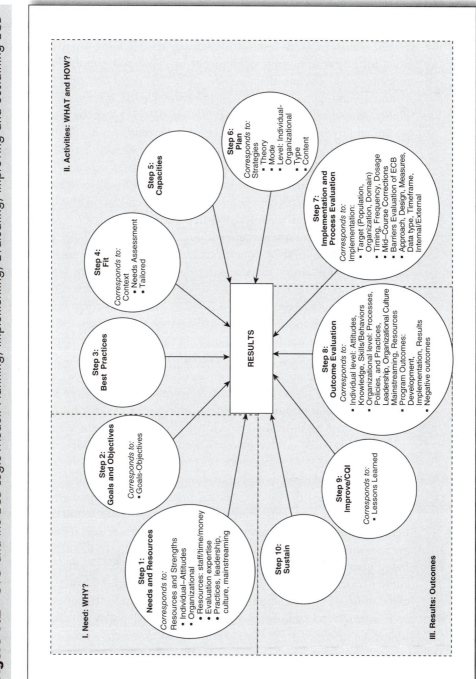

I. Need: WHY?

II. Activities: WHAT and HOW?

Step 1:
Needs and Resources
Corresponds to:
Resources and Strengths
  ▪ Individual–Attitudes
  ▪ Organizational
  ▪ Resources: staff/time/money
  ▪ Evaluation expertise
  ▪ Practices, leadership,
    culture, mainstreaming

Step 2:
Goals and Objectives
Corresponds to:
▪ Goals-Objectives

Step 3:
Best Practices

Step 4:
Fit
Corresponds to:
Context
  ▪ Needs Assessment
  ▪ Tailored

Step 5:
Capacities

Step 6:
Plan
Corresponds to:
Strategies
  ▪ Theory
  ▪ Mode
  ▪ Level: Individual-
    Organizational
  ▪ Type
  ▪ Content

Step 7:
**Implementation and
Process Evaluation**
Corresponds to:
Implementation:
  ▪ Target (Population,
    Organization, Domain)
  ▪ Timing, Frequency, Dosage
  ▪ Mid-Course Corrections
  ▪ Barriers Evaluation of ECB
  ▪ Approach, Design, Measures,
    Data type, Timeframe,
    Internal/External

RESULTS

Step 8:
Outcome Evaluation
Corresponds to:
  ▪ Individual level: Attitudes,
    Knowledge, Skills/Behaviors
  ▪ Organizational level: Processes,
    Policies, and Practices,
    Leadership, Organizational Culture
    Mainstreaming, Resources
  ▪ Program Outcomes:
    Development,
    Implementation, Results
  ▪ Negative outcomes

Step 9:
Improve/CQI
Corresponds to:
  ▪ Lessons Learned

Step 10:
Sustain

III. Results: Outcomes

159

GTO AND ACCOUNTABILITY ACROSS SYSTEMS

Often, multiple system levels are involved in addressing a particular problem area, for example, juvenile delinquency or childhood obesity. For example, in working with juvenile delinquency, there are programs and policies at the national, state, community, and organizational levels. It is easy to have accountability slippage between systems. We think GTO can be used to address accountability in each system. We graphically represent it in Table 9.2.

One way of using the table is to describe it as proposing a systematic accountability process that uses a standard approach (always uses the 10 steps) but is individualized for each situation (so it's not one size fits all). For example, if there is a problem in diabetes or in infant mortality or childhood obesity, the national level reports the overall country statistics. But we know that prevalence and incidence differ in different states and within a state (e.g., rural, inner city, suburban).

The GTO accountability questions are generic. The responses, however, can be different in different parts of the country or community. For example, the answers to question 1 (NEEDS/RESOURCES) about infant mortality will be different in a middle-class neighborhood in Manhattan compared with a lower income neighborhood in the Bronx. Therefore, answering questions 2 through 10 depends on the needs and resources in that particular system. The aim is to ensure that the process is individualized for that setting (i.e., it is customized and tailored to the needs and resources of each neighborhood). Additionally, it is important to address the interactive accountability between systems (across columns) to achieve outcomes. For example, in a health care clinic, a doctor may work with an individual patient who has been diagnosed with diabetes to develop goals based on that patient's needs and resources, identify an evidence-based practice that works best for the patient, evaluate the effectiveness of that best practice, and develop a plan for improving and sustaining the practice and outcomes. If a health clinic is treating many patients diagnosed with diabetes, the health clinic leadership may want to look for efficacy and efficiency practices that can be used for many diabetes patients; therefore, it conducts a needs and resource assessment and the staff collaboratively identify an evidence-based plan to purchase special equipment that will benefit the needs of many clinic patients with diabetes. GTO thinking can extend beyond the hospital or clinic to issues at the community, state, national, and international levels.

It is rarely possible for a higher system-level policy to affect individuals unless the intermediate systems are involved. A benefit of the GTO levels and accountability table is that it proposes that all systems are accountable and can have the same accountability language.

Table 9.2 GTO and Levels of Accountability

Accountability Question	Country	State	County	Agency/Organization	Provider	Client
1. NEEDS/RESOURCES						
2. GOALS						
3. EVIDENCE-BASED PRACTICES						
4. FIT						
5. CAPACITY						
6. PLAN						
7. IMPLEMENTATION/ PROCESS EVALUATION						
8. OUTCOME EVALUATION						
9. CQI						
10. SUSTAINABILITY						

CQI, Continuous quality implementation; GTO, Getting To Outcomes.

For example, the GTO approach to accountability is being used by the Philadelphia Department of Behavioral Health and Intellectual disAbility Services in the procurement and contracting processes of their $1 billion annual budget for public behavioral health system. The service provider contracts will reflect the department's commitment to evidence-based and outcome-driven priorities by using the 10 GTO steps in the contract, and the Department will be working with the service providers to help build their capacity to implement the 10 steps to achieve outcomes.

CONCLUSION

GTO represents a useful approach to facilitate a step-by-step process of planning, implementation, evaluation, CQI, and sustainability, using empowerment evaluation principles. Capacity building, accountability, and the achievement of outcomes are the most important components of this model, which are used nationally and internationally. Over the past two decades, there have been many success stories involving the use of GTO in developing and evaluating service programs. However, in the spirit of empowerment evaluation and CQI, GTO is continually being improved with the aim of helping people achieve desired outcomes based on a systematic set of actions. Additionally, we are working on deepening our work on each of the GTO steps (e.g., implementation science in step 7 on implementation/process evaluation; Meyers et al., 2012) and bringing GTO to additional content domains, including health care (Wandersman, Alia, Cook, & Ramaswamy, 2014).

In closing, the term accountability does not have to be relegated solely to whoever is to blame after a failure occurs (e.g., problems in the U.S. government's initial rollout of the health insurance website and Secretary Kathleen Sebelius's subsequent resignation or the Veterans Affairs scandal and subsequent resignation of Secretary Eric Shinseki). It actually makes sense to think that individuals and organizations should be proactive and strategic about their plans, implement the plans with quality, and evaluate whether or not the time and resources spent led to outcomes. It is logical to want to know why certain things are being done and others are not, what goals an organization is trying to achieve, that the activities are designed to achieve the goals, that a clear plan is put into place and carried out with quality, and that there be an evaluation to see if it worked. GTO was designed to provide funders, practitioners, and other key stakeholders with a results-based approach to accountability that helps them succeed.

REFERENCES

Chinman, M., Acosta, J., Ebener, P., Burkhart, Q., Clifford, M., Corsello, M., et al. (2013). Intervening with practitioners to improve the quality of prevention: One year findings from a randomized trial of Assets-Getting to Outcomes. *Journal of Primary Prevention, 34*(3), 173–191.

Chinman, M., Hunter, S. B., Ebener, P., Paddock, S. M., Stillman, L., Imm, P., et al. (2008). The Getting To Outcomes demonstration and evaluation: An illustration of the prevention support system. *American Journal of Community Psychology, 41*(3/4), 206–224.

Chinman, M., Imm, P., & Wandersman, A. (2004). *Getting To Outcomes*^{TM} *2004: Promoting accountability through methods and tools for planning, implementation, and evaluation* (Tech. Rep. No. TR101-CDC). Santa Monica, CA: RAND Corporation. Retrieved from http://www.rand.org/pubs/technical_reports/TR101.html

Chinman, M., Imm, P., Wandersman, A., Kaftarian, S. J., Neal, J., Pendleton, K. T., et al. (2001). Using the Getting To Outcomes (GTO) model in a statewide prevention initiative. *Health Promotion Practice, 2*(4), 302–309.

Chinman, M., Tremain, B., Imm, P., & Wandersman, A. (2009). Strengthening prevention performance using technology: A formative evaluation of interactive Getting To Outcomes. *American Journal of Orthopsychiatry, 79*(4), 469–481.

Fetterman, D., & Wandersman, A. (2005). *Empowerment evaluation principles in practice.* New York: Guilford Press.

Fisher, D., Imm, P., Chinman, M., & Wandersman, A. (2006). *Getting To Outcomes with developmental assets.* Minneapolis, MN: Search Institute.

Hannah, G., McCarthy, S., & Chinman, M. (2011). *Getting To Outcomes in services for homeless veterans: 10 steps for achieving accountability.* Philadelphia: National Center on Homelessness Among Veterans. Retrieved from http://www.va.gov/HOMELESS/NationalCenter_Additional_Information.asp

Imm, P., Chinman, M., Wandersman, A., Rosenbloom, D., Guckenburg, S., & Leis, R. (2006). *Preventing underage drinking: Using Getting To Outcomes*^{TM} *with the SAMHSA Strategic Prevention Framework to achieve results* (Tech. Rep. No. TR-403-SAMHSA). Santa Monica, CA: RAND Corporation. Retrieved from www.rand.org/pubs/technical_reports/TR403/

Labin, S., Duffy, J., Meyers, D., Wandersman, A., & Lesesne, C. (2012). A research synthesis of the evaluation capacity building literature. *American Journal of Evaluation, 33*(3), 307–338.

Lesesne, C. A., Lewis, K. M., Moore, C., Fisher, D., Green, D., & Wandersman, A. (2012). *Promoting science-based approaches to teen pregnancy prevention using Getting to Outcomes* [Draft 2007]. Atlanta, GA: Centers for Disease Control and Prevention.

Mattox, T., Hunter, S. B., Kilburn, M. R., & Wiseman, S. H. (2013). *Getting To Outcomes® for home visiting: How to plan, implement, and evaluate a program in your community to support parents and their young children* (Tech. Rep. No. TL-114-SNM). Santa Monica, CA: RAND Corporation.

Meyers, D. C., Katz, J., Chien, V., Wandersman, A., Scaccia, J. P., & Wright, A. (2012). Practical implementation science: Developing and piloting the Quality Implementation Tool. *American Journal of Community Psychology, 50*(3/4), 481–496.

Wandersman, A. (2014). Getting To Outcomes: An evaluation capacity building example of rationale, science, and practice. *American Journal of Evaluation, 35*(1), 100–106.

Wandersman, A., Alia, K., Cook, B., & Ramaswamy, R. (2014). *Empowerment evaluation, improvement science, and evidence-based interventions: Achieving outcomes in healthcare improvement*. Invited manuscript submitted for publication.

Wandersman, A., Chien, V., & Katz, J. (2012). Toward an evidence-based system for innovation support for implementing innovations with quality: Tools, training, technical assistance, and quality assurance/quality improvement. *American Journal of Community Psychology, 50*(3/4), 445–460.

Wandersman, A., Imm, P., Chinman, M., & Kaftarian, S. (1999). *Getting To Outcomes: Methods and tools for planning, self-evaluation and accountability*. Rockville, MD: Center for Substance Abuse Prevention.

Wandersman, A., Imm, P., Chinman, M., & Kaftarian, S. J. (2000). Getting To Outcomes: A results-based approach to accountability. *Evaluation and Program Planning, 23*(3), 389–395.

Wandersman, A., Snell-Johns, J., Lentz, B., Fetterman, D., Keener, D., Livet, M., et al. (2005). The principles of empowerment evaluation. In D. M. Fetterman & A. Wandersman (Eds.), *Empowerment evaluation principles in practice* (pp. 27–41). New York: Guilford Press.

CHAPTER 10

"No Excuses"

Using Empowerment Evaluation to Build Evaluation Capacity and Measure School Social Worker Effectiveness

Ivan Haskell

Mastery Charter Schools

Aidyn L. Iachini

University of South Carolina

Young people across the United States experience a number of challenges that influence their ability to attend school, engage in classroom learning, and achieve academic success (Adelman & Taylor, 2002). Significant risk factors for poor academic achievement include poverty, homelessness, unmet mental health needs, bullying and conflictual peer relationships, family discord, and neighborhood violence (Richman, Bowen, & Wooley, 2004). School mental health (SMH) programs and services are essential strategies to address these nonacademic barriers to student learning and to promote students' healthy development and success in school (Adelman & Taylor, 2002; Anderson-Butcher et al., 2010; Iachini, Dorr, & Anderson-Butcher, 2008).

School social workers serve critical roles within these SMH systems. A recently developed national practice model categorizes school social work practice according to three domains—promoting healthy learning environments, providing educationally important mental health services, and leveraging resources (Frey et al., 2012). Other models of school social work categorize social worker roles according to micro- or macro-level targets of change efforts (Frey & Dupper, 2005). Many school social workers work at both levels, providing services directly to students and families at the microlevel, and supporting school-wide systemic change and continuous improvement efforts (e.g., policy development, development of referral protocols) at the macrolevel. Depending on the school community, the roles and responsibilities of school social workers can vary greatly across these different targets and domains of practice.

Given this variability, many schools and researchers find it challenging to capture outcomes associated with school social work practice (Allen-Meares, Montgomery, & Kim, 2013; Daly et al., 2006). One common difficulty faced by school administrators is how to examine the impact of school social workers' mental health service provision with individual students. Because each student experiences unique challenges to learning, it is hard to identify a common measure (or set of measures) that applies in all cases. Without using common measures, it is difficult to aggregate data at the school or school-district levels to demonstrate the collective value of social workers' work with individual students. This in turn makes planning for school- or district-wide continuous improvement efforts problematic (Lyon, Borntrager, Nakamura, & Higa-McMillan, 2013).

These challenges require innovative solutions. These solutions are often best derived from the collective thinking of those involved in direct service provision, because they have to wrestle with the issue of how to measure their effectiveness on a daily basis. Empowerment evaluation offers a powerful approach for evaluating school social work programs. Empowerment evaluation is "an evaluation approach that aims to increase the likelihood that programs will achieve results by increasing the capacity of program stakeholders to plan, implement, and evaluate their own programs" (Fetterman & Wandersman, 2005, p. 27).

Empowerment evaluation involves moving through a three-step (Fetterman, 2007) or ten-step process (Chinman, Imm, & Wandersman, 2004). In the three-step empowerment evaluation model, the first step involves stakeholders identifying their collective mission and group values (i.e., "establishing the mission"); the second step involves prioritizing and identifying activities to achieve the group's mission, assessing their performance through ratings and/or group dialogue (i.e., "taking stock"); and the third step focuses on identifying goals and implementing related strategies, determining what type(s) of evidence will be needed to monitor impact, and monitoring implementation in order to foster continuous improvement (i.e., "planning for the future"; Fetterman, 2007). Empowerment evaluation is usually facilitated by an empowerment evaluator who helps to support and develop the evaluation capacity of stakeholders involved in the process (Fetterman, 2009; Fetterman, Deitz, & Gesundheit, 2010; Labin, Duffy, Meyers, Wandersman, & Lesesne, 2012). Evaluation capacity building (ECB) is defined as an "intentional process to increase individual motivation, knowledge, and skills, and to enhance a group or organization's ability to conduct or use evaluation" (Labin et al., 2012, p. 308).

The hallmark of an empowerment evaluation approach is a commitment to a set of 10 core principles throughout the evaluation process (Fetterman & Wandersman, 2005). These principles include:

- Improvement
- Community ownership
- Inclusion
- Democratic participation
- Social justice
- Community knowledge
- Evidence-based strategies
- Capacity building
- Organizational learning
- Accountability

Although empowerment evaluation has been used in a wide variety of service settings (e.g., community organizations and health service settings) and to examine a range of programs and issues (e.g., substance use prevention, HIV prevention, family support and functioning), relatively few studies have documented the use of empowerment evaluation within the context of schools (Miller & Campbell, 2006). Exceptions are found in the work of Levin (1996), Everhart and Wandersman (2000), and Fetterman (2005), who have published examples of empowerment evaluation applied within school settings.

The purpose of this chapter is to add to the emerging literature in this area and to share a case study of empowerment evaluation and ECB as it relates to an evaluation of a school social work program within one network of charter schools.

MASTERY CHARTER SCHOOLS BACKGROUND

Mastery Charter Schools (MCS), the site of this case study, is a network of high-performing charter schools in Philadelphia, PA. MCS started in 2001 with one school, now called the Mastery-Lenfest Campus, and expanded through the addition of three more schools between 2005 and 2009. The MCS network of schools now includes 15 schools, all within the city of Philadelphia. Twelve of the 15 schools were developed through what is commonly called a "school turnaround" model. For these schools, MCS acquired the buildings and the management of the schools from the School District of Philadelphia (SDP) and continued to serve as the neighborhood school for the students in those communities. The U.S. Department of Education describes this type of turnaround model, in which a new entity takes over an existing school, as a "school restart model" (U.S. Department of Education, 2009).

Beginning in the 2010–2011 school year, the SDP began a program called the Renaissance Initiative. Under this initiative, which has continued for 4 years, education management organizations and/or charter school operators have submitted proposals to take over management of neighborhood schools that have been underperforming as measured by a School Performance Index. These organizations agree to serve as the neighborhood school in perpetuity, by enrolling all current and future students drawn from the catchment areas surrounding the schools.

MCS has experienced substantial early successes at its full turnaround schools. At all of the schools that MCS opened under the SDP Renaissance Initiative, attendance has increased, student turnover has been reduced, violence has dropped, and academic performance (as measured by state exams) has improved, in some cases substantially (Mastery Charter Schools, 2013). On July 29, 2010, President Obama cited MCS as an example of school turnaround success in his speech to the National Urban League:

> There's a charter school called Mastery in Philadelphia. And in just two years, three of the schools that Mastery has taken over have seen reading and math levels nearly double—in some cases, triple . . . One school called Pickett went from just 14 percent of students being proficient in math to almost 70 percent. Now—and here's the kicker—at the same time academic performance improved, violence dropped by 80 percent—80 percent. And that's no coincidence. Now, if a school like Mastery can do it, if Pickett can do it, every troubled school can do it. But that means we're going to have to shake some things up. Setting high standards, common standards, empowering students to meet them; partnering with our teachers to achieve excellence in the classroom; educating our children—all of them—to graduate ready for college, ready for a career, ready to make most of their lives.

Together, MCS's 15 schools serve approximately 9,600 students. The great majority of MCS's schools are located in socioeconomically disadvantaged neighborhoods within Philadelphia. A total of 79% of the student population is eligible for free or reduced price lunch, and 88% of students are Black/African American. There also are high levels of risk exposure in the neighborhoods where MCS schools are located (Public Health Management Corporation et al., 2013). Of the 15 MCS schools, 6 are located within zip codes where

30.1% to 45% of adults report experiencing four or more adverse childhood experiences (ACEs), and 7 more of the schools are located within zip codes where more than 45.1% of adults reported four or more ACEs. ACEs have been shown to predict mental health problems, substance abuse, poor health, and early mortality (Felitti et al., 1998). These data suggest a much higher level of risk exposure than in the state of Pennsylvania as a whole, where only 13% of adults report exposure to four or more ACEs (Public Health Management Corporation et al., 2013).

Mastery Charter Schools Culture and Values

Together, the 15 MCS schools are guided by a set of core values and a "no excuses" culture. MCS's first and most important value is "Student Achievement—Above All." The desired outcome of any action taken at MCS is to be framed by staff and students in terms of how it ultimately contributes to student achievement. Another core value of MCS is continuous improvement. In MCS's teacher handbook and other school materials, this value is emphasized through statements such as "We seek a better way—always. We are engaged in an ongoing cycle of goal setting, action, measurement and analysis."

MCS's motto is "Excellence. No Excuses," which highlights its commitment to a no excuses philosophy toward urban education (Thernstrom & Thernstrom, 2003; Williams, 2002). Qualities of no excuses schools typically include a longer school day and a longer school year than most other schools, selective teacher hiring, strict behavior norms, and a pronounced emphasis on foundational reading and math skills (Angrist, Dynarski, Kane, Pathak, & Walters, 2012). In a no excuses culture, the belief is that staff members should look for ways to remove obstacles to student success, even if this means moving beyond one's usual mode of intervention and comfort zone.

MCS School Social Work Program

Currently, MCS employs at least one social worker at each of the schools in its network, and a number of schools employ two social workers. In MCS's earliest days, though, there were no social workers at all. As school personnel recognized the need to address student barriers to learning in order to promote academic achievement, MCS expanded its model for doing so by putting social workers in the forefront of providing these supports. At MCS, the school social workers hold a variety of responsibilities, which include supporting a caseload of students, serving as their school's homeless coordinator, handling behavioral health crises, developing and overseeing aftercare plans for students returning from residential treatment and inpatient hospitalization, making reports of suspected child abuse, and serving grieving students.

As the school social work program expanded at MCS, there was an identified need to employ someone at the network level that could help develop procedures and measurement strategies for the work of social workers, promote a climate of accountability, and focus on driving continuous improvement among school social work staff. This resulted in the creation of the director of social and psychological services (DSPS) position during the 2009–2010 school year, a position held by the first author of this chapter. From the perspective of the chief academic officer (CAO; now MCS's chief of schools), the DSPS position was created because there was no available method at the time to objectively determine how social workers were contributing to their schools. While anecdotal information supported the positive efforts of social workers, when principals were asked directly to comment on specific outcomes effected by social workers, they were usually unable to do so. At MCS, social work positions are funded based on the general school budget—not grant or externally funded. As full-time professionals not carrying a teaching load, social workers occupy positions that are fairly expensive. Therefore, the CAO felt that there needed to be additional "hard" evidence to justify continuing to fund them.

The DSPS was in an interesting position, since he had been hired to oversee the work of the social workers who had already been working at MCS and had developed, with the support of on-site supervisors, their own ways of prioritizing their work, had created their own forms, and were left to navigate issues of professional identity as social workers largely on their own. The next section of this chapter describes how the DSPS used an empowerment evaluation strategy to determine how best to measure and evaluate school social work effectiveness at MCS. The case study is organized by the three phases of empowerment evaluation.

EMPOWERMENT EVALUATION STEP 1: ESTABLISH THE MISSION

One of the first steps the DSPS took was to set up meetings with all of the existing social workers to interview them and learn about their current responsibilities and efforts. The DSPS also tried to achieve some "early wins" by responding to social workers' requests for form creation and research related to confidentiality and record keeping. During these meetings, the DSPS realized that while some overarching support for the implementation of a data collection and analysis process could be provided, the bulk of the ongoing work needed to be driven in large part by the social workers themselves. A primary consideration in making this decision was the knowledge that there were plans in place to substantially increase the number of schools and students served by MCS over the next 5 years (and therefore the number of social workers). However, there was no corresponding increase in infrastructure support planned for supporting social workers at the network level. As such, the DSPS and social workers identified that the primary mission was to create a decentralized evaluation system that could demonstrate the impact of school social work practice with individual students.

EMPOWERMENT EVALUATION STEP 2: TAKING STOCK

During the early conversations between the DSPS and social workers, the primary emphasis was on finding out which data collection strategies (if any) social workers had utilized and how social workers monitored student progress. In addition to these one-on-one conversations, the DSPS established monthly social work meetings, which have continued throughout the life of this project. A great deal of discussion at these early meetings was centered on how to measure school social workers' impact on individual student outcomes. Some of the themes that arose from these discussions were the following:

- While most social workers were looking at data periodically, the time periods varied. Some examined the data every week, while some looked at the data only on a monthly or report (marking) period basis (i.e., every 6 to 7 weeks).
- Due largely to requests from school administrators, social workers were primarily interested in examining data from MCS's school databases in three areas: attendance, school misbehavior, and academic performance. At most schools, this emphasis was part of an approach to serving at-risk students that had been passed down from MCS's initial schools. This approach to data tracking did not appear to have been developed in a collaborative way (e.g., as a joint decision-making process between social workers and their managers).
- Most social workers felt that measuring student progress through school records data had some limitations, including (1) some students did not have problems in all three areas; (2) sometimes progress was demonstrated in one or two areas, but not all three; (3) especially in the case of academic outcomes, social workers felt as though the reporting period and semester grades were probably too distal from their work to be

positively affected in some cases; and (4) for some students (e.g., for grieving students or students with a mood or anxiety disorders), none of the three types of metrics were particularly applicable.

- Social workers had not used global measures of student functioning (e.g., Strength and Difficulties Questionnaire [Goodman, 1997] or Achenbach System of Empirically Based Assessments [ASEBA; Achenbach, 2009; Achenbach & Rescorla, 2001]) in any systematic way. However, during the 2009–2010 school year, the school counselors/therapists, who were contracted employees working at MCS schools, had used the ASEBA to look at the outcomes of their student interventions. Despite students receiving about 30 to 45 minutes of counseling/therapy per week, and despite the significant investment involved in having students and teachers complete the ASEBA at three time intervals (at intake, at midyear, and at end of year), no consistent changes were noted on either the ASEBA Total Problems Scale, ASEBA internalizing subscale, or ASEBA externalizing subscale from the beginning until the end of the school year. In contrast, using Likert scale items, teacher and student survey ratings of these same therapists suggested that students had made progress on the problems that led to their referral to the counselors/therapists. Furthermore, feedback from the counselors/therapists (and social workers) pointed out that as a global measure, in most cases, the ASEBA did not tie directly in to the goals that they had set for their students.
- Social workers stated that any new data process should not involve a substantial amount of time spent collecting, scoring, entering, and analyzing data. Thus, whatever process was devised for examining outcomes, it had to be simple enough to be completed by the social workers without providing an undue time burden.

Selecting an Empowerment Evaluation Approach

Based on the feedback from social workers, the values of MCS, and considering the limited ability of the DSPS to run a large-scale outcome project on a continuing basis, the DSPS decided to employ an empowerment evaluation approach to outcome measurement for several reasons.

First and foremost, it was thought that using an empowerment evaluation approach would empower social workers to choose and take ownership of their own goals and outcomes. Furthermore, a benefit of using an empowerment evaluation approach (in comparison to a traditional evaluation approach) is that through ECB, social workers can learn to evaluate problems in a systematic manner and develop a feedback loop that contributes to continuous improvement (a core MCS value). At the outset of the project, there was also hope that social workers might eventually change the way they viewed many of the problems they encountered in their work—not just problems that caseload students brought to them, but dilemmas and concerns related to the many other tasks and responsibilities they engage in at MCS.

As noted earlier, use of a standardized global measure of emotional functioning (ASEBA) in a similar context at MCS had shown a lack of consistent results, despite significant effort spent collecting and analyzing data. Because empowerment evaluation is primarily concerned with finding ways that participants can demonstrate positive results, rather than with an academic exercise or idealized form of objectivity (Wandersman, Snell-Johns, Lentz, Fetterman, & Keener, 2005), a choice was made to forgo a centralized evaluation tool using a one-size-fits-all approach and instead to empower social workers to choose their own measures based on what they felt would provide the best fit. In addition, consistent with empowerment evaluation's focus on ECB, the hope was that over time, as social workers began to use and learn from the outcomes they derived, there would be less of a role for the DSPS—that ultimately, the project would become largely self-sustaining. Thus, the ultimate goal was for social workers to build their overall evaluation capacity, to learn for themselves what worked and what did not, and to modify their work over time to become more effective in producing real outcomes for their caseload students.

EMPOWERMENT EVALUATION STEP 3: PLAN FOR THE FUTURE

At the end of the second empowerment evaluation step, the DSPS had received a significant amount of information to sift through and incorporate in order to develop the goals of the project.

Goals

Ultimately, after considering the values of MCS as an organization and considering the need to empower social workers to buy in to any new evaluation tracking system, the following goals were decided on:

- Empowerment Evaluation Goal 1: To develop an objective caseload evaluation system that would produce the types of hard data that could meet the needs of MCS's decision makers and would justify the funding being spent on social workers

- Empowerment Evaluation Goal 2: To develop a caseload evaluation system that was flexible enough to adapt to the many different types of problems that students and school social workers worked on together
- Empowerment Evaluation Goal 3: To develop a caseload evaluation system that would maximize social-worker buy-in and empowerment
- Empowerment Evaluation Goal 4: To build the evaluation capacity of social workers so that a decentralized outcome-focused goal-setting process would be sustainable without an increase in centralized support

During the summer prior to the 2011–2012 school year, the DSPS devised a final plan to meet these goals. The plan was shared at an initial social work meeting at the beginning of the 2011–2012 school year, and is described next in more detail.

Strategy—Developing a Social Work Caseload Evaluation System

To meet the project goals outlined earlier, a caseload evaluation system needed to be developed for MCS social workers to set goals and monitor progress with their students. Development of this system required answering several questions through meetings and discussions between the DSPS and the social workers. Following are key questions and decisions made during this development process.

Who would be considered a student on a social worker's caseload?

Since social workers work with many students in the course of a given week or month, one of the initial questions raised by social workers was how they should determine which students should be included in the goal-setting process. For example, social workers are given the task of supporting (and acting as the school's liaison for) homeless students and providing support for students who have lost a close family member. Their support for these students may be transitory (e.g., one to two meetings over a 2-week span to assess and provide support for a grieving child) or may occur sporadically over a several week or month period (e.g., for a student who has involvement with the county children and youth agency).

After receiving feedback from social workers at a monthly social work meeting, a decision was made that caseload students should include any students in the following categories: (1) at-risk students assigned to the social worker's caseload as part of the school's student support and intervention process; (2) students seen by social workers for weekly counseling as mandated by the student's Individualized Education Plan (IEP); and/or (3) students with whom the social worker has regular contact at least once every 2 weeks for 6 weeks or longer.

How often would social workers collect data?

At the time that the project was first implemented, MCS's school year was divided into six reporting periods of about 6 to 7 weeks each. As such, the determination was made that goal cycles should coincide with every two report periods (i.e., in roughly 12-week cycles). As of the 2013–2014 school year, MCS moved to a four-report-period calendar and goals are now set four times per year (in 9- to 10-week cycles).

Where would social workers keep track of these data?

Before the DSPS was hired, some of the school social workers utilized a spreadsheet system to keep track of their work with individual students. It was decided that it would be best to continue utilizing this data tracking strategy, but to simplify the tracking spreadsheet to enhance ease of use. The spreadsheet was designed to serve both as a repository of data and as a tool to help structure social workers' goal setting, data collection, and data reporting. The columns included in the tracking spreadsheet are described in Table 10.1.

When and how would goals be set with individual students?

General guidelines for choosing goals were discussed with social workers at the outset of the project and the DSPS provided one-on-one support for all social workers during the first goal cycle. Social workers could choose a wide variety of goals, as long as they could be measured objectively. A general recommendation was made that goals should be set within the first 2 to 3 weeks of each goal cycle, as goals set earlier in the cycle would allow social workers more time for intervention with their students. After some time, documentation indicated that some social workers were not setting goals until fairly late in the goal cycle. This was negatively impacting their ability to meet their goals with individual students. Therefore, starting at the beginning of the second project year, there was a requirement that social workers had to submit their

Table 10.1 Caseload Evaluation System Tracking Spreadsheet Column Names and Descriptions

Metric Spreadsheet Column	Column Description
Student Name or Initials	
Current Status	Social workers chose the student's current status from a drop-down list (e.g., currently enrolled, in placement, etc.). An outcome metric was not required for non-active students.
On Intern Caseload?	Some social workers had master's-level social work interns work with some of the students on their caseload. Interns' success contributed to each social worker's individual goal attainment rating.
Start Date of Service	The date that the social worker started working with the student as a caseload student was noted, even if it was during a previous school year.
End Date of Period Assessed	The end date of the current goal-setting cycle was noted. This date was the same for all caseload students, but was updated each time a new goal cycle ended.
# of Days of Service	The number of days that students were receiving social work intervention was automatically calculated using a spreadsheet formula. If the number of days was less than 42 (i.e., 6 weeks), the goal(s) for that student was not part of the % of goals met statistic.
Closing Date	A closing date of service triggered the DSPS to not include the particular student's goal(s) in the analysis of whether 70% of goals were met.
The following columns were completed for EACH GOAL (up to 3 per student)	
Problem Name	Social workers chose from a drop-down list. A list of social work problems was generated based on a survey of social workers during the 2010–2011 school year. Social workers picked the best match from the list or "other."
Metric Name	Social workers entered a short name for their chosen metric, such as "Grades", "Level 2s", "Teacher Rating Scale", etc. If social workers used an already available measure (e.g., Abbreviated Social Skills Rating Scale), they entered the full name of the measure.
Metric Type	Social workers chose the type of metric from a drop-down list (e.g., general number; Likert scale). There were also five different rates that could be chosen (e.g., rate per week, rate per month, etc.).

Metric Spreadsheet Column	Column Description
Desired Change	Social workers chose "Increase" or "Decrease" from the drop-down list based on whether they were focused on reducing the problem or negative metrics or increasing positive metrics. Choosing either "Increase" or "Decrease" affected the color formatting of the outcome column.
Notes on Metric	The "Notes on Metric" column included enough detail so that the DSPS could interpret each goal/metric solely from the information included in the spreadsheet. The required parameters included: • A description of what the goal or metric meant (if it was not clear from the metric name or metric type). For example, if the metric Name was "Teacher Rating Scale", this section included a description of the scale (e.g., "10-point scale rating intensity for off-task behavior"). • The sources from which the data were derived (e.g., "Score is average of rating scales from teachers for all four major academic subjects"). • Information pertaining to when the baseline and outcome data were collected and/or the period covered by the data (e.g., "# of Level II's first 4 weeks of RP1 compared to # of Level II's last 4 weeks of RP2").
Baseline	Numerical baseline data were included here. For caseload students who had been included for at least one reporting cycle (and for which the goal/metric stayed the same), the baseline was typically the outcome number from the previous RP2 cycle.
Goal	Social workers noted the numerical goal they set for the student in this column. This number represented the bar that students needed to meet in order for the goal to be met.
Outcome	The final outcome number was included here. The spreadsheet was set up so that the cell would turn red if the goal was not reached and green if it was.

DSPS, Director of social and psychological services; *RP*, report period.

goal spreadsheets after the first or second week of the goal cycle to demonstrate that goals had been set for their caseload students. It is also important to note that weekly tracking of goals (which some social workers had been required to do in previous years) was not required as part of this process. This decision was made in part to minimize the administrative burden on social workers of collecting and reporting weekly data and also to allow for metrics where weekly progress was unlikely.

The goal-setting guidelines and parameters related to this process have continued to be refined and are now included in MCS's social worker manual (initially developed during the second half of the 2011–2012 school year). An example of a goal-setting guideline derived from social workers' experiences is that dichotomous metrics should generally be avoided. This guideline arose because social workers found that even if a student is generally improving and is on track to meet the goal, "one bad day" can lead to a failure to meet the goal.

What measurement tools would the social workers use to measure student goals?

At the beginning of implementation of this new caseload evaluation system, the DSPS believed that social workers would primarily use student records data (e.g., grades, behavioral incidences, absences) to track student progress, and that when student records data were not chosen, social workers would create simple rating scale measures or would search for and identify other measures for specific problems. Social worker feedback during the first few weeks of the project indicated that this idea needed to be reconsidered. Social workers were concerned about their ability and expertise to create measures on their own or to identify existing measures that were applicable for specific student problems.

Therefore, during the first goal cycle, the DSPS researched and compiled a list of measures that could be used for a majority of concerns or problems that were the focus of social work intervention. The list of measures has grown over time and now includes about 75 measures for 40 different problems. It is sorted alphabetically by topic (e.g., social skills) so that social workers can browse the measures by problem or goal type. Additional information for each measure includes measure name; recommended age or grade ranges (when available); whether the measure is youth self-report or completed by the parent or teacher; length of the measure; whether the measure is in the public domain; and brief notes on scoring or interpretation. Many of the listed measures came from a compendium of measures assembled by Dahlberg, Toal, Swahn, and Behrens (2005). The DSPS also created a sample teacher rating scale with different possible Likert scale ratings that could be adapted and used by the social workers.

What types of problems would social workers target and what methods of interventions would they use?

Because social workers work with students with a number of presenting concerns, no predefined methods of intervention were required. The DSPS encouraged social workers to use empirically supported treatments whenever possible, but the primary focus was on empowering social workers to choose their own interventions and on letting outcomes drive the process. Social workers were given the option of including between one and three goals per caseload student on the tracking spreadsheet.

It should be pointed out that individual counseling and therapy interventions were not necessarily the primary intervention methods used to support student success. For example, for a student who tended to get into the most trouble in one or two classes—a trend that can be discerned from examining school discipline data—intervening with the teacher was an intervention that was often chosen.

Given the variability across social workers, the tracking spreadsheet allowed for social workers to track specific identified target client problems, individual goals, and baseline and outcome data. Specifically, the tracking spreadsheet included a drop-down list from which social workers were able to choose a problem or concern. The list of problems was created by conducting a survey of social workers during the taking stock portion of this project. In a subsequent spreadsheet column, social workers were then asked to choose a more specific goal name.

How would "success" be defined?

During this step of the process, the DSPS worked with the CAO to discuss a benchmark that would be realistic for social workers in terms of the percentage of students on their caseload who might be expected to reach their goals. Ultimately, a decision was made that social workers would be expected to meet 70% of the goals they set during each goal cycle. Although this number was fairly arbitrary, MCS believes in setting a high bar for staff and student success. In fact, an even higher bar was considered—set at 80%—but it was ultimately determined by the DSPS and CAO that this bar might prove too difficult to reach. There was some discussion that if results were much higher or much lower, the 70% expectation could be adjusted at a later date.

For each student, social workers were then faced with the task of determining how difficult to make their goals (i.e., how to choose the numerical target that needed to be reached in order for the goal to be considered met for that student). Consideration was given to recommending a default level of change (i.e., a 50% increase or decrease) but the ultimate decision was to let social workers choose the difficulty level of the goals themselves. Because no absolute numerical target needed to be met, social workers were encouraged to think about what would be a clinical or functional level of improvement for the student and what would be a realistic amount of change that could be expected during the goal cycle. It also is important to note that the design of the tracking spreadsheet helped to provide visual progress to social workers about individual students' progress toward meeting their goals. After social workers completed the "outcome" column in the spreadsheet at the end of each goal cycle, the cell turned either red or green, depending on whether the proposed goal was met.

At the collective level, the DSPS needed to devise a way to track whether social workers were setting numerical goals that were easier, more difficult, or similar to other social workers. Social workers also needed a way to examine their own performance in light of the difficulty level they had chosen. As such, the DSPS calculated the overall difficulty level of social workers' goals at the end of each goal cycle using the following formula: *([absolute value [baseline—goal set]/baseline] × 100)*. The formula compared the total sum of all the social workers' baselines with the total sum of all of their projected outcomes.

Monitoring Progress

Table 10.2 contains descriptive data from the first 2 years of the project. Despite the fact that social workers were able to choose between one and three goals for each student, the vast majority of caseload students had only one goal set for them (95.4% and 94.3% in Years 1 and 2, respectively). On average, social workers' results were very close to the 70% rate of goal attainment that was the predetermined measure of social work success. This is quite high when compared to the effects of "mental health" interventions on academic outcomes noted in the literature (Hoagwood et al., 2007; Lyon, Borntrager, Nakamura, & Higa-McMillan, 2013; Michael et al., 2013; Pullman, Weathers, Hensley, & Bruns, 2013). One likely reason for this is that social workers did not confine their primary mode of intervention to therapy or counseling, as is the case in most other reported studies. In fact, MCS social workers often used similar intervention strategies as the mentors in the "Check and Connect" program (such as contracting for school attendance), which has been found to positively impact attendance and school persistence (Christenson, Stout, & Pohl, 2012; Sinclair, Christenson, & Thurlow, 2005). Another reason could be the ability of social workers in this project to choose a measure that fit their students' needs, rather than a one-size-fits-all model where students are assessed using the same measure.

Table 10.2 also lists the average difficulty levels (% change set) for two categories of goals—increase goals (i.e., goals in which a social worker worked with a student to increase a measure of positive functioning) and decrease goals (i.e., goals in which a social worker worked with a student to decrease a measure of poor functioning). Goal difficulty level (average % change) was highest during the initial goal cycle of the 2012–2013 school year (23% for increase goals and 40% for decrease goals). Not surprisingly, the first goal cycle also had the lowest percentage of social worker goals met (68%). These data indicate that social workers chose to set numeric targets somewhat lower in subsequent goal cycles. Doing so could have had the effect of boosting their number of goals met and helping them meet or surpass the 70% goal attainment benchmark. Goal difficulty level should be viewed in light of the fairly short goal cycles (about 12 to 13 weeks).

For each goal cycle, the average difficulty level set by social workers for increase goals was lower than for decrease goals. It is not clear why this is the case. One possibility is that there were a higher number of self-report or teacher rating scales (e.g., Abbreviated Social Skills Rating Scale) included as increase goals, whereas decrease goals tended to focus more on student data, such as disciplinary incidents. In general, rating scales seemed to be less amenable to change than student data measures, especially over the 12- to 13-week goal cycle time frames.

After each goal cycle, the DSPS analyzed each social worker's spreadsheet and summarized the data in an Excel spreadsheet table. Table 10.3 is an example of what the data looked like—it includes selected data from the first goal cycle of the 2012–2013 school year. (Note that the averages included in the table are based on a subset of the total data for that cycle. For this reason, they are not representative of the entire set of data from that goal cycle). The spreadsheet was accompanied by a document explaining how to interpret the data. This information is reproduced in Table 10.4.

Originally, these results were shared only with social workers and their supervisors during monthly social worker meetings and via e-mail. During the second year of the project, the data were also distributed via e-mail to principals and principal supervisors. Sharing the data with supervisors and principals helped the project gain traction. At first, supervisors were not used to discussing individual student goals and/or did not put a lot of weight into the process of goal setting and analysis. It took some time—well into Year 2 of the project— but eventually supervisors' and administrators' ability to understand and utilize these data became apparent.

Table 10.2 Descriptive Data From the First Two Years of the Caseload Evaluation System at MCS

Goal Cycle	# of Social Workers	Total Goals Set	Avg. % Change Set (Increase Goals Difficulty)	Avg. % Change Set (Decrease Goals Difficulty)	Avg. Goals per SW	% of Goals Met	% Goals Drawn From MCS Student Records
RP* 1 & 2 2011–2012	14	250	23%	40%	16	68%	74%
RP 3 & 4 2011–2012	14	283	12%	38%	20	66%	75%
RP 5 & 6 2011–2012	14	245	14%	33%	18	73%	77%
All of 2011–2012	14	778	15%	37%	56	70%	75%
RP 1 & 2 2012–2013	16	264	17%	28%	17	71%	64%
RP 3 & 4 2012–2013	17	315	13%	28%	19	72%	73%
RP 5 & 6 2012–2013	17	326	11%	24%	19	73%	84%
All of 2012–2013	17	905	13%	27%	53	71%	74%

MCS, Mastery Charter Schools; *RP*, reporting period; *SW*, social worker.

Table 10.3 Example of Post-Goal Cycle Feedback Provided to Social Workers and Supervisors

# SW	Grades	% Goals Met 1 & 2*	# Caseload Clients ≥ 6 weeks	# Caseload Clients Whole Year	# Goals Set	# Goals Met	# Increase Goals	# Decrease Goals	% Decrease Goals	Increase Baseline	Increase Goal Set	Overall % Increase Set	Decrease Baseline	Decrease Goal Set	Overall % Decrease Set	eSchool Data	Other Data	% eSchool Data
1	ES	80%	10	13	10	8	1	9	90%	10	15	50%	134	93	30%	6	4	60%
2	MS-HS	40%	15	17	15	6	9	6	40%	66	75	14%	50	25	50%	15	0	100%
3	ES	85%	17	19	26	22	1	21	81%	30	50	67%	207	163	21%	26	0	100%
4	MS-HS	69%	13	18	13	9	1	12	92%	30	40	33%	74	58	22%	10	3	77%
Group Avg.		69%	14	17	16	11	3	12	80%	34	45	32%	116	85	27%	14	2	84%

* In the original spreadsheet, the cells in this column were color coded: cells below 50% were colored red, 50%–59% were colored orange, 60%–65% were colored yellow, 66%–69% were colored light green, and 70% or greater were colored dark green.

ES, Elementary school, *MS-HS*, middle school–high school; *SW*, social worker.

Table 10.4 Explanation of Post–Goal Cycle Feedback

Spreadsheet Column	Description
SW #	SWs are assigned ID numbers to be able to provide schools with comparison feedback without identifying other schools' SWs.
Grades Served	Included in order to provide a reference for comparing metrics among SWs.
% Goals Met for Most Recent Data Cycle	Statistic calculated by dividing the number of goals met by the number of goals set for the most recent data cycle. Cell color is based on percentage of goals met; dark green, above 70%; light green, 65%–69%; yellow, 60%–69%; orange, 50%–59%; and red, below 50%.
# Caseload Clients $\geq$ 6 weeks	Only students who have worked with the social worker for 6 weeks or longer *during the current goals cycle* count toward outcome metrics.
# of Caseload Clients Whole Year	The SW metrics spreadsheet is cumulative. This number is the cumulative number of caseload students included on the spreadsheet for the current school year.
# Goals Set	At least one goal needs to be included on the spreadsheet for each student. SWs can choose to include more than one goal per student if they want.
# Goals Met for Most Recent Data Cycle	Number of outcome metrics meeting or exceeding the goals set by the SW during the most recent data cycle.
# of Increase Goals	SWs can choose to work with students to increase a positive metric (e.g., number of classes passed) or reduce a problem or negative metric (e.g., number of classes failed). This statistic represents the number of "Increase" goals set by the SWs.
# of Decrease Goals	The number of goals based on problem behaviors that were set to "decrease" by the SWs.
% Decrease Goals	% of total goals that are set to decrease (# of Decrease Goals divided by # of Goals Set)
Increase Baseline	This statistic was developed by adding together the entire baseline scores for the goals that the SW set to increase. Because goals of different types were combined, it is likely to be skewed in situations in which the SW did not have a lot of Increase goals or where different types of metrics that use larger numbers (e.g., semester grades) are combined with smaller numbers (e.g., a scale that ranges from 1–5, etc.).

Spreadsheet Column	Description
Increase Goal Set	This statistic was developed by adding together all of the goals set by the SW for increase goals.
Overall % Increase Set	For the goals/metrics spreadsheet, SWs determine the bar for students needed to meet their goals on a case-by-case basis. The "Overall % Increase Set" statistic is a percent change score based on a comparison of their total set of baseline scores with the total set of their goal scores *for Increase Goals only*. In other words, if the sum of the SW's baseline score for Increase Goals is 100 and the sum of Increase Goal scores is 150, on average, the SW's students would be required to increase by 50% to cumulatively meet their goals. On average, increase change scores set by SWs tend to be lower than decrease change scores.
Decrease Baseline	Same description as for "Increase Baseline" except for Decrease Goals instead of Increase Goals.
Decrease Goal Set	Same description as for "Increase Goal Set" except for Decrease Goals instead of Increase Goals.
Overall % Decrease Set	Same description as for "Overall % Increase Set" except for Decrease Goals instead of Increase Goals.
School Records Data	Number of metrics that are based on MCS school records data, such as grades; failed credits; Level 1s; Level 2s; absences or tardies, etc.
Other Data	Number of metrics that are not based on MCS school records data. These include already available measures of certain problems or strengths that SWs asked teachers or students to complete as well as SW-created teacher rating scales.
MCS School Records Data	The percentage of goals that are based on MCS student database data.

MCS, Mastery Charter Schools; *SW*, social worker.

DISCUSSION

Through development, implementation, and evaluation of this caseload evaluation system in MCS, many lessons have been learned. First, we examined the extent to which each of the project goals identified during the third empowerment evaluation step were met. Then, we discussed overall lessons learned while trying to achieve those goals.

Empowerment Evaluation Goal 1: To develop a more objective caseload evaluation system that would produce the types of hard data that could meet the needs of MCS's decision makers and would justify the funding being spent on social workers

Since the project start, MCS has increased the presence of social workers at its schools, even though per student reimbursement has dropped during the same period. During the 2010–2011 school year, MCS served 4,171 students and employed seven social workers—a ratio of 595 students per social worker. As of the 2013–2014 school year, MCS serves 9,626 students and employs 21 social workers—a ratio of 458 students per social worker. In fact, many MCS schools have added a second social worker during the term of this project. That social workers have been added at MCS during a time of declining funding appears to reflect this project's ability to generate evidence of social worker impact.

The goal of this project was not to generate data that might meet the rigorous standards required for publication, but instead to provide a real-world, flexible, and manageable way to get information about goals and outcomes. And yet, the data generated needed to be of sufficient quality to provide evidence of social worker effectiveness. As implemented, the caseload evaluation system clearly leaves room for measurement error and bias in reporting. For example, social workers could give a "boost" to their results by changing the type of goal or numerical target between the beginning of the goal cycle and the end of the goal cycle. Or, they could choose not to include all students who meet the definition of caseload students on the spreadsheet. The potential for diminished objectivity of an empowerment evaluation approach has in fact been noted (Wandersman et al., 2005). However, even at MCS, with a strong commitment to hard data, the benefits of an empowerment evaluation approach generated good enough data to outweigh the possible ways in which the goals could be manipulated if social workers chose to do so.

Empowerment Evaluation Goal 2: To develop a flexible system to support progress monitoring for the many different types of student-presenting concerns

A major theme that appeared during the "taking stock" step of empowerment evaluation was that social workers were interested in ways of measuring progress that did not rely exclusively on school records data (academics, behavior, and attendance/lateness). In the end, roughly 75% of student goals during the first 2 years of the project were based on student records data, but

25% were not. Of those 25%, various measures were used, including a number of teacher and student self-rating scales, as well as measures created by social workers (e.g., number of self-reported days abstinent from drug use). Overall, social workers reported that they were satisfied with the flexibility of the case-load evaluation system because it allowed them to choose measures that truly fit the presenting concerns and problems of their students.

And yet, the freedom to choose their own measures meant that social workers had to spend a lot more time and effort seriously considering what types of measures they wanted to use, compared to using one required global measure or measures that had been chosen for them ahead of time. Of course, spending time thinking about goals has a secondary benefit of focusing the social workers' thinking on how they are going to help the student achieve them, which likely helps them to improve the effectiveness of their interventions.

The caseload evaluation system described in this chapter also relies on the concept of continuous improvement. However, the need for continuous improvement can be problematic in situations in which students for whom goals have been met continue to stay on the social worker's caseload. When numerical outcome targets continue to be set higher for each subsequent goal cycle, there eventually comes a point when each student will hit a ceiling level of improvement. Theoretically, continued improvement should result in discharge of the student from the social worker's caseload. However, in reality, it is not so simple because students, parents, administrators, and social workers are often hesitant to discharge students from social workers' caseloads as soon as they start to do well.

Empowerment Evaluation Goal 3: To develop a system that would maximize social worker buy-in and empowerment

Social worker buy-in to the goal-setting system was generally good. A factor that may have contributed to this was that social workers were already aware of MCS's data orientation when they were hired. In other words, there was a degree of "readiness" at the outset of the project because social workers understood that some type of measurement of their work was a given. Furthermore, in subsequent school years (2011–2012 and 2012–2013), when the DSPS hired the social workers, openness toward social worker accountability for student outcomes was a contributing factor to their selection. Social workers also appreciated the use of an empowerment evaluation approach because they were asked to only set goals they thought were within their locus of control.

The current project is unique in that it marries an empowerment evaluation approach with a high-stakes, performance-based culture. In fact, social workers' goal attainment has implications for their employment status—their goal attainment results contribute to about one third of their end-of-year performance evaluations. Furthermore, all contracts at MCS are renewed annually based in part on the previous year's performance. In some ways, an empowerment evaluation approach is perfect for a high-stakes environment such as this, because it puts more control in the hands of those being evaluated than in a traditional evaluation system. It should be pointed out that in all cases so far, social workers who have participated in the caseload evaluation system have had their contracts renewed the subsequent school year.

Empowerment Evaluation Goal 4: To build the evaluation capacity of social workers so that a decentralized outcome-focused goal-setting process would be sustainable without an increase in centralized support

Overall, for social workers who had been through several goal-setting cycles, little technical assistance and support from the DSPS was needed other than calendar invite reminders to set goals. For these social workers, it was apparent that there was a clear increase in their evaluation capacity, and thus the goal-setting process became largely self-sustaining. However, for new social workers and for the few social workers who required additional support, there is still a significant role for the DSPS. Because there have been between two and four new social workers every year since the project began, the DSPS has had to spend significant time building the capacity of these new social workers to utilize this system.

KEY LESSONS LEARNED AND TARGETS FOR EVALUATION CAPACITY BUILDING

ECB is a core tenet of empowerment evaluation (Fetterman & Wandersman, 2005; Labin et al., 2012). This project demonstrated that there was fairly significant variation in the amount of support required to successfully build the capacity of social workers. Some social workers understood the goal-setting and data collection process well at the outset of the project and were able to utilize the system with little additional support. Other social workers required more substantial support in order to set goals.

One important lesson learned through this project is that the role of the DSPS as an evaluator was essential for project success. This person not only serves as a "salesperson" to enhance buy-in to the new caseload evaluation system, but also serves as a technical support provider, critical friend (Fetterman, 2007, 2009), and consultant for individual social workers as they try to navigate and learn the system. Others implementing evaluation systems like this should strongly consider identifying someone to serve in this role.

Another lesson learned through this project was that targeted capacity building and infrastructure support were needed to both design and improve the utility of the caseload evaluation system for social workers (Lyon et al., 2013). Over the 2 years of the project, the DSPS was able to discern a number of pitfalls that prevented social workers from meeting their goals. These included:

- *Spending time identifying the student problem and setting realistic student goals:* Social workers learned that failing to spend time during the assessment period to select goals that fit students' presenting concerns, are within the social workers' locus of control, and are amenable and sensitive to change efforts can result in poor outcomes at the end of the cycle.
- *Identifying appropriate interventions to help students improve over time:* In most cases, defining effective interventions required a good understanding of the root causes of the problem. In some situations, discussions with social workers suggested that they did not have a good theory or set of ideas about causes. This often led to ineffective or inconsistent interventions—and a lack of goal attainment. At other times, social workers defaulted to individual therapy approaches in situations in which working with a teacher or parent would likely have been more impactful.
- *Allowing sufficient time to provide intervention:* Social workers at MCS are very busy. It is easy for other pressing tasks to take up social workers' time and prevent them from spending sufficient time on interventions with caseload students.
- *Identifying an appropriate measurement strategy to measure student progress:* Social workers sometimes chose measures that were not a good fit for the problem that the student was dealing with. In other cases, they chose measures where the student scored well at baseline, leaving little room for improvement.
- *Continuously monitoring student improvement:* Some social workers did not realize that a student did not meet their goal until it was too late to change intervention strategies. In fact, Bickman, Kelley, Breda, de Andrade, and Riemer (2011) found that weekly feedback on goal progress is more effective than less frequent feedback in improving therapist goal attainment.

Identification of these key targets for ECB has been important, particularly as it has helped to guide and shape training and technical assistance provided to new social workers. For example, starting in the 2012–2013 school year, the DSPS began to meet with current social workers and their on-site supervisors if they did not meet the 70% benchmark in a given reporting period. The frequency and content of these meetings is determined based on a number of factors, such as how close the social worker was to meeting the 70% threshold. In all cases so far, with this additional support (and likely the extra focus from the social worker's on-site supervisor), social workers have been able to substantially increase their performance in the subsequent goal cycle. These key targets and ECB strategies are important for others to consider when designing similar evaluation systems.

CONCLUSION

This project was unique in that it attempted to marry a no excuses, high-stakes, and performance-oriented culture with an empowerment evaluation approach. The focus was both on understanding the impact of school social work services on youth at MCS and on improving social work practitioners' evaluation capacity in order to improve the effectiveness of their work with individual students. At MCS, social workers were actively engaged in the design of the system, encouraged to take ownership of the goal-setting process, and ultimately empowered as they continue to monitor the services they provide so that all students have the opportunity to achieve academic success.

REFERENCES

Achenbach, T. M. (2009). *The Achenbach system of empirically based assessment (ASEBA): Development, findings, theory, and applications.* Burlington: University of Vermont Research Center for Children, Youth and Families.

Achenbach, T. M., & Rescorla, L. A. (2001). *Manual for the ASEBA School-Age Forms & Profiles.* Burlington, VT: University of Vermont, Research Center for Children, Youth, & Families.

Adelman, H. S., & Taylor, L. (2002). Building comprehensive, multifaceted, and integrated approaches to address barriers to student learning. *Childhood Education, 78*(5), 261–268.

Allen-Meares, P., Montgomery, K. L., & Kim, J. S. (2013). School-based social work interventions: A cross-national systematic review. *Social Work, 58*(3), 253–262.

Anderson-Butcher, D., Lawson, H., Iachini, A. L., Flaspohler, P., Bean, J., & Wade-Mdivanian, R. (2010). Emergent evidence in support of a community collaboration model for school improvement. *Children & Schools, 32*(3), 160–171.

Angrist, J. D., Dynarski, S. M., Kane, T. J., Pathak, P. A., & Walters, C.R. (2012). Who benefits from KIPP? *Journal of Policy Analysis and Management, 31*(4), 837–860.

Bickman, L., Kelley, S. D., Breda, C., de Andrade, A. R., & Riemer, M. (2011). Effects of routine feedback to clinicians on mental health outcomes of youths: Results of a randomized trial. *Psychiatric Services, 62,* 1423–1429.

Christenson, S. L., Stout, K., & Pohl, A. (2012). *Check & Connect: A comprehensive student engagement intervention: Implementing with fidelity.* Minneapolis: University of Minnesota, Institute on Community Integration.

Dahlberg, L. L., Toal, S. B, Swahn, M., & Behrens, C. B. (2005). *Measuring violence-related attitudes, behaviors, and influences among youths: A compendium of assessment tools* (2nd ed.). Atlanta, GA: Centers for Disease Control and Prevention, National Center for Injury Prevention and Control.

Daly, B. P., Burke, R., Hare, I., Mills, C., Owens, C., Moore, E., et al. (2006). Enhancing No Child Left Behind–school mental health connections. *Journal of School Health, 76,* 446–451.

Everhart, K., & Wandersman, A. (2000). Applying comprehensive quality programming and empowerment evaluation to reduce implementation barriers. *Journal of Educational & Psychological Consultation, 11*(2), 177–191.

Felitti, V. J., Anda, R. F., Nordenberg, D., Williamson, D. F., Spitz, A. M., Edwards, V., et al. (1998). Relationship of childhood abuse and household dysfunction to many of the leading causes of death in adults: The Adverse Childhood Experiences (ACE) study. *American Journal of Preventive Medicine, 14*(4), 245–258.

Fetterman, D. M. (2005). Empowerment evaluation: From the digital divide to academic distress. In D. Fetterman & A. Wandersman (Eds.), *Empowerment evaluation principles in practice* (pp. 92–122). New York: Guilford Press.

Fetterman, D. M. (2007, Winter). Empowerment evaluation: A tool to facilitate a learning community and engage accreditation standards. *COMTA News,* 1–6.

Fetterman, D. M. (2009). Empowerment evaluation at the Stanford University School of Medicine: Using a critical friend to improve the clerkship experience. *Ensaio: Avaliação e Políticas Públicas em Educação, 17*(63), 197–204.

Fetterman, D. M., Deitz, J., & Gesundheit, N. (2010). Empowerment evaluation: A collaborative approach to evaluating and transforming a medical school curriculum. *Academic Medicine, 85*(5), 813–820.

Fetterman, D. M., & Wandersman, A. (Eds.). (2005). *Empowerment evaluation principles in practice.* New York: Guilford Press.

Frey, A. J., Alvarez, M. E., Sabatino, C. A., Lindsey, B. C., Dupper, D. R., Raines, J. C., et al. (2012). The development of a national school social work practice model. *Children & Schools, 34*(3), 131–134.

Frey, A. J., & Dupper, D. R. (2005). A broader conceptual approach to clinical practice for the 21st century. *Children & Schools, 27*(1), 33–44.

Goodman, R. (1997). The Strength and Difficulties Questionnaire: A research note. *Journal of Child Psychology and Psychiatry, 38*(5), 581–586.

Hoagwood, K. E., Olin, S. S., Kerker, B. D., Kratochwill, R. R., Crowe, M., & Saka, N. (2007). Empirically based school interventions targeted at academic and mental health functioning. *Journal of Emotional and Behavioral Disorders, 15,* 66–92.

Iachini, A. L., Dorr, C., & Anderson-Butcher, D. (2008). Fostoria Community Schools' innovative approach to refining and coordinating their school-based mental health service delivery system. *Report on Emotional and Behavioral Disorders in Youth, 8*(3), 69–75.

Labin, S. N., Duffy, J. L., Meyers, D. C., Wandersman, A., & Lesesne, C. A. (2012). A research synthesis of the evaluation capacity building literature. *American Journal of Evaluation, 33*(3), 307–338.

Levin, H. M. (1996). Empowerment evaluation and accelerated schools. In D. M. Fetterman, S. J. Kaftarian, & A. Wandersman (Eds.), *Empowerment evaluation: Knowledge and tools for self-assessment and accountability* (pp. 49–64). Thousand Oaks, CA: Sage.

Lyon, A. R., Borntrager, C., Nakamura, B., & Higa-McMillan, C. (2013). From distal to proximal: routine educational data monitoring in school-based mental health. *Advances in School Mental Health Promotion, 6*(4), 263–279.

Mastery Charter Schools. (2013). *Turnaround schools results: Statistics.* Retrieved from http://www.masterycharter.org/about/the-results.html

Michael, K. D., Albright, A., Jameson, J. P., Sale, R., Massey, C., Kirk, A., et al. (2013). Does cognitive behavioural therapy in the context of a rural school mental health programme have an impact on academic outcomes? *Advances in School Mental Health Promotion, 6*(4), 247–262.

Miller, R. L., & Campbell, R. (2006). Taking stock of empowerment evaluation: An empirical review. *American Journal of Evaluation, 27*, 296–319.

Public Health Management Corporation, Merritt, M. B., Cronholm, P., Davis, M., Dempsey, S., Fein, J., et al. (Eds.). (2013, September 8). *Findings from the Philadelphia Urban ACE Survey.* Princeton, NJ: Robert Wood Johnson Foundation. Retrieved from http://www.rwjf.org/en/research-publications/find-rwjf-research/2013/09/findings-from-the-philadelphia-urban-ace-survey.html

Pullman, M. D., Weathers, E. S., Hensley, S., & Bruns, E. J. (2013). Academic outcomes of an elementary school-based family support programme. *Advances in School Mental Health Promotion, 6*(4), 231–246.

Richman, J. M., Bowen, G. L., & Wooley, M. E. (2004). School failure: An eco-interactional developmental perspective. In Fraser, M. W. (Ed.), *Risk and resilience in childhood: An ecological perspective* (2nd ed., pp. 133–160). Washington, DC: NASW Press.

Sinclair, M. F., Christenson, S. L., & Thurlow, M. L. (2005). Promoting school completion of urban secondary youth with emotional or behavioral disabilities. *Exceptional Children, 71*(4), 465–482.

Thernstrom, A., & Thernstrom, S. (2003). *No excuses: Closing the racial gap in learning.* New York: Simon & Schuster.

U.S. Department of Education. (2009). *School Improvement Grants—American Recovery and Reinvestment Act of 2009; Title I of the Elementary and Secondary Education Act of 1965: Notice of proposed requirements.* Washington, DC: Author. Retrieved from: http://www2.ed.gov/legislation/FedRegister/other/2009-3/082609d.html

Wandersman, A., Snell-Johns, J., Lentz, B. E., Fetterman, D. E., & Keener, D. C. (2005). The principles of empowerment evaluation. In D. M. Fetterman & A. Wandersman (Eds.), *Empowerment evaluation principles in practice* (pp. 27–41). New York: Guilford Press.

Williams, B. (2002). A no-excuses approach to closing the achievement gap. In S. J. Denbo & L. M. Beaulieu (Eds.), *Improving schools for African American students: A reader for educational leaders* (73–79). Springfield, IL: Charles C Thomas.

CHAPTER 11
Empowerment Evaluation Conducted by Fourth- and Fifth-Grade Students[1]

Regina Day Langhout

University of California at Santa Cruz

Jesica Siham Fernández

University of California at Santa Cruz

As social-community psychologists, we are interested in engaging in practices that will help schools function better for students and families, especially for those who come from social groups that have historically experienced school as exclusionary (e.g., working-class and working-poor communities, communities of color, immigrant communities). Our examination of research on school reform indicates that transformational change is incredibly difficult to achieve (Kozol, 1991; McMillan, 1975; Ouellett, 1996; Rappaport, Moore, & Hunt, 2003; Sarason, 1971, 1995, 1997). Indeed, changes that are sustainable and alter role relationships among people such that communities have access to control over resources that affect them (both psychological and material) are challenging. In searching for solutions, we have considered lessons from community psychology

1. The authors wish to thank the Change 4 Good students, our school collaborator and principal at "Maplewood Elementary School," the school district superintendent, r2row, and Shile. We also thank Danielle Kohfeldt and Marina Castro for taking fieldnotes. This project was supported by grants to the first author from the Center for Justice, Tolerance, and Community; the Cowell Foundation; a Junior Faculty Social Science Research Grant; and University-Community Links. The second author was supported through a Eugene Cota-Robles Fellowship.

and organizing regarding empowerment and the action-reflection cycle (Rappaport, 1981; Speer & Hughey, 1995; Speer, Hughey, Gensheimer, & Adams-Leavitt, 1995; Warren & Mapp, 2011). Within this literature, we have identified what appear to be wins in some school districts across the United States, in places as varied as San José (CA), Chicago, Tucson, the Mississippi Delta, the Arkansas Delta, and New York City (Cammarota, 2007; Fetterman, 1994; Fetterman & Wandersman, 2007; Warren & Mapp, 2011).

These wins have taken place via two paths: (1) grassroots organizing using a set of processes that combine relational organizing, capacity building, and changing cultures between schools and communities such that all stakeholders feel it is their role to be involved in the school (Cammarota, 2007; Warren & Mapp, 2011); and (2) empowerment evaluation, which includes capacity building and transforming cultures as central components (Fetterman, 1994; Fetterman & Wandersman, 2007). Our interests and energy, therefore, are currently aligned with school reform models that are more bottom-up than top-down, with an emphasis on transformational change and the empirical outcomes of those processes, as well as advocacy. For these reasons, empowerment evaluation is an excellent fit for us because of its flexibility, collaborative underpinnings, grounding in empiricism, use in transformative processes, and value base (Fetterman, 1994, 1999; Fetterman & Wandersman, 2007).

Empowerment evaluation is an approach that is concerned with improvement and self-determination (Fetterman, 1994, 2010a; Wandersman et al., 2005). Therefore, there is an emphasis on the co-construction of knowledge and evaluation, capacity building for people, programs, and institutions. By evaluation capacity building (ECB), we mean engaging in processes that increase knowledge and skills to enhance an organization's ability to conduct and use evaluation (Labin, Duffy, Meyers, Wandersman, & Lesesne, 2012). This process includes assessing the organizational context, as well as evaluation needs and strengths of the individuals and organization (step 1), providing activities that address needs by building on identified strengths so that the individuals and organizations are prepared to conduct empowerment evaluation (step 2), and assessing individual and organizational outcomes to discern if evaluation capacity has been built (step 3; Labin et al., 2012).

In empowerment evaluation, a set of 10 principles help to drive the process. These principles are *improvement* (better results), *community ownership* (community makes important decisions), *inclusion* (participation of different stakeholder groups), *democratic participation* (non-tokenistic collaboration and transparency), *social justice* (fair and equitable allocation of resources, opportunities, and obligations and engagement in actions that address inequalities), *community knowledge* (community members are experts on their lives), *evidence-based strategies* (interventions with empirical support should be examined and modi-fied, when necessary, to be contextually and culturally relevant), *capacity build-ing* (the "giving away" of evaluation through increasing the knowledge base and skills of people, programs, and institutions), *organizational learning* (creating a culture where learning and transformational improvement is expected), and *accountability* (focusing on what can be done to get to desired outcomes; Fetterman, 2010a; Fetterman & Wandersman, 2007; Wandersman et al., 2005). These principles are put into practice through the empowerment evaluation cycle of taking stock, setting goals, developing strategies, and documenting progress; this all happens among a learning community (Fetterman, 1999; Fetterman & Wandersman, 2007).

In the rest of this chapter, we provide an example of empowerment evaluation from our own research, emphasizing the documenting progress phase. We begin with an overview of an ongoing collaborative community-based research project that completed its sixth year in 2013. We partnered with fourth- and fifth-grade students (ages 9–11) to enact change in their school. These 6 years represent two empowerment evaluation cycles. We first describe the context of this work, including the school, the background for how this collaboration developed, and our role. We then describe how students engaged in two complete empowerment evaluation cycles, with an emphasis on the two evaluation phases (one from each empowerment evaluation cycle) and our ECB efforts in those two evaluation phases. We describe two full cycles because ECB and empowerment evaluation are iterative processes, yet many descriptions appear more like a snapshot (Fetterman, 2010a; Labin, 2014; Suarez-Balcazar & Taylor-Ritzler, 2014); our goal is to illustrate dynamism. Specifically, we show how students took stock to discern a problem, set their goals, and develop a strategy to achieve their goals. We then go into greater detail regarding how they evaluated their first interven-tion (i.e., how they documented their progress). Next, we briefly describe how this evaluation shaped their strategy for their second intervention, and what that intervention was. Then, we detail their evaluation of their second intervention.

In each section, we outline how student actions aligned with empowerment evaluation principles. We provide several handouts/lesson plans and discuss in detail the documenting progress phase in an effort to make visible our ECB practices. We do this because we agree with both Leviton's (2014) claim that evaluators need to ask themselves about the guidance and assistance they offer when they engage in ECB and Clinton's (2014) statement that the "how to" of ECB is still being developed. We end the chapter with school improvement outcomes directly related to the students' empowerment evaluation effort. In addition, we discuss implications for ECB and empowerment evaluation given this specific collaborative context.

"CHANGE 4 GOOD" CONTEXT

Background

Maplewood Elementary School[2] is a public elementary school in an unincorporated area of California's central coast. It serves students from transitional kindergarten to fifth grade. According to school accountability data, during this project, Maplewood Elementary students were predominantly Latina/o (approximately 75%). Other students were white (15%), African American (2%), and Asian/Asian American (0.5%). Roughly two thirds were designated as English language learners. Also, more than three fourths qualified for free or reduced-price lunch. The school's faculty, on the other hand, are primarily white, and few speak Spanish.

The Community Psychology Research & Action Team (CPRAT) at the University of California at Santa Cruz (UC Santa Cruz) became involved with the school in 2006. The relationship began after a conversation between Gina (the first author and a UC Santa Cruz professor) and the (past) principal, (past) literacy specialist, and a fifth-grade teacher (our school collaborator, who is now the literacy specialist), who were involved with an Industrial Areas Foundation (IAF) community organizing group. We discussed the values and goals of our fields and institutions. Common ground included social justice, inclusion, improvement, evidence-based strategies, capacity building, and community ownership. We brainstormed a project to embody shared values and goals.

We decided to create a program that would teach leadership skills to elementary school students and facilitate opportunities for them to make changes at the school. We chose this course of action because school staff were dissatisfied with the limited leadership opportunities available to students (a student council) and felt that more students, from varying backgrounds, had ideas for school improvement. This program was conceptualized as addressing (a) inclusion (creating student leadership opportunities); (b) capacity building, evidence-based strategies, and improvement (students conduct social science research and evaluate their interventions, altering interventions as needed to work toward school improvement); (c) social justice (changes would benefit the growing Latina/o population, which was essential given the shifting demographics of the school and the school's desire for better outreach); and (d) community ownership (students would have major decision-making roles and carry out interventions).

---

2. The name of the school has been changed.

"Change 4 Good" is the name of the after-school program. It meets weekly for 1.25 hours. CPRAT runs the program, with the assistance of the school's literacy specialist. Most attendees are Latina/o, live in low-income families, and are categorized by their school as English language learners. They enter the program in fourth grade and graduate when they matriculate from elementary school, at the completion of fifth grade. In the program, students learn social science research methods that serve as the foundation for initiating and creating change in their school. Young people discern a problem, devise an intervention, and evaluate it. Hence, they participate in the empowerment evaluation cycle of taking stock, setting goals, developing strategies, and documenting progress.

CPRAT's Role

CPRAT follows the educational pyramid model (Seidman & Rappaport, 1974); a professor oversees 1 or 2 graduate students who supervise 4 to 10 undergraduates who all work together. Our goal is to facilitate student ownership of the Change 4 Good program, social justice, and ECB for students to carry out effective school changes.

Because students work with us for only 2 years, and because Western society tends to view children as people who are becoming capable rather than people who are already capable (Langhout & Thomas, 2010), we have unique roles. We, and our school collaborator, hold the institutional program knowledge and assist continuing students in teaching new students what has been done and why. Additionally, we provide options regarding the social science research methods that are best suited to youth's research questions, as well as information regarding which of their proposed interventions has empirical support. Finally, we teach technical skills to students to help them carry out their empowerment evaluation cycle. In short, we engage in ECB.

CHANGE 4 GOOD ENGAGES IN EMPOWERMENT EVALUATION

Empowerment Evaluation Cycle 1—Change 4 Good Students Define the Problem: Taking Stock

Step 1 in ECB includes assessing goals, context, and strengths (Labin et al., 2012). To do this, CPRAT needed to first devise an activity that would help students take stock of their current situation and discern an area of focus. This step warrants great attention because the area of focus, or mission, drives the rest of the process (Fetterman, 2010a). We decided to focus on photovoice because of its accessibility (Langhout, in press). Photovoice is a method where people are given a prompt (here, "What are your hopes and dreams for your school?") and take pictures based on that prompt (Wang & Burris, 1994, 1997). They then examine their pictures, select a few, write narratives, and discuss their chosen photos. The conversation is designed to help people see connections among one another's lives. Also, the discussion facilitates a broader structural analysis and possible policy solutions to problems (see Langhout, in press, for a description of the ECB photovoice curriculum). Students analyzed their pictures for themes and then discussed root causes through other structured activities. At the conclusion of this phase, Change 4 Good students decided that their problem definition was that the school was not connected to them and their families and, therefore, they did not have a sense of belonging (see Kohfeldt & Langhout, 2012, for a description of the ECB activity and process).

With this process, students practiced the community knowledge and social justice empowerment evaluation principles. As a method, photovoice is based on the premise that picture takers are experts in their community. Their community knowledge, once examined systematically by them, was considered useful scientific knowledge that would drive the process. The social justice empowerment evaluation principle is visible in their conceptualization of the problem. A premise of social justice is that there are social inequities in society; an implication of this fact is that social systems are in need of change. The students' problem definition points to a social system in need of change (i.e., the school) rather than a person or group of people (e.g., the students, the teachers).

Empowerment Evaluation
Cycle 1—Change 4 Good Students Set Goals

Students set a goal to increase the school's connection to themselves and their families. This was their goal because they thought it related directly to their conceptualization of the problem, and it held the appropriate system (the school) accountable. Their conceptualization of the problem and goal were therefore aligned with one another. This goal was consistent with the improvement empowerment evaluation principle because increasing student and family sense of belonging would improve the school.

Empowerment Evaluation Cycle 1— Change 4 Good Students Develop a Strategy

In strategizing, Change 4 Good students decided to create a mural based on students' stories, as a way to make the school more visibly welcoming to them. They chose creating a mural as their strategy for several reasons. First, they felt stories about them did not represent them or their families. Second, our school collaborator was interested in having a mural at the school; many other district schools had murals, but this school, labeled as unattractive by many, had none. Third, through the photovoice process, students engaged in ECB practices and learned about imagery, critical literacy, and how to tell a story through symbols. They were excited to put these skills to work by creating permanent imagery. CPRAT researched murals and concluded that there was empirical support for such a project. Specifically, if empowerment is about people having access to control the psychological and material resources that affect their lives (Rappaport, 1981), then the stories told about individuals and communities are an important psychological resource because these stories often serve as a foundation for what can and cannot be done. Art has been used to foster alternative narratives about subordinated communities for years (Baca, 2008; Langhout, in press; Thomas & Rappaport, 1996). For example, among the Mexican heritage community in the 1960s, murals were used to represent the politicized identity and cultural pride of Chicanas/os.

After the principal agreed to the making of a mural, the students underwent another round of photovoice, this time taking pictures "to document things that are meaningful to the people who live here" (Change 4 Good, 2010, p. 31). Students took pictures and analyzed their pictures and narratives by sorting them into categories. They then made posters for each category that included images and narratives. Based on their data analysis, they agreed on the following themes: community, nature, family and friends, peace, education, fun, and diversity. Although they had many ideas for symbols, they realized they had not included other students in the school in their data gathering process. Because of this, the other students' ideas were likely not represented in the symbols and images in the mural. In their book documenting their process (Change 4 Good, 2010, p. 37), they wrote:

> We also wanted to give other students in our school the opportunity to give input on what they wanted in the mural. This way the mural would really belong to everyone, not just Change 4 Good. One day during lunch we put out a giant piece of butcher paper for students to draw or write about images they wanted to

include in the mural. We also gave out surveys to students. After gathering their ideas we moved on to the next phase.

They then planned their mural, got it approved by the principal and superintendent, and, with the assistance of Arturo Rosette, a critical muralist and founder of Art 4 Change, they painted it. Afterward, they created a book that described their mural making process and the mural symbols. Considering organization-level ECB outcomes, the book is important because it is a resource for future Change 4 Good students and it increases organizational capacity. With respect to empowerment evaluation principles, creating the mural was most aligned with improvement. Specifically, the mural was created to improve the school by making it more welcoming to Latina/o students and families.

Empowerment Evaluation Cycle 1— Change 4 Good Students Document Their Progress: The "We Are Powerful" Mural

After completing their first mural, titled "We Are Powerful," the Change 4 Good students evaluated the impact on the school community. With the help of CPRAT, students decided to assess the following: "What do other students at Maplewood Elementary School feel and think about the mural?" and "What do students want to see in a future mural?"

Once the questions were determined, CPRAT engaged the students in ECB to ensure they were ready for data collection. Step 1 of ECB entails assessing needs and strengths (Labin et al., 2012). We first conducted a needs assessment by asking students what they knew about science and research. Most students discussed science as it related to biology (e.g., cells, the circulatory system) and connected research to looking up information in books. We built on this knowledge base to describe science more generally and in ways that were inclusive of social science. We also described the research process generally and discussed how social science research methods were aligned with the general research process, which made explicit the link between science and research. Through this process, CPRAT determined that students knew little about social science data collection. We therefore designed activities that would teach students about different methods to evaluate their mural. Methods included surveys, interviews, and focus groups. They decided to conduct focus groups with other students. They chose focus groups because they wanted to have more interaction with their peers, and they wanted an open discussion that would help facilitate the gathering of ideas and suggestions for what their next intervention should entail. Change 4 Good student interest in focus groups was also connected to their desire to create a sense of belonging among their peers and to create a more inclusive and participatory process that would allow for more students to have a say in future interventions.

This process was congruent with several empowerment evaluation principles. Change 4 Good students decided how to evaluate their mural, which was consistent with the community ownership empowerment evaluation principle. Moreover, because the young people were part of the school community, they knew how to interact with other students. This reliance on community knowledge (another empowerment evaluation principle) was valuable because it allowed them to potentially gain more trustworthy information.

Learning About and Conducting Focus Groups

After deciding on focus groups, students then had to learn how to collect and analyze data. Step 2 of ECB includes developing activities to increase empowerment evaluation knowledge (Labin et al., 2012). CPRAT developed a Focus Group Lesson Plan (see Appendix 11A) and performed focus group skits to demonstrate facilitation. The following fieldnote captures some of the interactions during a session.

> At this time we moved on to the skits. . . . RA [UCSC Research Assistant] Amy started out by saying hello to her focus group, and explaining what the topic was [What is your favorite TV show?]. Then, every so often, she would break one of the rules. The first time, she crossed her arms and slouched down while RA Ryan was talking. Several of the students immediately clapped [to indicate a broken rule]. I said, "freeze!" and called on one of the clappers, Lorena. She said that RA Amy had crossed her arms. I wrote this down on the easel and then told RA Amy to restart. RA Ryan explained that his favorite show was SpongeBob and RA Amy asked him why. As he answered, RA Amy leaned over to RA Maria and whispered something to her. Even more students clapped this time. . . . I froze the scene and called on someone different. I wrote down what they said, "whispering while someone else is talking." . . . When it was RA Terri's turn . . . she didn't want to do the focus group on TV shows and RA Amy asked if there was something else she would like to do. RA Terri said sing and dance. . . . I froze the scene. I explained that one thing to remember is that focus group participation is voluntary so if any one says they don't want to do it anymore they don't have to. . . . I went through the things that I wrote down. (DK fieldnote 1/13/2011)

In this abbreviated fieldnote, students tested their knowledge of focus group facilitation. They began to learn—through participatory observation—how to conduct focus groups, including facilitation.

Next, students wrote a focus group protocol that would help guide the discussion. They developed their protocol through conversations among themselves and CPRAT. After several sessions, students agreed on a set of questions (see Appendix 11B). These questions gave closure to their first action-evaluation cycle. Students then practiced facilitating focus groups on one another until CPRAT and students agreed that they were skilled facilitators. The young people then conducted four focus groups with students in the third through fifth grades. All participants were recruited by Change 4 Good youth. Each focus group had two facilitators and one note-taker, all of whom were Change 4 Good youth who chose their roles. Step 3 in the ECB process includes assessing outcomes. CPRAT and students jointly ensured they were ready to conduct focus groups through monitoring their practice sessions. Students then carried out their data collection.

In collecting focus group data, students engaged several empowerment evaluation principles. First, they were committed to making a change (community ownership). Second, they had insider knowledge about student experience and of local stories, which helped shape their questions (community knowledge). Lastly, their process allowed for the empowerment evaluation principles of democratic participation and inclusiveness by incorporating the voices and stories of the broader community.

Analyzing Findings From Focus Groups

The focus group notes were the students' data. The young people, with the help of CPRAT, then analyzed these data. With respect to ECB, CPRAT had already determined that students knew little about social science methods and would therefore need data analysis guidance (step 1; Labin et al., 2012). To learn how to analyze data, students participated in several activities (step 2 of ECB). Two endeavors that helped students move from data to codes, and then from codes to themes, were a candy sorting and messaging activity (see Foster-Fishman, Law, Lichty, & Auon, 2010, for a complete ECB lesson plan). The candy sorting activity involved students organizing candies according to different characteristics that they chose. It is important to note that the candy could be sorted in multiple ways. Students then participated in a messaging activity. They read through stanzas from song lyrics and organized these according to themes. Both activities allowed for students to learn about data analysis.

Through analyzing their focus group notes, students determined that their peers did not feel very connected to the first mural because the mural did not fully represent their experiences and because they did not help paint the mural. Considering ECB, the fact that students analyzed their focus group data is an outcome.

This process demonstrates some empowerment evaluation principles. Students were building capacity by learning a method of evaluation (e.g., focus groups) and acquiring the tools and skills to collect and analyze their data. Also, students were accountable to their community. Hence, they were better able to make an informed decision for their next intervention. In evaluating their first mural, students were accountable to their school, especially those who defined the problem in earlier phases of the empowerment evaluation cycle.

Empowerment Evaluation Cycle 2—Change 4 Good Students Take Stock

In evaluating their first action, Change 4 Good students determined that their peers did not feel very connected to the first mural. Students therefore concluded that a second mural that incorporated the stories and lived experiences of the school and broader community was not only important but also necessary. In this decision, students' actions came into closer alignment with their goals, which is what empowerment evaluation is designed to facilitate (Fetterman, 2010a).

Their commitment to create a sense of belonging within the school/community context through the creation of a second mural was founded on the empowerment evaluation principles of social justice, democratic participation, and inclusion. The students' decision to create a second mural was based on a desire to create an empowering and critical visual representation of their school and community stories. Raising these voices is a form of social justice. Moreover, their decision to engage the broader Maplewood community in the process was congruent with the empowerment evaluation principle of democratic participation because they wanted others to feel connected to the mural. Also, this desire to represent the community invoked the empowerment evaluation principle of inclusion. That is, Change 4 Good youth wished to include more students, teachers, families, and community members in the making of their next mural. They wanted others to feel connected, represented, and validated through the sharing of stories that were representative of the diversity within Maplewood.

Empowerment Evaluation Cycle 2— Change 4 Good Students Set Goals

Students set a goal to include more school and community members in their mural making process so that a second mural would represent the stories of success, hope, and struggle in their school and community. Creating opportunities for participation and therefore a sense of belonging was an important goal of Change 4 Good. This was especially important given the diversity within the Maplewood community and the changing demographics within the school setting.

Change 4 Good students' goals were aligned with the empowerment evaluation principles of accountability, inclusion, and improvement. First, the students viewed themselves as accountable to the original goal of the first intervention (i.e., first mural) to create a sense of belonging through the making of a mural at their school. This initial process, however, was not inclusive of the broader school or of the community. Thus, the students altered their methodological approach toward collecting data, by involving the community and the students, teachers, and parents at their school. By doing this, they hoped to increase sense of belonging, thereby improving the school.

Empowerment Evaluation Cycle 2— Change 4 Good Students Develop Strategies

Change 4 Good students first decided on a data collection method. They chose focus groups because they knew it was appropriate for collecting stories. Next, they developed a prompt to guide discussions. They examined their data from their prior focus groups and discussed other local stories to help them determine a prompt. With the help of CPRAT, the students decided to ask: *Tell us a story about a time when you felt you had (or did not have) the power to change something in Maplewood.* Over a 6-month period, Change 4 Good youth strengthened their focus group facilitation skills, recruited participants, and conducted seven focus groups with students, teachers, parents, family members, teens, and other adults. Considering ECB, CPRAT facilitated this activity process (ECB step 2) as described in the previous strategy development phase of empowerment evaluation cycle 1.

To discern themes for their mural, students analyzed their focus group notes. In addition to the candy sorting and messaging activities (Foster-Fishman et al., 2010), we developed a concept mapping activity (see Appendix 11C; for more information on the ECB concept mapping activity, see Fernández, Nguyen, &

Langhout, 2013). This activity was used to facilitate the students' process of connecting and organizing their experiences, the stories/data they collected, and other local stories to the themes they discerned when they analyzed their data. Through this process, students saw how all three sets of stories (i.e., their personal stories, their data, and other local stories) fit together and how the themes were connected to each other. Students then developed mural symbols.

After presenting two mural drafts to the school collaborator, principal, and superintendent, a final draft was approved with some modifications. The second mural, titled "Maplewood Stories," represented many community narratives. Stories included the history of Maplewood and the importance of community, peace, love, diversity, education, and creating opportunities for all. The making of their second mural, with the assistance of Shile from Art 4 Change, concluded their second intervention.

Change 4 Good student strategies were consistent with several empowerment evaluation principles. First, their outreach was congruent with the empowerment evaluation principles of community ownership and inclusion through the creation of a space where stories were shared and people's experiences were validated. Yet, the principal felt that too few teachers had been included in the process (two of the seven sessions were with teachers) and that parent outreach was exclusive rather than inclusive because recruitment happened through the English Learner Advisory Committee (a parent group who speak primarily Spanish at home) only and not also through the Parent Teacher Association (a parent group who speak primarily English at home). Second, by conducting focus groups with school and community members, and by analyzing their own data, Change 4 Good students were building capacity, as well as ownership of their empowerment evaluation process. They were viewed as experts and more knowledgeable about their school/community context and therefore better able to engage in the decision making that would improve not only their experience and sense of belonging in the school setting but also that of other students at their school.

Empowerment Evaluation Cycle 2— Change 4 Good Students Document Progress: Evaluating the "Maplewood Stories" Mural

Choosing a Method and Collecting Data to Document Progress

Because the principal had voiced some concerns about the inclusiveness of perspectives in the second mural, CPRAT paid special attention to research methods that could be used to survey a broad array of stakeholders. In our ECB step of designing activities to strengthen empowerment evaluation capacity, we presented Change 4 Good students with three options for mural evaluation: individual interviews, focus groups, and questionnaire distribution and collection. Students discussed the pros and cons of each method (see Appendix 11D for our handout). In the end, they decided to write questionnaires, which they knew would yield less depth from each person but would enable them to collect data from far more people. In this way, they viewed the questionnaires as more inclusive. They then focused on their research question, "Do people feel connected to the mural?" and in small groups they developed questionnaires for the following groups: (1) transitional kindergarten to third graders, (2) fourth and fifth graders, (3) school staff, (4) families, and (5) the broader community. Versions 4 and 5 were written in English and Spanish to increase inclusiveness. Next, they shared their questionnaires with our school collaborator and the other small groups. They edited their questionnaires based on one another's suggestions. The school collaborator also provided invaluable feedback. Finally, all versions went to the principal, who shared them with the school leadership team for comment and to gain approval for distribution. The leadership team agreed to a schoolwide data collection (see Appendix 11E for the final version of the school staff questionnaire). The schoolwide questionnaire distribution is an organization-level ECB outcome; it indicated the leadership team's openness to participate in evaluating an intervention at their school. This openness signals an organizational culture that values empiricism, student learning, and improvement; this culture is important for organizational change (Labin et al., 2012). Additionally, students creating the questionnaire was an ECB outcome.

Students developed data collection plans for each stakeholder group. With our school collaborator's help, the student data collection was announced at an assembly. Students said:

> Hello our names are [names]. We are a part of the Change 4 Good program, which made the new mural. We want to know what everyone thinks about it so we made some questionnaires. Your teacher will hand out the questionnaires for you to fill out later. When you are done filling out the questionnaire, please give it to your teacher. In one or two weeks, we will be passing out questionnaires during recess for you to give to your families. Come find us at that time. If your family fills them out, you will be in a raffle and could win prizes. Thank you. (Change 4 Good, 2013)

Teachers were responsible for turning in completed questionnaires to our school collaborator, who followed up to ensure a good response rate. Considering school staff, students placed a questionnaire in each person's mailbox after ensuring all school staff had mailboxes.

Family questionnaire data collection had a multi-pronged approach, with the goal of collecting 50 completed questionnaires. Change 4 Good students first approached other students at recess; they explained the questionnaire, told them that if they took it home, had a family member fill it out, and returned it, they would be entered into a raffle. In step 2 of ECB, a mid-course correction is sometimes needed, which means empowerment evaluation skills need to be bolstered (Fetterman, 2010a; Labin et al., 2012). Our school collaborator assessed that a mid-course correction was needed and acted accordingly. Specifically, Change 4 Good students were not actively approaching other students at recess and encouraging them to take a questionnaire home. Instead, they were standing in groups with one another, hoping other school students would approach them. Our school collaborator talked with the Change 4 Good students and worked with them to proactively approach other students. Once they did this, they were able to hand out many more questionnaires. To reach families of younger students (who had a different recess time), they approached families after school and asked them to fill out the questionnaire. Even with these efforts and this mid-course correction, they were unable to reach their goal of 50 returned questionnaires. To compensate for this, they distributed questionnaires at "Family Fun Night" and finally reached their goal. The fact that students were able to implement and reach their goal was an ECB outcome.

Community questionnaire distribution did not go as smoothly. Change 4 Good students wanted to collect data from nearby establishments (e.g., grocery store, family resource center, park) during our after-school time, but the school principal did not grant permission to leave the campus, citing liability concerns. Instead, students agreed to take community questionnaires and distribute them on their own time at events that they were already attending (e.g., soccer games, birthday parties). They also reached out to the director of the nearby Family Resource Center and asked her to put a stack of questionnaires at the front desk. Finally, they wrote a letter to the editor of the local weekly alternative paper, which was published. They thanked the community for voting for their mural, which had recently won first place as the best public art in the county, and asked community members to fill out the questionnaire, which could be found at the Family Resource Center. Even with this extensive approach, they only collected five questionnaires, so they dropped the community component from further consideration. This process signaled a negative ECB outcome, due largely to broader organizational realities around liability.

This process was consistent with several empowerment evaluation principles. First, the students had community ownership over the process. Indeed, they decided on the research question and method, designed the questionnaires, and were instrumental in collecting all data. The community knowledge empowerment evaluation principle was also central. Youth knew best how to ask other students about the mural. Additionally, they asked the school collaborator for help with the school staff version, and the school collaborator knew best how to increase the response rate. Democratic participation was a third empowerment evaluation principle. The school collaborator, principal, and school leadership team helped shape the questionnaires, and these were approved by the school leadership council as per the principal's desire. Finally, the process was inclusive. The entire school (i.e., approximately 350 students and 35 school staff) was asked to participate in the survey. Questionnaires were returned by 300 students and 17 staff. Also, 55 family members were surveyed, leading to 372 total responses.

Data Analysis

The next task was to enter and clean data. Consistent with ECB, CPRAT provided technical support by creating the codebooks. The ECB needs assessment includes assessing organizational context (Labin et al., 2013). Based on this assessment, we knew that there were not enough computers for all students and that the few school computers available were dated. We therefore decided to bring six laptops to the program. This organizational context created specific boundaries around activities for the session. Thus, we created different activity stations so that all students could engage in some aspect of skill building (e.g., data entry, creating a data analysis plan). Students rotated among activity stations, with free time at the end to spend at whichever activity station they preferred.

In their first data analysis session, students were enthusiastic to enter their data into Excel. As they approached the computers, CPRAT was able to assess their familiarity with computers and data entry (ECB step 1: Assess empowerment evaluation needs and strengths; Labin et al., 2012). CPRAT members worked one-on-one with students to ensure they knew how to navigate the track pad on the laptop and how to enter data into Excel (ECB step 2). They entered as much data as they could in the session, and then CPRAT completed the data entry, as a form of support and assistance. The following week, students learned how to clean data in SPSS (see Appendix 11F for the ECB handout). Data cleaning is important so that errors in data entry can be remedied. Students, again working one-on-one with CPRAT members, cleaned their data by examining frequencies for each variable to ensure all variables had data within the expected range. When a data point was out of range, students went back to the original questionnaire, looked up the appropriate number, and changed the value in SPSS. Students completed as much data cleaning as they could in the hour. CPRAT then cleaned the rest of the data before the next session, as a form of support and assistance. Data entry and cleaning combined the ECB steps 2 and 3. Specifically, students were learning how to conduct empowerment evaluation by doing it, and CPRAT was assessing their capacity to carry out empowerment evaluation by working one-on-one with students.

During the next two sessions, students broke up into small groups and finished their data analysis plan, with the help of CPRAT. Their questions guided the subsequent lessons on data analysis because we could assess their goals in their data analysis plans and tailor a lesson plan to help them answer their questions (ECB step 2). Students were interested in comparing older and younger students, as well as boys and girls, on several variables. They also were curious about teacher and student comparisons, as well as comparing family members depending on if they filled out the questionnaire in Spanish or English. It was clear that students needed to learn about *t*-tests, which is a way to compare two groups on a continuous variable. CPRAT then gave a lesson on *t*-tests, as described in the following abridged field note.

Gina began her talk with the students about means and variability. She asked the group what a mean was, and someone replied that it meant someone who wasn't nice. Gina smiled and said that that wasn't the mean she meant. There was some more silence, but finally someone answered with a definition of a mean. Gina used height as an example, and called up Mary and Lisette to show their differences in height. She also stood up front with them and asked the group what the average height of the group was. The students all suddenly seemed to understand what Gina was talking about, because they all let out a group, "Ohh!" She called for a few more volunteers and asked the students how they would go about finding the average. Someone said that they would take everyone's height, add it up, and divide it by the number of people up there. She thanked that student for the answer and asked everyone to sit down. She then asked what everyone's favorite food was. A few students answered ravioli. Then she asked, "Who gives you ravioli at your house?" A few students answered their dad, and a few answered their stepdad. She told students to make-believe certain situations in order to show what she was trying to explain. One she gave was to imagine that their dad always gave them exactly 10 raviolis, but their stepdad always gave them a different amount—sometimes 5, sometimes 7, sometimes 15. It was always different. She then asked them that if they got one more ravioli from their dad or their stepdad, would that be different or seem different or feel different from how many they usually got? She asked them to think about it, if they counted up their raviolis over several meals and then calculated the averages for dad and stepdad, how would they know if a difference actually mattered (i.e., if the difference was significant). . . . Some students said one ravioli wasn't enough to be more. She then turned on her projector to show them a picture . . . It was an image of different graphs showing what variability meant. She related it to getting different amounts of raviolis from their dad and their stepdad. She then had more students come to the front of the room and put them in two groups—one with everyone about the same height and another with students who were all different heights. She asked them which group had more variability. The students said the group with all different heights had more variability. Gina said that was right, even though the average heights might be really close. She then said that when we look at different groups, we need to know their mean (or average) and variability to decide if they are different from each other in a meaningful way. This will help us know if one ravioli is a meaningful difference, for example . . . . Gina opened up SPSS and started asking the students what they wanted to know about the data they collected. Right away, she mentioned their hypothesis from the other day about the older students liking the picture in the mural of the previous principal more than the younger students. She showed us how she was going to calculate this on her computer. She asked the students what the variable name was for the principal's picture and plugged it into the program. Then she compared the groups she had set up to represent the younger and older students. There was about a .2 difference, on a 3-point scale, in means between the two, so she asked them if they thought that difference mattered. She asked them which one was bigger, and the students seemed to struggle on this one . . . . Gina asked them what number is between 1 and 2, referencing the questionnaire's point system value we had given it. . . . Someone then answered 1.5, and then, with the help of SPSS, we were able to discern that the younger students' answer of 1.6 was quite different than the older students' 1.8. (MDC & RDL combined fieldnote, 5/25/13)

As should be clear, students were engaged in the capacity building empowerment evaluation principle through this process. Indeed, they learned how to enter and clean data. Perhaps more important, they learned to formulate questions that they could answer based on their collected data. In this process, they also considered possible results and developed arguments to support their expectations. Additionally, students behaved in ways that were consistent with the inclusion empowerment evaluation principle in that they wondered how different stakeholder groups experienced the mural. Students proceeded, over the next sessions, to answer questions they had developed.

Results

Change 4 Good students focused on several aspects of their results. We highlighted the examples below because they garnered the most student attention.

We asked if the 4th and 5th graders liked the mural more than the TK [transitional kindergarten]-3rd graders. TK-3 liked the mural more than 4–5 graders. We were surprised because we know more about the mural than they do. We think that the younger kids might have liked the mural more because it is pretty, colorful, and cartoonish.

We thought the younger students would like images that were pretty, colorful, or cartoon-like more than the other images. We talked about it a lot and decided the pretty, colorful, or cartoon-like images were the Diversity, Education, History, and Love circles. Therefore, the other grouping included Community, Working Together, Struggle, Opportunity, and Safety. We added together the items and took their averages because there was a different number of images in each group. This means that responses ranged from 0 (dislike) to 2 (like). We were correct in our guess . . . with the younger students liking the pretty/colorful/cartoonish images (average = 1.58) more than the other images (average = 1.43).

We asked, which group of students liked the "love" image better? We were interested in this question because the "love" image has a picture of the previous school principal, who died two summers ago. To make this comparison, the responses had to be put on the same response scale, which was from 0 (dislike) to 2 (like). We thought that the 4th and 5th grade students might like the image more than the TK-3rd grade students because the older students knew the previous principal, and so the image would be more meaningful to them. This was true . . . with the 4th and 5th grade students liking the image (average = 1.82) more than the younger students (average = 1.63).

When we looked at the teacher/staff questionnaire, we saw that the least liked image was the one representing struggle. We wanted to know if there was a difference in how much teachers/staff liked the image compared to students. There was a difference. Students liked the struggle image (average = 1.40) more than teachers/staff liked it (average = .80). . . . We thought that this was the case because students experienced a lot of struggles and so the image was more important to them. (Change 4 Good, 2013, pp. 1–3)

The creation of this report was an important individual- and organizational-level ECB outcome because children wrote it (with the assistance of CPRAT) and it codified their evaluation.

The results and report engaged the accountability empowerment evaluation principle. Specifically, students asked questions that pertained to each group of stakeholders and assessed differences in perceptions for different stakeholder groups. Some students were troubled by the results regarding school staff and wanted to ensure that school personnel felt as connected to future murals as students and families were. These conversations will continue when the students decide how this empowerment evaluation cycle will inform their next intervention.

CONCLUSION

Change 4 Good students—many of whom are Latina/o and from low-income and immigrant families—have a strong interest in creating a more welcoming school. To create change, they conducted empowerment evaluation. They took stock, set goals, developed strategies, and documented progress (Fetterman, 1999; Fetterman & Wandersman, 2007). Additionally, they used their findings as the foundation for further interventions at their school.

Considering ECB, some argue that more emphasis should be placed on evaluation planning and design than on data analysis when time is limited (Labin et al., 2012). We agree with this statement when the analysis is quantitative but disagree when it is qualitative. Quantitative data analysis is often deductive, or top-down, meaning that data are used to confirm or disconfirm ideas or predictions. When this is the case, evaluation planning and design set the framework for all other steps. Qualitative data analysis, however, can be deductive (top-down) or inductive (bottom-up) or a combination of both. If the data analysis is inductive, as it was in our examples, participation in this process from those conducting empowerment evaluation is essential because the analysis is foundational to theory building (Fetterman, 2010b). For example, if CPRAT had discerned themes from analyzing focus group data, these may have been similar to the themes chosen by students. Yet, these may also have been quite different because our social positioning and context is different than that of the students; we are not in the school regularly and many of us do not live in this same community. We are not arguing that CPRAT's analysis would have been invalid but that it likely would have been at least partially different from the students' analysis.

Our attention to ECB can put us in tension with some of our stakeholders. For example, once the first mural was painted, many teachers felt excited and asked if our program could help create a mural every year. Other university-based researchers within our funding network have also posed the same question. The answer is yes and no. Yes, we could paint a mural every year, but it would mean eschewing the focus on ECB. Indeed, condensing a 3-year cycle into 1 year would mean much less attention to data collection and analysis. On the other hand, some students are frustrated that they are not painting murals at the end of each year. Nevertheless, we have chosen to prioritize ECB because we believe an extremely important individual outcome is the relationship that young people have to knowledge production. This is best served through ECB because through it, students learn how to ask their own questions, collect and analyze data systematically, and answer those questions. Additionally, research indicates that attention to ECB increases the probability of achieving desired organizational outcomes (Clinton, 2014).

There are several implications for empowerment evaluation worth highlighting given the context of this work. As university-based researchers, we agree with the empowerment evaluation premise that the community should eventually be able to conduct empowerment evaluation on their own (Fetterman & Wandersman, 2007). Yet, our collaborators are young people who are in Change 4 Good for only 2 years. This presents a few challenges. The first is that youth often have less information about social science research than adults, usually because of lack of exposure. We therefore have more ECB work to do, which simply takes longer. Second, because of how young people are positioned in Western society, they are sometimes denied permission to carry out the work as they would like to. Often, this denial comes in the form of a custodial and/or bureaucratic rationale; young people must be protected from possible harm, so they cannot (in this case) collect data from the community because if anything happens, they could be harmed and the school would be held liable. These structures can serve as barriers to the empowerment evaluation process and require a great deal of creativity on the part of young people and CPRAT. Third, students are transitory, in that they graduate elementary school and move on to middle school. This means that the school collaborator and CPRAT hold the institutional memory and that CPRAT is constantly engaged in ECB.

To address this, CPRAT has assisted young people in writing the history of the program so that other students may refer to it. Examples include a book documenting the process of the first mural, a documentary explaining the second mural process, and the written report of the results from the second mural evaluation. These documents build organizational capacity. Given the context of this work, we also believe it makes sense to ensure a long-term collaboration. CPRAT has therefore made a commitment to continue to work with students as long as they would like, and we do not view our role as working ourselves out of our job.

It is also important to note that Change 4 Good goals sometimes put empowerment evaluation principles in tension with each other. We suspect this is the case for many intervention contexts. The two empowerment evaluation principles that seemed to be in tension most frequently in our program are inclusion and social justice, which may seem counterintuitive. Being more inclusive, for example, might mean giving teacher, parent, student, and community stories equal weight in the data collection and mural design process. Yet, based on the problem definition of students and families feeling disconnected from the school, it is also the case that the murals are being designed and painted with the explicit purpose of making visible student and family stories. Sometimes, to engage in social justice, certain perspectives that have been systematically excluded must be lifted up or highlighted. Therefore, CPRAT and Change 4 Good have decided to give social justice a higher priority than inclusion and democratic participation. Time will tell what priority each of these empowerment evaluation principles receive in the future because, as mentioned earlier, some students were disturbed by the school staff survey results regarding their (lower level of) connection to the second mural. It may be that, in the evaluation of their actions, students begin to think differently about their goals (Fetterman, 2013). This would be consistent with the assertion that engagement in the evaluation process can lead to organizations thinking differently about their processes and outcomes (Leviton, 2014).

Overall, we hope our telling of Change 4 Good's empowerment evaluation process has communicated two main points. The first is that elementary school students can engage in empowerment evaluation. Specifically, our students develop sophisticated and reflective ways to think about their interventions and their ability to create change in the world. They already are engaged in their community. Second, we hope this telling has demystified what can seem like a complicated and difficult process that only experts should attempt. Change 4 Good and CPRAT have learned from our reflexive evaluation. As the physical walls of the school have changed, so has the understanding of all of us engaged in this process: students, parents, teachers, and the professor alike.

Appendix 11A
Focus Group Lesson Plan

<u>Materials</u>: Hat for facilitator, whiteboard, markers, and paper and pen

<u>Number of Lessons</u>: 5–6, about 1 hour each

<u>Purpose</u>: Focus groups are designed to collect ideas and feedback from other people, in a group format. People talk about their ideas and experiences. Focus groups allow researchers to hear how people agree and disagree with one another and how their ideas might even change over the meeting. The goal of this lesson plan is to prepare elementary school students to conduct focus groups.

<u>Discussion</u>: Have a discussion about what focus groups are and why they are used. Have students ever participated in a group discussion that was about their experiences and opinions? What was it like? Discuss the role of the facilitator and how the facilitator should behave while conducting focus groups. Together, and based on a discussion of times when students have felt like they could share in a group versus times when they felt like they could not, develop a set of facilitator guidelines for a focus group.

They will probably look something like this:

1. Share guidelines with all participants in the focus group.
2. Make everyone feel comfortable.
3. Make eye contact and nod your head as participants speak.
4. Keep an open posture.
5. Use friendly body language.
6. Don't laugh at people's responses. There are no right *or* wrong answers.
7. People are allowed to disagree. In fact, disagreement is encouraged because with focus groups, we want to hear lots of different ideas.

8. Let others answer for themselves. Do not answer for other people.

9. Ask "clarifying questions" to help people make their responses more clear.

10. Let people know that their responses are "confidential." That means that you will share their answers, but you won't tell anyone the name of the person who said it.

11. Tell all participants that they should not talk with others about what happened in the focus group, and they should not gossip about what people said.

After the guidelines are set, discuss (with examples) the difference between open- and closed-ended questions. Closed-ended questions have a finite number of answers and do not allow the members of the focus group to go in-depth with the topic. Open-ended questions are preferred in a focus group because they allow more in-depth responses.

Skits: To show what the physical aspects of appropriate facilitating within a focus group would look like, have the research assistants (RAs; or another group who has been trained in focus groups) present a skit. One RA could wear a hat to differentiate herself or himself as the facilitator. During the skit, the facilitator practices asking each of the other RAs questions about their favorite TV shows.

Examples of *appropriate* facilitating include making direct eye contact, maintaining open posture, nodding, and asking more about each person's answer.

Examples of *inappropriate* facilitating include crossed arms, laughing at or making fun of answers, whispering to others in the group, and looking bored or interrupting the participant when answering the question.

Set the skit up like a game; every time the facilitator does something that breaks a guideline, have the students clap once, freeze the skit, write the problem they identify on the whiteboard, and continue on with the skit. When the RAs finish the skit, discuss with the students what the facilitator did and what the facilitator could improve on.

In the following lesson, perform another skit to focus on open-ended and closed-ended questions rather than focusing on the ethical aspects of facilitating. The facilitator should ask closed- and open-ended questions about a topic, such as ice cream. A question such as "Do you like ice cream?" can be used to show a closed-ended question, while a question like "What kind of ice cream do you like?" can be used to illustrate open-ended questions.

The RAs should give lengthier, in-depth answers in response to open-ended questions to demonstrate the wider array of answers. This time, do not have the students clap, but have them note the different types of questions that the facilitator asks and how the responses differ. After the skit, have the students discuss the differences between the responses to open- and closed-ended questions. Then have them practice turning the closed-ended questions into open-ended questions. For example, instead of asking, "Do you prefer chocolate or sprinkles on your ice cream?" they could ask, "What kind of toppings do you like on your ice cream?"

Practice Groups: After the skits, place the students into small groups (about four students each and one RA) and ask them to demonstrate the facilitating skills they learned. Choose a facilitator or two for each group, and have them choose various topics to discuss in their groups to practice applying good facilitating skills. Throughout these practice groups, a number of issues that weren't discussed in the larger group can be discussed. The students are reminded that they will be using these skills when they facilitate their own focus groups. With the small group, determine what other issues came up.

In the next lesson, bring all of the issues, concerns, and questions that came up in the practice groups and discuss how to handle these issues with all the students. Modify the facilitator role as necessary. Practice the focus groups again, with these new guidelines in mind.

In the next lesson, re-visit the reason for why the focus groups will be conducted and start to brainstorm a focus group protocol in small groups (this should include an introduction as to why the focus groups are happening, the guidelines for the discussion, and the questions to be asked, paying attention to open- and closed-ended questions). Once the protocol is set, have the students practice the protocol in small groups, with one RA in each group. With the students, the RA should note the issues, concerns, and problems that arise in the focus group. Bring these issues back to the large group and modify the protocol as necessary. Keep going with this iterative process until the protocol is set and all students are comfortable facilitating a focus group.

Appendix 11B
Focus Group Script

Ice-Breaker List

Facilitator and co-facilitator select the ice-breaker, either a "check-in" prompt OR a game.

What's your favorite (select one or two of these check-in prompts):

Hobby	Game/Ride
Movie/Cartoon/TV Show	Sport
Song/Artist/Singer	Food

These can be "acted out," as in the form of charade; or if the student didn't want to act it out, the student could say it.

Games (select one game):

Shabuya	Down by the bay (clapping game)
Hokie pokie	Patty cake (clapping game)
Simon says	Double this (clapping game)

Introduction

Hello! Thank you for participating in the focus group. My name is _____, I am in the _____ grade, and I will be the facilitator. My name is _____, and I am in the _____ grade, and I will be the co-facilitator. [switch to note-taker] And my name is_____, I am in the _____ grade, and I will be the note-taker.

We are the students from the "Change 4 Good" after-school program, and we want to see what students in the third, fourth, and fifth grades at

Maplewood Elementary think about the "We Are Powerful" mural. We want to do focus groups to assess how other students at our school feel and think about the mural, and what students want to see in a future mural at our school.

Focus groups are a method of social science research where people get into a group and they are asked questions about a topic. The themes that come out of these discussions will give us information about the mural and what other students think and feel about it. Your responses will be unknown. We will not share your answers, and we won't tell anyone your name and what you said. We will only take notes of what is said and happens in the focus group. You can decide to participate or not to participate in the focus group at any time.

Guidelines

1. Make everyone feel comfortable.

2. Make eye contact and nod your head as they speak.

3. Keep an open posture.

4. Use friendly body language.

5. Don't laugh at people's responses. There are no right or wrong answers.

6. People are allowed to disagree.

7. Let others answer for themselves. Do not answer for other people.

8. People's responses are "anonymous." That means that we will not share your responses.

9. What happens in the focus group is confidential and will not be tied to your name or who you are.

Discussion Questions

1. What does the mural mean to you? What is your favorite part of the mural? Why? What does your favorite part of the mural mean to you?

2. Have students created something at this school? [*Pause and wait for students to respond.*] Why do you think the mural was made? [*Pause and wait for students to respond.*] Who do you think made it? [*If they say "strangers," it's okay; remember there are no right or wrong answers.*]

3. What do you hear other students or adults say about the mural?

4. Have you noticed the Spanish and English words on the mural? [*Pause, and check to see what students respond; do they nod their head "yes" or shake their head "no"?*] Why do you think there are Spanish AND English words? [*Pause for student responses.*] How does having Spanish and English words on the mural make you feel? [*Pause for student responses.*] Do you think other languages should be included on the next mural? If so, which languages?

5. Do you think more people should be included in helping to plan the next mural? Who? [*Pause for student responses.*] How could we include them? [*Pause.*] Did you have a chance to include your ideas in the mural? Did you have a chance to help decide what the mural should look like?

6. Whose ideas should be included in the next mural at Maplewood Elementary School (MES)? Why? [*Pause for student responses.*] How could we include your ideas and the ideas of other students in the next mural at MES?

Appendix 11C
Concept Map Activity

A concept map allows one to see visually how different terms or concepts can be connected to each other. It is similar to a "brainstorm" or a "mind map" that generates and produces different ideas. For example, think of the word *community*. Next, think of how *community* is related to other words or how it connects with other themes from the list below. Then, once you have discussed in your groups how *community* can be tied to other words or themes, cluster it. Use the template below to help you guide your thinking.

Themes:

1. **Diversity** of culture, language, race, ethnicity, and generations deserve to be acknowledged, because these can create a sense of pride and appreciation for others.

2. **Safety** can be possible by having more knowledge about gangs and how members of gangs can recruit youth, and how violence and crime can lead to unsafe communities.

3. **Resources** such as money, more jobs, and programs for all people in the community involved are needed.

4. **Education** is what we learn in our classrooms about science, math, and technology, but also how we as students support and help each other learn.

5. **History** is a way of learning and sharing experiences from the past with the present and bringing the two together to present a story of what was once a farm town and is now the growing community of Maplewood.

6. **Love** can give others hope that there can be peace in the world.

7. **Opportunities** should be created that are just and fair, and do not perpetuate racism, ageism, sexism, heterosexism and classism.

8. **Powerlessness** can lead to helplessness and sadness, as well as poverty and hunger.

9. **Community** is the joining and coming together of people to help families and schools to learn about one another, especially to learn about the different cultures that make up the community.

10. **Struggle** is the fight for human rights, to be treated equally and have the same opportunities as others.

11. **Communication** with different members of the community can lead to a safe place to live and a caring environment.

12. **Schools** are lacking resources, some of which include Spanish-English bilingual teachers; nutritious, healthy, and high-quality lunch food; and more education programs for youth.

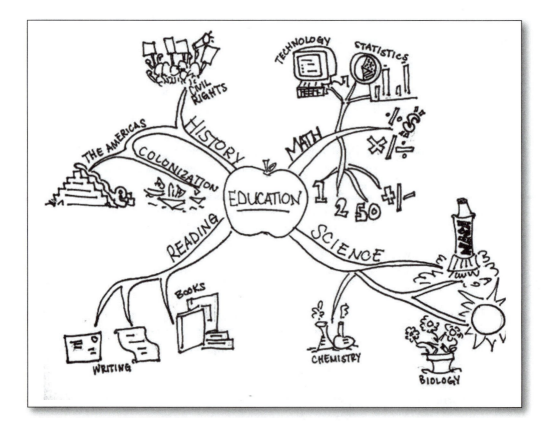

Appendix 11D
Ways to Collect Data

Our question:

Does the mural help people feel more connected to the school? Do people feel connected to the mural? Have they experienced something they see in the mural?

Possible methods

©iStockphoto.com/
pagadesign

1. Questionnaire: Having people answer questions that you've written on a piece of paper.

Which theme have you experienced that is in the mural? (Check all that apply.)

_____ Love   _____ Communication

_____ History   _____ Struggle

_____ Education   _____ Community safety

©iStockphoto.com/
Art-Y

2. Individual Interview: Asking people questions one-on-one

Have you experienced any of the themes in the mural? Can you tell me about that?

©iStockphoto.com/
cherezoff

3. Group Interview/Focus Groups/House Meetings:
Asking people questions in small groups

Have you experienced any of the themes in the mural? Can you tell me about that?

Appendix 11E

School Staff Questionnaire

We are students in the Change 4 Good after-school program and we have written this questionnaire so that we can understand better your reactions to the mural, Maplewood Stories.

					Yes
				Mostly	|
			Unsure	|	|
		A little	|	|	|
	No	↓	↓	↓	↓
1. Do you like the mural?	1	2	3	4	5
2. Do you feel good about the mural?	1	2	3	4	5
3. Do you feel confused by the mural?	1	2	3	4	5
4. Do you feel connected to the mural?	1	2	3	4	5
5. Do you understand the mural?	1	2	3	4	5
6. Did the mural change the school for the better?	1	2	3	4	5

Next, we ask some questions about the images in the mural. Please rank-order your responses, with 1 being the most/your #1 choice and 10 being the least/your last choice.

Theme and Image	I feel connected (1 = most connected; 10 = least connected)	I like it (1 = like it most; 10 = like it least)
7. History (Tree)		
8. Love (Previous principal and the horse)		
9. Education (Apple)		
10. Diversity (Rainbow and paint pallet)		
11. Communication (People talking)		
12. Working together (Clasped arms)		
13. Struggle (Megaphone and rally)		
14. Take opportunities (Graduation)		
15. Safe community (Hand making peace sign)		
16. Overall (Open book and world)		

Now, we have some questions about our next project.

17. Should Change 4 Good make another mural? (Circle one):
    Yes   No   Maybe

18. The goal of "Maplewood Stories" was to increase connection to the school by telling community stories. Do you think a future mural should tell community stories? (Circle one):   Yes   No   Maybe

Finally, we have some questions about you.

19. Did you help with the mural (for example, participate in a focus group/ house meeting, paint, provide feedback)? (Circle one):   Yes   No

20. What is your role in the school? (Circle one):

Teacher   Lunch helper   UCSC helper   Principal Nurse   Substitute teacher

Custodian   Yard duty   Teacher's aide   Secretary Librarian   Other _____

Appendix 11F

How to Clean Data

When we enter data by hand, we make errors. We need to <u>check</u> our data for errors. One way to do that is to check <u>frequencies</u>. We will assume that if all the values are within the range that we expect, then the data have been entered correctly. If the variable has values that are outside of the range, then we need to look more closely at the variable and find the error.

But what's a variable?

©iStockphoto.com/ nickylarson974

A variable is the name we give to one question we asked on the questionnaire. So, we asked people if they liked the mural, and then we named that question "like" in the dataset. "Like" is the variable name.

Okay! But what's a frequency?

In this case, a frequency is how often people answer in a certain way. So, if we asked 10 people if they liked the mural, 7 might have said "yes," 2 might have said "no," and 1 might have answered "unsure." So, for our "yes" response, our frequency is 7. For "no," it's 2. What is the frequency for "unsure"?

Got it. So how do we do this?

©iStockphoto.com/PeopleImages

First, make sure you have the questionnaires and that they are in ID order. Got it?

Now follow these instructions:

In SPSS, have your dataset open.

At the menu bar, go to <u>Analyze</u> → Descriptive statistics → Frequencies

A window will pop up and the variables will be listed there. Choose the variable you want (any variable but ID, which isn't a question we asked in our questionnaire but rather the unique number that we wrote on each questionnaire we got back. We'll see this again later).

Choose a variable by clicking on it, and then hit the right arrow. The variable will move into the "variable" column on the right. Next, click on "okay."

Whoa! What happened?

An "output" screen opened, and you can see the frequencies for each of your responses for your variable. Are all the numbers within the range you expected? Look at your codebook to see the range for that variable. If there are no errors, move on to the next variable.

I found an error. Now what?

Time to fix it! Click on the data screen. On the menu, click Data → Sort cases. Choose the variable you want (you can start to type the name of it and it'll pop up). Click on it and then click on the arrow. It'll move into the "sort by" box. Click "OK" and now look for your case that is out of range. Click on the out-of-range datum and see which number gets clicked on the left. Got it? Now scroll over and see the ID number. Now find that questionnaire and look up the variable. What should be there? FIX IT! Once you've fixed all the errors for that variable, it's time to check your work. Re-run the frequency. Is everything in range? If so, save your data and move on to the next variable. Great work!

REFERENCES

Baca, J. F. (2008). *La memoria de nuestra tierra: Sites of public memory* (Foreseeable Futures Position Paper No. 8). Retrieved from Imagining America website: http://imaginingamerica.org/fg-item/la-memoria-de-nuestra-tierra-sites-of-public-memory

Cammarota, J. (2007). A social justice approach to achievement: Guiding Latino students toward educational attainment with a challenging socially relevant curriculum. *Equity & Excellence in Education, 40,* 87–96.

Change 4 Good. (2010). *We are powerful: The story of a mural.* Unpublished book.

Change 4 Good. (2013). *Maplewood stories mural results.* Unpublished report.

Clinton, J. (2014). The true impact of evaluation: Motivation for ECB. *American Journal of Evaluation, 35*(1), 120–127.

Fernández, J. S., Nguyen, A., & Langhout, R. D. (2013). *What's the story? Concept mapping with elementary school-aged youth in a yPAR after-school program.* Manuscript submitted for publication.

Fetterman, D. M. (1994). Empowerment evaluation. *Evaluation Practice, 15*(1), 1–15.

Fetterman, D. M. (1999). Reflections on empowerment evaluation: Learning from experience. *Canadian Journal of Program Evaluation* [Special Issue], 5–37.

Fetterman, D. M. (2010a). Empowerment evaluation: An exercise in efficiency. In M. Segone (Ed.), *From policies to results: Developing capacities for country monitoring and evaluation systems* (pp. 279–288). UNICEF.

Fetterman, D. M. (2010b). *Ethnography: Step-by-step* (3rd ed.). Thousand Oaks, CA: Sage.

Fetterman, D. M. (2013). *Empowerment evaluation in the Digital Villages: Hewlett-Packard's $15 million race toward social justice.* Stanford, CA: Stanford University Press.

Fetterman, D. M., & Wandersman, A. (2007). Empowerment evaluation: Yesterday, today, and tomorrow. *American Journal of Evaluation, 28,* 179–198.

Foster-Fishman, P. G., Law, K. M., Lichty, L. F., & Aoun, C. (2010). Youth ReACT for social change: A method for youth participatory action research. *American Journal of Community Psychology, 46,* 67–83.

Kohfeldt, D. M., & Langhout, R. D. (2012). The 5 whys: A tool for defining problems in yPAR. *Journal of Community and Applied Social Psychology, 22,* 316–329.

Kozol, J. (1991). *Savage inequalities: Children in America's schools.* New York: Crown.

Labin, S. N. (2014). Developing common measures in evaluation capacity building: An iterative science and practice process. *American Journal of Evaluation, 35*(1), 107–115.

Labin, S. N., Duffy, J. L., Meyers, D. C., Wandersman, A., & Lesesne, C. A. (2012). A research synthesis of the evaluation capacity building literature. *American Journal of Evaluation, 33*(3), 307–338.

Langhout, R. D. (in press). Photovoice as a methodology. In M. B. Schenker, X. Castañeda, & A. Rodriguez-Lainz (Eds.), *Migration and health research methodologies: A handbook for the study of migrant populations.* Berkeley: University of California Press.

Langhout, R. D., & Thomas, E. (2010). Imagining participatory action research in collaboration with children: An introduction. *American Journal of Community Psychology, 46,* 60–66.

Leviton, L. C. (2014). Some underexamined aspects of evaluation capacity building. *American Journal of Evaluation, 35*(1), 90–94.

McMillan, C. B. (1975). Organizational change in schools: Bedford-Stuyvesant. *Journal of Applied Behavioral Science, 11,* 437–453.

Oullett, M. L. (1996). Systemic pathways for social transformation: School change, multicultural organization development, multicultural education, and LGBT youth. *Journal of Gay, Lesbian, and Bisexual Identity, 4,* 273–294.

Rappaport, J. (1981). In praise of paradox: A social policy of empowerment over prevention. *American Journal of Community Psychology, 9,* 1–25.

Rappaport, J., Moore, T., & Hunt, G. (Cochairs) (with E. Mattison, N. Pearce, J. Bracey, & M. Reyes Cruz). (2003, June). *It's not about education: Schooling for African-American and Latino students.* Symposium conducted at the Ninth Biennial Conference on Community Research and Action, Las Vegas, NM.

Sarason, S. B. (1971). *The culture of the school and the problem of change.* Boston: Allyn & Bacon.

Sarason, S. B. (1995). *School change: The personal development of a point of view.* New York: Teachers College Press.

Sarason, S. B. (1997). The public schools: America's Achilles heel. *American Journal of Community Psychology, 25,* 771–785.

Seidman, E. J., & Rappaport, J. (1974). The educational pyramid: A paradigm for training, research, and manpower utilization for community psychology. *American Journal of Community Psychology, 2,* 119–130.

Speer, P. W., & Hughey, J. (1995). Community organizing: An ecological route to empowerment and power. *American Journal of Community Psychology, 23,* 729–748.

Speer, P. W., Hughey, J., Gensheimer, L. K., & Adams-Leavitt, W. (1995). Organizing for power: A comparative case study. *American Journal of Community Psychology, 23,* 57–73.

Suarez-Balcazar, Y., & Taylor-Ritzler, T. (2014). Moving from science to practice in ECB. *American Journal of Evaluation, 35*(1), 95–99.

Thomas, R. E., & Rappaport, J. (1996). Art as community narrative: A resource for social change. In M. B. Lykes, A. Banuazizi, R. Liem, & M. Morris (Eds.), *Myths about the powerless: Contesting social inequalities* (pp. 317–336). Philadelphia: Temple University Press.

Wandersman, A., Snell-Johns, J., Lentz, B. E., Fetterman, D. M., Keener, D. C., Livet, M., et al. (2005). The principles of empowerment evaluation. In D. M. Fetterman & A. Wandersman (Eds.), *Empowerment evaluation principles in practice* (pp. 27–41). New York: Guilford Press.

Wang, C., & Burris, M. A. (1994). Empowerment through photo novella: Portraits of participation. *Health Education and Behavior, 21,* 171–186.

Wang, C., & Burris, M. A. (1997). Photovoice: Concept, methodology, and use for participatory needs assessment. *Health Education and Behavior, 24,* 369–387.

Warren, M. R., & Mapp, K. L. (2011). *A match on dry grass: Community organizing as a catalyst for school reform.* New York: Oxford University Press.

CHAPTER 12

Building Evaluation Capacity to Engage in Empowerment Evaluation

A Case of Organizational Transformation

Yolanda Suarez-Balcazar

University of Illinois at Chicago

Tina Taylor-Ritzler

Dominican University

Gloria Morales-Curtin

El Valor Corporation

INTRODUCTION

Community-based organizations (CBOs) in the United States provide a range of services to vulnerable individuals with a variety of needs and conditions, including individuals with disabilities and those with chronic health conditions. Social services are designed to meet basic needs, provide life skills, and promote wellness and/or well-being and full participation in the community. In 1993, the U.S. government passed the Government Performance and Results Act (GPRA), which holds federal agencies accountable for outcomes exerting pressure on social service programs receiving federal funding (Kravchuk & Schack, 1996).

The pressure for accountability extended beyond programs receiving government funding. By the time the GPRA was introduced, United Way and other funders of social programs had already introduced outcome measurement systems, making funding contingent on providing evidence of outcomes (Kaplan & Garrett, 2005).

CBOs have experienced many challenges in responding to accountability mandates. Few CBOs providing disability and other health and social services evaluate outcomes or measure performance (Carman, 2007). This deficiency of attention to evaluation is rooted in a lack of knowledge and skills about how to design or implement evaluation activities, along with an absence of capacity in the systems needed to sustain evaluation activities (Suarez-Balcazar, Orellana-Damacela, Portillo, Lanum, & Sharma, 2003). Such challenges are related to the difficulty of discerning the differences between types of evaluation (such as needs assessment, monitoring, management practices, and/or outcome evaluation), as well as related to the specific skills necessary to develop tools and collect and analyze information to document program processes and successes (Carman, 2007; Garcia-Iriarte, Suarez-Balcazar, & Taylor-Ritzler, 2011). To address these challenges, many CBOs have chosen to invest in building partnerships with collaborators who can assist in building evaluation capacity (see Fetterman, 2001; Fetterman, Kaftarian, & Wandersman, 1996).

Empowerment evaluation was selected as an approach for the CBO that is the focus of this case study for several reasons. The CBO wanted to minimize reliance on external consultants and institutionalize evaluation by building the evaluation skills of staff in order to meet funders' pressure to report program outcomes. The university partners introduced the organization to empowerment evaluation because the empowerment evaluation principles of *social justice* and *inclusion* fit well with the organization's mission, values, and efforts to meet the needs of a vulnerable population. Additionally, the principle of *capacity building* fit the organization's desire to mainstream and institutionalize evaluation activities. As described by Labin, Duffy, Meyers, Wandersman, and Lesesne (2012), capacity building is designed to enhance staff evaluation skills and knowledge so that they have the ability to conduct their own evaluations.

The purpose of this chapter is to describe the process of organizational transformation, as experienced by a CBO over a 7-year partnership with a team of evaluators from the University of Illinois at Chicago. We describe the transformation process according to the three-step empowerment evaluation approach (Fetterman, 2013): (1) redefine the mission and purpose; (2) take stock of current efforts; and (3) plan for the future (see Fetterman & Wandersman, 2005, 2007). We also describe the CBO's transformation through the facets of empowerment evaluation—training for capacity building, facilitation, advocacy, illumination, and liberation. We discuss how the organization embraced empowerment evaluation principles of *capacity building, improvement, organizational learning, inclusion, social justice, evidence-based strategies,* and *accountability* as they mainstreamed and institutionalized evaluation activities (see Fetterman & Wandersman, 2005). As stated by Lentz et al. (2005), building the capacity of a CBO to integrate evaluation within its daily activities—"mainstreaming"—requires transformative learning. Evidence of transformative learning is captured through the voice of the CBO partner, represented by the third author, included in quotes throughout the chapter. In addition, Table 12.1 provides a brief summary of the empowerment evaluation principles that are relevant to and intertwined within the case study, with examples that illustrate their evidence and a quote from the third author.

Table 12.1   Putting It All Together: Empowerment Evaluation Principles at Work

Principles	Example of Evidence	Voices From Stakeholders
Capacity Building	The evaluators provided training and brainstorming sessions, ongoing technical assistance, and ongoing feedback on outcome indicators, logic models, and outcomes tracking forms.	"Training activities and brainstorming sessions helped us understand the importance of evaluation and how to develop logic models and measure outcomes."
Organizational Learning	The organization established regular meetings to review evaluation outcomes, logic models are posted on walls for everyone to see, staff share outcomes with each other, staff use evaluation language.	"Twice a week staff has time to reflect on outcomes and enter outcome data. We have meetings every quarter to look at where we are as an organization and review our participants' outcomes."
Improvement	Staff modified the outcomes tracking forms and updated evaluation forms to inform continuous improvement in services.	"I now have a comprehensive understanding of how evaluation works and how to use results to improve our programs."
Inclusion	The voices of participants are included in the evaluation process. Staff ran focus groups with participants. Participants are asked to choose their own goals and speak up. Family members are being included as well.	"Participants are part of the process and are always engaged in making their choices and as peer-to-peer support. Lead participants are now teaching sign language classes to new participants."

(Continued)

Table 12.1 (Continued)

Principles	Example of Evidence	Voices From Stakeholders
Social Justice	Staff changed the way they conceive of outcomes of interest. The organization facilitated self-determination and advocacy skills in participants with disabilities.	"We provide opportunities for participants to make their own choices, know their rights, make choices independent from a parent, choice of meals, clothing, relationships, things they want to do."
Accountability	Evaluation reports are produced for the Board, funders, and accreditation bodies. All programs are currently being evaluated.	"All staff has documentation requirements and participates in monthly reviews of progress and outcomes. Evaluations are also used to gain funding and political support."
Evidence-based Strategies	The organization is using results to plan future actions. The organization is also expanding their collaborations with other local academic institutions to enhance their access to evidence-based strategies and practices.	"We are expanding our partnerships to help us stay connected and stay abreast with what is being published and what works."
Democratic Participation	Staff, participants, and their family members are invited to provide input and participate in the decisions that impact programming.	"We are including our participants and families in decision making more than ever before."

BACKGROUND AND CONTEXT

El Valor is a CBO located in a predominantly Latino neighborhood that provides an array of programs to over 1,000 individuals with intelectual and developmental disabilities and their families with the mission of assisting them in becoming fully integrated and involved in their comunities. The organization provides developmental training, vocational evaluation and employment services, community residential options, family respite services, and brain injury case management, among other services. El Valor is largely funded by grants from United Way, state funding, and not-for-profit and private foundations.

When we began the partnership, the CBO was preparing for an accreditation visit from the Commission on Accreditation of Rehabilitation Facilities (CARF), whose reviews often impact opportunities for funding. The organization was experiencing challenges documenting program outcomes and integrating evaluation requirements from CARF as well as other funders including United Way and the Illinois Department of Human Services (see Suarez-Balcazar et al., 2010).

THE PROCESS OF ORGANIZATIONAL TRANSFORMATION THROUGH EVALUATION CAPACITY BUILDING

Empowerment Evaluation Steps

1. Redefine the mission and purpose

According to Fetterman (2005), during this step the organization's staff clarifies its mission and its purpose and identifies common ground and common interests. To achieve this, we engaged in several activities, including facilitating two brainstorming sessions; interviewing and shadowing staff and program participants to obtain stakeholders' views of the program's mission, vision, and goals; and reviewing past evaluation and accreditation reports. Preskill and Boyle (2008) and Taut (2007) noted that these are preliminary activities that help gauge an organization's readiness for evaluation capacity building (ECB).

The following quote from the third author illustrates the organizational context at that time:

> We started thinking about our need to get some evaluation training when CARF accreditation was coming and I was pulling my hair out. We had a consultant that came, gave us some tools that did not address the funders standards and left. We also had an opportunity to work with United Way and they were requesting a logic model and we did not have one. We were focusing on *activities* and not focusing on *outcomes*. We were looking into moving participants within the program and yet, not including participants' voices in the evaluation process. We did not know what to do. We were trying to incorporate (in the evaluation) the requirements of CARF, United Way, and the Department of Human Services (funders at the time) and it was hard. (G. Morales-Curtin, personal communication, 2013)

Clarifying the organization's mission and purpose was key to helping the CBO rethink how they were facilitating the inclusion, self-determination, and independence of individuals with developmental disabilities as they struggled to respond to pressures for accountability from various funding entities. From this initial step, it became clear that the CBO needed to rethink participant outcomes and how to translate their values of fostering independence and self-determination among participants into action.

2. Take stock of current efforts

During this step, the organization identifies priorities and strategies that will assist in achieving its mission (Fetterman, 2005). To facilitate the process of identifying priorities and identifying areas for ECB, we used the Evaluation Capacity Assessment Instrument (ECAI, see Table 12.2), developed and

Table 12.2 Evaluation Capacity Assessment Instrument

EVALUATION CAPACITY ASSESSMENT INSTRUMENT

Please circle the number that best corresponds to your level of agreement with each of the statements in the sections that follow. Base your ratings on <u>the program where you work</u> as a staff person.

SECTION I: About You

Thoughts about Evaluation

I think that an evaluation...	Strongly Disagree	Disagree	Agree	Strongly Agree
1. Will help me understand my program.	1	2	3	4
2. Will inform the decisions I make about my program.	1	2	3	4
3. Will justify funding for my program.	1	2	3	4

I think that an evaluation...	Strongly Disagree	Disagree	Agree	Strongly Agree
4. Will help to convince managers that changes are needed in my program.	1	2	3	4
5. Will inform changes in our documentation systems.	1	2	3	4
6. Is absolutely necessary to improve my program.	1	2	3	4
7. Should involve program participants in the evaluation process.	1	2	3	4
8. Will influence policy relevant to my program.	1	2	3	4
9. Will help improve services to people from diverse ethnic backgrounds who also have disabilities.	1	2	3	4
10. Is unnecessary because we already know what is best for our participants.	1	2	3	4
11. Is too complex for our staff to do.	1	2	3	4

Motivation to Engage in Evaluation

I am motivated to...	Strongly Disagree	Disagree	Agree	Strongly Agree
1. Learn about evaluation.	1	2	3	4
2. Start evaluating my program.	1	2	3	4
3. Support other staff to evaluate their program.	1	2	3	4
4. Encourage others to buy into evaluating our program.	1	2	3	4

(Continued)

Table 12.2 (Continued)

Evaluation Knowledge and Skills

I know how to...	Strongly Disagree	Disagree	Agree	Strongly Agree
1. Develop an evaluation plan.	1	2	3	4
2. Clearly state measurable goals and objectives for my program.	1	2	3	4
3. Identify strategies to collect information from participants.	1	2	3	4
4. Define outcome indicators of my program.	1	2	3	4
5. Decide what questions to answer in an evaluation.	1	2	3	4
6. Decide from whom to collect the information.	1	2	3	4
7. Collect evaluation information.	1	2	3	4
8. Analyze evaluation information.	1	2	3	4
9. Develop recommendations based on evaluation results.	1	2	3	4
10. Examine the impact of my program on people from diverse ethnic/racial backgrounds and/or people with disabilities.	1	2	3	4
11. Write an evaluation report.	1	2	3	4
12. Conduct an evaluation of my program on my own.	1	2	3	4

I know how to...	Strongly Disagree	Disagree	Agree	Strongly Agree
13. Conduct an evaluation of my program with support from others.	1	2	3	4
14. Present evaluation findings orally.	1	2	3	4

SECTION II: About Your Organization

Leadership

	Strongly Disagree	Disagree	Agree	Strongly Agree
1. I provide effective leadership.	1	2	3	4
2. Staff understands how everyone's duties fit together as part of the overall mission of the program.	1	2	3	4
3. I communicate program goals and objectives clearly.	1	2	3	4
4. I have a clear plan for accomplishing program goals.	1	2	3	4
5. I have realistic expectations of what staff can accomplish given the resources they have available.	1	2	3	4

Learning Climate

The program where I work fosters an environment in which...	Strongly Disagree	Disagree	Agree	Strongly Agree
1. Evaluation information is shared in open forums.	1	2	3	4
2. Staff is supported to introduce new approaches in the course of their work.	1	2	3	4

(Continued)

Table 12.2 (Continued)

The program where I work fosters an environment in which...	Strongly Disagree	Disagree	Agree	Strongly Agree
3. It is easy for staff to meet regularly to discuss issues.	1	2	3	4
4. Staff is provided opportunities to assess how well they are doing, what they can do better, and what is working.	1	2	3	4
5. Staff can encourage managers and peers to make use of evaluation findings.	1	2	3	4
6. Staff respects each other's perspectives and opinions.	1	2	3	4
7. Staff errors lead to teachable moments rather than criticisms.	1	2	3	4
8. Staff participates in making long-term plans for their program.	1	2	3	4
9. Staff concerns are ignored in most decisions regarding strategic planning and evaluation.	1	2	3	4

Resources for Evaluation

In my program...	Strongly Disagree	Disagree	Agree	Strongly Agree
1. Resources are allocated to provide accommodations for people from diverse ethnic	1	2	3	4

In my program...	Strongly Disagree	Disagree	Agree	Strongly Agree
backgrounds and for people with disabilities to collect evaluation information (e.g., interpreters, translated documents).				
2. Staff has time to conduct evaluation activities (e.g., identifying or developing a survey, collecting information from participants).	1	2	3	4
3. Staff has access to technology to compile information into computerized records.	1	2	3	4
4. Staff has access to adequate technology to produce summary reports of information collected from participants (e.g., computerized database).	1	2	3	4
5. Resources are allocated for staff training (e.g., money, time, bringing in consultants).	1	2	3	4
6. Technical assistance is available to staff to address questions related to evaluation.	1	2	3	4
7. Funders provide resources (e.g., training, money, etc.) to conduct evaluation.	1	2	3	4
8. Funders provide leadership for conducting evaluation.	1	2	3	4
9. Agency leadership engages in ongoing dialogue with funders regarding evaluation.	1	2	3	4

(Continued)

Table 12.2 (Continued)

SECTION III: About Your Work				
Evaluation as Part of Your Job				
	Strongly Disagree	Disagree	Agree	Strongly Agree
1. My program gathers information from diverse stakeholders to gauge how well the program is doing.	1	2	3	4
2. My program has adequate records of past evaluation efforts and what happened as a result.	1	2	3	4
3. I have access to the information I need to make decisions regarding my work.	1	2	3	4
4. I am able to integrate evaluation activities into my daily work practices.	1	2	3	4
5. The evaluation activities I engage in are consistent with funders' expectations.	1	2	3	4

Use of Evaluation Findings

Please indicate the extent to which your program currently uses evaluation results for the following purposes:	Not at All	To Some Extent	To a Considerable Extent	To a Very Great Extent
1. To report to a funder.	1	2	3	4
2. To improve services or programs.	1	2	3	4

Please indicate the extent to which your program currently uses evaluation results for the following purposes:	Not at All	To Some Extent	To a Considerable Extent	To a Very Great Extent
3. To get additional funding.	1	2	3	4
4. To design ongoing monitoring processes.	1	2	3	4
5. To assess implementation of a program.	1	2	3	4
6. To assess quality of a program.	1	2	3	4
7. To improve outreach.	1	2	3	4
8. To make informed decisions.	1	2	3	4
9. To train staff.	1	2	3	4
10. To develop best practices.	1	2	3	4
11. To eliminate unneeded services or programs.	1	2	3	4

Have you been involved in past efforts to evaluate a program at your agengy?

☐ No

☐ Yes. If Yes, please explain your role:

_____

_____

Have you had any previous training in evaluation? (1) No (2) Yes

If your answer is yes, please indicate the type of training:

(1) Course about evaluation as a part of your educational/college training

(2) Workshops

(3) Talks/conferences

(4) Experience conducting/collaborating in evaluations

SOURCE: Taylor-Ritzler, Suarez-Balcazar, Garcia, Henry, & Balcazar. (2013), American Journal of Evaluation (34, 2), pp. 202–204, © 2013 by Sage Publications. Reprinted by Permission of SAGE Publications.

empirically validated by Taylor-Ritzler, Suarez-Balcazar, Garcia-Iriarte, Henry, and Balcazar (2013). The ECAI was derived from the empirical and theoretical literature on ECB (e.g., Labin et al., 2012; Preskill & Boyle, 2008). The application of the ECAI with this CBO identified leadership as crucial to successful ECB efforts. Specifically, the organization's leader and one staff member became the catalysts for change within the organization (see Garcia-Iriarte et al., 2011).

From the ECAI assessment, interviews, and our review of documents, it became clear that despite the CBO's strengths, staff were experiencing several challenges. Specifically, we identified very high levels of self-reported awareness of the need for evaluation and high levels of motivation to engage in evaluation from senior administrators of the program, with more moderate levels from program staff. Some of the program staff were initially very resistant to the idea of evaluating their programs. Although senior administrators were clear with staff about the need for program documentation and evaluation, staff questioned why evaluation was important and how program participants would benefit from their efforts at program documentation.

Moreover, responses on the ECAI and our review of documents also indicated consistently lower levels of self-reported knowledge related to evaluation. There was confusion in understanding the terms *output* and *outcome*. These terms were used interchangeably and typical outputs, such as the type and number of activities offered to participants, were reported as outcomes. Other evaluation researchers have noted that distinguishing these terms and applying an outcomes approach is often a challenge for CBOs (Wandersman, 2014; Wandersman, Imm, Chinman, & Kaftarian, 2000). Staff members had difficulty conceptualizing the purpose of their activities with participants as processes related to desired outcomes. Staff understood that their funders required them to focus on five key areas of services with participants that included activities of daily living; financial/monetary skills; community integration; socialization and communication skills; and health and safety skills. It became clear to the staff that attendance at a math class does not ensure that a participant knows how to purchase a bus ticket at a local station to visit a museum located in the city's downtown area. The forms and processes that were in place were not tracking indicators of the impact of the program's services. Rather, program staff were only tracking activities that their consumers engaged in. This is well illustrated by the following statement from the third author:

> We thought we were doing all this great work for people with disabilities as we were so busy doing and recording "activities" we did with participants as our out-

comes. We did not know that our activities were not necessarily outcomes. (G. Morales-Curtin, personal communication, 2013)

The ECAI also revealed that the CBO routinely did not use evaluation processes and results to inform decision making and program improvement. Instead, program records were kept solely for accreditation purposes, recorded by hand and kept in large binders. As a result, the information was not easily useful to assess program outcomes across participants. Moreover, the staff realized that the recording formats and tracking sheets they used were redundant, in part, due to the multiple forms required by funders. Due to the large volume of paperwork required to document each contact with each participant, the administration had granted each staff member time twice a week to devote to completing paperwork. This resulted in frustration from staff and frequent missing fields on forms. The following quote summarizes the state of evaluation at the CBO:

> Until [the evaluators] came here I did not see the connection between documentation processes and program improvement. There were forms and paperwork, but there was no link to the logic model or outcomes. I would count my numbers and put it in a binder for CARF when they came. (G. Morales-Curtin, personal communication, 2013)

Based on interviews and informal brainstorming sessions we also noted that the CBO was not receiving support or guidance from their funders, who required evaluation reports. Overall, the identification of strengths and areas of need enabled the CBO to take stock of the need for ECB. Most important, staff was open and ready to learn and use evaluation in an empowering way. The staff identified the development of logic models as a very important process about which they needed a critical friend who could provide them with feedback and input.

3. Plan for the future

During this step, the organization used the priorities identified through taking stock to plan an organizational transformation process (Fetterman, 2005). Once the CBO took stock of the priorities related to evaluation of their programs—areas of strength and areas of need—we developed a plan for capacity building that would lay a foundation for empowerment evaluation.

Training for Capacity Building

According to Fetterman and Wandersman (2005), capacity building is one of the core principles of empowerment evaluation that enables an organization to conduct its own evaluations. Our capacity building approach, informed by the assessment activities reported earlier, was multifaceted. The plan included group training and brainstorming sessions, one-on-one coaching with specific staff in leadership positions, and ongoing input. Through training sessions we built awareness and understanding of the need for evaluation, developed basic evaluation competencies among staff (e.g., understanding the difference between an output and an outcome, developing a logic model, and identifying outcome indicators), and strengthened leadership related to evaluation. The CBO's leaders supported the development of a learning climate wherein data were used to inform decision making, improve programs, and support staff to innovate. In addition, the evaluation allowed the CBO to reallocate resources to support improved evaluation capacity.

Capacity building for empowerment evaluation is a cyclical and continuous process of program improvement (see Fetterman, Deitz, & Gesundheit, 2010; Fetterman & Wandersman, 2007; Livet & Wandersman, 2005), especially in light of resource shortages, staff workload, and staff turnover. We used the ECAI after capacity building activities were implemented to evaluate their impact, serving as a feedback loop in the process to inform additional planning. During the early years of the partnership, the CBO was faced with the layoffs of six critical staff members due to budget cuts. According to the third author, many changes impacted the organization, increasing their desire to mainstream evaluation practices and activities:

> Over this time period many changes with the State happened that impacted our work. Programs and budgets were cut, delayed payment to vendors, and state conversion from grants to agencies to fee-for-services. To stay competitive, we made the decision to maintain CARF accreditation to ensure quality programming and of course evaluation became critical. (G. Morales-Curtin, personal communication, 2013)

Over the course of 7 years, our team worked closely with the program administrators and staff on several initiatives that were designed to strengthen overall evaluation capacity and result in authentic empowerment evaluation. We held brainstorming sessions to discuss the challenge of staff completing what were at that time burdensome documentation requirements. During the first brainstorming session, staff expressed having an epiphany—they more clearly understood the need to track progress toward goals, rather than solely tracking activities. These brainstorming sessions helped demystify evaluation activities. Discussion then centered around how to support the redesign of the CBO's documentation systems and forms to capture relevant information about activities and related outputs, as well as goals and related outcomes.

We spent several sessions having staff develop, share, and refine their logic models with one another. We ran logic model review sessions and outcomes training refresher sessions as regularly as once a semester or as requested by the organization. In these ways, we found evidence that evaluation capacity was being built. These capacity building activities led to other facets of empowerment evaluation— facilitation, advocacy, illumination, and liberation.

Facilitation

To facilitate ongoing organizational transformation, we have provided regular support to the CBO and played the role of critical friend in several ways. We have sat on accreditation reviews and provided input when requested by the leader of the CBO; we have provided feedback on grant proposals; matched graduate students (enrolled in a program evaluation course) with the CBO to assist with evaluations of specific programs; facilitated refresher sessions on logic models; provided input on documentation forms and protocols; and we have assisted with data analysis of evaluation surveys that were developed and conducted by staff. The facilitation process has also been reciprocal. The CBO's leader and staff have lectured at our graduate seminars at the university on empowering participants with developmental disabilities through evaluation and discussed the challenges and benefits of engaging in empowerment evaluation at the individual and organizational levels.

Reassessment of evaluation capacity using the ECAI, ongoing conversations with staff, and observations of evaluation processes within the CBO have revealed improvements in staff members' awareness, motivation, and competence related to evaluation, as well as improvements in leadership, learning climate, and resources allocated to evaluation. Specifically, staff became interested in learning about evaluation and ways to improve their documentation processes so that these would reflect the impact of their services and supports on program participants. The CBO embraced empowerment evaluation principles including creating an organizational learning climate that supports evaluation. We observed that CBO staff post their logic models on the walls to elicit feedback and to discuss evaluation plans at meetings. The organization also embraced the principle of accountability by requiring all programs to measure and document outcomes with the goal of improving programs (see Table 12.1).

Advocacy

At the core of advocacy in empowerment evaluation is the link between self-evaluation and advocacy activities at the level of the individual participant (Fetterman, 2001). The CBO has a very strong commitment to promoting advocacy skills among program participants, yet at the beginning of the partnership they were struggling with how to engage participants with developmental and intellectual disabilities in advocating for their wishes, identifying their own goals, and evaluating their goal achievement. Traditionally, the direct support staff and counselor assigned to each participant played a critical role in identifying goals *for* the participant. Our team worked with the program administrators and staff to support their adoption of procedures that would allow for the development of more authentic and individualized goals identified *by* participants.

During our partnership, one of our graduate students developed her dissertation study on empowerment evaluation with CBO participants as they took control of their own Individual Service Plans (ISP). She built on the foundation that had been laid through our earlier work and used a capacity building approach to train staff to empower participants to advocate for themselves and take control of their own choices (see Garcia-Iriarte, 2009). She helped the staff design goal evaluation forms that reflected the views of program participants and that were more culturally appropriate and fully accessible for individuals with intellectual and developmental disabilities, taking into consideration literacy levels and disability issues. The use of these visual tools was designed to promote inclusion, self-determination, and decision making by participants. Once developed, the staff and participants took the goal-tracking forms, tweaked them, and made them their own. These tools assist participants in selecting goals, tracking progress toward goals, and promoting inclusion by bringing their voices into the evaluation process. Currently the staff and participants are utilizing these evaluation forms. Figure 12.1 illustrates two examples (out of 24) of possible life skills supported at the organization from which the participant chooses his/her goals.

> Participants are now expressing their needs, speaking about their rights and making choices. Opportunities are being presented to the participants to speak out and participate in community events. This is the key change the CBO is seeing; community participation, volunteering in their communities and working, being independent at home and at work (travel, trips) and giving the participant the right to choose what he/she wants. (G. Morales-Curtin, personal communication, 2013)

To support advocacy efforts, the CBO facilitated the involvement of participants in the national People First Movement, which has chapters across the United States. The main focus of People First is to promote independence and

Figure 12.1   Examples of goals accessible to participants with developmental disabilities

Medication Management   Money Management

©iStockphoto.com/ AndrewSoundarajan, ©iStockphoto.com/ AlexKalina

self-determination by increasing members' skills, as well as knowledge and awareness of their rights. The movement addresses members' needs for socialization and full participation in society, as well as building a national agenda for inclusion of people with intellectual disabilities in all aspects of community life. The inclusion of El Valor's participants in this movement had an impact on family members and service providers' attitudes and behaviors, as they became more supporting of self-advocacy and self-determination efforts (see Kramer, Kramer, Garcia-Iriarte, & Hammel, 2011).

> State cuts eliminated leisure/recreational activities for participants. Therefore supporting the People First movement was important for us. This was a critical area where participants were not "programmed" but had clear opportunity for growth. The CBO supports the movement with staff time and fund raising efforts to take trips, Camp Confidence and attend conferences such as "Speak Up Speak Out." (G. Morales-Curtin, personal communication, 2013)

Illumination

Several "eye-opening, revealing, and enlightening experiences" (Fetterman, 2001, p. 37) have taken place at the CBO throughout the empowerment evaluation process. Program staff transformed their ways of thinking about evaluation from something they had to do for an external source or as a result of a mandate, to a tool they could use to better understand and improve their programs. The organization's staff acquired evaluation knowledge and was able to accurately use evaluation terms and identify evaluation uses. For example, program staff understood the usefulness of writing SMART participant goals (specific, measurable, attainable, realistic, and timely; see also Getting To Outcomes, Chinman, Imm, & Wandersman, 2004). The staff embraced and consistently used evaluation language.

Most significant, through the empowerment evaluation process, the staff realized that the core values of the CBO—fostering independence, self-determination, inclusion, and social justice for individuals with disabilities—were not reflected in the planning, implementation, and evaluation of the organization's programs. In fact, the voices of participants were not included in programming and programs were fostering dependency rather than interdependence or independence, as indicated by this quote:

> We were thinking that by serving vulnerable people we were being inclusive and achieving our outcomes. We were not asking participants what they wanted. Now things are different. Participants tell us what they want and we listen. They choose their own goals. (G. Morales-Curtin, personal communication, 2013)

This realization was followed by discussions among staff and focus groups with participants conducted by the staff. As a result of these sessions, a satisfaction survey was developed by staff and participants that is currently being utilized regularly. An example of one question is illustrated in Figure 12.2. The organization now uses these more accessible evaluation forms (Figures 12.1 and 12.2) on a regular basis.

Liberation

As articulated by Fetterman (2001), liberation frees the individual and/or organization from preexisting roles, constraints, and preconceived ideas or frameworks that can hinder empowerment evaluation efforts. At the organizational level, staff, counselors and managers, and administrators began to reconceptualize the notions of advocacy and independence. Given that most of the participants are from Latino backgrounds, culturally speaking, family members tend to embrace more paternalistic and interdependent ways of relating to their family member with a disability, despite the fact that the CBO prides itself on promoting advocacy, empowerment, and independence. Through the empowerment evaluation process, the organization transformed their own views and

Figure 12.2 Example of an evaluation question

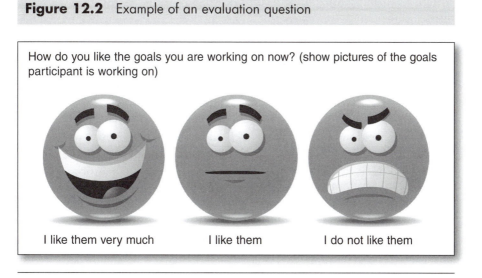

How do you like the goals you are working on now? (show pictures of the goals participant is working on)

I like them very much   I like them   I do not like them

©iStockphoto.com/ mstay

ways of providing services from a paternalistic perspective to one that is culturally sensitive and fosters both interdependence and independence, allowing the
participant to speak for himself/herself despite their intellectual or developmental disability. They also began to focus more on educating family members
about the notion of rights, advocacy, and independence. In this way they
embraced the empowerment evaluation principles of social justice, democratic
participation, and inclusion (see Table 12.1).

Key to this process was that the CBO's leader transformed her views and
practices by allowing staff and participants to have more autonomy in the
evaluation process itself. This action liberated her from controlling the process and liberated participants and staff by providing them with more
choices.

Also critical at this stage was the liberation of the CBO from reliance on the
evaluators. In the role of critical friend, the evaluators have been able to stay
connected with the organization given the level of reciprocity and support that
has been built for one another's work, but the CBO is fully and independently
engaged in evaluation that is mainstreamed and institutionalized into its daily
activities. They make their own decisions about when and what type of assistance to request from evaluation experts.

As part of the liberation process, the CBO is expanding its partnerships
and relationships with funders, the community, and different academic units

within local universities. Liberation takes many forms as illustrated by the third author:

> The CBO is expanding its role seeking out funding from other sources utilizing the management reporting and outcomes to seek additional funding sources and minimize state dependence, liberating us from state dependency because it has many strings attached. (G. Morales-Curtin, personal communication, 2013)

The organization is bringing together diverse disciplines and partners to support evidence-based models that will improve outcomes for individuals with disabilities. Currently, the organization is in a state of expansion, continuous improvement, and creating natural learning environments as they embrace several principles of empowerment evaluation (see Table 12.1).

> It is a liberating feeling to take on challenges that appear to be unattainable and with strong relationships working together and willing to embrace change— we were able to change a system. (G. Morales-Curtin, personal communication, 2013)

Empowerment Evaluation Outcomes

Empowerment evaluation is intended to promote successful programs by helping organizations to mainstream evaluation practices that allow them to assess and continually improve their programs (Livet & Wandersman, 2005). As noted in Table 12.1, in this case study we gathered evidence that these intended outcomes were achieved. Based on several pieces of evidence, including repeated scores on the ECAI completed by staff (about midway [$N = 17$] through the partnership when the ECAI was developed and again 4 years later [$N = 16$]), direct observations, and review of products (e.g., evaluation reports), critical improvements were achieved. The average ratings on the 4-point ECAI improved significantly for the following subscales: individual staff motivation (mid mean = 3.00, SD = .43; post mean = 3.45, SD = .44; $t(30) = -2.93$, $p < .05$), organizational leadership related to evaluation (mid mean = 2.18, SD = .58; post mean = 2.76, SD = .36; $t(31) = -3.40$, $p < .05$), and the critical evaluation capacity outcome of mainstreaming evaluation into work processes (mid mean = 2.39, SD = .46); post mean = 2.89, SD = .66; $t(31) = -2.50$, $p < .05$). Furthermore, staff demonstrated evaluation skills through their evaluation reports, application of the participant satisfaction survey, and application of empowerment evaluation principles in the process of supporting the participant's goal selection (see Garcia-Iriarte et al., 2011; Suarez-Balcazar et al., 2010). As noted earlier, the CBO experienced improved leadership related to championing evaluation, and also committed more resources to evaluation processes (including improved access to technology to produce summary reports of program information: mid mean = 2.12, SD = .70; post mean = 2.69, SD = .79; $t[31]$ = −2.20, $p < .05$), and developed a stronger learning climate that supported improved management and accountability (evaluation information was shared significantly more in open forums: mid mean = 2.06, SD = .68; post mean = 2.68, SD = .87; $t[31]$ = −2.26, $p < .05$). Despite the methodological limitations—small sample size and lack of control group—the results of the ECAI were encouraging.

Strengthening all of these elements of evaluation capacity led to organizational self-assessment related to planning and implementing program services that was mainstreamed throughout the CBO and institutionalized over time. The CBO developed its own evaluation dashboard that clearly states participants' goals, benchmarks, current baseline levels, and goal accomplishments (see Fetterman, 2005; Fetterman & Wandersman, 2007). In addition, a software system was implemented to move all paper evaluations to electronic form.

Other outcomes achieved included an increase in participants' accomplishment of goals that foster self-determination, defined by the organization as providing participants the opportunity to identify and accomplish their personal goals. The CBO received rave reviews from accreditation review boards and funders because of their more comprehensive evaluation plan, logic models, and actual goal attainment by participants. Increases in participants' levels of satisfaction with the services provided and with progress toward their own goal accomplishment have been noted as well. Furthermore, the organization received additional funding to expand their brain injury program and to support transition services for youth with disabilities.

Role of the Evaluators

Our role as partners shifted from facilitators and coaches early in the partnership to critical friends as the empowerment evaluation process evolved. As stated by Fetterman (2001), a critical friend believes in the program, poses important and honest questions, facilitates the empowerment process, and supports the organization's efforts, enabling the program to achieve its goals. We facilitated some of the early brainstorming sessions and capacity building trainings; then staff gradually took on these roles and relied on us less as the empowerment process unfolded. We played the role of critical friends when there was a need to ask probing questions and provide scholarly expertise to support a goal or strategy. Furthermore, we trained our students to play that role as well. Through empowerment evaluation efforts, we were ready to wear different hats, be sensitive and respectful of the culture of the organization, and be transformed by the experience. Finally, we engaged in several cycles of reflection and action, typical in empowerment evaluation (Fetterman et al., 2010), as we utilized data and practical experience to inform future plans and actions with the CBO.

CONCLUSIONS

The case study illustrated in this chapter was grounded in the theoretical and empirical literature on empowerment evaluation. This grounding informed our collective understanding of the cyclical nature of ECB as part of an empowerment evaluation approach. The illustration of this case study of empowerment evaluation has important implications for practice and demonstrates the importance of using science to inform practice and practice to inform science (Suarez-Balcazar & Taylor-Ritzler, 2014). Although the case is illustrated across the steps, facets, and principles of empowerment evaluation, these did not necessarily happen in a precise linear form. Empowerment evaluation is a dynamic and interactive process and calls for ongoing cycles of reflection and action.

The take home messages from this example of empowerment evaluation transformation effort are many. Empowerment evaluation, when it works, results in liberation. Our work involved facilitating the CBO's process of rethinking outcomes, reconceptualizing what they do, redesigning forms and processes to support inclusion and liberation, and supporting their efforts to reconceptualize their understanding of their roles in social change processes. Throughout the process of transformation as it relates to evaluation, the CBO embraced many principles of empowerment evaluation including capacity building, social justice, accountability, inclusion, and program improvement.

Empowerment evaluation can take a considerable amount of time, depending on the complexity of the organization. Our roles in this process shifted over time from facilitators, coaches, and occasionally as consultants to critical friends. This included work with specific individual staff members, with small and large groups, and with organizational leaders.

ECB is a critical aspect of empowerment evaluation. We incorporated multiple methods for assessing the CBO's evaluation capacity to inform the process of our empowerment evaluation work. These methods included the use of a validated instrument for assessing evaluation capacity (the ECAI), interviews and shadowing of key stakeholders, and record reviews. The ECAI proved to be a very useful tool in helping the organization take stock of its strengths and priorities for capacity building. This tool can be utilized by CBOs in full (entire instrument) or by sections (e.g., thoughts about evaluation, motivation, skills) to plan evaluation activities.

It is noteworthy that this effort was funded only initially. During the first 4 years of the 7-year partnership the ECB work was funded by NIDRR (National Institute on Disability and Rehabilitation Research; which covered a portion of the salaries of the evaluators, as well as assistantships for graduate students). By the end of the funding cycle, the CBO was well into the illumination phase and was in control of the evaluation processes. This has been a win-win opportunity for the CBO leadership, staff, and participants, and for the university faculty and students. CBOs in partnership with universities are continuously creating natural learning environments with a focus on "peer-to-peer" support, with participants, staff, and researchers developing relationships with each other and sharing their abilities and talents.

REFERENCES

Carman, J. (2007). Evaluation practice among CBOs. *American Journal of Evaluation, 28,* 60–75.

Chinman, M., Imm, P., & Wandersman, A. (2004). *Getting To Outcomes 2004: Promoting accountability through methods and tools for planning, implementation, and evaluation.* Santa Monica, CA: RAND Corporation.

Fetterman, D. M. (2001). *Foundations of empowerment evaluation.* Thousand Oaks, CA: Sage.

Fetterman, D. M. (2005). Empowerment evaluation: From digital divide to academic distress. In D. M. Fetterman & A. Wandersman (Eds.), *Empowerment evaluation principles in practice* (pp. 92–122). New York: Guilford Press.

Fetterman, D. M. (2013). Empowerment evaluation: Learning to think like an evaluator. In M. Alkin (Ed.), *Evaluation roots: A wider perspective of theorists' views and influences* (pp. 304–322). Thousand Oaks, CA: Sage.

Fetterman, D. M., Deitz, J., & Gesundheit, N. (2010). Empowerment evaluation: A collaborative approach to evaluating and transforming a medical school curriculum. *Academic Medicine, 85*(5), 813–820.

Fetterman, D. M., Kaftarian, S., & Wandersman, A. (Eds.). (1996). *Empowerment evaluation: Knowledge and tools for self-assessment and accountability.* Thousand Oaks, CA: Sage.

Fetterman, D. M., & Wandersman, A. (Eds.). (2005). *Empowerment evaluation principles in practice.* New York: Guilford Press.

Fetterman, D. M., & Wandersman, A. (2007). Empowerment evaluation: Yesterday, today and tomorrow. *American Journal of Evaluation, 28*(2): 179–198.

Garcia-Iriarte, E. (2009). *Participation of people with intellectual disabilities in empowerment evaluation.* Dissertation project, University of Illinois, Chicago.

Garcia-Iriarte, E., Suarez-Balcazar, Y., & Taylor-Ritzler, T. (2011). A catalyst for change approach to evaluation capacity. *American Journal of Evaluation, 32*(2), 168–182.

Kaplan, S. A., & Garrett, K. E. (2005). The use of logic models by community-based initiatives. *Evaluation and Program Planning, 28*, 167–172.

Kramer, J. M., Kramer, J. C., Garcia-Iriarte, E., & Hammel, J. (2011). Following through to the end: The use of inclusive strategies to analyse and interpret data in participatory action research with individuals with intellectual disabilities. *Journal of Applied Research in Intellectual Disabilities, 24,* 263–273.

Kravchuk, R. S., & Schack, R. W. (1996). Designing effective performance measuring systems under the Government Performance and Results Act of 1993. *Public Administration Review, 56*(4), 348–358.

Labin, S., Duffy, J., Meyers, D., Wandersman, A., & Lesesne, C. A. (2012). A research synthesis of evaluation capacity building literature. *American Journal of Evaluation, 33*, 307–338.

Lentz, B. E., Imm, P. S., Yost, J. B., Johnson, N. P., Barron, C., Lindberg, M. S., et al. (2005). Empowerment evaluation and organizational learning: A case study of a community coalition designed to prevent child abuse and neglect. In D. Fetterman & A. Wandersman (Eds.), *Empowerment evaluation principles in practice* (pp. 155–182). New York: Guilford Press.

Livet, M., & Wandersman, A. (2005). Organizational functioning: Facilitating effective interventions and increasing the odds of programming success. In D. M. Fetterman & A. Wandersman (Eds.), *Empowerment evaluation principles in practice* (pp. 123–154). New York: Guilford Press.

Preskill, H., & Boyle, S. (2008). A multidisciplinary model of evaluation capacity building. *American Journal of Evaluation, 29*(4), 443–459. doi:10.1177/1098214008324182

Suarez-Balcazar, Y., Orellana-Damacela, L., Portillo, N., Lanum, M., & Sharma, A. (2003). Implementing an outcomes model in the participatory evaluation of community initiatives. *Journal of Prevention and Intervention in the Community, 26*, 5–20.

Suarez-Balcazar, Y., & Taylor-Ritzler, T. (2014). Moving from science to practice in evaluation capacity building. *American Journal of Evaluation, 35*(1), 95–99.

Suarez-Balcazar, Y., Taylor-Ritzler, T., Garcia-Iriarte, E., Keys, C. B., Kinney, L., Ruch-Ross, H., et al. (2010). Evaluation capacity building: A culturally- and contextually-grounded interactive framework and exemplar. In F. Balcazar, Y. Suarez-Balcazar, T. Taylor-Ritzler, & C. B. Keys (Eds.), *Race, culture and disability: Rehabilitation science and practice* (pp. 307–324). Sudbury, MA: Jones & Bartlett.

Taut, S. (2007). Studying self-evaluation capacity building in a large international development organization. *American Journal of Evaluation, 28*(1), 45–59.

Taylor-Ritzler, T., Suarez-Balcazar, Y., Garcia-Iriarte, E., Henry, D., & Balcazar, F. (2013). Understanding and measuring evaluation capacity: A model and instrument validation study. *American Journal of Evaluation, 34*, 190–206.

Wandersman, A. (2014). Getting To Outcomes: An evaluation capacity building example of rationale, science and practice. *American Journal of Evaluation, 35*(1), 100–106.

Wandersman, A., Imm, P., Chinman, M., & Kaftarian, S. (2000). Getting To Outcomes: A results-based approach to accountability. *Evaluation and Program Planning, 23*(3), 389–395.

CHAPTER 13

An Empowerment Evaluation Approach to Implementing With Quality at Scale

The Quality Implementation Process and Tools

Andrea E. Lamont

University of South Carolina

Annie Wright

Wright Consulting, LLC

Abraham Wandersman

University of South Carolina

Debra Hamm

Richland School District Two, Columbia, South Carolina

Despite growing evidence of program effectiveness in research trials, communities and organizations (e.g., schools) continue to struggle to reach the same desirable outcomes when implemented in their local context (Wandersman et al., 2008). This is the crux of the gap between research and practice. The historical record documents the long line of health and human service and education programs that are viewed as nonproductive, even as failures. Wandersman (2009) presents four reasons why desirable outcomes of an innovation are difficult to achieve: (1) incomplete or inconsistent theory or idea, (2) poor quality implementation, (3) inadequate evaluation, and (4) lack of support for the innovation. Quality implementation stands out as a particularly prevalent problem. Placing this issue in a real-world context, Debra Hamm, the superintendent of the school district that is the focus of this chapter, explains:

> So much of what we are asked to do in modern education systems involves large-scale, high-stakes programs. Expectations that all students will be college and career ready are coming at the same time that demands for services to end obesity, prevent bullying, and better serve families as a whole are increasing. These are important issues that require thoughtful consideration. However, in reality, schools are often expected to get up to speed and implement multiple programs in short timeframes with limited capacities. Failure to do so can result in major consequences. This is a formidable issue for school leaders. Programs are typically expensive to implement—and not addressing them well can be even more costly. There is a need to implement each program with quality. This is a challenge for today's schools.

There are many ideas that are good (or sound good) but fail due to a lack of quality in implementation (implementation failure). There is sufficient evidence that programs work under resource-rich experimental conditions. The challenge is how to translate these processes and outcomes into everyday settings, which can be challenged by resource limitations, lack of fit between the program and host setting, conflicting priorities, and overall "messy realities." The failure to achieve comparable outcomes to those seen in research trials is a major concern of funders and the public alike. We know that quality implementation is a critical component of program success; however, given real-world complexities, how can communities implement interventions with quality?

In this chapter, we describe an empowerment evaluation approach to supporting quality implementation of evidence-based programs in real-world settings. The approach blends empirical findings from the implementation science literature with an empowerment evaluation perspective in order to support schools (or other community organizations) in the process of quality implementation.

In the first half of this chapter, we briefly describe empowerment evaluation and the quality implementation process. The information presented is applicable to any innovation (defined as a program, policy, or practice that is new to an organization), regardless of context or content area. In particular, we highlight a user-friendly tool—the Quality Implementation Tool (QIT)—that was specifically designed to facilitate quality implementation. In the second half of this chapter, we describe how the QIT facilitated an empowerment evaluation approach to support quality implementation of a large-scale, high-stakes technology integration initiative in a large school district.

EMPOWERMENT EVALUATION APPROACH

Empowerment evaluation is an evaluation approach that aims to both assess the overall effectiveness of a given program or innovation, as well as increase the likelihood of achieving desired outcomes by building the capacities of the host organization (e.g., schools) to plan, implement, and evaluate the program over time (Fetterman & Wandersman, 2005). Empowerment evaluation is based on a set of guiding principles that differentiate empowerment evaluation from other, more traditional evaluation approaches; these guiding principles are (1) improvement, (2) community ownership, (3) inclusion, (4) democratic participation, (5) social justice, (6) community knowledge, (7) evidence-based strategies, (8) capacity building, (9) organizational learning, and (10) accountability. Table 13.1 highlights the guiding principles of empowerment evaluation. These principles are referred to throughout this chapter to illustrate how the evaluation was grounded in the core values of an empowerment approach.

THE QUALITY IMPLEMENTATION PROCESS

A basic axiom of implementation science is that to achieve outcomes, programs need to be implemented with quality (Durlak & DuPre, 2008; Wandersman, 2009). Quality implementation refers to the process of putting an innovation into practice that meets the necessary standards for reaching the innovation's desired outcomes (Meyers et al., 2012). The distinction between quality implementation and fidelity of implementation is important. Quality implementation is a broader concept than fidelity alone. Although it involves fidelity to program components, quality implementation also involves consideration of how the program fits within the organizational context and establishes conditions conducive to implementation. The quality implementation process involves more than being adherent to program design. It involves adopting a big-picture perspective to *proactively plan* for implementation, *monitor* implementation over time, and *evaluate* the quality of implementation.

Table 13.1 Empowerment Evaluation (EE) Principles as Applied to Implementation Support Work

Principles	Description of Principle	How Our Work Adhered to EE Principles
Improvement	• EE values improvement in people, programs, organizations, and communities in order to achieve outcomes.	• Implementation support involved regular feedback on the QIT process. • QIT data were used to make data-informed decisions to improve the quality of implementation of 1TWO1. To facilitate continuous quality improvement, data were provided in a timely manner and used to inform potential solutions. The regular availability of data during key stages of implementation was helpful in terms of improving program implementation. This was a new approach for the district staff, who saw the advantages of the regular, ongoing data review and who used it for immediate planning and making mid-course corrections, when needed. • It is noteworthy that this use of data for improvement purposes was unfamiliar to many school members (particularly those at the school level) who are used to typical evaluation practices and educational data being used in punitive ways (e.g., states issuing school report card ratings based on standardized test scores). We used our strong relationship with the district and focused on relationship-building strategies with schools in order to circumvent these concerns.
Community Ownership	• EE values the community's right to make decisions that affect their lives, and believes that evaluation is most effective when the community is empowered to exercise its decision-making rights.	• We believe in the transparency of data and provided the district with all available data needed to make critical decisions. We helped facilitate discussions about potential areas for improvement, but all decisions about how to proceed were directed by the district.

Principles	Description of Principle	How Our Work Adhered to EE Principles
	• Decision-making power is owned by the community, not the funder or evaluator.	• At the school level, the QIT process was designed to provide a structure for implementation, but it was the responsibility of the school to determine what implementation of 1TWO1 would look like for their school. Each school had ownership over the initiative in their school. One concrete example of schoollevel decisions is the choice of devices. Although schools were mandated to select personalized computing devices for each student, they had the option of which device to select. Another example is the method of professional development offered to teachers. Professional development is recommended, but how it is enacted at each school may vary. Evaluation data are used to promote effective professional development practices. • The district had direct input into all aspects of the evaluation. All evaluation tasks were planned for and completed collaboratively. District input was highly valued, as they were the experts in what works in their schools. Regular feedback on the evaluation process was elicited from the district and schools.
Inclusion	• EE values community ownership that is inclusive and involves key stakeholders in decision-making processes.	• Our work with the district involved persons from all levels. We did not work solely with the program champion or district leaders. Instead, we regularly elicited feedback from ITSs in schools, persons with expertise in academics, information technology personnel, principals, teachers, and even students/parents. We valued the importance of understanding how implementation was proceeding from a range of persons. • Regular team meetings consist of persons with varying job responsibilities. Decisions are often made through conversations with this diverse group.

(Continued)

263

Table 13.1 (Continued)

Principles	Description of Principle	How Our Work Adhered to EE Principles
		• An early adaptation to our work with the district was made as a result of this inclusive process. During early discussions of implementation with primarily technology persons, it was realized that integrating academic personnel into the discussion would greatly enhance the evaluation and use of QIT. Academics were invited to follow-up meetings and were more directly brought into the implementation process.
Democratic Participation	• EE assumes that stakeholders have the capacity for intelligent judgment and action when provided with appropriate information. • EE values authentic collaboration as a means to maximize diverse areas of knowledge and skill. • EE values fairness and due process as integral parts of the process.	• We provided expertise in the area of evaluation; however, the input and feedback from key stakeholders was regularly elicited. School members and district staff were seen as experts in their own content areas. The diversity of areas of expertise helped move our evaluation forward and deepen the quality of the work. • Our relationship was characterized by authentic collaboration. We specifically focused on relationship building throughout the course of the project. This resulted in a single, unified team ("us"), rather than "the evaluators" and "the district."
Social Justice	• EE values social justice, or the fair and equitable distribution of resources.	• 1TWO1 is a district-level initiative. A primary goal of the initiative is to equalize access to technology among all students. This equality of access is regularly tracked as part of the evaluation.

Principles	Description of Principle	How Our Work Adhered to EE Principles
		• One of the primary areas assessed as part of the process evaluation is "Reach," or the extent to which the initiative is delivered to all students. This is assessed quantitatively though the examination of differential effects (or differences in the effects of the initiative on program outcomes) across different populations of youth (e.g., low SES) and through differences in implementation across schools. It is also assessed qualitatively through discussions of implementation across schools.
Community Knowledge	• EE values community-based knowledge and wisdom and balances this local expertise with scientific knowledge. • EE assumes that people are generally aware of their own problems and have the capacity to generate sustainable solutions.	• We valued the expertise of the individual schools throughout the implementation process. The flexibility of the QIT takes advantage of schools' knowledge of "what works" for their schools. We were not prescriptive; rather, we offered a structure that each school could use to identify, and generate solutions for, their own implementation challenges. This was very important, given the differing identities and values of each school. • We regularly assessed fit and capacity issues for all evaluation tasks. Although scientific best practices may have dictated a certain strategy, we balanced this scientific knowledge with district knowledge of what is feasible and most effective for their district.
Evidence-Based Strategies	• EE values the role of science and empirical information about what works in a particular area.	• The QIT is an example of a translation of the empirical literature on implementation. Use of the QIT was adapted to fit the needs of the schools, yet the scientific underpinnings and core components of the tool were maintained.

(Continued)

265

Table 13.1 (Continued)

Principles	Description of Principle	How Our Work Adhered to EE Principles
	• EE understands the value of fit and adaptation in bringing evidence-based strategies to local contexts.	• Our approach to process evaluation followed QIT Component 6 (Evaluate the effectiveness of implementation), rooting the entire process evaluation in an evidence-based framework. • We regularly consult the implementation science literature to improve the quality of implementation and evaluation work.
Capacity Building	• EE values the role of the community in the evaluation process and sees participation as critical to mainstreaming evaluation processes. • EE is designed to enhance stakeholders' capacities to conduct evaluation and to improve program planning and implementation.	• The collaborative nature of our relationship easily facilitated participation of district leaders in the evaluation process. We regularly elicited feedback for evaluation methods and engaged the district in discussions/interpretations of data to both ensure meaningful use of the data (community expertise and knowledge was valued) and increase capacity for using data to inform decisions. • Part of our process evaluation involved classroom observations. The GTO team provided a structure for conducting these observations, collaborated with district experts on content, and then trained district leaders in how to conduct the observations themselves (in addition to evaluation team observations). The number of classrooms observed was doubled by including the district leaders in this data collection. District leaders expressed how helpful the observation protocol and the classroom observation experience were for improving implementation over time. This will likely become a regular practice beyond our evaluation, thereby increasing sustainability of program outcomes over time.
Organizational Learning	• EE values a process that encourages learning as a means for program improvement.	• A major strength of the district prior to our involvement was their value of and high level of capacity for data-informed decision making. This value likely contributed to the positive fit with the GTO approach and underlies our solid relationship.

Principles	Description of Principle	How Our Work Adhered to EE Principles
	• EE values the use of data to inform decision making and the use of reflection to encourage meaningful learning.	• All data on implementation are presented to the district team in a timely manner. Although the EE team synthesizes the data, interpretation of the data and reflections about what the data mean for program improvement are seen as primarily the responsibility of the district. During EE and district meetings, the EE team provides discussion prompts to facilitate effective conversations about the data. All decision making and processing come from district leaders.
Accountability	• EE values accountability to ultimate program outcomes and the process of implementation.	• We established a culture of mutual accountability with the district. We were held accountable for producing objective and meaningful data, and they were accountable for using these data for continuous quality improvement. The EE team and district were also held accountable to the community at large, and regularly presented data to the broader community (e.g., parent meetings, steering committees) and posted findings in public places (e.g., Internet). • One example of accountability at the school level was evident in the QIT process. Schools indicated that large group discussions on implementation progress, "turning in" completed tools to the EE team, and seeing the compiled data increased their accountability to using the tool to implement with quality. • The accountability approach advocated in EE was consistent with a long-standing interest in accountability and an outcome orientation of the district.

GTO, Getting To Outcomes; IT, information technology; ITS, Instructional Technology Specialist; 1TWO1, district-wide initiative to provide each student with a mobile computer; QIT, Quality Implementation Tool; SES, socioeconomic status.

The assumption underlying this process is, given sufficient capacity and support, implementing organizations (e.g., communities, schools, organizations) are capable of engaging in the quality implementation process, thereby creating a pathway for outcomes to be achieved. Failure to attend to the process of implementation may result in program failure, despite strong program planning and design (Wandersman, 2009). Fortunately, the quality implementation process is a malleable process that can be strengthened; in particular, support for quality implementation falls nicely under the purview of the empowerment evaluator. Typically, the empowerment evaluator *supports* the organization's capacity to *deliver* a program to intended recipients through capacity building and formalized support, for example, technical assistance. By providing implementation support, organizations and communities that have generally low capacity to implement programs have the opportunity to increase their capacity and reach outcomes.

The Quality Implementation Tool (QIT)

The quality implementation process should follow program development (e.g., a strategic plan). High-quality implementation cannot make up for poor program design. A systematic process, such as Getting To Outcomes® (see Wandersman, Chapter 9, this volume; Chinman, Acosta, Hunter, & Ebener, Chapter 15, this volume) or Fetterman's three-step approach (see Fetterman, Chapters 2 & 7, this volume), should be used prior to implementation to ensure that the program being implemented is an appropriate method to achieve results. Implementation follows planning. Once a plan is established, the Quality Implementation Tool (QIT) is a consultative tool that provides a systematic method for supporting the quality implementation process (see Meyers et al., 2012, for a more detailed description of the tool and its development). The QIT guides organizations through factors that are consistently deemed to be important for high-quality implementation, as reported in the implementation science literature. Specifically, the QIT breaks the process down into six components, each addressing an important area of implementation:

1. Develop an implementation team. This component focuses on establishing a formal structure for overseeing aspects of implementing the innovation.

2. Foster supportive organizational/communitywide climate and conditions. This component focuses on creating an overall climate that facilitates change and is conducive to implementing the innovation.

3. Develop and monitor an implementation plan. It is assumed that a plan for performing an intervention was created prior to the start of implementation. This component focuses on refining and monitoring this plan for implementation.

4. Receive training and technical assistance. This component focuses on the type, quality, and quantity of innovation support provided to an organization to implement an innovation.

5. Practitioner-developer collaboration in implementation. This component supports implementation by having experts in the innovation work hand in hand with practitioners to address challenges.

6. Evaluate the effectiveness of the implementation. This component provides an evidence-informed method for conducting a process evaluation of implementation over time. It focuses on important process indicators (dosage, quality, fidelity, adaptation, program reach, and program differentiation); this provides information that can be used to make midcourse corrections, if needed.

Each of the six components "drills down" into specific action steps intended to enact quality implementation. Each action step is designed to prompt organizations to develop concrete behavioral strategies that will improve the quality of implementation over time. A complete list of action steps is presented in Table 13.2. To maintain applicability to any innovation or organizational context, the action steps in the QIT are generic and can be customized to a particular innovation.

A notable advantage of the QIT is its flexibility, which can be particularly useful for multisite initiatives and for bringing evidence-based or evidence-informed interventions to scale. Based on the empowerment evaluation principle of community ownership, the QIT provides a systematic method for implementation, but it is not prescriptive. It provides a common language across sites and ensures that important implementation factors are not overlooked; however, it allows the individual sites to develop their own strategies and plans for implementation. Each site determines what implementation will look like *for them*. Thus, although the same tool may be used at multiple sites, the ways in which different sites "bring each QIT component to life" may differ. This ensures that implementation fits the local context and represents the integral balance between empirically based knowledge (empowerment evaluation principle of empirically based strategies) and stakeholder expertise of what will work best for them (empowerment evaluation principles of community ownership and community knowledge).

Table 13.2   Quality Implementation Tool Action Steps

Component 1: Develop an Implementation Team

Action Steps:

1. Identify an implementation team leader.

2. Identify and recruit content area specialists as team members.

3. Identify and recruit other agencies and/or community members (e.g., family members, clergy, and business leaders) as team members.

4. Assign team members documented roles, processes, and responsibilities.

5. Decide on structure of team overseeing implementation (e.g., steering committee, advisory board, community coalition, work groups).

Component 2: Foster Supportive Organizational Climate and Conditions

Action Steps:

1. Communicate the perceived need for the innovation within the organization/community.

2. Communicate the perceived benefit of the innovation within the organization/community.

3. Create policies that counterbalance stakeholder resistance to change.

4. Create policies that enhance accountability (to help ensure that stakeholders complete implementation tasks).

5. Create policies that foster shared decision making and effective communication (vertical and lateral).

6. Ensure that implementation has adequate administrative support. Address administrative support needs.

7. Identify and foster a relationship with a champion for the innovation.

Component 3: Develop and Monitor an Implementation Plan

Action Steps:

1. List specific tasks required for implementation.

2. Establish timeline for implementation tasks.

3. Assign implementation tasks to specific stakeholders.

4. Consider including client input.

Component 4: Receive Training and Technical Assistance (TA)

Action Steps:

1. Determine specific needs for training and/or TA.

2. Identify and foster relationship with trainers and/or TA provider(s).

3. Ensure that your trainers and/or TA provider(s) have sufficient knowledge about your organization/community's needs and resources.

4. Ensure that your trainers and/or TA providers have sufficient knowledge about your organization/community's goals and objectives.

5. Work with TA providers to implement the innovation.

Component 5: Practitioner-Developer Collaboration in Implementation

Action Steps:

1. Collaborate with expert developers about factors impacting quality of implementation in your organization/community.

2. Engage in problem solving. (Note: In some cases, the innovation's developer may be the TA provider.)

Component 6: Evaluate the Effectiveness of Implementation

Action Steps:

1. Measure fidelity of implementation (i.e., the extent to which you followed your implementation plan).

2. Measure dosage of the innovation (i.e., the extent to which the innovation has been delivered).

3. Measure the quality of innovation delivery (i.e., how well the innovation's components have been delivered).

4. Measure participant responsiveness to the implementation process (i.e., the extent to which the innovation holds the interest and attention of participants).

5. Measure degree of program differentiation (i.e., the extent to which the targeted innovation differs from other innovations in the community organization).

6. Measure program reach (i.e., the extent to which the innovation was delivered to the people it was designed to reach).

7. Measure adaptation (i.e., the extent to which adjustments were made to the original innovation in order to fit your setting's needs and resources).

Application of the Quality Implementation Process

The QIT is a tool that allows evaluators and communities to translate *planning*, *monitoring*, and *evaluating* implementation into actionable steps.

Planning. At the beginning of implementation, the QIT can be used to systematize thinking and help plan for implementation. To do this, organizations (with the possible support of an empowerment evaluator) consider how each action step applies to their organization and innovation, and then they create a plan for completing the action step in a timely manner.

Monitoring. Once implementation begins, the QIT provides a means to monitor implementation over time. Often, certain aspects of implementation are more easily integrated into practice than others. By monitoring how implementation is progressing, the QIT provides the opportunity for real-time feedback on the implementation process and allows for systematic mid-course corrections to be made. This monitoring is seen as a critical part of the implementation process by revealing any potential areas of concern before substantial implementation problems arise.

Evaluating. The QIT can be used to evaluate the process of implementation. Organizations are prompted to think about what went well in terms of implementation, what could be improved, and what lessons were learned. This supports the process of continuous quality improvement of programs over time. In multisite initiatives, the evaluative features of the QIT can also be used to help interpret outcome findings such as understanding why some sites performed better or worse than others. Retroactively determining factors underlying variability in programmatic success across sites can assist organizations in planning for and improving their next big implementation phase or cycle.

The three phases of implementation (planning, monitoring, evaluating) are highly related and dynamic. Organizations are encouraged to jointly consider all three phases of implementation. For example, after determining what went well and/or can be improved, organizations should plan for future implementation and then monitor these changes over time.

A SCHOOL DISTRICT'S EDUCATIONAL TECHNOLOGY INTEGRATION INNOVATION: A CASE EXAMPLE OF THE QUALITY IMPLEMENTATION PROCESS

The quality implementation process was successfully used in a school district's educational technology integration initiative. This case example highlights how the process was used to guide the initiative.

The Initiative: "1TWO1
Computing: A computer for every student!"

In their book, *Disrupting Class*, Cristensen, Horn, and Johnson (2008) write,

> A primer on the theory of disruptive innovation reveals that schools in the United States have in fact constantly improved. Society just keeps moving the goalposts on schools by changing the definition of quality and asking schools to take on new jobs. Even in the new landscapes, where most successful organizations fail, schools have adapted remarkably well. (pp. 10–11)

Indeed, the goalposts for American education are moved with regularity, and the urgency of change is a theme commonly heard by educators. In this decade alone, K–12 education has experienced significant shifts in national and state policies that change curriculum, instruction, and assessment. Ranging from implementation of the Common Core State Standards to sophisticated integration of technology into learning, all of these demands challenge teachers and administrators to implement multiple efforts quickly, simultaneously, and successfully. Yet, called on to serve as agents for significant change, few educators have any formal training about change leadership.

The school district in our case example undertook a 3-year rollout of an individualized computing initiative that provides all students in Grades 3 through 12 with their own mobile computing device. Although this sounds like a computer procurement and distribution effort, the underlying goal was to provide technology and professional development as a strategy to change how teachers teach and students learn, ultimately leading to increased student engagement and learning outcomes. In particular, the school district wanted to personalize learning to reflect students' own strengths and interests, to increase the authenticity of learning experiences by grounding them in real-world problem solving and projects, and to encourage collaboration to enhance learning. All of this would take place in 39 schools and centers, with approximately 22,000 students and 1,000 teachers, and in a setting where schools have considerable autonomy for site-based management.

While the sheer scale of the project suggested that a clear execution plan was needed, the fact that it would occur in 39 different locations, each with different leaders, also suggested the need for common implementation strategies and accountability at the district and school levels. As Adam Frankel, founding CEO of Digital Promise, said in a TED talk, "Sophisticated technologies that are implemented poorly won't make a difference" (Frankel, 2013).

Bringing 1TWO1 to Scale With Quality

1TWO1 Computing is a district-wide initiative aimed at transforming education through the integration of educational technology in the classroom. As stated earlier, introducing technology into the classroom does not inherently transform education. Implementation of 1TWO1 required explicit attention to supporting pedagogical change—a huge task by itself that was compounded by the number of implementation sites and the flexibility afforded to schools in customizing implementation. This variability in schools (e.g., programmatic, grade level, and leadership differences) made planning for, monitoring, and evaluating implementation a challenge for both the district and the empowerment evaluators. The district team and the evaluators found themselves asking, "How can we ensure quality implementation at each school, when implementation is largely determined by the school itself?"

The quality implementation process provided a straightforward answer to these implementation concerns. Use of the process and tools (as described in the next subsection and in Table 13.3) was phased in over time, starting with the district level and then moving to individual schools. This allowed the district to "grow into" the quality implementation process and integrate it into district practice.

Setting the Stage for the Quality Implementation Process

As with all tools, they are most effective when used appropriately. Thus, before describing how the tool was used, it is important to point out a few key "contextual ingredients" that contributed to its ultimate effectiveness.

First, the QIT was used on an already well-defined program that was based on best practices and promising practices in the educational technology literature and fit within the broader district culture. As part of an overall Getting To Outcomes® (GTO®) approach to empowerment evaluation (e.g., Wandersman, Chapter 9, this volume; Chinman et al., Chapter 15, this volume), the district and evaluation team had previously assessed needs/resources, established goals, explored best practices, addressed issues with fit and capacity, and developed an implementation plan. Use of the QIT fits primarily within Step 7: Implementation and Process Evaluation in the 10-step GTO process. The program was well conceived, and an overall rollout scheme had been carefully worked out with stakeholders. This is critical because quality implementation will not compensate for a poor quality program in reaching outcomes. This type of foundational work should be done before implementation begins.

Table 13.3 Overview of Phased-In Process of Implementation Support

Stage of Implementation Support	Key Activities
1. Introduction to quality implementation at the district level	• Initiative leader at the district completed the QIT and shared with other team leaders. • GTO team facilitated a workshop where district leaders (approximately $n = 30$) worked through the QIT for planning and monitoring 1TWO1 at the district level.
2. Piloting the QIT at the school level	• Piloted use of the QIT with selected elementary schools. Focus was on monitoring and planning implementation within schools and sharing ideas across schools. • District leaders used the QIT (independent of the GTO team) to address challenges with implementation at the middle school level.
3. Engaging all schools in the quality implementation process	• Use of the QIT with all schools. Support for use of the QIT was provided via training and group technical assistance.

Further, the district had a long-standing commitment to technology, a strong organizational structure, and a high level of readiness for the innovation. District leadership had a strong interest in understanding implementation and a history of data-informed decision making. This facilitated use of a process that tracked implementation data. Use of the QIT was an excellent fit with their organizational system. Particular contextual strengths of the district are described by Superintendent Hamm:

> The district was fortunate to have both a relatively clear plan for 1TWO1 implementation and considerable capacity to support the initiative. The plan was developed by a large and representative implementation team, which improved the quality of the plan and generated a knowledgeable and enthusiastic base of support for implementation. The project also benefited from the district's history of encouraging the use of technology in classrooms; each school has an Instructional Technology Specialist to provide professional development and support for its teachers, a Tech Mentors program which focuses on teachers helping teachers

had been in place for over a decade, and Technology Integration Specialists are available to provide district-level leadership, training, and support.

The district also has a history of using a variety of data to inform decision making. Early in the process of planning the 1TWO1 initiative, a consensus was reached among district leaders to include program evaluation as a means for increasing the chances for success and for documenting outcomes. As the project kicked off, project leaders particularly wanted access to timely data that could inform adjustments to school and district plans and services as they were being phased in so that the roll-out would go as smoothly as possible.

The delivery system was composed of those responsible for providing 1TWO1 instruction in the classroom—all teachers, Instructional Technology Specialists (ITSs; who also played a support role), and administrators. The support system for the initiative was multitiered and addressed various aspects of support. At the school level, each school had at least one ITS, whose primary role was implementation support in the school. ITSs provided the bulk of school-specific professional development and supported teachers in their transition to teaching with technology. Additionally, principals were expected to provide support to the teachers in changing classroom pedagogy via establishing schoolwide conditions conducive to 1TWO1 implementation and change. At the district level, support was provided in multiple domains. Information technology (IT) personnel ensured technical aspects (e.g., wireless bandwidth, device troubleshooting) functioned appropriately. District technology experts (referred to as Technology Integration Specialists [TISs]) provided overall support to schools and oversaw implementation across the district. TISs provided both direct support to teachers and school administration (via district-wide professional development) and indirect support via work to support school-based ITSs. This well-established structure laid an important foundation to introduce the quality implementation process and facilitated use of the QIT.

Empowerment Evaluators' Role: The Getting To Outcomes (GTO) Team

The empowerment evaluators were first introduced to 1TWO1 as formative and outcome evaluators. A solely "external" role was relatively short-lived. By employing the principles of empowerment evaluation and placing explicit focus on relationship building, the evaluation team quickly formed a strong, collaborative relationship with the district. According to Hamm, the superintendent,

> The district elected to use the services of Abraham Wandersman and the Getting To Outcomes (GTO) evaluation group and relatively quickly the relationship between the evaluators and the district became such that the evaluators were very much a part of the 1TWO1 team effort. The district found the GTO findings to be useful and because the findings were frequently utilized, the GTO team worked even harder to provide information that would help the project to succeed. The relationship contributed much to program quality, since all data and feedback were seen through the perspective of a unified team interested in continuous quality improvement and program outcomes.

An Empowerment Evaluation Approach to Ensuring Quality Implementation

District leaders knew that the scope of their project demanded a clear implementation strategy if it was to reach the student-level outcomes they desired. The challenge was *how* to ensure quality implementation at each school. As described earlier, because of problems with implementation, schools nationwide struggle to achieve desired outcomes. Therefore, the district wanted to adopt a systematic approach to implementation. Concerns arose about the sheer number of schools (how to bring the innovation to scale) and about known differences across teachers in terms of technology knowledge, experience, and level of buy-in. These concerns were compounded by the site-based management system that gave schools significant autonomy over implementation. The district needed support in ensuring quality implementation at both the district level and within individual schools.

Collaboratively, the GTO team and district decided to use the QIT to support the district in a quality implementation process. The QIT was introduced in multiple stages, each iteration increasing the role of district staff in QIT completion as they became more and more empowered to utilize the QIT independent of the evaluation team. The purpose of this multistaged process was to increase familiarity with the tool by the district, thereby increasing their ownership of the tool and the implementation process. To illustrate how the QIT was used within an empowerment evaluation approach, principles of empowerment evaluation are parenthetically inserted into the following subsection (see also Table 13.1).

Applying the QIT

Stage 1: Introduction to Quality Implementation at the District Level

The district and the GTO team decided to first use the QIT to help the district-level technology team assess and improve its own part in the implementation of 1TWO1. District staff knew from the beginning of the 1TWO1 initiative that reaching their goal of transforming classroom instruction would only happen with strategic support provided to the delivery system (teachers, ITSs, and principals). They were motivated to be systematic and effective in this provision of support. At first, this process was guided by the evaluation team, who was familiar with the QIT as a consultative tool. It was ultimately the district's choice of whether and how the tool was used to support implementation (principles of *community knowledge* and *community ownership*). The decision to use the QIT was first guided by the chief information officer, Debra Hamm, who later became the superintendent. She completed a brief worksheet version of the QIT to see how it applied to 1TWO1. This increased her buy-in for use of the tool immediately. In the spirit of inclusion, however, a decision about whether or not to use the tool came after input from other district staff. In a core team meeting (comprised of the chief information officer, district technology leaders, the director of accountability and evaluation, the director of IT services, and the executive director of curriculum and professional development), the quality implementation process, the QIT, and how the process could be used to support work at the district level were discussed (principles of *inclusion* and *community knowledge*). Collaboratively, the group decided that the tool would be useful for helping the district create a plan and a process for supporting the schools.

The district team determined that the best way to introduce the QIT was via a single workshop for district leaders (principles of *community [school] ownership* and *community knowledge*). All technology leaders were invited to attend. Approximately 30 people with varying positions and areas of expertise attended the session (principles of *democratic participation* and *inclusion*). At the workshop, district leaders were oriented toward the importance of quality implementation by both the GTO team and the core district team. It was important to convey that this process was initiated collaboratively between district leaders and the evaluation team. It was not simply a part of the "external evaluation" or a performance review (as in a traditional evaluation approach); rather, the tool was intended to help the schools reach their outcomes. It was a joint decision to use the QIT as a means for support. After the QIT was introduced, participants collaboratively completed a customized version of the QIT. This customization involved use of an electronic form, which matched the district's value on collaborative technology, as well as adapting the QIT action steps into items that were relevant for 1TWO1. For example, instead of using the prompt "Identify and recruit content area specialists as team members," we created a Google web-form in which participants were guided through a series of items that prompted them to reflect on current members of the leadership team (monitoring membership). In addition, the form provided a list of potential roles (e.g., principals, teachers, technology leaders) that they may consider adding in the future (planning). The worksheets were designed to stimulate thinking and conversation about each QIT component.

After the workshop, the evaluation team compiled data from the workshop, looking for domains of quality implementation that were particularly strong and those that needed the schools' attention. These data were largely focused on identifying areas of implementation concern and generating potential solutions (principle of *improvement*). The data were then presented to the core district leadership team (principles of *improvement* and *accountability*). The district team prioritized suggestions for areas of future work and discussed specific ways to go about achieving the prioritized suggestions. The end-product was a concrete plan for what the district needed to do to support quality implementation at the district level, for example, what needed to be done, by whom, by when, and what the plan is for moving forward and for follow-up (principle of *accountability*).

Leaders at the district describe the value of the tool at this stage as twofold: First, it was instructive in that it presented a new perspective on what implementation science suggests is essential for successful project implementation. Whereas some of the concepts were familiar to the district, implementation science was new. Second, it was a guide. It pointed the district to work that needed to be done, some of which had not been thought of, and all of which could be considered when they decided to use the QIT as a self-accountability tool. Use of the QIT confirmed strengths in their use of an implementation leadership team and in professional development and support, but it also identified areas that could be improved to foster a supportive climate. Over time, district leaders referred back to the QIT as a way to monitor work, make adjustments as needed, and encourage accountability. A current priority is to add a separate teacher advisory group to ensure that the expertise of teachers is fully incorporated and as an enhancement to efforts to maintain a supportive environment for innovative uses of technology. As described by the executive director of curriculum and professional development, Nancy Gregory,

> The QIT helped us take big tasks that we knew we had to do and break them down into smaller, more actionable pieces. It helped us not only understand what needed to be done—but also how to do it.

Stage 2: Piloting the QIT at the School Level

Utilizing data from the ongoing formative assessment of 1TWO1 computing being conducted by the GTO team, the district noted that there was a great deal of variability in *how* and *what* was being implemented across schools. In particular, as the 3-year rollout of computing devices continued, there was a need to support not-yet-1TWO1 teachers and schools in proactively planning for implementation as well as an opportunity to share implementation ideas across schools (principles of *improvement* and *evidenced-based strategies*). Using the QIT with schools was a logical next step. The district worked with the GTO team to develop a 1TWO1-specific version of the QIT. This 1TWO1 QIT was first used in a group activity with four elementary schools. Each school implementation team included a small group of school personnel and a district TIS. The GTO staff led the teams through the QIT in a day-long session. Each team completed the QIT for its own school, and debriefing allowed schools to share information. The QIT served not only as a planning tool for each school but also turned out to be an engine for communication and collaboration. With the school teams, people volunteered to take on new roles to complete tasks that emerged from the QIT process; between teams, strategies were shared.

Not only did this process support implementation at the individual school level, it also had an indirect effect of giving the district more control over the implementation process at the school level (principles of *ownership* and *capacity building*). Due to scheduling constraints, only two members of the GTO team were available to facilitate this meeting. Inadvertently, this laid a nice foundation for empowerment evaluation because the GTO team had to rely on district-level staff to facilitate conversations with the four teams. At the meeting, a district-level technology leader paired up with a school to guide them through the QIT worksheets. Even though schools maintained autonomy over implementation in their own school, the district was able to exert influence via recommendations based on the QIT. In the true sense of empowerment evaluation, the TISs' experience working with the school teams allowed them to learn to use the QIT and to feel confident doing so.

At the end of the day, the feedback from the schools was that the QIT was beneficial in two key respects: first, to clarify work to be done; and second, to foster communication by providing the structure and dedicated time to work together.

Expanding the scope of QIT. Based on positive experiences with the elementary schools, the school district felt empowered to conduct a similar session with the middle schools (principle of *capacity building*). This use of the QIT was led by the TISs. Under site-based management, middle schools had selected a variety of devices (e.g., iPADs, Chromebooks) and the differences among these devices were hampering efficient implementation. The district leadership team believed that by focusing on the implementation process, rather than the sometimes contentious complications of the school differences, the schools would make progress. An afternoon of work with the QIT proved that this was the case; in essence, the QIT provided neutral ground for work to be done. Completing the QIT provided information, not judgment. Regardless of device choice, the schools faced common implementation needs; this was a fact that minimized the effect of their differences. Schools again assembled small teams to participate, and schools that were using the same devices formed groups that shared findings and suggestions that emerged from the QIT. This turned out to be an active session; some schools even phoned and e-mailed individuals back at their schools to assign tasks and get input. At the end of the process, schools had better plans for moving forward, and staff felt more informed and communicated more effectively within their own school and with other schools. The information obtained from using the QIT resulted in substantial midcourse corrections to the middle school implementation plan—for example, delayed rollout, rethinking plans to bring devices home, and increased district support (principles of *organizational learning* and *accountability*). According to the chief technology officer, Tom Cranmer,

> The tool allows key players to step back, take a deep breath, and apply clear and structured logical steps to working through a challenge . . . . The QIT tool seems to position the elements of the project (and the challenges) externally in a way that the key team members can see through the hype and work in logical ways that lead to better outcomes. Also, many times in education . . . we begin with the end-game in mind and struggle to work backwards to force the end game — sometimes with incorrect practices — without any structured guide to step through sequentially. The QIT helps people realize details of what's really important during implementation. It is effective in taking

complex and potentially convoluted projects and converting the variables to their lowest common denominator.

Stage 3: Engaging All Schools in the Quality Implementation Process

In the phases of QIT use described so far, the QIT was used to facilitate a single implementation session or workshop with selected schools. There was little follow-up with schools regarding how the implementation process progressed as a result of using of the QIT. Acknowledging the need for greater focus on the *process* of implementation, the district expressed an interest in expanding this preliminary work to support all schools in a full quality implementation process (principle of *inclusion*). The aim was to use the QIT to give schools greater ownership for the project and less dependence on the district. To sustain the project over time, this shift was essential; but to accomplish it, some schools still needed guidance on implementation and others needed accountability. A plan was developed to have each school work with their implementation team to use the QIT to guide their work. School ITSs worked with their principals and 1TWO1 implementation teams to complete one component of the QIT per month. This process was facilitated by the GTO team, but schools completed the task largely on their own. To provide additional support, TISs provided assistance as needed. The GTO team summarized findings from each month's QIT tasks and the results were discussed at the ITS monthly meetings as a way to share information for improvement and to foster motivation and accountability.

A model for large-scale support. By this time, the relationship between the GTO team and the district was very strong, and collaboration was typical practice. Together, it was decided that a formal system of support would be needed in order to guide schools through the quality implementation process. The team considered best practices (e.g., evidence-based system of innovation support; Wandersman, Chien, & Katz, 2012) and discussed how these approaches fit within the current structure of support and with current capacities. Ultimately, it was decided to focus on providing tools, training, technical assistance, and quality assurance/quality improvement to schools as part of a comprehensive system of support. The basic premise was that all four support components would be necessary for high-quality support; any one component alone may be insufficient for producing change.

The team started with the development of a manual (a tool) for individual schools. The manual contained a customized version of the QIT that focused primarily on the monitoring and planning aspects of the tool. Worksheets guided schools through each action step. The purpose was to give schools a means to complete the QIT without the need for direct consultation, since capacity limitations reduced the team's ability to provide one-on-one support to each school. A major component of the manual was the inclusion of "lessons learned" and "shared information" from previous phases of the QIT. This provided practice-based evidence and functioned as a stimulus for schools to generate their own ideas. The manual for the QIT was created by the evaluation team and was distributed to the ITSs at each school by the district and evaluation team (principle of *evidence-based strategies*).

Yet, the GTO team and district recognized that simply distributing this self-directed manual would be insufficient for supporting change (Wandersman et al., 2012). Distribution was therefore accompanied with a QIT training session for all schools, which was developed by the evaluation team with regular feedback from the district (principles of *community [school] knowledge, improvement*, and *ownership*). Due to time limitations, the training was conducted in a single, hour-long session (with an additional "orientation session" a week beforehand to prepare schools for the training). All school ITSs were in attendance. Principals were invited to the sessions to increase their ownership over the implementation of 1TWO1 in their schools and to support an inclusive and democratic participation process at each individual school. A key aspect of the training (and accompanying orientation session) was the initial introduction to the QIT. It was decided that the introduction to the QIT should come from district leaders in order to generate buy-in from schools. The aim was to emphasize that use of the QIT was not simply an evaluative or data collection tool but, rather, a tool that was selected by the district as a way to provide systematic support (principle of *ownership*). District leaders spoke about how the process had been useful for them and expressed their excitement about bringing it to the school level. Additionally, schools that had previously participated in QIT pilots were prompted to discuss their experience with the tool. Participating schools expressed to peer schools how the QIT specifically helped them in their schools. Only after this discussion were the details of the QIT introduced. A member of the evaluation team described the theoretical base of the QIT and described each component in detail.

The training session was followed up with technical assistance (TA) for use of the QIT. Ideally, one-to-one, proactive TA would be provided to each school; however, given the large scale of the initiative, there were not sufficient capacities to implement such an approach. Thus, the district and evaluation team collaboratively decided that a group TA format that was integrated into preexisting ITS meetings would be the most feasible option. As such, a member from the evaluation team attended regularly scheduled, monthly ITS meetings and guided schools through the QIT in a step-by-step manner. Each month, schools were responsible for completing one QIT component at their schools. District-level support was available between meetings. Progress and challenges on each component were then discussed at the monthly ITS meetings. Group discussions were intended to establish a system of peer support for implementation, facilitate collaboration, and generate ideas for implementation based on practice-based evidence. Discussions involved school ITSs, district support staff, and the evaluation team.

This opportunity to share ideas and learn from other schools on a monthly basis was reported by schools to be a helpful process. Feedback indicated that these discussions not only generated ideas for improvement but also held schools accountable for QIT completion (principles of *accountability* and *organizational learning*). Accountability and organizational learning were further supported through regular review of the data collected on the QIT worksheets. Each month, the evaluation team compiled these data for the district team's review. These data (along with other evaluation data) were used to plan for ongoing support (principles of *accountability* and *organizational learning*).

Reflections on the Use of the QIT

Throughout the academic year, the evaluation team and district regularly reflected on the level and quality of support provided to schools. Two important aspects of support are worth highlighting, as they played a critical role in the QIT success. First, the process of using the QIT with individual schools was designed to provide individual schools with flexibility in how implementation would look in their school (principle of *school ownership*). This ensured that implementation fit within their local context, while simultaneously providing a systematic way to ensure that implementation remained proactive and systematic (principle of *evidenced-based strategies*). Second, the district played an active role in setting expectations throughout the quality implementation process and modeled use of the QIT to improve implementation over time (principles of *school ownership, accountability, capacity building,* and *organizational learning*). District leaders regularly discussed the QIT at technology-related meetings and fully supported the process. This level of support was critical. We are certain that the tool would not have been as effective without this type of leadership support.

Several challenges also arose. In particular, helping 1TWO1 school leaders embrace the QIT as a useful tool, rather than viewing it as one more piece of paperwork to be done for the district, needed to be addressed. As part of the plan for using the QIT, the district and evaluation team strategically included an orientation workshop for principals and ITSs. The intent was to introduce the QIT in a way that would predispose them to value the QIT to improve 1TWO1 implementation and to emphasize the usefulness of the QIT and implementation science in their larger roles as school leaders. Still, because the QIT came through the evaluation effort, some held initial perceptions that they were being asked to do additional work "just because of the evaluation." A second challenge came from the customized tool itself. The fact that an electronic form was created to simplify QIT reporting made the process easier and more effective for some but invited others to simply fill in the blanks without much work behind the words. It was quickly realized that meaningful use of the QIT would require deliberate, ongoing action to change attitudes about informed decision making and even the role of the implementation team. By regularly sharing evaluation findings, exemplifying how data were being used to improve the 1TWO1 roll-out, and providing time for collaboration regarding the data and their implications, dispositions about the use of data and the QIT changed over time.

Of course, as empowerment evaluators, it was important for us to "practice what we preached" and regularly monitor and evaluate how the QIT process was working over time. As a team, we strongly believe in continuous quality improvement and took the quality assurance/quality improvement seriously in using the QIT with individual schools. Each month, the evaluation team discussed potential areas for improvement with the district and schools. Over the course of the academic year, various mid-course corrections were made to the quality implementation process to better support schools. For example, a few changes (nonexhaustive list) were the following:

1. Presentation of QIT data to ITSs each month. This was intended to further increase accountability for QIT completion by schools and to stimulate discussions about common implementation themes across schools.

2. Presentation of data at principal meetings and to additional district staff (e.g., academics), as deemed appropriate by the district. This transparency of QIT data served a secondary purpose of making the QIT a familiar, internal process across the district. It also increased principal involvement in the implementation process.

3. Adaptation of all QIT forms to an electronic document to facilitate completion.

4. Increased discussion time at meetings.

The evaluation team and district are engaging in a systematic continuous quality improvement process to further improve implementation support for next year. This process involves using a GTO approach to plan, monitor, and evaluate implementation support for the next academic year.

CONCLUSION

One major reason for failure to achieve intended results in large-scale, "real-world" projects stems from a lack of quality regarding implementation of key program aspects. The quality implementation process is designed to specifically address this research-practice gap. Developed from the empirical literature, these tools are user-friendly and designed to be highly accessible for use by support and delivery systems, regardless of a context or program content area.

The use of the quality implementation process in a large-scale educational technology integration initiative illustrates the utility of the process and tool. A phased-in process helped the district and schools to implement the initiative with quality. The school district personnel and evaluators developed a strong collaborative relationship. This process helped the district break down the seemingly insurmountable task of monitoring (and influencing) implementation of 1TWO1 in all schools into smaller, achievable tasks. Each time the QIT was used, the district took more control over the process, thereby empowering district personnel to plan for, monitor, and evaluate implementation over time.

Next Steps

Implementation with quality is not a simple task. It requires a great deal of effort by a team of implementers. The quality implementation process involves a systematic focus on planning, monitoring, and evaluating all aspects of implementation over time. This approach to high-quality implementation involves sizable resources in time and energy. We recognize that all organizations may not be ready to engage in such a process. Some may prefer to simply complete a single, brief self-assessment to monitor implementation at a single time point or may wish to simply complete QIT forms as a means to stimulate discussion or for data collection purposes. For this reason, a brief self-assessment of implementation status—referred to as the Quality Implementation Self-Assessment Rating Scale (QISARS)—has been developed. It is based on the QIT and is included in the chapter appendix with the caveat that we have not fully used this tool. Completion of this self-assessment rating is intended to stimulate discussion about implementation and may inspire organizations to engage in a full quality implementation process.

In conclusion implementation is an ongoing process—for both the delivery and support systems. Empowerment evaluators are well positioned to support quality implementation of evidenced-based and evidenced-informed programs in real-world settings so that program outcomes can be achieved.

Appendix 13A

The Quality Implementation Self-Assessment Rating Scale

Please think about a current innovation you and your organization are considering implementing or are in the process of implementing.

This brief self-rating scale provides a quick diagnostic about the current status of implementing an innovation in an organization (an *innovation* is a program, policy, or practice that is new to an organization). Items in this self-rating scale are based on implementation science and empirical evidence on what promotes quality implementation.

The self-rating scale is based on theory and practice related to a synthesis of the implementation science literature—the quality implementation framework (Meyers, Durlak, & Wandersman, 2012) and the comprehensive and consultative quality implementation process (Lamont, Wright, Wandersman, & Hamm, Chapter 13, this volume; Meyers, Chien, Katz, Wandersman, Wright, & Scaccia, 2012), which involves ongoing planning, monitoring, and evaluating implementation quality over time. However, this self-rating scale does not supplant the more comprehensive quality implementation process. The Quality Implementation Self-Assessment Rating Scale (QISARS) provides a point-in-time assessment of the quality of implementation and should be used to inform next steps for implementation support. It is intended to provide insight into areas of strength and areas in which your organization may need additional support and may point to the direction of undertaking a quality implementation process.

For each item, rate the current status of your organization as in "early stage," "transitional stage," or "advanced stage" based on the following descriptions:

Early Stage: You may have considered this as part of your plan to implement but have not yet taken specific steps to put it into place.

Middle Stage: You have begun taking steps to incorporate this into your overall implementation process.

Advanced Stage: You have taken steps to make this an integral and ongoing part of your implementation.

SECTION 1: PREPARING FOR IMPLEMENTATION

Before implementing a new innovation, it is important that your organization has a clear vision and plan for implementation. Quality implementation is part of a larger process of planning, monitoring, and evaluating an innovation. Jumping to implementation without first developing a concrete plan for implementation may prevent quality implementation in the long term.

Where do you think your organization is on each of the following?

	Early	*Transitional*	*Advanced*
1. Our organization has conducted a needs and resource assessment to identify the underlying needs we are trying to address.	☐	☐	☐
2. Our organization has a set of identified goals and desired outcomes to meet needs.	☐	☐	☐
3. My organization has considered best practice ways to meet goals and objectives.	☐	☐	☐
4. We have considered how evidence-based strategies fit with our organization.	☐	☐	☐
5. We have assessed our organization's capacity to implement best practices in our organization (e.g., support personnel, costs for professional development, staff skills).	☐	☐	☐
6. Based on the above items, we have selected an innovation and developed a concrete plan for implementing this innovation in our organization.	☐	☐	☐

Briefly describe the innovation or transition you and your organization are considering implementing or have begun implementing.

_____

_____

_____

SECTION 2: DEVELOP AN IMPLEMENTATION TEAM

The quality of any implementation is improved when there is oversight and input from a team of organization members, rather than the responsibility of a single person. An implementation team that utilizes many different people and skills in the organization will be helpful for quality implementation of your chosen innovation.

Where is your organization in each of the following items?

	Early	Transitional	Advanced
1. Our organization has a team responsible for overseeing the transition to this innovation.	☐	☐	☐
2. There is a team leader for the implementation team.	☐	☐	☐
3. The team leader has a clear role and responsibilities.	☐	☐	☐
4. Our team includes staff from different departments or content areas who work collaboratively.	☐	☐	☐
5. Considerations have been made to ensure that the team leader has sufficient time and resources to effectively oversee the transition to this innovation.	☐	☐	☐
6. We have considered inviting community members or other external persons (e.g., business leaders, other agencies) as team members.	☐	☐	☐

	Early	Transitional	Advanced
7. Members of our transition team know their roles and responsibilities.	☐	☐	☐
8. We have collaborations with persons (internal and/or external) with extensive knowledge and/or expertise relevant to the specific content of this innovation.	☐	☐	☐
9. We have an agreed upon structure(s) for our team overseeing transition (e.g., steering committees, advisory committees, workgroups).	☐	☐	☐

SECTION 3: FOSTER SUPPORTIVE CLIMATE AND CONDITIONS FOR YOUR INNOVATION IN YOUR ORGANIZATION

Having an organizational climate that is supportive of change will greatly facilitate quality implementation of innovations. When the organizational climate is favorable to the innovation, quality implementation is more likely.

What steps has your organization taken to create supportive climate and conditions?

	Early	Transitional	Advanced
1. This innovation has at least one "champion" who is excited about it and shows leadership for the project.	☐	☐	☐
2. We have communicated the need for this innovation throughout the organization.	☐	☐	☐
3. We have communicated the benefits of this innovation throughout the organization.	☐	☐	☐
4. We regularly assess resistance to this innovation in our organization.	☐	☐	☐

(Continued)

(Continued)

	Early	Transitional	Advanced
5. We have created policies and procedures/practices for dealing with resistance to this innovation.	☐	☐	☐
6. We have created policies and procedures/practices that enhance staff accountability to implementing the innovation.	☐	☐	☐
7. We use a shared decision-making approach to planning and implementing the transition to this innovation. We use a collaborative approach and consider input from many levels before making decisions.	☐	☐	☐
8. We have adequate support from our organization's administration for this implementation.	☐	☐	☐

SECTION 4: MONITOR IMPLEMENTATION

The plan your organization has for the transition to your chosen implementation will act as a road map. Quality plans include a clear strategy for monitoring how the transition is progressing over time.

What does your transition plan include?

	Early	Transitional	Advanced
1. Our plan for implementation includes specific, actionable tasks.	☐	☐	☐
2. Each task on our implementation plan includes:			
• a person responsible for overseeing completion	☐	☐	☐
• an expected timeline for completion	☐	☐	☐
3. We regularly revisit plans and make mid-course corrections, as needed.	☐	☐	☐

SECTION 5: RECEIVE AND PROVIDE
TRAINING AND TECHNICAL ASSISTANCE

Training and technical assistance is a critical component to supporting quality implementation.

Rate your organization on the following aspects of training and technical assistance:

	Early	Transitional	Advanced
1. We have assessed and prioritized support needs specifically related to this innovation.	☐	☐	☐
2. We have a designated person(s) responsible for providing training/ technical assistance to organization members.	☐	☐	☐
3. We have fostered a relationship with external persons and resources to support training/technical assistance.	☐	☐	☐
4. The person(s) providing training/technical assistance understands our organization's needs/resources.	☐	☐	☐
5. The person(s) providing training/technical assistance understands our organization's goals/objectives.	☐	☐	☐
6. The person(s) providing professional development/training has a sufficient level of content knowledge specifically related to this innovation to adequately train members of our organization.	☐	☐	☐
7. Our transition team works collaboratively with the person(s) responsible for professional development/training.	☐	☐	☐

SECTION 6: COLLABORATION WITH PROGRAM DEVELOPERS

Direct communication between program experts and community organizations can help improve the quality of implementation.

Rate your organization on the following dimensions:

	Early	Transitional	Advanced
1. We regularly collaborate with the developers of this innovation.	☐	☐	☐
2. We regularly engage in problem solving related to implementation with program developers.	☐	☐	☐

REFERENCES

Cristensen, C., Horn, C., & Johnson, C. (2008). *Disrupting class: How disruptive innovation will change the way the world learns.* New York: McGraw-Hill.

Durlak, J. A., & DuPre, E. P. (2008). Implementation matters: A review of research on the influence of implementation on program outcomes and the factors affecting implementation. *American Journal of Community Psychology, 41*(3/4), 327–350. doi:10.1007/s10464–008–9165–0

Fetterman, D. M., & Wandersman, A. (2005). *Empowerment evaluation principles in practice.* New York: Guilford Press.

Frankel, A. (2013, May 16). *Accelerating innovation in education.* [TED Talk]. Retrieved from http://www.digitalpromise.org/ted-talk-accelerating-innovation-in-education-by-adam-frankel

Meyers, D. C., Durlak, J. A., & Wandersman, A. (2012). The quality implementation framework: A synthesis of critical steps in the implementation process. *American Journal of Community Psychology, 50*(3/4), 462–480. doi:10.1007/s10464–012–9522-x

Meyers, D. C., Katz, J., Chien, V., Wandersman, A., Scaccia, J. P., & Wright, A. (2012). Practical implementation science: Developing and piloting the Quality Implementation Tool. *American Journal of Community Psychology, 50*(3/4), 481–496. doi:10.1007/s10464–012–9521-y

Wandersman, A. (2009). Four keys to success (theory, implementation, evaluation, and resource/ system support): High hopes and challenges in participation. *American Journal of Community Psychology, 43*(1/2), 3–21. doi:10.1007/s10464–008–9212-x

Wandersman, A., Chien, V. H., & Katz, J. (2012). Toward an evidence-based system for innovation support for implementing innovations with quality: Tools, training, technical assistance, and quality assurance/quality improvement. *American Journal of Community Psychology, 50*(3/4), 445–459. doi:10.1007/s10464–012–9509–7

Wandersman, A., Duffy, J., Flaspohler, P., Noonan, R., Lubell, K., Stillman, L., et al. (2008). Bridging the gap between prevention research and practice: The interactive systems framework for dissemination and implementation. *American Journal of Community Psychology, 41*(3/4), 171–181. doi:10.1007/s10464–008–9174-z

CHAPTER 14

Empowerment Evaluation and Evaluation Capacity Building in a 10-Year Tobacco Prevention Initiative

David M. Fetterman

Fetterman & Associates and Stanford University

Linda Delaney

LFD Consulting, LLC

Beverly Triana-Tremain

Public Health Consulting, LLC

Marian Evans-Lee

University of Arkansas at Pine Bluff

INTRODUCTION

The purpose of this chapter is to highlight the process of building evaluation capacity in a 10-year tobacco prevention initiative in Arkansas. Capacity building is one of the most important principles guiding empowerment evaluations. Capacity building in this tobacco prevention initiative was primarily learning by doing, with the guidance of empowerment evaluators. Grantees conducted their own monitoring and self-assessment activities. One of the most useful monitoring tools used was the Empowerment Evaluation Dashboard. It consisted of setting goals and benchmarks or milestones, and collecting base-line and actual performance data. The dashboard was used to help grantees monitor their own performance and make midcourse corrections. The dash-board also provided funders, legislators, grant coordinators, and empowerment evaluators with a window into grantee performance. They used it to monitor grantee performance and progress, as well as a gauge to alert them to the need to offer assistance. This dashboard has been adapted and used in many other empowerment evaluations. Additional capacity building methods included workshops, training, and mentorship. This initiative was conducted in accor-dance with the Centers for Disease Control and Prevention (CDC) guidelines and recommendations and resulted in significant outcomes ranging from con-tributions to policy to saving millions in excess medical costs.

PROBLEM

A brief review of the problem on international, domestic, and state levels pro-vides a context in which to view the empowerment evaluation work being conducted primarily by community-based organizations throughout the state of Arkansas. It also helps to highlight the empowerment evaluation principle of social justice.

International. Tobacco use is the leading cause of preventable death in the world, according to the World Health Organization (2008). It is responsible for the deaths of more than 100 million people in the 20th century, killing between 5 and 6 million people each year. Secondhand smoke is responsible for the deaths of more than 600,000 people each year (Öberg, Jaakkola, Woodward, Peruga, & Prüss-Ustün, 2011). The cost of tobacco use is estimated at more than $500 billion each year (Shafey, Eriksen, Ross, & Mackay, 2009). The high-est cigarette consuming countries include China, Russia, United States, Japan, and Indonesia (Campaign for Tobacco-Free Kids, 2014).

United States. Paralleling the international statistics, the CDC (2011) found that "tobacco use is the single most preventable cause of disease, disability, and death in the United States" (p. 1). It is responsible for the deaths of more than 400,000 Americans each year. This is more than AIDS, alcohol, car accidents, illegal drugs, murders, and suicides combined (Campaign for Tobacco-Free Kids, 2014). The cost of health care directly attributable to tobacco use is more than $96 billion each year. The tobacco industry spends more than $8.8 billion annually in marketing alone (Evans, Farkas, Gilpin, Berry, & Pierce, 1995; Pierce, Choi, Gilpin, Farkas, & Berry, 1998; Pollay et al., 1996; U.S. Federal Trade Commission, 2013).

Arkansas. In Arkansas, 25% of adults smoke (559,500). Approximately 4,900 adults die each year in the state as a result of smoking. The annual health care costs in Arkansas directly attributable to smoking are $812 million, according to the Arkansas Department of Health (2014) and the Campaign for Tobacco-Free Kids (2014). The tobacco industry's marketing expenses in Arkansas alone amount to $107.4 million each year.

The tobacco industry's marketing practices, internationally, nationally, and on a state level, target low-socioeconomic-status minority groups. Point of sale tobacco marketing disproportionately affects ethnic minorities (U.S. Department of Health and Human Services, 2012). Retailers provide more storefront advertising in minority communities than nonminority neighborhoods (Henriksen, Feighery, Schleicher, Haladjian, & Fortmann, 2004; Henriksen, Schleicher, Dauphinee, & Fortmann, 2012; Laws, Whitman, Bowser, & Krech, 2002; Novak, Reardon, Raudenbush, & Buka, 2006; Seidenberg, Caughey, Rees, & Connolly, 2010). Menthol cigarettes, favored by African American smokers,[1] are promoted more heavily in low-income minority communities (court records document the tobacco industry's efforts to incentivize local retailers to promote menthol cigarettes in communities of color). Mentholated cigarettes may increase the risk of lung and bronchial cancer. As a result, African American men are 34% more likely to develop lung cancer than are white men (U.S. Department of Health and Human Statistics, 2006). The results are nothing short of a public health disaster.

While highlighting the scale, size, and severity of the problem, this brief overview only begins to scratch the surface of the tobacco industry's power to persuade people to use tobacco. They are well resourced and deploy highly sophisticated marketing campaigns. This is the context for the tobacco prevention work being conducted in the state of Arkansas.

Tobacco Prevention and Cessation in Arkansas

In spite of the tobacco industry's wealth of resources, marketing acumen, and history of deception about the dangers of tobacco use (Advocacy Institute, 1998; Glantz, Slade, Bero, Hanauer, & Barnes, 1998; U.S. House of Representatives Subcommittee on Health and the Environment, 1994), the

---

1. National Cancer Institute. (2008). *The role of the media in promoting and reducing tobacco use* (Tobacco Control Monograph No. 19, NIH Publication No. 07-6242, pp. 56–57). ("Roughly three-fourths of African-American smokers consume mentholated cigarettes, with Newport, Kool, and Salem representing the most popular brands.")

tobacco industry lost a pivotal legal battle that resulted in the historic Master Tobacco Settlement in 1998. This was an agreement between the four largest tobacco companies and 46 state attorneys general to pay a minimum of $206 billion over 25 years (Wikipedia, 2013). These funds have been used to support tobacco prevention and cessation programs across the United States.

The Arkansas Department of Health used a portion of these funds to launch the Tobacco Prevention and Cessation Program in 2001. This program was charged with the responsibility of implementing a comprehensive tobacco education, prevention, and cessation program. The Arkansas Department of Health initially appropriated 31.6% of Arkansas' Master Tobacco Settlement revenue to this program. Funding for tobacco prevention and cessation efforts in the state, at present, is approximately $16 million to $17 million. This is half of the CDC's recommendation of $36.4 million for comprehensive tobacco prevention and cessation programs (see Arkansas Department of Health, 2014).

The Arkansas Department of Health allocated a portion of this funding specifically for tobacco prevention and cessation programs in minority communities, because of the disproportionate impact of tobacco use on minorities (American Lung Association, 2010; U.S. Department of Health and Human Services, 1998).

These funds were used to establish the Minority Initiative Sub-Recipient Grant Office (MISRGO) at the University of Arkansas at Pine Bluff. MISRGO's mission is specifically to prevent and reduce tobacco use in minority communities.

Empowerment Evaluation Conducted by MISRGO

MISRGO has awarded grant funds to more than 50 Arkansas organizations for tobacco prevention and cessation programs. Grantees typically receive awards for 1 to 2 years. MISRGO currently sponsors empowerment evaluations and provides technical assistance for 20 grantees across the state of Arkansas.

The grantees have ranged from faith-based agencies to hospitals. However, most of them have been community-based social service agencies. MISRGO grantees have broad-based support across the state for their tobacco prevention and cessation work (Fetterman, Tremain, & Delaney, 2011).[2]

A few key events in this 10-year empowerment evaluation initiative highlight the value of empowerment evaluation principles guiding the effort. The empowerment evaluation capacity building (ECB) principle, in particular, was

---

2. MISRGO grantees also have a strong track record of success based on past performance. For example, in 2011, the majority of MISRGO grantees met or exceeded their annual performance goals (see Fetterman, Delaney, & Tremain, 2013; Fetterman, Tremain, & Delaney, 2012).

a dominant theme throughout the decade. ECB is defined as an "intentional process to increase individual motivation, knowledge, and skills, and to enhance a group or organization's ability to conduct or use evaluation" (Labin, Duffy, Meyers, Wandersman, & Lesesne, 2012, p. 308). The MISRGO grantees' ECB largely consisted of (1) conducting their own evaluation (learning by doing), (2) using an empowerment evaluation tool called a dashboard, and (3) other formal training, ranging from qualitative methods to the use of technological tools. This chapter provides an insight into how empowerment evaluation helped maximize community-based potential. The approach also helped the group become more focused, self-determined, and productive.

Launching the Evaluation

The MISRGO grantees adopted an empowerment evaluation approach in 2005. They used a three-step empowerment evaluation approach, which included (1) clearly defining their mission, (2) taking stock of the work, and (3) planning for the future. In addition, they monitored their plans for the future, made midcourse corrections based on their performance data, and produced tobacco prevention and cessation results (see Fetterman, Chapter 1, this volume, 2001, 2013; Fetterman, Deitz, & Gesundheit, 2010; Fetterman & Wandersman, 2005).

Mission. The mission focused on creating a healthier Arkansas, reducing illness, saving the state money (in excess medical costs), improving the quality of life in Arkansas, and serving as a model for other communities committed to combating the consumption of tobacco.

Taking stock. This step included assessing the following activities: developing an evaluation plan, increasing community support, building evaluation and organizational capacity, using best practices, and using media to inform the public about the dangers of tobacco consumption (Figure 14.1).

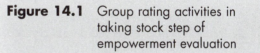

Figure 14.1   Group rating activities in taking stock step of empowerment evaluation

Courtesy of David M. Fetterman

The group rated how well they were doing on these activities at three points during the year, providing the group with multiple opportunities to engage in dialogues about their ratings for each activity. The dialogues provided the group with concrete activities to follow up on as they started to plan for the future.

Planning for the future. Based on their mission and taking-stock exercises, the group decided to do the following:

- Adopt an empowerment evaluation plan (agreeing to learn by doing, complemented with formal training activities).
- Build additional community support (by working with ministers and partnering with schools and local social service providers).
- Build their evaluation and organizational capacity (with additional workshops and training activities).
- Adopt best practices (by contacting the CDC).
- Use media (to expand their reach and impact).

Empowerment evaluation principles that served as driving forces during this phase of the effort are the following:

- *Improvement* (to improve their capacity to plan, implement, and evaluate their programs)
- *Community ownership* (to take control of their own monitoring and evaluation activities)
- *Inclusion* (including all grantees funded by the sponsor and engaging their communities)
- *Social justice* (addressing important social and health disparities)
- *Community knowledge* (relying on their own knowledge about their county's needs and surveying community members)
- *Evidence-based strategies* (acknowledging the value of the CDC's work in this area)
- *Capacity building* (adopting a three-step approach to monitoring and assessing their own performance)
- *Accountability* (rating their performance in their taking-stock exercises, establishing clear goals in their plans for the future, monitoring progress, and assessing performance)

Implementing the Empowerment Evaluation

As part of the "planning for the future" step, MISRGO grantees established their goals, specified their strategies to accomplish their goals, and agreed on credible evidence to determine if their strategies were being implemented with quality and accomplishing specified goals.

They also adopted CDC guidelines, priorities, and outcome indicators (Starr, Rogers, Schooley, Porter, Wiesen, & Jamison, 2005). Later they adopted CDC's *Best Practices for Comprehensive Tobacco Control Programs* (CDC, 2007). They focused specifically on four CDC intervention areas:

1. Preventing the initiation of tobacco use among youth

2. Promoting cessation among youth and adults

3. Eliminating exposure to secondhand smoke

4. Identifying and eliminating disparities in tobacco use among different population groups

Grantees aligned their activities with these four CDC intervention areas. A sample of grantee activities is listed under each CDC area in Table 14.1.

GRANTEE ACTIVITIES

Critical empowerment evaluation principles shaping this phase of the empowerment evaluation included *improvement* (improving ECB by establishing goals and baselines and adopting CDC guidelines); *community ownership* (taking responsibility for their own self-assessments); *inclusion* (including all grantees in the empowerment evaluation steps); *democratic participation* (equal vote and role in establishing mission, rating activities, engaging in dialogues about ratings, and recommending plans for the future); *social justice* (prioritizing and implementing a plan to address disparities in tobacco use among different groups); *community knowledge* (grantee organizations selecting relevant target populations and implementing programs reflecting community interests); *evidence-based strategies* (adopting and adhering to CDC guidelines; using Arkansas Department of Health and U.S. Census data); *capacity building* (implementing their own empowerment evaluation); and *accountability* (establishing verifiable baselines and holding themselves accountable to specific goals on a specified timeline).

Monitoring Progress

Once the MISRGO grantees established their mission, took stock or rated how well they were doing, and agreed on plans for the future, it was necessary

Table 14.1   CDC Intervention Areas and MISRGO Tobacco Prevention

CDC Intervention Area	Grantee Activities
1. Preventing the initiation of tobacco use among youth	• Conduct storefront surveys (to identify marketing tactics of cigarette companies and determine if they are targeting youth). • Provide training in prevention strategies through media outreach, gorilla marketing campaigns, and youth rallies. • Encourage youth and young adults to pledge not to initiate tobacco use. • Conduct compliance checks on retailer sales to minors.
2. Promoting cessation among youth and adults	• Increase the use of the Quitline service (telephone hotline to help counsel people trying to stop their smoking habit). • Encourage African Americans and Latinos to participate in cessation programs. • Increase community partners to combat tobacco consumption. • Increase the number of people participating in the 40 Days to Freedom program (faith-based smoke cessation program).
3. Eliminating exposure to secondhand smoke	• Encourage voluntary smoke-free perimeter policies. • Educate parents and law enforcement officers about the benefits of smoke-free environments in cars (Act 811). • Gather petition signatures for smoke-free environments. • Establish smoke-free parks.
4. Identifying and eliminating disparities in tobacco use among different population groups	• Develop point of purchase policies to reduce advertising. • Increase African American and Latino post-test scores in awareness (concerning tobacco consumption). • Share information about current tobacco laws with African Americans and Latinos. • Improve access to existing cessation resources for Hispanic males.

for them to monitor their strategies to determine if they were accomplishing their goals.

The diversity of programs and grantee turnover rate (every 1 to 2 years) made traditional training problematic or at least repetitive. The Empowerment Evaluation Dashboard became a useful tool to help grantees monitor and then assess their programs. (It also served as an informal approach to evaluation training.)

Empowerment Evaluation Dashboard

The Empowerment Evaluation Dashboard consisted of the following components: goals, baseline, benchmarks or milestones, and actual performance (see Table 14.2). For example, in this initiative, one of the goals was to create smoke-free parks to reduce the dangers of secondhand smoke. This is in alignment with CDC guidelines and is part of the CDC intervention area to "Eliminate Exposure to Secondhand Smoke." According to the CDC, "Creating tobacco-free policies in workplaces, other public places, and homes and vehicles not only protects nonsmokers from involuntary exposure to toxins in tobacco smoke, but also may have the added benefit of reducing tobacco consumption by smokers and increasing the number of smokers who quit" (Starr et al., 2005, p. 147).

One grantee's goal was to establish seven smoke-free parks in their county by the end of the year. Their baseline was zero since there were no smoke-free

Table 14.2 Dashboard Components and Common Definitions

Dashboard Components	Definitions
Baselines	"Where they started"
Goals	"Where they would like to go"
Benchmarks or Milestones	"Intermediate steps" or milestones along the way toward goal
Actual Performance	"Where they are now"—what they have accomplished at present compared with benchmarks or milestones and goals

parks in their county when they started. They established the following benchmarks or milestones: two in the first quarter of the year, four in the second quarter, six in the third, and seven by the end of the year.

They compared their actual performance with their goals and benchmarks or milestones throughout the year. During the first quarter, they established one smoke-free park. This alarmed them (as they were not reaching their benchmark or milestone of two smoke-free parks by that time). They reached out for assistance from grantees successful in establishing smoke-free parks. This was less threatening than "looking up the ladder" or chain of command to the grant coordinators or sponsors. One of the most successful grantees shared their strategy in this area:

> We got the kids together for a "clean up the park day." They picked up all the cigarette butts off the ground. It really cleaned the parks up. But we didn't stop there. We had them put the butts in garbage bags and then we arranged for them to bring them to a city council meeting. They delivered the bags of butts at the council meeting and explained how cigarette butts litter their play area and leach into the ground water. They also reminded the council members that when people were smoking in the park they filled the lungs of children playing in the park with second-hand smoke. They asked the council to ban smoking from the parks for these reasons and they did it. It also did not hurt that we invited the press to the city council meeting. (MISRGO grantee, 2011)

The less successful grantees followed the strategy of the more successful ones and exceeded their benchmarks the next quarter. They secured five more smoke-free parks, as compared with their benchmark or milestone of a total of four smoke-free parks by that time. The same group continued to build on their success and added one more smoke-free park in the third quarter, for a grand total of seven smoke-free parks before the end of the year (see Table 14.3 and Figure 14.2).

As grantees became more experienced, they were able to establish more realistic goals, better approximations of their benchmarks or milestones, and more precise projections of their progress on the dashboard. The use of the Empowerment Evaluation Dashboard helped grantees compare their actual performance with their benchmarks or milestones. Instead of neglecting or ignoring the problem, they used the Empowerment Evaluation Dashboard to monitor their own performance. It often served as a wake-up call, letting them know that they needed help.

Table 14.3 Individual Grantee Dashboard

	1st Qtr	2nd Qtr	3rd Qtr	4th Qtr
Baseline	0	0	0	0
Goals	7	7	7	7
Benchmarks	2	4	6	7
Actual Performance	1	6	7	7

Figure 14.2 Bar chart to monitor individual grantee progress

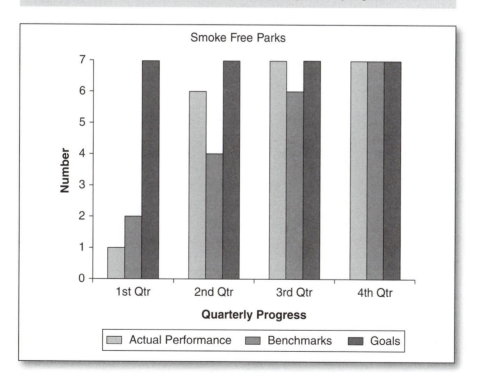

As grantees matured, they became more comfortable in asking for and offering help to other grantees. They understood that the legislature was going to assess their performance collectively across the state, not based on their

individual agency's performance. (The funding crisis that helped to crystallize this collaborative spirit is described later in this chapter.) They used the Empowerment Evaluation Dashboard information to help them meet and exceed their benchmarks or milestones and goals before the end of the year.

Aggregating the Data

The use of the Empowerment Evaluation Dashboard was invaluable as a tool for individual agencies/grantees to monitor their performance and trigger required interventions as needed. However, the legislature was more interested in the grantees' cumulative progress and accomplishments throughout the state. The dashboard data were rolled up to serve precisely that purpose.

Instead of focusing on individual grantee performance, the legislative report focused on the entire MISRGO grantees' progress concerning each CDC intervention area. The grantees' performance was categorized as met, exceeded, or not met benchmarks/milestones and goals. The dashboard measurements helped the legislature know that 70% of the grantees met or exceeded their annual goals concerning a reduction in secondhand smoke. The same approach was applied to each CDC intervention area (Figure 14.3).

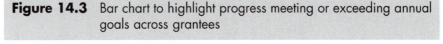

Figure 14.3 Bar chart to highlight progress meeting or exceeding annual goals across grantees

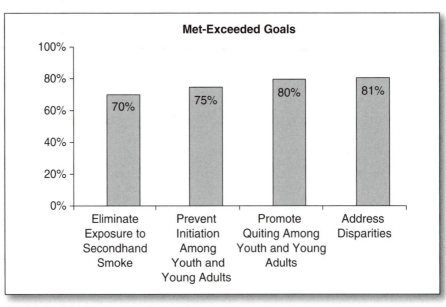

In short, the dashboard enabled legislators, sponsors, grant coordinators, and evaluators to see if progress was being made across grantees, fulfilling both knowledge and accountability objectives.

Formal Training

In addition to learning how to monitor their performance by doing it, grantees periodically requested additional formal training to improve data collection, analysis, and reporting, as well as tools to help implement their programs. For example, one of the group's goals was to improve their ability to solicit youth perspectives about smoking. Another was to improve their outreach or ability to reach youth with their message about tobacco consumption. In both cases, additional skills were needed. They asked for additional training in ethnographic (Fetterman, 2010) or qualitative approaches, specifically interviewing and observing (to solicit the youths' perspectives). They applied the training, and the data derived from the interviews were used to get a better handle on youth views about tobacco use, levers to reinforce or change their views, and ways to communicate with them, including specific types of social media.

Once the MISRGO grantees became aware of how important social media was as an outreach tool (in part from their interviews with youth), they requested workshops on how to use social media to communicate with youth, including Facebook, Twitter, Google+, and YouTube. Some of the grantees immediately applied the training to their work and produced YouTube videos to reach youth in their counties.

These training activities snowballed. After receiving training about social media, grantees requested broader training about the use of the Internet to communicate with each other and reach their target populations. Training expanded into a variety of tech areas including videoconferencing on the net (Skype, ooVoo, and Google Hangouts); online surveys (SurveyMonkey); word clouds (Wordle); digital photography; picture file sharing (Picassa and Flickr); online shared documents and spreadsheets (Google Drive); blogs; and infographics and data visualization. We also had a training session devoted to the use of Google Glass (Figure 14.4). Glass is a voice- and gesture-activated pair of glasses that lets you connect with the world through the Internet. You can take a picture, record a video, send a message, listen to music, or make a telephone or video call—all hands free. The group immediately recognized the potential for evaluation use. They saw how it could be used to document site visits, share preliminary findings, and even stream video for spontaneous training opportunities (see the blog "AEA365" April 17 and 18 and http://tobaccoprevention

Figure 14.4 Dr. Charity Smith learning to use Google Glass at tobacco prevention empowerment evaluation training

Courtesy of David M. Fetterman

.blogspot.com/2014/04/google-glass-and-empowerment-evaluation.html).

One of the grantees was motivated to produce and post their Air Quality Study in Smoking Bars in Fayetteville on YouTube after these sessions (see http://www.youtube.com/watch?v=0_2Lhpi07-0). Another grantee also produced and posted an antitobacco message on YouTube shortly after their training. A record of the training, facilitation, accomplishments, and reports are maintained on the MISRGO empowerment evaluation blog (tobaccoprevention.blogspot.com).

Detours

Challenges are inevitable in any evaluation. Empowerment evaluations are no different. One of the earliest diversions was a legislative effort to divest MISRGO of its funding. A leading legislative figure in the state attempted to shift tobacco prevention funding to the fight against obesity. Obesity is an increasingly important public health issue. However, the plan to divert the tobacco funds was not based on data. It was largely based on this politician's political aspirations. He thought this would be an excellent topic to spearhead his campaign.

MISRGO grantees were faced with a dilemma. They had made much progress. Individually many grantees could demonstrate their effectiveness. They were helping prevent youth from smoking and helping others to stop smoking. However, they were in a fledgling stage when it came to cooperation and collaboration. The grantees were still very competitive, often vying for the same funding.

In desperation, a suggestion from the group was made to begin pooling their data. There were protests and arguments. However, they were able to come to a consensus about pooling the number of people they were able to help quit smoking. The cumulative totals were impressive. However, that number needed to be translated into a language policymakers understood if the grantees were to survive this fiscal attack. The numbers were translated into dollars. The group provided data showing they were saving the state more than $84 million in excess medical expenses. This saved the day and created a completely new spirit of collaboration and cooperation across grantees. They saw personally the power of the collective impact.

Another effort to divert funds from tobacco prevention helped unify grantees and strengthen MISRGO efforts. This time, another politician tried to transfer tobacco prevention funds to the drug courts (judicially supervised programs to provide treatment for nonviolent drug law offenders). Drug courts are an equally important service in the public health domain. However, the effort to divert funds from tobacco prevention to drug courts was not based on Arkansas data. The argument in favor of tobacco prevention work was based on evaluation data. The MISRGO grantees had developed an enviable track record, which was documented with evaluation data. Evaluation data helped support the need for this programming; however, it was not the only reason the funds were retained. This politician's efforts helped catalyze MISRGO into action. Grantees were organized to present their case in the legislature. Political "watchdogs" monitored the legislative proceedings. This proved to be instrumental. For example, a few days after this politician was defeated in his efforts to divert the funds, he tried again. He was temporarily in a position to rule on a vote to consider his bill to shift the funds to his pet program. He asked for a yea or nay vote instead of an actual count, since he knew he did not have the required number of votes. A tobacco prevention watchdog remained on guard and observed the maneuver and called him on it, requiring an actual count. He was defeated again.

Both of these political challenges were important. They led to a mobilization that strengthened the initiative. The first battle helped unify the grantees as a team. It served as a catalyst for sharing and collaborating across grantee agencies. They learned how to pool data for a common purpose. They also learned an old but timeless lesson, that "united we stand and divided we fall." There is strength in numbers.

The second effort to divert tobacco funds taught MISRGO to be more politically savvy and defend itself from political attack. They used evaluation findings to defend their work, but they also learned how important it was to keep their eye on the political process as well.

MISRGO's response to these challenges highlights a few of the guiding principles of empowerment evaluations, including improvement (learning how to pool data to improve reporting); community ownership (MISRGO grantees came together to respond to attacks on their funding as a group, demonstrating that they owned the larger initiative and its evaluation); inclusion (everyone was invited to share their data); democratic participation (the group discussed and agreed to pool their data to protect themselves, and participated in legislative debates to ensure their work was represented); social justice (they defended a worthwhile program devoted to ameliorating health-related inequities); community knowledge (adding what they learned about the legislative language and customs and incorporating it within their own body of knowledge); evidence-based strategies (relying on evaluation data, and reviewing the research on drug courts in the state); capacity building (learning to navigate in legislative waters); organizational learning (learning how important it was to function in legislative environments); and accountability (providing the legislature with performance data).

Serendipity

Empowerment evaluation, although sequential and typically focused on outcomes, is also a creative, emergent, and iterative experience. In the scramble to assemble relevant data when faced with fiscal assaults in the legislature, MISRGO evaluators learned that the data for their purposes were neither of high quality nor easy to come by. The immediate response involved pooling data to survive—demonstrating strength in numbers, literally. However, once the crisis had subsided, the group reflected on the experience and came to the conclusion that there was a paucity of readily accessible tobacco prevention data and that they lacked the tools to collect and analyze relevant data.

The group came to an unexpected conclusion. They decided that Arkansas needed an evaluation center. They needed a centralized place for evaluation training, evaluation projects, conferences, and scholarship. The consensus was that a center could help them be better prepared to document grantee accomplishments and defend their programs before legislative hearings in the future.

The MISRGO office and the empowerment evaluation team provided support and leadership in this effort. The bill for the center was drafted and passed in both the House and the Senate of the Arkansas legislature. Later, it was signed into law by the governor. The center provided the first large-scale evaluation training in the state. Faculty included Stewart Donaldson, dean and director of the Claremont Evaluation Center, teaching about program theory; Tarek Azzam, also from Claremont, focusing on technology in evaluation; Rosalie Torres, independent evaluator, providing guidance on interviewing; and David Fetterman, facilitating an empowerment evaluation workshop. Charles Gasper also provided insights into foundation perspectives during the training.

This is an excellent example of the serendipity and synergy that empowerment evaluation can generate. The establishment of the center was not a planned part of the process. This idea emerged from their experience—in addition to monitoring, assessing, and producing outcomes, an entire evaluation center was born.

Empowerment principles reflected in this phase of the evaluation include improvement (recognizing and acting on the need for better training); community ownership (taking the steps together as a group to establish a center and shape future training); inclusion (inviting all grantees to the table to discuss the idea of a center and marshal resources required to establish one); democratic participation (ensuring open and fair deliberations about the purpose of the center); social justice (focused on training minority evaluators); community knowledge (grantees assessing their own needs, e.g., evaluation training as applied to their local communities and circumstances); evidence-based strategies (recognizing the value of evaluation expertise and center-based scholarship); capacity building (pursing formal evaluation training at the center); organizational learning (learning how a center can provide them with more credibility and sustainability); and accountability (recognizing they were accountable to the legislature for the quality of their work and the role of the center in refining their skills).

CONCLUSION

This decade-long tobacco prevention empowerment evaluation initiative has produced a steady stream of accomplishments. The grantees have empowered themselves. They contributed to policy changes on the state level, including the passage of Act 811. It has strengthened Arkansas' smoke-free car law (Act 13 of 2006) by increasing the age of children protected from secondhand smoke from 6 to 14 years of age, impacting more than 827,411 children. It has saved the state more than $84 million in excess medical expenses. In addition, grantees have been successful in creating smoke-free parks across the state and increasing the number of people pledging to quit smoking. According to the CDC, "Attempting to quit is an essential step in the process of becoming tobacco-free" (Starr et al., 2005, p. 246).

MISRGO grantees have used newspaper, radio, and television media to successfully communicate with the public. Through their media campaigns they have substantially contributed to smokers calling the Quitline to assist them in their efforts to stop smoking. These efforts are all in alignment with CDC guidelines and recommendations: "Tobacco control programs need to foster the motivation to quit through policy changes and media campaigns and promote their Quitline services" (2007, p. 41).

External evaluations of the tobacco prevention work in Arkansas also suggest they have been effective. For example, cigarette use has been cut by one third in the state, according to a 10-year study conducted by RAND (Engberg, Scharf, Lovejoy, Yu, & Tharp-Taylor, 2012). Reductions have been particularly significant in the Delta, a region of the state with a high minority population. They also noted a reduction in tobacco-related illness such as heart attack and stroke. These are solid accomplishments validated by external assessments. It also highlights how internal and external assessments are not mutually exclusive. Empowerment evaluations embrace external assessments.

The empowerment evaluation and program efforts have also produced numerous unintended positive outcomes, including the creation of the Arkansas Evaluation Center focusing on training for minority evaluators. This chapter demonstrates that empowerment evaluation contributes to a broad spectrum of outcomes beyond the initial goals established at the beginning of the initiative, because people, projects, and systems evolve over time.

Empowerment evaluation principles have been instrumental in guiding this initiative and documenting significant outcomes. Evaluation capacity building was highlighted in this chapter. It focused on the (1) experiential—learning by doing; (2) technical—technical assistance and training; and (3) pragmatic—Empowerment Evaluation Dashboard. The dashboard was used to help people monitor their own performance and make midcourse corrections as needed. It also provided donors and coordinators with a tool to assist them with their oversight, supervision, and accountability responsibilities. The dashboard (aggregated findings) was also used to inform legislative bodies about the group's progress and accomplishments. In addition, the dashboard was useful in defending attacks on future funding for the program.

This brief description of a decade of tobacco prevention work highlights the value and utility of empowerment evaluation to build capacity and address significant social justice issues in public health.

REFERENCES

Advocacy Institute. (1998). *Smoke & mirrors: How the tobacco industry buys and lies its way to power and profits*. Washington, DC: Author.

American Lung Association. (2010). *African Americans*. Retrieved from http://www.lung.org/stop-smoking/about-smoking/facts-figures/african-americans-and-tobacco.html

Arkansas Department of Health. (2014). *Tobacco prevention and cessation program: Arkansas strategic plan to prevent and reduce tobacco use 2009–2014*. Little Rock: Author. Retrieved from http://www.healthy.arkansas.gov/programsServices/tobaccoprevent/Documents/TPCP StrategicPlan.pdf

Campaign for Tobacco-Free Kids. (2014). *The toll of tobacco in Arkansas*. Retrieved from http://www.tobaccofreekids.org/facts_issues/toll_us/arkansas

Centers for Disease Control and Prevention, National Center for Chronic Disease Prevention and Health Promotion. (2007). *Best practices for comprehensive tobacco control programs*. Atlanta, GA: Author.

Centers for Disease Control and Prevention, National Center for Chronic Disease Prevention and Health Promotion. (2011). *Tobacco use: Targeting the nation's leading killer*. Atlanta, GA: Author. Retrieved from http://www.cdc.gov/chronicdisease/resources/publications/aag/osh.htm (See also http://www.cdc.gov/chronicdisease/resources/publications/aag/pdf/2011/Tobacco_AAG_2011_508.pdf)

Engberg, J., Scharf, D. M., Lovejoy, S. L., Yu, H., & Tharp-Taylor, S. (2012). *Evaluation of the Arkansas Tobacco Settlement Program: Progress through 2011*. Santa Monica, CA: RAND Corporation.

Evans, N., Farkas, A., Gilpin, E., Berry, C., & Pierce, J. P. (1995). Influence of tobacco marketing and exposure to smokers on adolescent susceptibility to smoking. *Journal of the National Cancer Institute, 87*(20), 1538–1545.

Fetterman, D. M. (2001). *Foundations of empowerment evaluation*. Thousand Oaks, CA: Sage.

Fetterman, D. M. (2010). *Ethnography: Step-by-step* (3rd ed.). Thousand Oaks, CA: Sage.

Fetterman, D. M. (2013). *Empowerment evaluation in the digital villages: Hewlett-Packard's $15 million race toward social justice*. Stanford, CA: Stanford University Press.

Fetterman, D. M., Deitz, J., & Gesundheit, N. (2010). Empowerment evaluation: A collaborative approach to evaluating and transforming a medical school curriculum. *Academic Medicine, 85*(5), 813–820.

Fetterman, D. M., Delaney, L., & Tremain, B. (2013). *MISRGO evaluation: Annual report 2012–2013*. San Jose, CA: Fetterman & Associates.

Fetterman, D. M., Tremain, B., & Delaney, L. (2011). *MISRGO empowerment evaluation: June 2011 annual report*. San Jose, CA: Fetterman & Associates.

Fetterman, D. M., Tremain, B., & Delaney, L. (2012). *MISRGO evaluation annual report 2011–2012*. San Jose, CA: Fetterman & Associates.

Fetterman, D. M., & Wandersman, A. (2005). *Empowerment evaluation principles in practice*. New York: Guilford Press.

Glantz, S. A., Slade, J., Bero, L. A., Hanauer, P., & Barnes, D. E. (1998). *The cigarette papers*. Berkeley: University of California Press.

Henriksen, L., Feighery, E. C., Schleicher, N. C., Haladjian, H. H., & Fortmann, S. P. (2004). Reaching youth at the point of sale: Cigarette marketing is more prevalent in stores where adolescents shop frequently. *Tobacco Control, 13*(3), 315–318.

Henriksen, L., Schleicher, N. C., Dauphinee, A. L., & Fortmann, S. P. (2012). Targeted advertising, promotion, and price for menthol cigarettes in California high school neighborhoods. *Nicotine & Tobacco Research, 14*(1), 116–121.

Labin, S. N., Duffy, J. L., Meyers, D. C., Wandersman, A., & Lesesne, C. A. (2012). A research synthesis of the evaluation capacity building literature. *American Journal of Evaluation, 33,* 307–338.

Laws, M. B., Whitman, J., Bowser, D. M., & Krech, L. (2002). Tobacco availability and point of sale marketing in demographically contrasting districts of Massachusetts. *Tobacco Control, 11*(Suppl. 2), ii71–ii73.

Novak, S. P., Reardon, S. F., Raudenbush, S. W., & Buka, S. L. (2006). Retail tobacco outlet density and youth cigarette smoking: A propensity-modeling approach. *American Journal of Public Health, 96*(4), 670–676.

Öberg, M., Jaakkola, M. S., Woodward, A., Peruga, A., & Prüss-Ustün, A. (2011). Worldwide burden of disease from exposure to second-hand smoke: A retrospective analysis of data from 192 countries. *Lancet, 377*(9760), 139–146.

Pierce, J. P., Choi, W. S., Gilpin, E. A., Farkas, A. J., & Berry, C. C. (1998). Tobacco industry promotion of cigarettes and adolescent smoking. *Journal of the American Medical Association, 279*(7), 511–515.

Pollay, R., Siddarth, S., Siegel, M., Haddix, A., Merritt, P. K., Giovino, G. A., et al. (1996). The last straw? Cigarette advertising and realized market shares among youths and adults. *Journal of Marketing, 60*(2), 1–16.

Seidenberg, A. B., Caughey, R. W., Rees, V. W., & Connolly, G. N. (2010). Storefront cigarette advertising differs by community demographic profile. *American Journal of Health Promotion, 24*(6), e26–e31.

Shafey, O., Eriksen, M., Ross, H., & Mackay, J. (2009). *The tobacco atlas* (3rd ed.). Atlanta, GA: American Cancer Society.

Starr, G., Rogers, T., Schooley, M., Porter, S., Wiesen, E., & Jamison, N. (2005). *Key outcome indicators for evaluating comprehensive tobacco control programs.* Atlanta, GA: Centers for Disease Control and Prevention.

U.S. Department of Health and Human Services, Centers for Disease Control and Prevention, National Center for Chronic Disease Prevention and Health Promotion, Office on Smoking and Health. (1998). *Tobacco use among U.S. racial/ethnic minority groups—African Americans, American Indians and Alaska Natives, Asian Americans and Pacific Islanders, and Hispanics: A report of the Surgeon General.* Atlanta, GA: Author.

U.S. Department of Health and Human Services, Centers for Disease Control and Prevention, National Center for Chronic Disease Prevention and Health Promotion, Office on Smoking and Health. (2012). *Preventing tobacco use among youth and young adults: A report of the Surgeon General.* Atlanta, GA: Author.

U.S. Department of Health and Human Services, U.S. National Institutes of Health, National Cancer Institute. (2006). *SEER Cancer statistics review, 1975–2005.* Bethesda, MD: Author.

U.S. Federal Trade Commission. (2013). *Federal Trade Commission cigarette report for 2011.* Retrieved from http://www.ftc.gov/os/2013/05/130521cigarettereport.pdf

U.S. House of Representatives Subcommittee on Health and the Environment. (1994, May 26). *How the tobacco industry launched its disinformation campaign.* Presented to 103rd Congress of the United States. Retrieved from http://www.ttlaonline.com/HKWIS/hksplash.htm

Wikipedia. (2013). *Tobacco master settlement agreement.* Retrieved from http://en.wikipedia.org/wiki/Tobacco_Master_Settlement_Agreement

World Health Organization. (2008). *Report on the global tobacco epidemic, 2008: The MPOWER package.* Geneva, Switzerland: Author.

PART IV
RESEARCH AND REFLECTIONS

CHAPTER 15

Getting To Outcomes®

Evidence of Empowerment Evaluation and Evaluation Capacity Building at Work

Matthew Chinman

Joie Acosta

Sarah B. Hunter

Patricia Ebener

RAND Corporation

INTRODUCTION

Getting To Outcomes® (GTO®[1]) is an implementation support strategy that operationalizes empowerment evaluation. The GTO system provides tools (e.g., manuals), training, and technical assistance to increase the capacity of community-based practitioners to implement programs with quality and achieve outcomes. Empowerment evaluation and GTO share a focus on program improvement for the public good, the value of working collaboratively with programs and communities, and the use of traditional and rigorous evaluation methods. GTO also embodies concepts from evaluation capacity building (ECB; Labin, Duffey, Meyers, Wandersman, & Lesesne, 2012), as empowerment evaluation can be viewed as an approach to ECB and GTO is a specific case of empowerment evaluation. Although GTO's primary goal is to build capacity for a range of activities involved in high-quality programming, research shows that it places a heavy emphasis on

---

1. Getting To Outcomes and GTO are trademarks registered jointly by the RAND Corporation and the University of South Carolina.

ECB. Helping organizations integrate and utilize ongoing, high-quality evaluation is ECB's goal.

Over the past decade or so, GTO research has focused on the relationships between the support GTO provides and capacity, program performance, and, ultimately, program outcomes. These relationships are highlighted in the implementation support logic model presented in Figure 15.1 (Chinman et al., 2005). This logic model begins with an implementation support strategy (i.e., GTO). The strategy is designed to build capacity (i.e., the knowledge and skills) for a full range of program activities. Improvements in capacity, in turn, improve implementation quality (i.e., performance of key tasks in prevention programming, such as demonstrating program fidelity). Theoretically, if a program is delivered with high quality, it should produce positive outcomes. Consistent with social cognitive theories of behavioral change (Ajzen & Fishbein, 1977; Bandura, 2004; Fishbein & Ajzen, 1974, 1975), we theorize that exposure to GTO (e.g., training) leads to stronger knowledge, attitudes, and skills in performing GTO-related activities ("capacity" in the logic model). This in turn can lead to enhanced performance of more GTO-related behaviors, which supports successful program implementation (Durlak & DuPre, 2008).

In this chapter, we describe GTO and discuss GTO's relationship to empowerment evaluation and ECB. We review how GTO has developed over the past decade and been applied in a variety of different social service settings, as supported by different federal and state initiatives. We discuss GTO research and

Figure 15.1   Implementation support logic model

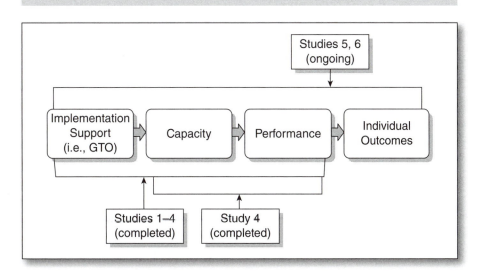

how it demonstrates evidence for the implementation support logic model presented in Figure 15.1. We conclude with a discussion of future directions of this work.

Nature of the Problem

Youth substance use and teen pregnancy are two of the social problems that GTO has been designed to address. Recent data suggest that youth continue to be at risk for problem alcohol and drug use. For example, a recent large-scale national survey found that by the time adolescents reach 12th grade, 22% of youth report heavy drinking in the past 2 weeks and over 45% report using marijuana (Johnston et al., 2012). It is well known that regular use of these substances during adolescence is associated with serious negative consequences, such as the increased likelihood of psychosocial, health, emotional, and financial problems in early and late adulthood (Aseltine & Gore, 2005; Brown et al., 2009; Jackson & Sartor, in press; Oesterle, Hill, Hawkins, Guo, & Catalano, 2004; Patton et al., 2007). Regarding adolescent sexual behavior, the United States has the highest pregnancy rate among all industrialized nations (Singh & Darroch, 2000; Solomon-Fears, 2013). Practicing unsafe sex and having children as a teen come with a great cost to society in terms of lost productivity and increased health care spending because young parents and their children experience a range of poor health and educational outcomes (Haveman, Wolfe, & Peterson, 1997; Hoffman, 2006; Kaye & Chadwick, 2006; Levine, Pollack, & Comfort, 2001; Perper, Peterson, & Manlove, 2010; Terry-Human, Manlove, & Moore, 2005).

Although evidence-based prevention programs (EBPs) are available to address these social problems, many communities often face challenges in adopting and implementing the programs with the fidelity needed to achieve outcomes demonstrated by researchers (Backer, 2002; Cassell et al., 2005; Chervin et al., 2005; Department of Health and Human Services [DHHS], 2002; Kramer et al., 2005). For example, a recent report of drug prevention programs in U.S. public schools showed that less than 10% of the nearly 6,000 schools surveyed reported using an EBP and less than half of those were implementing the program with proper fidelity (Crosse et al., 2011). Challenges to EBP use include limited resources, program complexity, and a lack of capacity (i.e., the knowledge and skills) needed to adopt and implement "off-the-shelf" EBPs (Green, 2001; Wandersman, 2003; Wandersman & Florin, 2003). All of these challenges have contributed to the large "gap" between research and practice at the local level (Altman, 1995; Backer, 2000; Mrazek & Haggerty, 1994; Wandersman & Florin, 2003).

Getting To Outcomes (GTO) was designed to address this "gap" between research and practice by building capacity for implementing programs with high quality.

GTO consists of 10 steps that are linked to 10 questions (Table 15.1) that, when answered, promote accountability. There are six steps that assist with

Table 15.1 The Ten Accountability Steps in GTO Manuals (Guided by Key Questions)

1. What are the needs and resources to address? GTO step 1 provides information about conducting a community *needs* assessment to help inform program planning.
2. What are the goals and objectives? GTO step 2 has worksheets for creating measurable *goals & objectives* from the needs identified in step 1.
3. Which evidence-based programs can be useful in reaching the goals? GTO step 3 overviews *evidence-based programming* and how to select a program to address the goals outlined in step 2.
4. What actions need to be taken so the selected program *fits* the community context? GTO step 4 prompts readers to reduce duplication and facilitate collaboration with other programs.
5. What capacity is needed for the program? GTO step 5 prompts readers to ensure there is sufficient organizational *capacity* to conduct the selected program.
6. What is the plan for this program? GTO step 6 assists with *planning* the selected program.
7. How will implementation be assessed? GTO step 7 assists with conducting a program *process evaluation*.
8. How well did the program work? GTO step 8 assists with conducting a program *outcome evaluation*.
9. How will continuous quality improvement (CQI) strategies be incorporated? GTO step 9 prompts practitioners to reassess accountability steps 1–8 after completing the program to *improve* the program.
10. If the program is successful, how will it be sustained? GTO step 10 presents several ideas to consider when attempting to *sustain* an effective program.

SOURCE: Adapted from Chinman, Imm, and Wandersman (2004).

program planning (i.e., steps 1–6), two steps that address evaluation (i.e., step 7 for process evaluation and step 8 for outcome evaluation), and two steps on the use of data to improve and sustain programs (steps 9 and 10). The tasks outlined in the GTO manuals to address the question in each step are known to be critical for high-quality implementation, and addressing each question is facilitated by three types of support: the GTO manuals, face-to-face training, and onsite technical assistance (TA).

In the next sections, we discuss GTO's relation to empowerment evaluation and ECB. We then discuss how GTO has been applied and disseminated by a number of different federal and state initiatives. Finally, we discuss the GTO research to date and the goals of future projects. This work demonstrates GTO's success as an implementation support model to improve program delivery and outcomes in a variety of settings.

GETTING TO OUTCOMES AND EMPOWERMENT EVALUATION PRINCIPLES

Empowerment evaluation theory states there will be a greater probability of achieving positive results when evaluators collaborate with program implementers and provide them with the tools and opportunities to plan, implement with quality, and evaluate outcomes themselves (Fetterman & Wanderman, 2005). GTO operationalizes, or "brings to life," the principles of empowerment evaluation. More specifically, GTO's primary focus is on program improvement to enhance the health, education, and general well-being of youth and adults (empowerment evaluation principle 1: *Improvement*) through the use of a systematic process of planning, implementation, evaluation, and quality improvement activities. Further, GTO is designed to improve organizational capacity (principle 8: *Capacity Building*). It internalizes and integrates the use of data and evaluation into routine operations contributing to a learning organization (principle 9: *Organizational Learning*). Like empowerment evaluation, when GTO is used, the community programs and staff from multiple levels are "in charge" (principles 2, 3: *Community Ownership, Inclusion*) through as democratic a decision-making process as the community organizations allow (principle 4: *Democratic Participation*). GTO guides rather than dictates how to best plan, implement, and evaluate programming. As part of the collaborative nature of GTO, knowledge of communities is valued (principle 6: *Community Knowledge*) and balanced with knowledge and use of programs, shown through research to be effective in improving outcomes, as well as strategies known to be effective in planning, implementing, and evaluating those programs (principle 7: *Evidence-Based Strategies*). Finally, GTO, in alignment with empowerment evaluation, promotes accountability not only by helping programs generate evaluation data that can be used to assess success, but also by enhancing program capacity to produce desired outcomes by asking and answering 10 accountability questions (principle 10: *Accountability*). GTO also plays a role in advocating for good practice in all areas of programming.

GETTING TO OUTCOMES AND EVALUATION CAPACITY BUILDING

GTO and ECB are similar in many respects. For example, GTO and ECB overlap in their end goals regarding the use of evaluation by community practitioners to improve program outcomes. A key ECB model, the integrative evaluation capacity building (IECB) model (Labin et al., 2012) specifies that the context, strengths, and resources are important when considering the need for ECB. Similarly, GTO is designed to address these factors as well. For example, in our GTO studies (four large-scale studies completed to date), we have found it useful for TA provision to begin with an assessment of the existing context, strengths, and resources of the setting in which the TA is planned to be provided. Assessing the motivations of staff targeted to engage in ECB is another factor in the IECB model. Motivation is not explicitly specified in the existing GTO approach and could improve future GTO use. In addition, research into ECB's impact on both capacity for evaluation specifically and improved outcomes of programs more broadly is just beginning (Suarez-Balcazar, 2014), and, as shown later, GTO research is contributing to the ECB literature (see also Wandersman, Chapter 9, this volume).

APPLICATION AND DISSEMINATION OF GTO

GTO has been used in several content domains and disseminated widely

GTO was developed to be used by communities and its uptake is, in part, an indicator of its utility in these settings. After the first GTO manual was developed to support drug abuse prevention (Chinman, Imm, & Wandersman, 2004), other manuals were developed that focused on underage drinking prevention (Imm et al., 2007), positive youth development (Fisher, Imm, Chinman, & Wandersman, 2006), teen pregnancy prevention (Lesesne et al., 2008), homelessness (Chinman, Hannah, & McCarthy, 2012), and home visiting

(Mattox, Hunter, Kilburn, & Wiseman, 2013). Most manuals are available at no cost from the RAND Corporation website: http://www.rand.org/health/projects/getting-to-outcomes./documents.html. As described in more detail later, GTO research has been conducted in most of these domains in dozens of locations across the United States.

In addition to the GTO research, GTO has also been adopted by various government agencies at the state and federal levels, demonstrating its utility in addressing the gap between research and practice. For example, the Substance Abuse and Mental Health Services Administration (SAMHSA) chose GTO as the theme for its biennial underage drinking "Town Hall Meeting" initiative, which is designed to help communities conduct high-profile town hall meetings as a way to kick-start prevention efforts. SAMHSA continues to provide information from the GTO underage drinking manual to support the work of the local town halls,[2] of which 1,500 were conducted in 2012. In another SAMHSA initiative, SAMHSA supported GTO training and manual dissemination to several communities awarded "systems of care" grants in 2009 to improve outcomes for children with serious emotional disturbance and their families.[3] In addition to SAMHSA's efforts, the Centers for Disease Control and Prevention (CDC) has also adopted GTO to assist grantees in its 5-year multistate Teen Pregnancy Prevention Initiative.[4] Both the SAMHSA and CDC initiatives show that GTO can be useful as an implementation support model in large-scale dissemination efforts.

State governments have also adopted GTO to improve programming. For example, the New Hampshire Division for Children, Youth and Families and the Division of Juvenile Justice used GTO to help incorporate evidence-based practices into their work (Barbee, Christensen, Antle, Wandersman, & Cahn, 2011).[5] In addition, the New York Office of Child and Family Services selected GTO to help design effective performance-based contracting in county departments of social services as required by a new law (Hannah, Ray, Wandersman, & Chien, 2010). Moreover, the Children, Youth and Families Department of the State of New Mexico partnered with RAND to secure a federal Maternal, Infant, Early Childhood Home Visiting grant, which included developing a GTO manual to support home visiting programs. Home visiting programs

2. https://www.stopalcoholabuse.gov/townhallmeetings/tips-resources/proven-prevention.aspx
3. http://digitallibraries.macrointernational.com/gsdl/collect/evaluati/index/assoc/HASHce52.dir/doc.pdf
4. http://www.cdc.gov/TeenPregnancy/PreventTeenPreg.htm
5. http://muskie.usm.maine.edu/helpkids/tele_pastdetail.htm

offer family-focused services to expectant parents and families with children up to the age of 5 years. These state-level projects in particular show that GTO can easily be adapted to address a number of community service challenges with the ultimate goal to improve program delivery.

GTO has begun to be used within the Department of Veterans Affairs (VA) and Department of Defense (DoD). For example, the DoD asked RAND to review the scientific literature and create a toolkit to support the DoD's suicide prevention efforts. The RAND Suicide Prevention Program Evaluation Toolkit[6] (Acosta, Ramchand, Becker, & Felton, 2013; Acosta, Ramchand, Becker, Felton, & Kofner, 2013) was designed to help DOD suicide prevention staff determine whether their programs have beneficial effects and where improvements are needed. The toolkit focuses on GTO steps 7 through 9 and can be downloaded at no cost from RAND's website (Acosta, Ramchand, Becker, & Felton, 2013; Acosta, Ramchand, Becker, Felton, & Kofner, 2013). In addition, GTO was piloted within the Pittsburgh VA Homelessness Center, which included the development of a GTO manual specifically for VA homelessness providers[7] (Chinman, Hannah, et al., 2012). The VA work further demonstrates GTO's flexibility and its applicability to a variety of social service program areas.

GTO has led to the development of a statewide ECB network called the Research and Evaluation Assistance for Change (REACH) in the state of Maine. This network is comprised of universities and colleges in the state that provide no-cost ECB support to community-based programs. REACH began as a way to continue the gains in evaluation capacity made by community-based prevention programs participating in GTO research (see Study 4, later in this chapter) and is an example of how GTO typifies empowerment evaluation and ECB.

COMPLETED RAND GTO RESEARCH PROJECTS

GTO research has been important to demonstrate its impact as an implementation support model, that is, GTO's impact on improving capacity, performance, and outcomes. Next, we summarize four completed studies and their relation to the implementation support logic model outlined in Figure 15.1. Where appropriate, the study results are also discussed in relation to empowerment

---

6. http://www.rand.org/pubs/tools/TL111.html

7. http://www.endveteranhomelessness.org/education/getting-outcomes%C2%AE-gto-services-homeless-veterans

evaluation and ECB. More details about the studies are available in the cited literature, which can be downloaded from the RAND Corporation website: http://www.rand.org/health/projects/getting-to-outcomes.html.

Study 1: The GTO-2004 Drug Prevention Program Study

This CDC-funded (Chinman et al., 2008), quasi-experimental study compared drug prevention programs in two community-based substance use prevention coalitions that did ($n = 6$) or did not receive ($n = 4$) GTO. The GTO intervention included access to the GTO manuals, GTO training, and on-site TA for up to 2 years. The 10 programs that participated were different in focus (i.e., the target population, program activities, and expected outcomes varied). The capacity of practitioners and performance of the 10 programs were assessed at baseline and after 1 and 2 years of GTO implementation. The capacity of practitioners was assessed by surveys on their knowledge and skills in performing key programming tasks prescribed by the GTO 10 steps (including evaluation, an overlap with ECB). Prevention performance was defined and assessed, through a structured interview, as how well a program carried out key programming tasks. We hypothesized that staff and programs assigned to the GTO condition would improve their capacity and performance as compared to programs not assigned to receive the GTO support.

Surprisingly we found that the GTO and non-GTO assigned staff did not differ in their capacity over time. However, we also found staff who reported using GTO experienced a significant improvement in capacity compared to those who did not. Analyses at the program level showed that the programs assigned to GTO improved performance more than programs not assigned to GTO. Related to this finding, we found that programs that used more GTO TA had greater performance improvements. Some of the largest gains in performance were observed in the GTO evaluation steps, consistent with ECB. Staff indicated that GTO helped increase their capacity, but the requirements to use GTO was at times difficult to maintain. Finally, we examined what factors led to GTO use. Training and perceived complexity were found to be key factors to using GTO, suggesting the importance of ongoing training and TA (Hunter, Paddock, Ebener, Burkhart, & Chinman, 2009). The study's sample size (i.e., 10 programs) and quasi-experimental (i.e., non-randomized) design limits the study's conclusiveness, but it was an appropriate initial examination of GTO's impact on staff capacity and program performance.

Study 2: The Internet-Based Getting To Outcomes Study

In this study, we developed an Internet-based Getting To Outcomes (called "iGTO") to assist states and other entities manage a large portfolio of prevention programs. Consistent with empowerment evaluation and ECB approaches, iGTO provides online help to carry out and document progress on each of the 10 GTO steps. iGTO generates reports that can be shared among program practitioners and stakeholders. The National Institute on Alcoholism and Alcohol Abuse funded the research on iGTO (Chinman, Tremain, Imm, & Wandersman, 2009). The research goals were to understand how iGTO was used among substance use prevention practitioners across two states (Missouri and Tennessee) and to evaluate iGTO's impact on program performance.

When the research was initiated, both Missouri and Tennessee were receiving funds from SAMHSA to support substance use prevention coalitions and programs. Some programs in both states received the iGTO intervention ($n = 33$ in Tennessee and $n = 21$ in Missouri), whereas others did not ($n = 21$ in Tennessee and $n = 9$ in Missouri). In the iGTO sites, prevention staff received training in the GTO approach and iGTO and had ongoing monthly TA meetings.

The results showed that most iGTO-assigned programs completed activities on all of the 10 GTO steps. Findings showed that programs receiving iGTO improved their prevention performance over non-iGTO programs, demonstrating the association between GTO and quality prevention practices, including evaluation similar to the goals of ECB. The results also indicated that most participants did not plan to use iGTO after the demonstration period—that is, when they would have to pay for it themselves. In interviews, practitioners mentioned certain limitations, including difficulty extracting and incorporating iGTO's information, aesthetics of the reports, design issues, and lack of detail on the evidence-based programs and strategies available. Despite these limitations, iGTO helped improve program performance, and yet this study indicated that more work is needed before an Internet-based GTO system is ready for large-scale prevention efforts.

Study 3: The Getting To Outcomes-Underage Drinking (GTO-UD) Study

To address underage drinking, a significant public health problem costing the United States $53 billion annually, we developed a Getting To Outcomes-Underage Drinking (GTO-UD) toolkit (Imm et al., 2007). The toolkit focuses on evidence-based strategies targeting "environmental" factors such as alcohol availability, policy and enforcement, community norms, and media messages.

Funded by the CDC, we conducted a study of the GTO-UD intervention with six prevention coalitions in South Carolina (Chinman et al., in press). The coalitions were implementing two environmental alcohol prevention strategies: (1) responsible beverage service, that is, training alcohol servers to comply with laws on the appropriate sale of alcohol; and (2) compliance checks, that is, the use of "undercover" minors by law enforcement to assess whether a retail outlet sells to minors. Assigned randomly, three coalitions received the GTO-UD intervention (i.e., GTO toolkit, training, and TA), and three coalitions followed their usual practices. A sample of alcohol merchants in the six counties served by the coalitions was surveyed before and after the intervention period to assess their attitudes toward underage drinking and alcohol selling practices. Similar to the previous GTO studies, interviews of program performance were conducted before and after the intervention period.

The results showed improvement in prevention performance in the GTO-UD coalitions as compared to the coalitions that did not receive the GTO-UD intervention. For example, the coalitions that received GTO-UD carried out compliance checks more systematically than the coalitions without GTO-UD support. Findings showed that program performance changes were related to the amount of TA received; that is, more TA was related to greater improvements in program performance. There were no significant differences in the attitudes between the two groups of merchants in the different areas. However, merchants located in the counties that received the GTO-UD support improved their rate of refusals to minor alcohol purchases, whereas merchants in the counties that did not receive GTO-UD support showed no such change. These findings are consistent with previous research demonstrating that GTO can improve prevention program quality. The findings regarding merchant attitudes and behaviors were modest, but they suggest that the prevention program quality can result in changes at the community level.

Study 4: The Getting To Outcomes and Developmental Assets (AGTO) Study

Building on the results from the previous research, this study was GTO's first large-scale randomized controlled trial (RCT; Chinman, Acosta, et al., 2012). The study was designed to evaluate GTO applied to developmental assets (Benson & Scales, 2011), an approach developed by the Search Institute to support mobilization and collaboration among a wide range of community stakeholders to promote positive youth development. A manual published by the Search Institute with input from RAND called *Getting To Outcomes With Developmental Assets: Ten Steps to Measuring Success in Youth Programs and Communities* (Fisher et al., 2006) was utilized in this study.

Study participants were from 12 community coalitions in Maine that had a positive youth development mission. Each of the 12 coalitions nominated up to five prevention programs to participate. The programs varied widely, but they generally promoted healthy development in middle school and high school youth. Most programs were not evidence based. Six coalitions and their respective 30 programs were randomly assigned to receive the AGTO intervention, and the other six maintained routine operations. Using similar measures from earlier projects, the study assessed capacity (knowledge and skills) of individual practitioners, exposure to and use of AGTO, practitioner perceptions of AGTO, and program performance.

Results showed that greater pre-intervention capacity (in particular, knowledge) predicted better program performance, a key link in the implementation support logic model in Figure 15.1. Our study also showed that improvements in capacity led to improvements in performance, as described in the implementation support logic model. Similar to the GTO-2004 Drug Prevention Program Study, we found that practitioners who reported using AGTO showed greater improvements in capacity as compared to practitioners that did not report using it, regardless of assignment to the AGTO intervention. Also consistent with previous studies, we found that programs receiving the largest amount of TA consistently showed the most performance improvement. These findings suggest that AGTO can be an important ECB intervention. Despite these gains in capacity and performance, however, we also learned from staff that although AGTO helped them to better plan and evaluate their programs, doing so required significant resources. These findings are also consistent across the GTO studies.

The AGTO study is especially significant because it was the first study to show that the *use* of an implementation support intervention yielded improvements in practitioner capacity and consequently in program performance on a large sample of practitioners and programs using a RCT study design (Acosta, Chinman, et al., 2013; Chinman, Acosta, Ebener, Burkhart, et al., 2013). During the course of the study, several new AGTO implementation tools were developed, including online e-learning modules that provide a brief training for each AGTO step and a bank of tested outcome measures.[8]

---

8. Available for free at http://agto.search-institute.org

ONGOING GETTING TO OUTCOMES RESEARCH: A FOCUS ON EVIDENCE-BASED PROGRAMS

Whereas past research on GTO leveraged existing programs and worked with staff regardless of their current program quality or evidence base, the designs of current projects involve testing GTO with a single EBP across multiple sites. This approach addresses certain challenges faced in past studies. First, in the previous studies, it was challenging to assess program fidelity (i.e., the quality of program delivery) because different types of programs were involved in the study. Studying the implementation of a single EBP allows us to utilize a single measure of program fidelity, making it easier to make comparisons across sites. Second, it was difficult to assess GTO's impact on program outcomes (e.g., changes in youth knowledge or behavior), the last link in the implementation support logic model, because the outcomes varied widely by program type, quality, and intensity. Using a single EBP allows us to better isolate the effects of GTO as the program type and quality is the same across sites. Next, we highlight two ongoing studies that are testing GTO with EBPs.

Study 5: Promoting Healthy Sexuality GTO Study

Funded by a grant from the National Institute of Child Health and Development, this is the first GTO study to systematically collect program fidelity and youth outcome data, attempting to demonstrate the last link in the implementation support logic model (Chinman, Acosta, Ebener, Driver, et al., 2013). Started in 2011, this RCT compares 16 Boys & Girls Clubs (BGCs) implementing an evidence-based teen pregnancy prevention program called Making Proud Choices (MPC) with 16 BGCs implementing MPC augmented with GTO. Sites are located in the Metro Atlanta area and in the state of Alabama. MPC is a well-researched pregnancy and HIV/STI risk-reduction EBP with multiple trials demonstrating its effectiveness (Jemmott, Jemmott, Fong, & Morales, 2010). Consistent with the community-based replication of MPC (Jemmott et al., 2010), all sites receive MPC training and resources. In addition to the MPC training and support, sites assigned to receive GTO were provided with training, onsite TA, and *Promoting Science-Based Approaches to Teen Pregnancy Prevention* (Lesesne et al., 2007), a manual developed by CDC that applies GTO to the domain of teen pregnancy prevention. In this study, we will collect data on performance (like past GTO studies), fidelity of MPC, and sexual health outcomes of youth participants.

Preliminary findings from the first year of MPC implementation show that the GTO sites demonstrate better program fidelity and performance ratings than the non-GTO sites. More complete findings on how GTO impacts performance ratings, MPC fidelity, and youth outcomes will be available as the study progresses.

Study 6: The GTO Continuous Quality Improvement Study

Over the past two decades, health care organizations have applied continuous quality improvement (CQI) approaches to improve health care delivery (Laffel & Blumenthal, 1989). While CQI has been utilized in traditional health care settings, such as hospitals and primary care clinics, the uptake has not been widespread in community-based settings, where the majority of substance use prevention and treatment services are delivered. A CQI strength is that it has the potential to equip community-based programs with the ability to self-evaluate and utilize more data-driven decision making. To address this lag, we are pilot testing a newly developed GTO-CQI manual, along with training and TA, among eight programs that are part of one of the largest publicly funded substance use treatment organizations serving Los Angeles County (Hunter, Ober, Paddock, Hunt, & Levan, 2014). The soon-to-be-published manual expands CQI support beyond the original GTO manual. Using the Plan-Do-Study-Act (PDSA) framework (Langley, Nolan, Nolan, Norman, & Provost, 2009), the GTO-CQI manual provides support for using available process and outcome data to systematically plan and undertake changes and document the impact of those changes to ultimately enhance service delivery and outcomes.

In this study, eight sites are randomized to receive GTO-CQI either in the first or second year of the study. We are measuring the feasibility, process, and extent of GTO-CQI use. We are estimating the effect of the GTO-CQI intervention by examining staff and client outcomes. Costs of conducting GTO-CQI are being documented. In the second year, we will examine GTO-CQI sustainability among the first cohort of programs who are no longer receiving TA and training to examine how feasible it is for organizations to continue GTO-CQI after the initial TA support ends.

To date, we have randomized the sites and delivered the GTO-CQI intervention to the first cohort ($n = 4$). Staff assigned to the intervention participated in monthly meetings to review program process and outcome data to help plan a program change. Next, staff implemented a change and studied its impact. Finally, staff determined whether the change they made to their program would be modified, continued, or discontinued, consistent with the PDSA approach. The next steps in the study are to continue data collection and shift the intervention to the second cohort.

FUTURE DIRECTIONS

Research on GTO is ongoing. Much has been accomplished in demonstrating GTO as an implementation support model, but more work needs to be done to understand GTO's feasibility in real-world settings. In studies ranging from small pilots to larger randomized trials, we have demonstrated support for the implementation support logic model presented earlier in this chapter. For example, we have shown that the GTO intervention improves capacity (Studies 1, 3, 4) and performance (Studies 1–4) of key programming activities, consistent with the goals of empowerment evaluation. In addition, we have shown empirically that program capacity is related to program performance (Study 4). However, the GTO research to date has involved a variety of programs serving different populations, with different activities, measures, and expected outcomes, thus making it challenging to assess the impact of GTO on individual program participants, the last link in the implementation support logic model. Studies are currently under way that address whether program performance is related to participant outcomes, as specified in the implementation support logic model.

Along with other commentaries (Wandersman, 2014), this review of studies shows how GTO is related to ECB. For example, GTO is very specific in how it addresses the three domains (strategies, implementation, and evaluation) in the *activities* column of the IECB (see Labin et al., 2012, p. 309). As stated earlier, GTO uses certain theories, has a specific set of implementation strategies to build capacity (e.g., manuals, training, face-to-face TA), and the GTO research shows how it builds evaluation capacity. These studies have examined some of the ECB implementation variables (e.g., amount of TA) mentioned by Labin et al. and how those variables impact ECB *results*, the third column of the IECB.

Further, GTO studies address many of the factors in the *results* column of the IECB. As discussed earlier, GTO research targets change in capacity at the individual level (knowledge, behavior) and change in performance at the organizational level (*practices* in IECB terms). These changes include evaluation but also include many types of programming activities. In addition, more recent GTO research has started to assess the relationships between these levels by examining whether individual capacity and/or resources predict organizational performance. Although both GTO and ECB help programs demonstrate outcomes (participant outcomes was added to the IECB although it was not included in their literature synthesis), it could be argued that this factor has even greater importance for GTO than ECB, given that GTO also focuses on program planning and implementation as well as evaluation. As discussed in earlier sections of this chapter, GTO research is now focused on understanding its impact on program outcomes. Finally, all of the GTO studies have documented lessons learned, in large part by a strong emphasis on qualitative assessments of the barriers and facilitators.

Research is still needed in several areas that apply not only to GTO but also to any kind of implementation support system. For example, research on the optimal level of resources to engage in the type of capacity building GTO provides is needed. One type of "resource" is readiness of the practitioners and the host organization. In our previous work, we have found that programs with the highest performance at baseline (i.e., pre-intervention) used more TA than programs with the lowest performance ratings. These findings suggest that a certain level of capacity is needed to experience additional benefits from an intervention like GTO. "Readiness," as a concept, is gaining more attention. For example, building on multiple literatures, a recent article suggested a new definition of readiness that is made of motivation, general capacities (e.g., leadership, climate), and program-specific capacities (Scaccia et al., in press). However, much still needs to be learned about these factors' relationships with one another, how to measure them, and the minimal amount needed for successful capacity building.

Another type of resource, TA, seems to impact the use of GTO and improvement in capacity and performance. Although we know that more TA hours are associated with greater gains in performance, in some areas, it is not known what the minimum investment needs to be. It is still not known what training TA providers must have to be effective. Some of the completed studies used highly knowledgeable PhD-level researchers and evaluators as TA providers, which is not likely to be sustainable. The last completed GTO study and some of the current ones are using TA providers with BA degrees, which appears to be sufficient with proper training and supervision (Chinman, Acosta, et al., 2012).

Research is needed to find the "sweet spot" that produces desirable outcomes at a cost that can be reasonably afforded by local, state, and federal agencies. In that vein, the GTO team at RAND has begun a GTO cost-effectiveness study called Preparing to Run Effective Prevention (PREP). Similar to Study 5, it is a 30-site RCT comparing an evidence-based drug prevention program called Project Choice (D'Amico et al., 2012) with and without GTO support.

However, this will be one of the first studies to examine capacity and performance improvements in relation to the costs of providing GTO.

Finally, we believe an important next step in GTO research is a very large–scale study, one that truly replicates how a state or large grant program would utilize GTO. Although we believe that GTO can help "scale up" communities to conduct quality prevention, and it has been used by SAMHSA and CDC to do so, GTO itself has not been evaluated in this way. An online system like iGTO could play an important role; however, iGTO needs to be improved and updated prior to large-scale dissemination. Many state and federal agencies are providing this type of support for evidence-based programs (e.g., technical assistance centers), yet there has been little rigorous research on whether the support yields outcomes in a cost-effective manner at that scale.

CONCLUSIONS

Over the past decade, we have learned several lessons. First, GTO alone cannot guarantee successful prevention program implementation and outcomes. Communities need sufficient resources to utilize GTO and to implement programs with quality. Also, we have learned that GTO's impact is maximized when some type of accountability is already in place. That is, GTO can *promote* accountability by helping programs and funders generate data needed to assess performance, but if a program is operating without any consequences for positive or negative performance, it is more challenging to motivate GTO use.

Second, the choice of the program is critical to GTO utilization. Although the first GTO steps are designed to assist communities in selecting a program, GTO is oftentimes used by existing programs to become more consistent with principles of effective programs (Robertson, David, & Rao, 2003). In several of these cases, although individual practitioners experienced increased capacity (improved knowledge and skills) by using GTO, the programs themselves were "only" able to improve in certain domains, namely planning and evaluation, leaving program quality (i.e., program delivery) relatively unchanged.

Third, capturing the impact of GTO is an ongoing challenge. For example, in one coalition, the executive director reported that GTO assisted her in resisting pressures to change a program that would have made it less evidence-based. While this decision was an improvement of sorts in how the program continued to be implemented, it was hard to discern this in the study's results. In other cases, practitioners learned skills through the GTO approach that they did not put into action until after the research had ended. We continue to refine our measures and use qualitative methods to capture some of the gains not currently documented by the quantitative measures.

In sum, GTO support through the manuals, trainings, and TA have come a long way over the past decade, guided by research and community input. The research has shown that GTO can build evaluation capacity using the principles of empowerment evaluation. However, much is yet to be accomplished. In the next phase, we are tackling the remaining questions about impact on individuals, cost-effectiveness, and operation at large scales. It is only then that it will be known how well GTO accomplishes all the principles of empowerment evaluation.

REFERENCES

Acosta, J., Chinman, M., Ebener, P., Malone, P. S., Paddock, S., Phillips, A., et al. (2013). An intervention to improve program implementation: Findings from a two-year cluster randomized trial of Assets-Getting To Outcomes. *Implementation Science, 8*, 87.

Acosta, J., Ramchand, R., Becker, A., & Felton, A. (2013). *Development and pilot test of the RAND Suicide Prevention Program Evaluation Toolkit.* Santa Monica, CA: RAND Corporation.

Acosta, J., Ramchand, R., Becker, A., Felton, A., & Kofner, A. (2013). *RAND Suicide Prevention Program Evaluation Toolkit.* Santa Monica, CA: RAND Corporation.

Ajzen, I., & Fishbein, M. (1977). Attitude-behavior relations: A theoretical analysis and review of empirical research. *Psychological Bulletin, 84*, 888–918.

Altman, D. G. (1995). Sustaining interventions in community systems: On the relationship between researchers and communities. *Health Psychology, 14*, 526–536.

Aseltine, R. H., Jr., & Gore, S. (2005). Work, postsecondary education, and psychosocial functioning following the transition from high school. *Journal of Adolescent Research, 20*(6), 615–639.

Backer, T. (2000). The failure of success: Challenges of disseminating effective substance abuse prevention programs. *Journal of Community Psychology, 28*(3), 363–373.

Backer, T. (2002). *Finding the balance: Program fidelity and adaptation in substance abuse prevention.* Rockville, MD: Center for Substance Abuse Prevention.

Bandura, A. (2004). Health promotion by social cognitive means. *Health Education & Behavior, 31*(2), 143–164.

Barbee, A. P., Christensen, D., Antle, B., Wandersman, A., & Cahn, K. (2011). Successful adoption and implementation of a comprehensive casework practice model in a public child welfare agency: Application of the Getting To Outcomes (GTO) model. *Children and Youth Services Review, 33*, 622–633.

Benson, P. L., & Scales, P. (2011). Developmental assets. In R. J. R. Levesque (Ed.), *Encyclopedia of adolescence.* New York: Springer.

Brown, S. A., McGue, M., Maggs, J., Schulenberg, J., Hingson, R., Swartzwelder, S., et al. (2009). Underage alcohol use: Summary of developmental processes and mechanisms: Ages 16–20. *Alcohol Research & Health, 32*(1), 41–52.

Cassell, C., Santelli, J., Gilbert, B. C., Dalmat, M., Mezoff, J., & Schauer, M. (2005). Mobilizing communities: An overview of the Community Coalition Partnership Programs for the Prevention of Teen Pregnancy. *Journal of Adolescent Health, 37*, S3–S10.

Chervin, D. D., Philliber, S., Brindis, C. D., Chadwick, A. E., Revels, M. L., Kamin, S. L., et al. (2005). Community capacity building in CDC's Community Coalition Partnership Programs for the Prevention of Teen Pregnancy. *Journal of Adolescent Health, 37*, S11–S19.

Chinman, M., Acosta, J., Ebener, P., Burkhart, Q., Clifford, M., Corsello, M., et al. (2012). Establishing and evaluating the key functions of an interactive systems framework using an Assets-Getting To Outcomes intervention. *American Journal of Community Psychology, 50*(3/4), 295–310.

Chinman, M., Acosta, J., Ebener, P., Burkhart, Q., Clifford, M., Corsello, M., et al. (2013). Intervening with practitioners to improve the quality of prevention: One year findings from a randomized trial of Assets-Getting To Outcomes. *Journal of Primary Prevention, 34*, 173–191.

Chinman, M., Acosta, J., Ebener, P., Driver, J., Keith, J., & Peebles, D. (2013). Enhancing Quality Interventions Promoting Healthy Sexuality (EQUIPS): A novel application of translational research methods. *Clinical and Translational Science, 6*, 232–237.

Chinman, M., Hannah, G., & McCarthy, S. (2012). Lessons learned from a quality improvement intervention with homeless veteran services. *Journal of Health Care of the Poor and Underserved, 23*(3 Suppl), 210–224.

Chinman, M., Hannah, G., Wandersman, A., Ebener, P., Hunter, S., Imm, P., et al. (2005). Developing a community science research agenda for building community capacity for effective preventive interventions. *American Journal of Community Psychology, (35)*3/4, 143–157.

Chinman, M., Hunter, S. B., Ebener, P., Paddock, S., Stillman, L., Imm, P., et al. (2008). The Getting To Outcomes demonstration and evaluation: An illustration of the Prevention Support System. *American Journal of Community Psychology, 41*, 206–224.

Chinman, M., Imm, P., & Wandersman, A. (2004). *Getting To Outcomes 2004: Promoting accountability through methods and tools for planning, implementation, and evaluation.* Santa Monica, CA: RAND Corporation.

Chinman, M., Tremain, B., Imm, P., & Wandersman, A. (2009). Strengthening prevention performance using technology: A formative evaluation of interactive Getting To Outcomes. *American Journal of Orthopsychiatry, 79*, 469–481.

Crosse, S., Williams, B., Hagen, C. A., Harmon, M., Ristow, L., DiGaetano, R., et al. (2011). *Prevalence and implementation fidelity of research-based prevention programs in public schools.* Washington DC: U.S. Department of Education Office of Planning.

D'Amico, E. J., Tucker, J. S., Miles, J. N. V., Zhou, A. J., Shih, R. A., & Green, H. D. J. (2012). Preventing alcohol use with a voluntary after school program for middle school students: Results from a cluster randomized controlled trial of CHOICE. *Prevention Science, 13*, 415–425.

Department of Health and Human Services (DHHS). (2002). Program announcement 2145—Coalition capacity building for teen pregnancy prevention. *Federal Register, 67*(119), 42018–42022.

Durlak, J. A., & DuPre, E. P. (2008). Implementation matters: A review of research on the influence of implementation on program outcomes and the factors affecting implementation. *American Journal of Community Psychology, 41*, 327–350.

Fetterman, D. M., & Wandersman, A. (2005). *Empowerment evaluation principles in practice.* New York: Guilford Press.

Fishbein, M., & Ajzen, I. (1974). Atitudes toward objects as predictive of single and multiple behavioral criteria. *Psychological Review, 81*, 59–74.

Fishbein, M., & Ajzen, I. (1975). *Belief, attitude, intention, and behavior: An introduction to theory and research.* Reading, MA: Addison-Wesley.

Fisher, D., Imm, P. S., Chinman, M., & Wandersman, A. (2006). *Getting To Outcomes with developmental assets: Ten steps to measuring success in youth programs and communities.* Minneapolis, MN: Search Institute.

Green, L. (2001). From research to "best practices" in other settings and populations. *American Journal of Health Behavior, 25*(3), 165–178.

Hannah, G., Ray, M., Wandersman, A., & Chien, V. H. (2010). Developing performance-based contracts between agencies and service providers: Results from a Getting To Outcomes support system with social service agencies. *Children and Youth Services Review, 32,* 1430–1436.

Haveman, R., Wolfe, B., & Peterson, E. (1997). Children of early child bearers as young adults. In R. Maynard (Ed.), *Kids having kids* (pp. 257–284). Washington, DC: Urban Institute Press.

Hoffman, S. (2006). *By the numbers: The public costs of teen childbearing.* Washington, DC: National Campaign to Prevent Teen Pregnancy.

Hunter, S. B., Ober, A. J., Paddock, S. M., Hunt, P. E., & Levan, D. (2014). Continuous quality improvement (CQI) in addiction treatment settings: Design and intervention protocol of a group randomized pilot study. *Addiction Science and Clinical Practice, 9*(1), 4.

Hunter, S. B., Paddock, S., Ebener, P., Burkhart, Q., & Chinman, M. (2009). Promoting evidence-based practices: The adoption of a prevention support system in community settings. *Journal of Community Psychology, 37*(5), 579–593.

Imm, P., Chinman, M., Wandersman, A., Rosenbloom, D., Guckenburg, S., & Leis, R. (2007). *Preventing underage drinking: Using Getting to Outcomes with the SAMHSA strategic prevention framework to achieve results.* Santa Monica, CA: RAND Corporation.

Jackson, K. M., & Sartor, C. E. (in press). The natural course of substance use and dependence. In K. J. Sher (Ed.), *The Oxford handbook of substance use disorders.* New York: Oxford University Press.

Jemmott, J. B., Jemmott, L. S., Fong, G. T., & Morales, K. H. (2010). Effectiveness of an HIV/STD risk-reduction intervention for adolescents when implemented by community-based organizations: A cluster randomized controlled trial. *American Journal of Public Health, 100,* 720–726.

Johnston, L. D., O'Malley, P. M., Bachman, J. G., & Schulenberg, J. E. (2012). *Monitoring the Future national results on adolescent drug use: Overview of key findings, 2011.* Ann Arbor: University of Michigan, Institute for Social Research.

Kaye, K., & Chadwick, L. (2006). *The lives of teen parents after welfare reform and the role of TANF.* Washington, DC: U.S. Department of Health and Human Services, Assistant Secretary of Planning and Evaluation.

Kramer, J. S., Philliber, S., Brindis, C. D., Kamin, S. L., Chadwick, A. E., Revels, M. L., et al. (2005). Coalition models: Lessons learned from the CDC's Community Coalition Partnership Programs for the Prevention of Teen Pregnancy. *Journal of Adolescent Health, 37,* S20–S30.

Labin, S. N., Duffey, T., Meyers, D. C., Wandersman, A., & Lesesne, C. A. (2012). A research synthesis of the evaluation capacity building literature. *American Journal of Evaluation, 33*(3), 307–338.

Laffel, G., & Blumenthal, D. (1989). The case for using industrial quality management science in health care organizations. *JAMA, 262,* 2869–2873.

Langley, G. L., Nolan, K. M., Nolan, T. W., Norman, C. L., & Provost, L. P. (2009). *The improvement guide: A practical approach to enhancing organizational performance* (2nd ed.). San Francisco: Jossey-Bass.

Lesesne, C. A., Lewis, K. M., Moore, C., Fisher, D., Green, D., & Wandersman, A. (2007, June). *Promoting science-based approaches to teen pregnancy prevention using Getting To Outcomes* [Draft, unpublished manual].

Lesesne, C. A., Lewis, K. M., White, C. P., White, D. C., Green, D. C., Duffy, J. L., et al. (2008). Promoting science-based approaches to teen pregnancy prevention: Proactively engaging the three systems of the interactive systems framework. *American Journal of Community Psychology, 41*, 379–392.

Levine, J. A., Pollack, H., & Comfort, M. E. (2001). Academic and behavioral outcomes among the children of young mothers. *Journal of Marriage and Family, 63*, 355–369.

Mattox, T., Hunter, S., Kilburn, M. R., & Wiseman, S. H. (2013). *Getting To Outcomes for home visiting: How to plan, implement and evaluate a program in your community to support parents of young children.* Santa Monica, CA: RAND Corporation.

Mrazek, P., & Haggerty, R. (1994). *Reducing risks for mental disorders: Frontiers for preventive intervention research.* Washington, DC: National Academy Press.

Oesterle, S., Hill, K. G., Hawkins, J. D., Guo, J., & Catalano, R. F. (2004). Adolescent heavy episodic drinking trajectories and health in young adulthood. *Journal of Studies on Alcohol, 65*(2), 204–212.

Patton, G. C., Coffey, C., Lynskey, M. T., Reid, S., Hemphill, S., Carlin, J. B., et al. (2007). Trajectories of adolescent alcohol and cannabis use into young adulthood. *Addiction, 102*(4), 607–615.

Perper, K., Peterson, K., & Manlove, J. (2010). *Diploma attachment among teen mothers* [Fact sheet]. Washington, DC: Child Trends.

Robertson, E. B., David, S. L., & Rao, S. A. (2003). *Preventing drug use among children and adolescents: A research-based guide for parents, educators, and community leaders* (NIH Publication No. 04-4212[A]). Bethesda, MD: National Institute of Health.

Scaccia, J. P., Cook, B. S., Lamont, A., Wandersman, A., Castellow, J., Katz, J., & Beidas, R.S. (in press). A practical implementation science heuristic for organizational readiness: R=MC². *Journal of Community Psychology.*

Singh, S., & Darroch, J. E. (2000). Adolescent pregnancy and childbearing: Levels and trends in developed countries. *Family Planning Perspectives, 32*(1), 14–23.

Solomon-Fears, C. (2013). *Teenage pregnancy prevention: Statistics and programs.* (Rep. No. RS20301). Washington, DC: Congressional Research Service.

Suarez-Balcazar, Y. (2014). Moving from science to practice in evaluation capacity building. *American Journal of Evaluation, 35*(1), 95–99.

Terry-Human, E., Manlove, J., & Moore, K. A. (2005). *Playing catch-up: How the children of teen mothers fare.* Hyattsville, MD: National Center for Health Statistics.

Wandersman, A. (2003). Community science: Bridging the gap between science and practice with community-centered models. *American Journal of Community Psychology, 31*(3/4), 227–242.

Wandersman, A. (2014). Getting To Outcomes: An evaluation capacity building example of rationale, science, and practice. *American Journal of Evaluation, 35*(1), 100–106.

Wandersman, A., & Florin, P. (2003). Community interventions and effective prevention: Bringing researchers/evaluators, funders and practitioners together for accountability. *American Psychologist, 58*(6/7), 441–448.

PART V
CONCLUSION

CHAPTER 16
Conclusion

Reflections on Emergent Themes and Next Steps Revisited[1]

David M. Fetterman

Fetterman & Associates and Stanford University

Abraham Wandersman

University of South Carolina

Shakeh J. Kaftarian

Kaftarian & Associates

All good things must come to an end. This maxim also applies to this collection. We began this book as a revision of the original *Empowerment Evaluation* (1995) book, which helped launch empowerment evaluation. It ended up being a completely new collection. The dialogue and engagement among the contributors helped refine important insights and understandings. Three chapters include program staff members as coauthors, reflecting the empowerment evaluation principles of inclusion and community knowledge. We encourage this type of publishing partnership. Like empowerment evaluation, and process use in particular, the creation of this book had an impact on many of us in the process of completing it. This collective engagement also served to further strengthen a committed community of learners.

---

1. This was the title we used in the conclusion of the first empowerment evaluation book 21 years ago. We now revisit the same concept. The underlying themes of capacity building and accountability remain, while entirely new next steps are needed.

This collection reflects the international scope of the approach, including empowerment evaluations conducted in Peru, the Visible Learning program operating in 10 countries, and work conducted in the United States. Youth as empowerment evaluators were included in this collection to emphasize the value of the often neglected voice of youth in community planning, implementation, and evaluation. Examples were drawn from both health and education, including schools and community-based organizations, to demonstrate the breadth of empowerment evaluation's reach. Since foundations are often viewed as catalysts of social change, two authors from foundations were invited to share their views about the power of empowerment evaluation to improve people's lives.

The projects selected for inclusion ranged from small local efforts to $15 million tech-oriented engagements and beyond. Some of the projects were of relatively short duration, whereas other empowerment evaluation initiatives have been operating for a decade. Although low-income communities of color were highlighted throughout the collection, many socioeconomically mainstream middle-class communities were also included. The fact that empowerment evaluation operates in government, corporate, non-profit, and foundation-funded settings speaks to the appeal and scope of the approach.

CONCEPTUAL CLARITY AND METHODOLOGICAL SPECIFICITY[2]

One of the most significant features of this book is the conceptual clarity and methodological specificity it offers. Empowerment evaluation theories, concepts, principles, and even steps have been described. Evaluation capacity building (ECB), a fundamental empowerment evaluation principle, was a central theme explicitly discussed in most chapters. The prominence of ECB merited a change in the title of this book to include evaluation capacity building. Additional clarity was added by providing greater methodological specificity. The standardized 3-step and 10-step empowerment evaluation approaches were presented and discussed in many of the chapters in this collection. This collection also highlights the central theme of accountability in empowerment evaluation.

---

2. One part of contributing to conceptual clarity is addressing misunderstandings. See chapter appendix for a discussion about common misunderstandings about empowerment evaluation.

ACCOUNTABILITY

From its inception, accountability has been a driving force and the bottom line in empowerment evaluation. A few paramount questions are: Did you do it? Did you accomplish your objectives? Did you produce the results you desired and promised? Each chapter speaks to these accountability questions. For example, the Tribal Digital Village built one of the largest wireless systems in the country. The other Digital Villages were responsible for transforming the curriculum and pedagogy in public schools and stimulating the development of local minority-owned small businesses. Minority-focused tobacco prevention programs saved millions of dollars in excess medical expenses, contributed to smoke-free policies, and led to the creation of the Arkansas Evaluation Center. Empowerment evaluation contributed to producing these programmatic and community-based initiative outcomes. In addition, each of the chapters focusing on tools was designed to address issues of accountability, ranging from social workers measuring their effectiveness to teachers "knowing their impact." Getting To Outcomes® (GTO®) explicitly tackles the issue of what it means to be accountable. The threads of evaluation capacity building and accountability, woven through these chapters, help define the fabric of empowerment evaluation.

INTERNAL VERSUS EXTERNAL EVALUATION

Although the focus of this book is on internal forms of evaluation, we want to reinforce the message that internal and external forms of evaluation can be used in tandem and can be mutually reinforcing. For example, RAND was responsible for conducting a meta-evaluation of GTO for over a decade (see Chapter 15, this volume). Similarly, RAND assessed tobacco prevention efforts in Arkansas, documenting progress made in reducing tobacco consumption in the same counties as the Minority Initiative Sub-Recipient Grant Office (MISRGO) tobacco prevention empowerment evaluation (see Chapter 14, this volume). In both cases, they helped validate empowerment evaluation efforts.

Internal and external forms of evaluation are not mutually exclusive. The only caveat is that external evaluations should be rooted in internal concerns; otherwise, they may be irrelevant or mislead program staff members. In addition, they might divert resources from the most important issues and problems, given the organization's stage of development.

NEXT STEPS

Empowerment evaluation is firmly rooted in the field of evaluation. It has been tested and contested. It has contributed to the literature. All three editors of this collection have received awards for their contributions to empowerment evaluation. In fact, empowerment evaluation is of sufficient maturity that it has become the focus of much research and evaluation. This begs the question: What's next?

BUILDING AND EXPANDING

Empowerment evaluation will build on its multisite work, determining the optimal balance between the flexibility needed to work in communities with emergent issues and the structures required to facilitate comparisons across programs and communities. Empowerment evaluators will continue to expand the reach of empowerment evaluation, operating in more countries and settings than ever before, because the demand for sensitivity, flexibility, self-determination, and results is growing every day.

PLACE-BASED EVALUATIONS

In place-based initiatives,[3] stakeholders are "engaged in a collaborative process to address issues as they experience within a geographic space," typically in a neighborhood or a region, where they create "shared plans and dreams" (Bellefontaine & Wisener, 2011, chap. 1). Place-based initiatives operate as "open systems where things change, people adapt to these changes which can change the outcomes" (Bellefontaine & Wisener, 2011, chap. 3). They employ a theory of change, a description of the change people want to see, and a theory of action, a description of the strategies that will actually produce the targeted outcomes (Rasmussen, 2013). Empowerment evaluations are philosophically aligned and methodologically robust enough to work in established and emergent place-based environments.

Empowerment evaluation has been engaged in place-based initiatives, such as those sponsored by Hewlett-Packard (Fetterman, 2013) and the Casey

---

3. They are also referred to as comprehensive community initiatives, community economic development, and complex adaptive systems.

Dr. Fetterman and a Latin America and Caribbean group enjoying a light moment during their empowerment evaluation. Courtesy of David M. Fetterman.

Family Foundation. Place-based work will continue to be an important home for empowerment evaluation to operate. For example, the W. K. Kellogg Foundation's board of trustees approved the use of empowerment evaluation as part of its evaluation repertoire in 2013. Linh Nguyen, Chief Operating Officer and vice president of Learning and Impact, the evaluation heart of the foundation, and the Kellogg Foundation's Latin America and Caribbean group invited Fetterman to facilitate empowerment evaluation exercises in Mexico City. The exercises were designed to help grantees monitor and assess their place-based initiatives, building on their own efforts in their micro-regions. The approach resonated with the grantees and complemented their own efforts.

It is no accident that Ricardo Millet, when he was the W. K. Kellogg Foundation director of evaluation, endorsed the approach in the foreword of *Empowerment Evaluation Principles in Practice* (Fetterman & Wandersman, 2005). It resonated with the foundation's commitment to helping people help themselves, and it continues to resonate today.

STAKEHOLDER INVOLVEMENT APPROACHES

Empowerment evaluation can benefit from an ongoing dialogue with similar stakeholder involvement approaches. *Stakeholder involvement approaches* is an umbrella term for similar (but different) approaches to evaluation that involve stakeholders in the evaluation, such as collaborative, participatory, and empowerment approaches to evaluation. Distinguishing evaluator roles across approaches has been useful. For example, collaborative evaluators are in charge of the evaluation, but they create an ongoing engagement between evaluators and stakeholders. Participatory evaluators jointly share control of the evaluation. Empowerment evaluators view program staff members, program participants, and community members as in control of the evaluation. However, empowerment evaluators serve as critical friends or coaches to help keep the process on track, rigorous, responsive, and relevant.

Collaborative, participatory, and empowerment evaluators have already made significant contributions to clarifying similarities and differences between approaches (Cousins, Whitmore, & Shulha, 2014; Fetterman, Rodríguez-Campos, Wandersman, & O'Sullivan, 2014). These distinctions help evaluators select the most appropriate approach for the task at hand. They also help establish appropriate expectations for grantees, community members, and sponsors.

The next challenge, however, is to begin to think about how best to apply these approaches in various combinations within the same large-scale place-based initiatives, where one approach may not be sufficient. In the process, empowerment evaluation will continue to refine its focus on outcomes, broadening the concept and enlarging the scope of what it means to reach goals and produce results in large-scale community or place-based initiatives.

Admittedly, there is much work ahead. The size of the task ahead, like the social and economic problems before us, should not discourage us from moving forward. As Thomas Edison said: "Opportunity is missed by most people because it is dressed in overalls, and looks like work." We, on the contrary, are eager to seize this opportunity to continue to work with communities and colleagues as co-equals, as we all expand our understanding and insight into empowerment evaluation.

Appendix 16A

Clarifying Empowerment Evaluation Issues

There have been a number of questions, concerns, and misunderstandings about empowerment evaluation over the past couple of decades. They have been addressed in various exchanges, as discussed in the first two chapters of this book. However, a summary of our responses to some of the most common questions or misunderstandings is presented here to assist practitioners as they respond to these issues in their own practice.

1. **Empowerment.** A common misconception about empowerment evaluation is that it empowers either individuals or groups. Empowerment evaluation can't empower anyone. People empower themselves. Empowerment evaluation simply provides the tools and environment conducive to empowering oneself.

2. **Objectivity and advocacy.** The question of whether empowerment evaluation is objective or promotes advocacy are legitimate questions. There should be no illusion, however; evaluation has never been neutral or free from political, social, cultural, or economic influences. Empowerment evaluation addresses many of these concerns by being transparent, bringing bias to the surface, and generating meaningful data to inform decision making. Moreover, these data are used by staff, community members, and other relevant parties to advocate for their programs or communities as data merit.

3. **Consumer focus.** Though evaluators and donors should be an integral part of empowerment evaluation, consumers (community members, program staff, and participants) are a (but not the only) driving force.

4. **Purpose.** There are multiple purposes for evaluation, including program improvement or development of programs, accountability, and knowledge production (Chelimsky, 1997). Empowerment evaluation contributes to all three purposes. It makes a strong contribution to external

accountability primarily by cultivating internal accountability, which remains long after an episodic and often anticipated external examination. The research on empowerment evaluation by Christie (2003), Miller and Campbell (2006), and Chinman, Acosta, Hunter, and Ebener (Chapter 15, this volume) represent important contributions to knowledge production, highlighting in part the rapidity of empowerment evaluation knowledge transfer into practice. (See Chelimsky & Shadish, 1997, concerning the multiple purposes of evaluation.)

5. **Bias**. Internal evaluations are often seen as biased and self-serving. This is not the case in quality empowerment evaluations. To the contrary, empowerment evaluations are often more critical of their own programs than are external examinations (which are concerned about being asked to return for a follow-up or extended engagement). Empowerment evaluations provide people with a window of opportunity to address long-standing issues of dysfunction and inefficiency in their own organizations in a nonthreatening and supportive atmosphere. Empowerment evaluations are not used to highlight individual inadequacies. Instead, they help organizations seize the opportunity to "make things work." In addition, the process is inclusive and transparent, open to critique and review, which makes it difficult to keep people from publically "speaking their truth."

6. **Outcomes**. Empowerment evaluations are highly collaborative and participatory in nature. However, the bottom line remains: Did you accomplish the desired results? Empowerment evaluations are conducted within the context of what people are already being held accountable for in their communities or workplaces. This makes the entire process more credible, authentic, and meaningful.

7. **Sociopolitical or psychological dimensions**. Much of the richness of empowerment evaluation is found in the social and psychological arena. Glass (personal communication, 1977) was one of the first evaluators to observe this phenomenon. He explained, "For people who know you, empowerment evaluation is first and foremost a psychological phenomenon, much more than a political act." It offers a supportive and nonjudgmental atmosphere, conducive to learning.

8. **Constituent communities**. Some colleagues have argued that empowerment evaluation should be limited to the disenfranchised. Empowerment evaluators, however, believe that everyone can benefit from being more empowered, particularly from a positive social and psychological growth perspective.

These points about conceptual clarity, as well as additional discussion about methodological specificity and outcomes are discussed in greater detail in the literature (Fetterman, 2001; Fetterman & Wandersman, 2005, 2007).[4]

REFERENCES

Bellefontaine, T., & Wisener, R. (2011). *The evaluation of place-based approaches*. Policy Horizon Canada. Retrieved from http://www.horizons.gc.ca/eng/content/evaluation-place-based-approaches

Center for Theory of Change. (2013). *What is theory of change?* Retrieved from http://www.theoryofchange.org/what-is-theory-of-change/#4

Chelimsky, E. (1997). The coming transformation in evaluation. In E. Chelimsky & W. Shadish (Eds.), *Evaluation for the 21st century: A handbook*. Thousand Oaks, CA: Sage.

Chelimsky, E., & Shadish, W. (Eds.). (1997). *Evaluation for the 21st century: A handbook*. Thousand Oaks, CA: Sage.

Christie, C. (2003, Spring). What guides evaluation? A study of how evaluation maps on to evaluation theory. *New Directions for Evaluation, 97*, 7–36.

Cousins, B., Whitmore, E., & Shulha, L. (2014). Let there be light: Response to Fetterman et al. 2014. *American Journal of Evaluation, 35*(1), 149–153.

Fetterman, D. M. (2001). *Foundations of empowerment evaluation*. Thousand Oaks, CA: Sage.

Fetterman, D. M. (2013). *Empowerment evaluation in the Digital Villages: Hewlett-Packard's $15 million race toward social justice*. Stanford, CA: Stanford University Press.

Fetterman, D. M., Rodríguez-Campos, L., Wandersman, A., & O'Sullivan, R. (2014). Collaborative, participatory, and empowerment evaluation: Building a stronger conceptual foundation for stakeholder involvement approaches to evaluation (A response to Cousins, Whitmore, and Shulha, 2013). *American Journal of Evaluation, 35*(1), 144–148.

Fetterman, D. M., & Wandersman, A. (2005). *Empowerment evaluation principles in practice*. New York: Guilford Press.

Fetterman, D. M., & Wandersman, A. (2007). Empowerment evaluation: Yesterday, today, and tomorrow. *American Journal of Evaluation, 28*(2), 179–198.

Miller, R. L., & Campbell, R. (2006). Taking stock of empowerment evaluation: An empirical review. *American Journal of Evaluation, 27*(9), 296–319.

Rasmussen, H. T. (2013). *What's a theory of action and why do we need one?* Retrieved from http://www.abeoschoolchange.org/blog/whats-a-theory-of-action-and-why-do-we-need-one

---

4. Christie (2003) has also revealed a unique contribution empowerment evaluation has made to the field and how to differentiate its contribution from contributions of similar approaches. (See also Fetterman, Rodríguez-Campos, Wandersman, & O'Sullivan, 2014.)

Index

About the Editors

David M. Fetterman is president and CEO of Fetterman & Associates, an international evaluation consulting firm. He has 25 years of experience at Stanford University, serving as a senior administrator, School of Education faculty member, and School of Medicine director of evaluation. Fetterman is the director of the Arkansas Evaluation Center and concurrently a professor at San Jose State University, the University of Charleston, and the University of Arkansas. He was a professor and research director at the California Institute of Integral Studies, principal research scientist at the American Institutes for Research, and a senior associate at RMC Research Corporation. Fetterman is a past president of the American Evaluation Association. He received both the Paul Lazarsfeld Award for Outstanding Contributions to Evaluation Theory and the Myrdal Award for Cumulative Contributions to Evaluation Practice. Fetterman also received the American Educational Research Association Research on Evaluation Distinguished Scholar Award. Fetterman is the founder of empowerment evaluation. He has published 16 books, including *Empowerment Evaluation in the Digital Villages: Hewlett-Packard's $15 Million Race Toward Social Justice*, *Empowerment Evaluation Principles in Practice* (with Wandersman), *Foundations of Empowerment Evaluation*, and *Empowerment Evaluation: Knowledge and Tools for Self-assessment and Accountability* (with Kaftarian and Wandersman).

Shakeh J. Kaftarian, Ph.D., is president and CEO of Kaftarian & Associates, a consulting firm offering empowerment evaluation services to national and international organizations. Her interests include community coalition building, substance abuse prevention programming, and women's health research. She has held positions as a research and evaluation scientist at the National Institutes of Health, Substance Abuse and Mental Health Administration, and Agency for Healthcare Research and Quality of the U.S. Department of Health and Human Services. She has served as senior advisor at the White House Office of National Drug Control Policy, and adjunct research professor at the Uniformed Services University of the Health Sciences. She is the coeditor (with Fetterman and Wandersman) of the first edition of *Empowerment Evaluation: Knowledge and Tools for Self-Assessment and Accountability* (Sage, 1996) and has authored a number of peer-reviewed articles and federal evaluation research reports. She has also served as guest editor for the *Journal of Primary Prevention, Prevention Science, Evaluation and Program Planning,* and *Journal of Community Psychology.*

Abraham Wandersman is a professor of psychology at the University of South Carolina–Columbia. Wandersman performs research and program evaluation on citizen participation in community organizations and coalitions and on interagency collaboration. He is a coeditor of three books on empowerment evaluation, and a coauthor of several Getting To Outcomes® accountability books (how-to manuals for planning, implementation, and evaluation to achieve results). Wandersman collaborated with CDC to develop the interactive systems framework for dissemination and implementation—the subject of two special issues of a peer-reviewed journal (2008, 2012). In 1998, he received the Myrdal Award for Evaluation Practice from the American Evaluation Association. In 2000, he was elected president of the Society for Community Research and Action (SCRA). In 2005, he was awarded the Distinguished Theory and Research Contributions Award by SCRA. In 2008, Getting To Outcomes won the American Evaluation Association's Outstanding Publication Award. In 2013, he was a visiting scholar at the Center for Injury Prevention of the Centers for Disease Control and Prevention.

About the Contributors

Joie Acosta is a behavioral scientist at the RAND Corporation and has a degree in community and cultural psychology from the University of Hawai'i. She specializes in participatory research and empowerment evaluations of health promotion, prevention and intervention, and community development projects. She has 11 years of experience developing and conducting community-based research and strategic planning. Acosta is currently the principal investigator (PI) on a National Institutes of Health research project grant (NIH R01) assessing the effectiveness of restorative practices, a whole-school positive youth development intervention. She is also co-PI on two NIH R01s funded to evaluate Getting To Outcomes®, an implementation support intervention to improve the implementation of evidence-based programs. She has led large-scale analyses of qualitative data, including interviews, videos, and document review, using Atlas.ti, NVivo, and Ethnograph qualitative analysis software. She received a Diversity Supplement from NIH to conduct a study assessing organizational networks formed to support prevention programs in 12 communities. Her network analysis expertise was applied to adapt the PARTNER tool for use by Hospital Preparedness Program (Office of the Assistant Secretary for Preparedness and Response, Department of Health and Human Services) and in New York City after Hurricane Sandy.

Matthew Biewener is project associate for the U.S. Substance Abuse and Mental Health Services Administration's (SAMHSA's) Center for the Application of Prevention Technologies (CAPT), where he directs SAMHSA's Service to Science (STS) subcontract process, including project planning and implementation, overseeing proposal submission and review, and assessing progress and outcomes. He coordinates development of systems, communications products, and other resources to support the efforts of local-level prevention programs to build their capacity to demonstrate greater evidence of effectiveness. Biewener also has special interest in developing and leveraging online technologies to enhance project management and information dissemination, including interactive databases that track planning and delivery of training and technical assistance services and those that provide state epidemiologists with access to inventories of behavioral health indicators. His work also focuses on a variety of public health topics, including mental health and school-based health promotion. He has developed, designed, and disseminated training and technical assistance tools related to evaluation capacity building, pandemic influenza preparedness, HIV in educational settings, and substance abuse prevention. Biewener earned his M.P.H. in maternal and child health from Boston University School of Public Health and his B.A. in public health from Johns Hopkins University.

Matthew Chinman is a senior behavioral scientist at the RAND Corporation and a research scientist at the Veterans Affairs (VA) Pittsburgh Healthcare System. Chinman has a degree in clinical/community psychology from the University of South Carolina. Chinman leads a program of research focusing on the implementation of evidence-based practices, which focuses on the Getting To Outcomes® (GTO®) model and implementation support intervention. This work has been supported by funding from the Centers for Disease Control and Prevention (CDC), Substance Abuse and Mental Health Services Administration (SAMHSA), U.S. Department of Veterans Affairs (VA), and National Institute of Health (NIH). GTO has been adopted by SAMHSA, CDC, VA's National Center for Homelessness Among Veterans, and several state agencies to support their own work in the areas of drug prevention, underage drinking prevention, homelessness, and teenage pregnancy prevention. Chinman has published and presented extensively on Getting To Outcomes research and implementation science.

Janet Clinton is an associate professor and the director of the Centre for Program Evaluation at the University of Melbourne. She is a psychologist and educator with an extensive publication record and is currently the coeditor of the *Evaluation Journal of Australasia*. Her evaluation experience extends across national and international contexts and includes more than 150 different evaluation projects. Her evaluation work focuses on the use of standard setting as a methodological tool, including the development of useable standards for a variety of sectors. She also has considerable experience in evaluation capacity building.

Kim Dash is a senior project director and scientist with Education Development Center, Inc. (EDC). She currently leads the Substance Abuse and Mental Health Services Administration's (SAMHSA's) Service to Science (STS) initiative, a national program that focuses on strengthening the evaluation capacity of innovative, field-grown substance abuse prevention programs. Dash has served on several research efforts, including two federally funded projects in EDC's Center for Research on High Risk Behavior—Reach for Health Middle Childhood Risk Prevention Study and Multi-level Bystander Strategies—to develop and pilot innovative prevention programs to reduce early sexual initiation and youth violence, respectively. Her work also focuses on programs designed to improve delivery of health care services, and she has collaborated with nursing and medical professionals to develop and evaluate programs on managing delirium and dementia in older adults; adopting and implementing clinical protocols to improve outcomes of hospitalized older adults; improving immunization practices; enhancing cancer risk assessment and screening of women of color; and increasing the number of racial and ethnic minority youth choosing to pursue careers in professional nursing. She earned her M.P.H. from the University of North Carolina, Chapel Hill, and her Ph.D. in social policy from Brandeis University.

Linda Delaney is the president of LFD Consulting, LLC, an organizational management consulting agency. She has an M.B.A., with more than 18 years of organizational/ employee development, leadership, and management experience. Delaney provides results-oriented proficiency training, applied to program evaluation, asset mapping, proposal reviews, technical writing, strategic planning, and implementation. Delaney is a workshop facilitator, workforce development provider, and skill/principle-based trainer. She also provides community outreach planning and development. She is a certified empowerment evaluator and cofacilitates evaluations with David M. Fetterman for the Minority Initiative Sub-Recipient Grant Office. Delaney also provides training at the American Evaluation Association annual meetings with Fetterman. She currently serves as the Learning Coordinator for the City of Memphis Office of Talent Development. Her books include *Stewardship: A Matter of Principle* and *In the Shadows of Greatness.*

José María Díaz-Puente is a professor at the Universidad Politécnica de Madrid. His line of research is focused on participatory methodologies for planning, evaluation, and management of public policies, programs, and projects, especially with regard to rural and socioeconomic development. He is the 2003 recipient of the Europe Prize for his contributions to the evaluation and planning of European policies. In addition, he was a Fulbright Scholar at Stanford University. He has participated in several projects at the international and European levels and has cooperated with governments, universities, and firms in the development of frameworks for the evaluation of public policies and development programs. Publications include book chapters and articles published in scientific journals such as *Community Development Journal*, *American Journal of Evaluation*, *Evaluation Review*, *European Planning Studies*, *Perspectives in Education*, *Procedia*, *Agrociencia*, *Cuadernos de Desarrollo Rural*, and *Estudios Geográficos*. He is certified as a project management director by the International Project Management Association (IPMA) and is a member of the research group GESPLAN, the Spanish Association of Project Engineering, and the American Evaluation Association.

Patricia Ebener is a senior survey director with the Survey Research Group and a senior researcher at the RAND Corporation in Santa Monica, California. Her research interests include the epidemiology and consequences of alcohol and other drug use; quality of behavioral health prevention, early intervention, and treatment services; community-based research; and survey research methods. Ebener is active in community research in collaboration with behavioral health treatment providers, school districts, law enforcement, local governments, and community-based organizations. She directed data collection for Centers for Disease Control and Prevention–funded studies of Getting To Outcomes® (GTO®) interventions in substance abuse coalitions in California and South Carolina and a National Institute on Drug Abuse–funded study of the Assets-Getting to Outcomes model tested in 12 communities in Maine. She continues to work with GTO colleagues on the dissemination and evaluation of GTO in a National Institute of Child Health and Human Development–funded study of GTO in combination with a pregnancy and STD/HIV prevention program for young teens; a mental health prevention and early intervention technical assistance project; and a National Institute on Alcohol Abuse and Alcoholism–funded evaluation of GTO with a substance abuse prevention program, Project CHOICE.

Marian Evans-Lee is the coordinator for the Minority Initiative Sub-Recipient Grant Office (MISRGO) at the University of Arkansas at Pine Bluff (UAPB). Evans-Lee has 15 years of experience in program planning and development, capacity building, and program evaluation. Evans-Lee completed a master's degree in public health from Tulane University in New Orleans and a doctorate degree in public health leadership from the University of Arkansas for Medical Sciences Fay W. Boozman College of Public Health. Evans-Lee is a certified health education specialist, a certified grant evaluator, and a member of the American Evaluation Association. She has served on the board of directors for the Boys and Girls Club of Jefferson County and the Arkansas Coalition for Excellence.

 **Jesica Siham Fernández** is a Ph.D. candidate in social psychology with a designated emphasis in Latin American & Latino Studies (LALS) at the University of California, Santa Cruz. Fernández's research spans several perspectives, including social-community psychology, LALS, education, and youth studies. Broadly, her programmatic line of research centers on exploring the role of settings in facilitating empowerment and *conscientización* among subordinated individuals and groups; specifically, how settings, such as schools and/or communities, shape and support opportunities to engage in social action. Additionally, she is interested in Latina/o communities and in social constructions of citizenship for children and youth. Currently, she is working on her dissertation, which will explore cultural citizenship among Latina/o youth in a youth participatory action research (yPAR) after-school program. Fernández is a joint teaching associate in the departments of psychology and LALS. She is a long-standing member of the Society for Community Research and Action (SCRA, Division 27 of APA) and the Society for the Psychological Study of Social Issues (SPSSI, Division 9 of APA). Fernández is a graduate student fellow of the American Association of Hispanics in Higher Education (AAHHE), recipient of the Eugene Cota-Robles Fellowship, and recipient of the UC President's Dissertation Year Fellowship.

 **María José Fernández-Moral** is a doctoral student at the Universidad Politécnica de Madrid and scholarship holder of the research group GESPLAN. Her research focuses on the evaluation of rural development programs and projects. Her emphasis is on facilitation processes and governance, especially at the local and regional levels. She has published articles in scientific journals.

Debra Hamm serves as the superintendent of Richland School District Two, the largest school district in the Midlands area of South Carolina. Hamm received a B.A. in sociology from the University of California, Santa Barbara, and an M.A. and Ph.D. in educational research from the University of South Carolina. Hamm's career as an educator spans nearly 40 years. In addition to teaching in public schools, she worked at the South Carolina Department of Education, where she served as the supervisor of teacher assessment and oversaw the development of teacher evaluation systems and licensure examinations. Hamm has taught at the University of South Carolina as an adjunct professor for graduate courses in research, statistics, assessment, and program evaluation. She has served in multiple administrative positions in Richland School District Two, including the position of chief information officer, overseeing the Office of Accountability and Evaluation and the Department of Information Technology Services. While in that position, Hamm received the District Level Administrator of the Year award from the South Carolina Association of School Administrators.

Ivan Haskell, Ph.D. in clinical-community psychology from the University of South Carolina, focuses on the design, implementation, and oversight of child and family community mental health services. Haskell has served as the clinical and administrative director of several publically funded mental health programs in Philadelphia. These programs have been located in traditional clinics as well as school-based settings. In 2010, he assumed the role of director of Social and Psychological Services for Mastery Charter Schools (MCS). At MCS, he created the social work and counseling/therapy programs and directed the reconfiguring of in-school student support systems. Haskell is interested in the implementation of social and emotional learning programs in schools, the application of evidence-based practice in community and school settings, and the evaluation of community and school-based mental health programs in order to drive continuous program improvement.

John Hattie is director of the Melbourne Educational Research Institute at the University of Melbourne. His areas of interest are measurement models and their applications to educational problems, and models of teaching and learning. Previous appointments were in Auckland, North Carolina, Western Australia, and New England. He was chief moderator of the NZ Performance Based Research Fund, is immediate past president of the International Test Commission, and associate editor of *British Journal of Educational Psychology* and *American Educational Research Journal*. He has published and presented more than 550 papers and supervised 180 theses students.

Sarah B. Hunter is a senior behavioral scientist at the RAND Corporation and professor at the Pardee RAND Graduate School of Public Policy. Hunter has a degree in psychology from the University of California, Santa Barbara. She has extensive experience in community empowerment and participatory program evaluation. As part of the Getting To Outcomes® projects, Hunter provided multiple trainings and hundreds of technical assistance hours to community-based organizations to build evaluation capacity and conduct continuous quality improvement. She has written about the elements of technical assistance and capacity building. Hunter uses both qualitative and quantitative methods to study program implementation. Hunter has served as the lead evaluator on several community service projects supported by the Substance Abuse and Mental Health Services Administration. They are designed to provide mental health and/or substance use treatment to vulnerable populations. Hunter is currently leading the development and testing of a Getting To Outcomes manual to support continuous quality improvement in community-based social service settings. She assisted in the development of the GTO manual to support home visiting.

Aidyn L. Iachini, Ph.D., M.S.W., L.S.W., is an assistant professor in the College of Social Work at the University of South Carolina. She has her Ph.D. in sport and exercise management and her M.S.W. with a concentration in school social work. She has experience working in schools, as well as in nonprofit and youth development settings. Her research interests include positive youth development, leadership and administration within youth development and human service organizations, school mental health service delivery systems, and program evaluation.

Pamela Imm is affiliated with the University of South Carolina and the Lexington Richland Alcohol and Drug Abuse Agency in Columbia, South Carolina. Imm is a trained community psychologist and has extensive experience in the areas of program development, program evaluation, and applied research.

Imm has worked as a consultant and evaluator with various local, state, and national agencies, including the Center for Substance Abuse Prevention, the Center for Substance Abuse Treatment, the Centers for the Application of Prevention Technologies, the Department of Education, and Community Anti-Drug Coalitions of America. Imm is a coauthor of the award-winning empowerment evaluation manual *Getting to Outcomes (GTO): Methods and Tools for Planning, Self-Assessment, and Accountability,* funded as a joint project between the Center for Substance Abuse Prevention and the RAND Corporation. Imm works closely with community coalitions and provides training and technical assistance in the areas of prevention programming, evaluations and monitoring, and strategies for community change.

Andrea E. Lamont is a community and quantitative psychologist working as a program evaluator. She received her Ph.D. in clinical-community psychology from the University of South Carolina; M.A. in psychology in education from Teachers College, Columbia University; M.A. in clinical-community psychology from University of South Carolina; and M.S. in applied statistics from University of South Carolina. Currently, Lamont is working as a predoctoral intern in community psychology as an empowerment evaluator on a variety of projects. Her primary interest is in the implementation process and organizational readiness for implementation. Her work aims to bridge the gap between research and practice by focusing on support for quality implementation of evidence-based/evidence-informed programs and practices. She works to synthesize and translate the implementation science research into usable forms for communities and organizations so that high-quality implementation can be attained. She also is interested in developing ways to inform and evaluate the work of the support system.

Regina Day Langhout's commitment to issues and concerns of social justice has informed her study of empowerment in educational and neighborhood settings. Her research addresses the following questions: (1) What characteristics within settings inhibit or promote—either intentionally or unintentionally—thriving? (2) How do race, ethnicity, social class, and gender influence experience, and how do these experiences influence subjectivity? (3) How do individuals and groups experience, cope with, and resist negative stereotypes? (4) What conditions are necessary for individuals to change their ideological perspectives and become inspired to work toward social justice? (5) How can researchers facilitate systemic, sustainable change that increases individual and group thriving, and support people identifying as agents of social change? Langhout's primary research takes place in elementary schools and neighborhoods that serve working-class and working-poor African American, Latina/o, and white students. She uses empowerment evaluation and participatory action research (PAR) to critically examine schools and neighborhoods. With empowerment evaluation and PAR, stakeholder groups collaborate to determine problems and interventions. She has been the PI of a youth empowerment evaluation and participatory action research program that has been running since 2006. She has published more than 30 articles on these topics.

Laura C. Leviton is senior advisor for evaluation at the Robert Wood Johnson Foundation in Princeton, New Jersey, a position that the foundation created for her to advise and consult on evaluations across its many initiatives and national programs. She has been with the foundation since 1999, overseeing more than 100 national and local evaluations. She was formerly a professor at two schools of public health, where she collaborated on the first randomized experiment on HIV prevention, and later on two large, place-based randomized experiments on improving medical practices. Leviton was president of the American Evaluation Association in the year 2000 and has coauthored two books: *Foundations of Program Evaluation* and *Confronting Public Health Risks*. She received the 1993 award from the American Psychological Association for Distinguished Contributions to Psychology in the Public Interest. She has served on three Institute of Medicine committees, evaluating preparedness for terrorist attack (2001), occupational hearing loss research (2006), and obesity prevention (2013). She was appointed by the secretary of the Department of Health and Human Services to the National Advisory Committee on HIV and STD Prevention of the Centers for Disease Control and Prevention. She is interested in all aspects of evaluation methodology and practice.

Gloria Morales-Curtin is the vice president for adult programs at El Valor Corporation. El Valor is a community-based organization that provides various programs to individuals with disabilities. Morales-Curtin supervises several programs, including the employment program, brain injury program, and other services. She is a graduate of the University of Illinois at Chicago.

Dawn Oparah is the cofounder and vice president of Amadi Leadership Associates, Inc., founded in 1995. She is a consultant and trainer and serves as a workshop presenter at regional, state, and national conferences. Oparah has worked in the United States and abroad as a university administrator/instructor, teacher, school principal, and government administrator. Oparah is the coauthor of an educational video titled *How to Raise and Teach a Thinking Child*. In 2005, the Search Institute invited her to write the book *Make a World of Difference*, full of activities to help teens explore issues of diversity. Currently Oparah serves as the Resource Development and Compliance Consultant for AVPRIDE, a youth-serving leadership organization that she cofounded in 1996. She has served on 16 boards of directors. Currently she is Chamber board member and cochair for the Education Partnership Initiative and a member of the Fayette Visioning Steering Committee. Oparah is also a board member of the Fayette/Coweta YMCA board and for Fayette FACTOR, an organization committed to strengthening families and children.

Susana Sastre-Merino, forestry engineer and Ph.D. candidate, is a researcher at the Universidad Politécnica de Madrid. Her research is focused on bottom-up approaches for planning, management, and evaluation of rural projects and programs. She focuses on socioeconomic development in rural areas, including capacity development and leadership for endogenous and sustainable development. She has participated in several national and international projects, with special focus on women in Latin America. She has published articles in scientific journals such as *Cuadernos de Desarrollo Rural* and *Procedia* and has participated in several international conferences. She is certified as a project management associate by the International Project Management Association and is a member of the research group GESPLAN.

Yolanda Suarez-Balcazar is professor and head of the Department of Occupational Therapy, College of Applied Health Sciences at the University of Illinois at Chicago (UIC). She is an affiliated faculty member in the Department of Disability and Human Development and the Department of Psychology at UIC. Trained as a community psychologist, Suarez-Balcazar's research focuses on the nexus between race, culture, and disability. She studies community-based organizations' capacity to evaluate service outcomes and provide culturally sensitive services to Latinos and African Americans. She also studies empowerment and participatory evaluation of obesity prevention interventions for people of color and people with disabilities and rehabilitation outcomes for people with disabilities. In her studies, she uses mixed methods and community-based participatory research approaches.

Tina Taylor-Ritzler is an assistant professor in the Department of Psychology at Dominican University and an affiliated research assistant professor in the Department of Disability and Human Development at the University of Illinois at Chicago. Taylor-Ritzler is a community psychologist by training, whose work focuses on conceptualizing, measuring, and building evaluation capacity within nonprofit organizations. Her recent work includes the development and validation of the Evaluation Capacity Assessment Instrument (ECAI), which is used to assess, strategically plan, and reassess evaluation capacity building efforts within organizations. Her work focuses on evaluation capacity building with organizations that support the community participation of individuals with disabilities in the Chicago area.

Beverly Triana-Tremain has 20 years of public health teaching, research, and consulting experience. Her background and skill set blends theoretical and practical approaches in evaluation, research, and quality improvement processes. She is a fellow in the National Public Health Leadership Institute and, in 2006, established Public Health Consulting, LLC, to assist agencies in improving the public health system. She serves as a technical consultant to various local, state, and national agencies in evaluation, research, and quality improvement. In 2009, she was appointed a member of the Quality Improvement Technical Assistance Panel for the National Association of City and County Health Officials (NACCHO). She is the evaluator or quality improvement consultant on grants received from Robert Wood Johnson Foundation, Centers for Disease Control and Prevention, Substance Abuse and Mental Health Administration (SAMSHA), RAND, Health Resources and Services Administration, and various state and local health departments. Currently, she serves as regional epidemiologist for SAMHSA for nine states in the south and southwest United States. There she assists states with evidence-based decision making for increasing shared protective factors that decrease the likelihood of substance abuse.

Pablo Vidueira received an undergraduate degree in agricultural engineering at the Universidad Politécnica de Madrid and an M.S. in project planning for rural development and sustainable management, an official master's degree from the Erasmus-Mundus Program of the European Commission. He is a doctoral candidate in the Projects and Rural Planning Department at the Universidad Politécnica de Madrid. His research is focused on methodologies used to determine the socioeconomic impact of evaluations of policies, programs, and projects. He has presented several papers at international conferences and has published several book chapters and papers in indexed journals. He has participated in national and international projects and has worked with governments, academic institutions, and firms. Vidueira also lectures in undergraduate- and master's-level courses at the Universidad Politécnica de Madrid.

Annie Wright is a clinical-community psychologist and program evaluator. She also owns and operates the independent consulting firm Wright Consulting, LLC. Wright graduated Phi Beta Kappa from Rhodes College in Memphis, with a major in psychology and a minor in urban studies. She completed her master's and doctorate degrees in clinical-community psychology at the University of South Carolina. Her work focuses on educational settings, including examining school climate, as well as school-based violence prevention and classroom technology integration programs. Additionally, she works with nonprofit organizations that provide educational supports to students and schools, including after-school programs, community gardens, and museums. She specializes in the implementation of high-quality programming that results in measurable and sustainable change for organizations and families.

Janice B. Yost, Ed.D., became the founding president of The Health Foundation of Central Massachusetts in 1999. The foundation's grantmaking focuses on taking evidenced-based strategies to scale by advocating for systems change to sustain the strategies. To assist that process, the foundation employs an empowerment evaluation approach called Results-Oriented Grantmaking and Grant-Implementation (ROGG), a planning and evaluation system that she codeveloped with Abraham Wandersman. ROGG's effectiveness has been recognized in several reports, including *Evaluation in Philanthropy: Perspectives From the*

Field, coreleased in 2009 by Grantmakers for Effective Organizations and the Council on Foundations. The foundation has made grants totaling $26 million, which focused on multiyear projects that achieved substantive public policy accomplishments such as impacting preschool children's mental health, improving access to dental services and mental health services, reducing hunger and homelessness, and guiding prisoner reentry and public housing tenants toward self-sufficiency. Yost previously served as the founding president of Mary Black Foundation and as a trustee of the Spartanburg Regional Hospital System. Her earlier career as a college professor and administrator included serving as Associate Chancellor for University Relations at the University of South Carolina–Spartanburg campus. She earned a doctorate in speech education from the University of Georgia.